# Lecture Notes in Computer Science 3622

*Commenced Publication in 1973*
Founding and Former Series Editors:
Gerhard Goos, Juris Hartmanis, and Jan van Leeuwe

T0216287

Varmo Vene   Tarmo Uustalu (Eds.)

# Advanced
# Functional
# Programming

5th International School, AFP 2004
Tartu, Estonia, August 14 – 21, 2004
Revised Lectures

 Springer

Volume Editors

Varmo Vene
University of Tartu
Department of Computer Science
J. Liivi 2, EE-50409 Tartu, Estonia
E-mail: varmo@cs.ut.ee

Tarmo Uustalu
Institute of Cybernetics
Akadeemia tee 21, EE-12618 Tallinn, Estonia
E-mail: tarmo@cs.ioc.ee

Library of Congress Control Number: 2005931987

CR Subject Classification (1998): D.1.1, D.1, D.3, F.3, D.2

| | |
|---|---|
| ISSN | 0302-9743 |
| ISBN-10 | 3-540-28540-7 Springer Berlin Heidelberg New York |
| ISBN-13 | 978-3-540-28540-3 Springer Berlin Heidelberg New York |

Springer is a part of Springer Science+Business Media

springeronline.com

© Springer-Verlag Berlin Heidelberg 2005
Printed in Germany

Typesetting: Camera-ready by author, data conversion by Scientific Publishing Services, Chennai, India
Printed on acid-free paper      SPIN: 11546382      06/3142      5 4 3 2 1 0

# Preface

This volume contains the revised lecture notes corresponding to nine of the lecture courses presented at the 5th International School on Advanced Functional Programming, AFP 2004, held in Tartu, Estonia, August 14–21, 2004.

The goal of the AFP schools is to inform the wide international communities of computer science students and software production professionals about the new and important developments in the area of functional programming. The schools put a special emphasis on practical applications of advanced techniques. The Tartu school was preceded by four earlier schools in Båstad, Sweden (1995, LNCS 925), Olympia, WA, USA (1996, LNCS 1129), Braga, Portugal (1998, LNCS 1608) and Oxford, UK (2002, LNCS 2638).

The scientific programme of AFP 2004 consisted of five preparatory ("intermediate") courses, given by John Hughes (Chalmers University of Technology, Göteborg, Sweden), Doaitse Swierstra (Universiteit Utrecht, The Netherlands) and Rinus Plasmeijer (Radboud Universiteit Nijmegen, The Netherlands), and nine regular ("advanced") courses, presented by Atze Dijkstra (Universiteit Utrecht, The Netherlands), Doaitse Swierstra, John Hughes, Conor McBride (University of Nottingham, UK), Alberto Pardo (Universidade de la República, Montevideo, Uruguay), Rinus Plasmeijer, Bernard Pope (University of Melbourne, Australia), Peter Thiemann (Universität Freiburg, Germany), and Simon Thompson (University of Kent, UK). There was also a student session.

The school attracted a record number of 68 participants from 16 countries (inclusive of the lecturers and organizers).

This volume contains the notes for the advanced courses. Following the school, the lecturers revised the notes they had prepared for the school. The revised notes were each carefully checked by two or three second readers selected from among the most qualified available and then revised once more by the lecturers. We are proud to commend the final texts to everyone wishing to acquire firsthand knowledge about some of the exciting and trendsetting developments in functional programming.

We are grateful to our sponsors, to the Faculty of Mathematics and Computer Science of the University of Tartu, to the lecturers and the second readers for their hard work on the oral presentations, and the notes, and to all our participants. You made the school what it was.

Tartu and Tallinn, June 2005                                     Varmo Vene
                                                                 Tarmo Uustalu

# Organization

## Host Institution

AFP 2004 was organized by the Department of Computer Science of the University of Tartu in cooperation with the Center for Dependable Computing (CDC), an Estonian center of excellence in research.

## Programme Committee

Varmo Vene (University of Tartu, Estonia) (chairman)
Johan Jeuring (Universiteit Utrecht, The Netherlands)
Tarmo Uustalu (Institute of Cybernetics, Tallinn, Estonia)

## Organizing Committee

Varmo Vene (University of Tartu, Estonia) (chairman)
Härmel Nestra (University of Tartu, Estonia)
Vesal Vojdani (University of Tartu, Estonia)
Tarmo Uustalu (Institute of Cybernetics, Tallinn, Estonia)

## Second Readers

Venanzio Capretta (University of Ottawa, Canada)
James Cheney (University of Edinburgh, UK)
Catarina Coquand (Chalmers University of Technology, Sweden)
Jeremy Gibbons (University of Oxford, UK)
Thomas Hallgren (Oregon Graduate Institute, Portland, OR, USA)
Michael Hanus (Christian-Albrechts-Universität zu Kiel, Germany)
Johan Jeuring (Universiteit Utrecht, The Netherlands)
Jerzy Karczmarczuk (Université Caen, France)
Ralf Lämmel (CWI, Amsterdam, The Netherlands)
Andres Löh (Universiteit Utrecht, The Netherlands)
Nicolas Magaud (University of New South Wales, Sydney, Australia)
Simon Marlow (Microsoft Research, Cambridge, UK)
Ross Paterson (City University, London, UK)
Simon Peyton Jones (Microsoft Research, Cambridge, UK)
Colin Runciman (University of York, UK)
Tim Sheard (Portland State University, Portland, OR, USA)
Joost Visser (Universidade do Minho, Braga, Portugal)
Eric Van Wyk (University of Minnesota, Minneapolis, MN, USA)

## Sponsoring Institutions

Tiigriülikool programme of the Estonian Information Technology Foundation

National Centers of Excellence programme of the Estonian Ministry of Education and Research

EU FP5 IST programme via the thematic network project APPSEM II

# Table of Contents

# Typing Haskell with an Attribute Grammar

Atze Dijkstra and S. Doaitse Swierstra

Institute of Information and Computing Sciences,
Utrecht University, P.O.Box 80.089,
3508 TB Utrecht, Netherlands
{atze, doaitse}@cs.uu.nl

**Abstract.** A great deal has been written about type systems. Much less has been written about implementing them. Even less has been written about implementations of complete compilers in which all aspects come together. This paper fills this gap by describing the implementation of a series of compilers for a simplified variant of Haskell. By using an attribute grammar system, aspects of a compiler implementation can be described separately and added in a sequence of steps, thereby giving a series of increasingly complex (working) compilers. Also, the source text of both this paper and the executable compilers come from the same source files by an underlying minimal weaving system. Therefore, source and explanation is kept consistent.

## 1 Introduction and Overview

Haskell98 [31] is a complex language, not to mention its more experimental incarnations. Though also intended as a research platform, realistic compilers for Haskell [1] have grown over the years and understanding and experimenting with those compilers is not an easy task. Experimentation on a smaller scale usually is based upon relatively simple and restricted implementations [20], often focusing only on a particular aspect of the language and/or its implementation. This paper aims at walking somewhere between this complexity and simplicity by

- Describing the implementation of essential aspects of Haskell (or any other (functional) programming language), hence the name Essential Haskell (EH) used for simplified variants of Haskell[1] in these notes.
- Describing these aspects separately in order to provide a better understanding.
- Adding these aspects on top of each other in an incremental way, thus leading to a sequence of compilers, each for a larger subset of complete Haskell (and extensions).
- Using tools like the Utrecht University Attribute Grammar (UUAG) system [3], hereafter referred to as the AG system, to allow for separate descriptions for the various aspects.

---

[1] The 'E' in EH might also be expanded to other aspects of the compiler, like being an Example.

V. Vene and T. Uustalu (Eds.): AFP 2004, LNCS 3622, pp. 1–72, 2005.
© Springer-Verlag Berlin Heidelberg 2005

The remaining sections of this introduction will expand on this by looking at the intentions, purpose and limitations of these notes in more detail. This is followed by a short description of the individual languages for which we develop compilers throughout these notes. The last part of the introduction contains a small tutorial on the AG system used in these notes. After the introduction we continue with discussing the implementation of the first three compilers (sections 2, 3 and 4) out of a (currently) sequence of ten compilers. On the web site [11] for this project the full distribution of the code for these compilers can be found. We conclude these notes by reflecting upon our experiences with the AG system and the creation of these notes (section 5).

## 1.1   Purpose

For whom is this material intended?

- For students who wish to learn more about the implementation of functional languages. This paper also informally explains the required theory, in particular about type systems.
- For researchers who want to build (e.g.) a prototype and to experiment with extensions to the type system and need a non-trivial and realistic starting point. This paper provides documentation, design rationales and an implementation for such a starting point.
- For those who wish to study a larger example of the tools used to build the compilers in these notes. We demonstrate the use of the AG system, which allows us to separately describe the various aspects of a language implementation. Other tools for maintaining consistency between different versions of the resulting compilers and the source code text included in these notes are also used, but will not be discussed.

For this intended audience these notesprovide:

- A description of the implementation of a type checker/inferencer for a subset of Haskell. We describe the first three languages of a (currently) sequence of ten, that end in a full implementation of an extended Haskell.
- A description of the semantics of Haskell, lying between the more formal [16,14] and more implementation oriented [21,33] and similar to other combinations of theory and practice [34].
- A gradual instead of a big bang explanation.
- Empirical support for the belief that the complexity of a compiler can be managed by splitting the implementation of the compiler into separate aspects.
- A working combination of otherwise usually separately proven or implemented features.

We will come back to this in our conclusion (see section 5).

We restrict ourselves in the following ways, partly because of space limitations, partly by design:

- We do not discuss extensions to Haskell implemented in versions beyond the last version presented in these notes. See section 1.3 for a preciser description of what can and cannot be found in these notes with respect to Haskell features.
- We concern ourselves with typing only. Other aspects, like pretty printing and parsing, are not discussed. However, the introduction to the AG system (see section 1.4) gives some examples of the pretty printing and the interaction between parsing, AG code and Haskell code.
- We do not deal with type theory or parsing theory as a subject on its own. This paper is intended to describe "how to implement" and will use theory from that point of view. Theoretical aspects are touched upon from a more intuitive point of view.

Although informally and concisely introduced where necessary, familiarity with the following will make reading and understanding these notes easier:

- Functional programming, in particular using Haskell
- Compiler construction in general
- Type systems, $\lambda$-calculus
- Parser combinator library and AG system [3,38]

For those not familiar with the AG system a short tutorial has been included at the end of this introduction (see section 1.4). It also demonstrates the use of the parser combinators used throughout the implementation of all EH versions.

We expect that by finding a balance between theory and implementation, we serve both those who want to learn and those who want to do research. It is also our belief that by splitting the big problem into smaller aspects the combination can be explained in an easier way.

In the following sections we give examples of the Haskell features present in the series of compilers described in the following chapters. Only short examples are given, so the reader gets an impression of what is explained in more detail and implemented in the relevant versions of the compiler.

## 1.2   A Short Tour

Though all compilers described in these notes deal with a different issue, they all have in common that they are based on the $\lambda$-calculus, most of the time using the syntax and semantics of Haskell. The first version of our series of compilers therefore accepts a language that most closely resembles the $\lambda$-calculus, in particular typed $\lambda$-calculus extended with **let** expressions and some basic types and type constructors such as *Int*, *Char* and tuples.

*EH version 1: λ-calculus.* An EH program is a single expression, contrary to a Haskell program which consists of a set of declarations forming a module.

> **let** $i :: Int$
> $\quad i = 5$
> **in** $i$

All variables need to be typed explicitly; absence of an explicit type is considered to be an error. The corresponding compiler (EH version 1, section 2 ) checks the explicit types against actual types.

Besides the basic types *Int* and *Char*, composite types can be formed by building tuples and defining functions:

> **let** $id :: Int \rightarrow Int$
> $\quad id = \lambda x \rightarrow x$
> $\quad fst :: (Int, Char) \rightarrow Int$
> $\quad fst = \lambda(a, b) \rightarrow a$
> **in** $id \ (fst \ (id \ 3, \text{'\textbf{x}'}))$

Functions accept one parameter only, which can be a pattern. All types are monomorphic.

*EH version 2: Explicit/implicit typing.* The next version (EH version 2, section 3 ) no longer requires the explicit type specifications, which thus may have to be inferred by the compiler.

The reconstructed type information is monomorphic, for example the identity function in:

> **let** $id = \lambda x \rightarrow x$
> **in** **let** $v = id \ 3$
> $\qquad$ **in** $id$

is inferred to have the type $id :: Int \rightarrow Int$.

*EH version 3: Polymorphism.* The third version (EH version 3, section 4 ) performs standard Hindley-Milner type inferencing [8,9] which also supports parametric polymorphism. For example,

> **let** $id = \lambda x \rightarrow x$
> **in** $id \ 3$

is inferred to have type $id :: \forall \ a.a \rightarrow a$.

## 1.3   Haskell Language Elements Not Described

As mentioned before, only a subset of the full sequence of compilers is described in these notes. Currently, as part of an ongoing work [11], in the compilers following the compilers described in these notes, the following Haskell features are dealt with:

**EH 4.** Quantifiers everywhere: higher ranked types [36,32,7,28] and existentials [30,25,27]. See also the longer version of these notes handed out during the AFP04 summerschool [13].

**EH 5.** Data types.

**EH 6.** Kinds, kind inference, kind checking, kind polymorphism.

**EH 7.** Non extensible records, subsuming tuples.

**EH 8.** Code generation for a GRIN (Graph Reduction Intermediate Notation) like backend [6,5].

**EH 9.** Class system, explicit implicit parameters [12].

**EH 10.** Extensible records [15,22].

Also missing are features which fall in the category syntactic sugar, programming in the large and the like. Haskell incorporates many features which make programming easier and/or manageable. Just to mention a few:

– Binding group analysis
– Syntax directives like infix declarations
– Modules [10,37].
– Type synonyms
– Syntactic sugar for **if, do**, list notation and comprehension.

We have deliberately not dealt with these issues. Though necessary and convenient we feel that these features should be added after all else has been dealt with, so as not to make understanding and implementating essential features more difficult.

## 1.4   An AG Mini Tutorial

The remaining part of the introduction contains a small tutorial on the AG system. The tutorial explains the basic features of the AG system. The explanation of remaining features is postponed to its first use throughout the main text. These places are marked with $\mathcal{AG}$. The tutorial can safely be skipped if the reader is already familiar with the AG system.

*Haskell and Attribute Grammars (AG).* Attribute grammars can be mapped onto functional programs [23,19,4]. Vice versa, the class of functional programs (catamorphisms

[39]) mapped onto can be described by attribute grammars. The AG system exploits this correspondence by providing a notation (attribute grammar) for computations over trees which additionally allows program fragments to be described separately. The AG compiler gathers these fragments, combines these fragments, and generates a corresponding Haskell program.

In this AG tutorial we start with a small example Haskell program (of the right form) to show how the computation described by this program can be expressed in the AG notation and how the resulting Haskell program generated by the AG compiler can be used. The 'repmin' problem [4] is used for this purpose. A second example describing a 'pocket calculator' (that is, expressions) focusses on more advanced features and typical AG usage patterns.

*Repmin a la Haskell.* Repmin stands for "replacing the integer valued leaves of a tree by the minimal integer value found in the leaves". The solution to this problem requires two passes over a tree structure, computing the miminum and computing a new tree with the minimum as its leaves respectively. It is often used as the typical example of a circular program which lends itself well to be described by the AG notation. When described in Haskell it is expressed as a computation over a tree structure:

```
data Tree = Tree_Leaf Int
          |  Tree_Bin   Tree Tree
          deriving Show
```

The computation itself simultaneously computes the minimum of all integers found in the leaves of the tree and the new tree with this minimum value. The result is returned as a tuple computed by function *r*:

```
repmin :: Tree → Tree
repmin   t
   = t'
  where (t', tmin)            = r t tmin
          r (Tree_Leaf i   ) m = (Tree_Leaf m   ,i            )
          r (Tree_Bin   lt rt) m = (Tree_Bin lt' rt',lmin 'min' rmin)
                            where (lt', lmin)  = r lt m
                                  (rt', rmin) = r rt m
```

We can use this function in some setting, for example:

```
tr    = Tree_Bin (Tree_Leaf 3) (Tree_Bin (Tree_Leaf 4) (Tree_Leaf 5))
tr'   = repmin tr
main :: IO ()
main = print tr'
```

The resulting program produces the following output:

```
Tree_Bin (Tree_Leaf 3) (Tree_Bin (Tree_Leaf 3) (Tree_Leaf 3))
```

The computation of the new tree requires the minimum. This minimum is passed as a parameter *m* to *r* at the root of the tree by extracting it from the result of *r*. The result tuple of the invocation *r t tmin* depends on itself via the minimum *tmin* so it would seem we have a cyclic definition. However, the real dependency is not on the tupled result of *r* but on its elements because it is the element *tmin* of the result tuple which is passed back and not the tuple itself. The elements are not cyclically dependent so Haskell's laziness prevents a too eager computation of the elements of the tuple which might otherwise have caused an infinite loop during execution. Note that we have two more or less independent computations that both follow the tree structure, and a weak interaction, when passing the *tmin* value back in the tree.

*Repmin a la AG.*  The structure of *repmin* is similar to the structure required by a compiler. A compiler performs several computations over an *abstract syntax tree* (*AST*), for example for computing its type and code. This corresponds to the *Tree* structure used by *repmin* and the tupled results. In the context of attribute grammars the elements of this tuple are called *attribute*'s. Occasionaly the word *aspect* is used as well, but an aspect may also refer to a group of attributes associated with one particular feature of the AST, language or problem at hand.

Result elements are called *synthesized* attributes. On the other hand, a compiler may also require information that becomes available at higher nodes in an AST to be available at lower nodes in an AST. The *m* parameter passed to *r* in *repmin* is an example of this situation. In the context of attribute grammars this is called an *inherited attribute*.

Using AG notation we first define the AST corresponding to our problem (for which the complete compilable solution is given in Fig. 1):

```
DATA Tree
  | Leaf int : {Int}
  | Bin  lt : Tree
         rt : Tree
```

The **DATA** keyword is used to introduce the equivalent of Haskell's **data** type. A **DATA**⟨*node*⟩ defines a *node* ⟨*node*⟩ (or *nonterminal*) of an AST. Its alternatives, enumerated one by one after the vertical bar |, are called *variants*, *productions*. The term *constructor* is occasionally used to stress the similarity with its Haskell counterpart. Each variant has members, called *children* if they refer to other nodes of the AST and *fields* otherwise. Each child and field has a name (before the colon) and a type (after the colon). The type may be either another **DATA** node (if a child) or a monomorphic Haskell type (if a field), delimited by curly braces. The curly braces may be omitted if the Haskell type is a single identifier. For example, the **DATA** definition for the repmin problem introduces a node (nonterminal) *Tree*, with variants (productions) *Leaf* and *Bin*. A *Bin* has children *lt* and *rt* of type *Tree*. A *Leaf* has no children but contains only a field *int* holding a Haskell *Int* value.

The keyword **ATTR** is used to declare an attribute for a node, for instance the synthesized attribute *min*:

> **ATTR** *Tree* [|| *min* : *Int*]
> **SEM** *Tree*
> | *Leaf* **lhs**.*min* = @*int*
> | *Bin*   **lhs**.*min* = @*lt*.*min* '*min*' @*rt*.*min*

---

**DATA** *Tree*
  | *Leaf int*  : {*Int*}
  | *Bin*  *lt*   : *Tree*
       *rt*   : *Tree*
**ATTR** *Tree* [|| *min* : *Int*]
**SEM** *Tree*
  | *Leaf* **lhs** . *min*  = @*int*
  | *Bin*  **lhs** . *min*  = @*lt*.*min* '*min*' @*rt*.*min*
**ATTR** *Tree* [*rmin* : *Int* ||]
  -- The next SEM may be generated automatically
**SEM** *Tree*
  | *Bin*  *lt*   . *rmin* = @**lhs**.*rmin*
       *rt*   . *rmin* = @**lhs**.*rmin*
**DATA** *Root*
  | *Root tree* : *Tree*
**SEM** *Root*
  | *Root tree*. *rmin* = @*tree*.*min*
**ATTR** *Root Tree* [|| *tree* : *Tree*]
**SEM** *Tree*
  | *Leaf* **lhs** . *tree*  = *Tree_Leaf* @**lhs**.*rmin*
  | *Bin*  **lhs** . *tree*  = *Tree_Bin* @*lt*.*tree* @*rt*.*tree*
  -- The next SEM may be generated automatically
**SEM** *Root*
  | *Root* **lhs** . *tree*  = @*tree*.*tree*
**DERIVING** *Tree* : *Show*
{
*tr*  = *Tree_Bin* (*Tree_Leaf* 3) (*Tree_Bin* (*Tree_Leaf* 4) (*Tree_Leaf* 5))
*tr'* = *sem_Root* (*Root_Root tr*)
*main* ::  *IO* ()
*main* =  *print tr'*
}

---

**Fig. 1.** Full AG specification of repmin

A synthesized attribute is declared for the node after **ATTR**. Multiple declarations of the same attribute for different nonterminals can be grouped on one line by enumerating the nonterminals after the **ATTR** keyword, separated by whitespace. The attribute declaration is placed inside the square brackets at one or more of three different possible places. All attributes before the first vertical bar | are inherited, after the last bar synthesized, and in between both inherited and synthesized. For example, attribute *min* is a result and therefore positioned as a synthesized attribute, after the last bar.

Rules relating an attribute to its value are introduced using the keyword **SEM**. For each production we distinguish a set of input attributes, consisting of the synthesized attributes of the children referred to by @⟨*child*⟩.⟨*attr*⟩ and the inherited attributes of the parent referred to by @**lhs**.⟨*attr*⟩. For each output attribute we need a rule that expresses its value in terms of input attributes and fields.

The computation for a synthesized attribute for a node has to be defined for each variant individually as it usually will differ between variants. Each rule is of the form

| ⟨*variant*⟩   ⟨*node*⟩.⟨*attr*⟩ = ⟨*Haskell expr*⟩

If multiple rules are declared for a ⟨*variant*⟩ of a node, the ⟨*variant*⟩ part may be shared. The same holds for multiple rules for a child (or **lhs**) of a ⟨*variant*⟩, the child (or **lhs**) may then be shared.

The text representing the computation for an attribute has to be a Haskell expression and will end up almost unmodified in the generated program, without any form of checking. Only attribute and field references, starting with a @, have meaning to the AG system. The text, possibly stretching over multiple lines, has to be indented at least as far as its first line. Otherwise it is to be delimited by curly braces.

The basic form of an attribute reference is @⟨*node*⟩.⟨*attr*⟩ referring to a synthesized attribute ⟨*attr*⟩ of child node ⟨*node*⟩. For example, @*lt.min* refers to the synthesized attribute *min* of child *lt* of the *Bin* variant of node *Tree*.

The ⟨*node*⟩. part of @⟨*node*⟩.⟨*attr*⟩ may be omitted. For example, *min* for the *Leaf* alternative is defined in terms of @*int*. In that case @⟨*attr*⟩ refers to a locally (to a variant for a node) declared attribute, or to the field with the same name as defined in the **DATA** definition for that variant. This is the case for the *Leaf* variant's *int*. We postpone the discussion of locally declared attributes.

The minimum value of *repmin* passed as a parameter corresponds to an inherited attribute *rmin*:

**ATTR** *Tree* [*rmin* : *Int* ||]

The value of *rmin* is straightforwardly copied to its children. This "simply copy" behavior occurs so often that we may omit its specification. The AG system uses so called copy rules to automically generate code for copying if the value of an attribute is not specified explicitly. This is to prevent program clutter and thus allows the programmer to focus on programming the exception instead of the usual. We will come back to this later; for now it suffices to mention that all the rules for *rmin* might as well have been omitted.

The original *repmin* function did pass the minimum value coming out *r* back into *r* itself. This did happen at the top of the tree. Similarly we define a *Root* node sitting on top of a *Tree*:

**DATA** *Root*
    | *Root tree* : *Tree*

At the root the *min* attribute is passed back into the tree via attribute *rmin*:

**SEM** *Root*
    | *Root tree.rmin* = @*tree.min*

The value of *rmin* is used to construct a new tree:

**ATTR** *Root Tree* [||| *tree* : *Tree*]
**SEM** *Tree*
    | *Leaf* **lhs**.*tree* = *Tree_Leaf* @**lhs**.*rmin*
    | *Bin*  **lhs**.*tree* = *Tree_Bin*  @*lt.tree* @*rt.tree*

**SEM** *Root*
    | *Root* **lhs**.*tree* = @*tree.tree*

For each **DATA** the AG compiler generates a corresponding Haskell **data** type declaration. For each node ⟨*node*⟩ a data type with the same name ⟨*node*⟩ is generated. Since Haskell requires all constructors to be unique, each constructor of the data type gets a name of the form ⟨*node*⟩_⟨*variant*⟩.

In our example the constructed tree is returned as the one and only attribute of *Root*. It can be shown if we tell the AG compiler to make the generated data type an instance of the *Show* class:

**DERIVING** *Tree* : *Show*

Similarly to the Haskell version of *repmin* we can now show the result of the attribute computation as a plain Haskell value by using the function *sem_Root* generated by the AG compiler:

```
{
tr  = Tree_Bin (Tree_Leaf 3) (Tree_Bin (Tree_Leaf 4) (Tree_Leaf 5))
tr' = sem_Root (Root_Root tr)
main :: IO ()
main = print tr'
}
```

Because this part is Haskell code it has to be delimited by curly braces, indicating that the AG compiler should copy it unchanged into the generated Haskell program.

In order to understand what is happening here, we take a look at the generated Haskell code. For the above example the following code will be generated (edited to remove clutter):

```
data Root = Root_Root (Tree)
-- semantic domain
type T_Root = ( (Tree))
-- cata
sem_Root :: (Root) -> (T_Root)
sem_Root ((Root_Root (_tree)))
  = (sem_Root_Root ((sem_Tree (_tree))))
sem_Root_Root :: (T_Tree) -> (T_Root)
sem_Root_Root (tree_) =
    let ( _treeImin,_treeItree) = (tree_ (_treeOrmin))
          (_treeOrmin) = _treeImin
          (_lhsOtree) = _treeItree
    in  ( _lhsOtree)


data Tree = Tree_Bin (Tree) (Tree)
          | Tree_Leaf (Int)
            deriving ( Show)
-- semantic domain
type T_Tree = (Int) -> ( (Int),(Tree))
-- cata
sem_Tree :: (Tree) -> (T_Tree)
sem_Tree ((Tree_Bin (_lt) (_rt)))
  = (sem_Tree_Bin ((sem_Tree (_lt))) ((sem_Tree (_rt))))
sem_Tree ((Tree_Leaf (_int))) = (sem_Tree_Leaf (_int))
sem_Tree_Bin :: (T_Tree) -> (T_Tree) -> (T_Tree)
sem_Tree_Bin (lt_) (rt_) =
    \ _lhsIrmin ->
        let ( _ltImin,_ltItree) = (lt_ (_ltOrmin))
             ( _rtImin,_rtItree) = (rt_ (_rtOrmin))
             (_lhsOmin) = _ltImin 'min' _rtImin
             (_rtOrmin) = _lhsIrmin
             (_ltOrmin) = _lhsIrmin
             (_lhsOtree) = Tree_Bin   _ltItree _rtItree
        in  ( _lhsOmin,_lhsOtree)
sem_Tree_Leaf :: (Int) -> (T_Tree)
sem_Tree_Leaf (int_) =
    \ _lhsIrmin ->
        let (_lhsOmin) = int_
             (_lhsOtree) = Tree_Leaf   _lhsIrmin
        in  ( _lhsOmin,_lhsOtree)
```

In general, generated code is not the most pleasant[2] of prose to look at, but we will have to use the generated functions in order to access the AG computations of attributes from the Haskell world. The following observations should be kept in mind when doing so:

- For node $\langle node \rangle$ also a type $T\_\langle node \rangle$ is generated, describing the function type that maps inherited to synthesized attributes. This type corresponds one-to-one to the attributes defined for $\langle node \rangle$: inherited attributes to parameters, synthesized attributes to elements of the result tuple (or single type if exactly one synthesized attribute is defined).
- Computation of attribute values is done by semantic functions with a name of the form $sem\_\langle node \rangle\_\langle variant \rangle$. These functions have exactly the same type as their constructor counterpart of the generated data type. The only difference lies in the parameters which are of the same type as their constructor counterpart, but prefixed with $T\_$. For example, data constructor $Tree\_Bin :: Tree \rightarrow Tree \rightarrow Tree$ corresponds to the semantic function $sem\_Tree\_Bin :: (T\_Tree) \rightarrow (T\_Tree) \rightarrow (T\_Tree)$.
- A mapping from the Haskell **data** type to the corresponding semantic function is available with the name $sem\_\langle node \rangle$.

In the Haskell world one now can follow different routes to compute the attributes:

- First construct a Haskell value of type $\langle node \rangle$, then apply $sem\_\langle node \rangle$ to this value and the additionally required inherited attributes values. The given function *main* from AG variant of repmin takes this approach.
- Circumvent the construction of Haskell values of type $\langle node \rangle$ by using the semantic functions $sem\_\langle node \rangle\_\langle variant \rangle$ directly when building the AST instead of the data constructor $\langle node \rangle\_\langle variant \rangle$ (This technique is called deforestation [42].).

In both cases a tuple holding all synthesized attributes is returned. Elements in the tuple are sorted lexicographically on attribute name, but it still is awkward to extract an attribute via pattern matching because the size of the tuple and position of elements changes with adding and renaming attributes. For now, this is not a problem as *sem_Root* will only return one value, a *Tree*. Later we will see the use of wrapper functions to pass inherited attributes and extract synthesized attributes via additional wrapper data types holding attributes in labeled fields.

*Parsing directly to semantic functions.* The given *main* function uses the first approach: construct a *Tree*, wrap it inside a *Root*, and apply *sem_Root* to it. The following example takes the second approach; it parses some input text describing the structure of a tree and directly invokes the semantic functions:

---

[2] In addition, because generated code can be generated differently, one cannot count on it being generated in a specific way. Such is the case here too, this part of the AG implementation may well change in the future.

**instance** *Symbol Char*
*pRepmin :: IsParser p Char ⇒ p T_Root*
*pRepmin = pRoot*
      **where** *pRoot = sem_Root_Root ⟨$⟩ pTree*
              *pTree = sem_Tree_Leaf ⟨$⟩ pInt*
                      ⟨|⟩ *sem_Tree_Bin*  ⟨$ *pSym 'B' ⟨*⟩ pTree ⟨*⟩ pTree*
           *pInt*  *= (λc → ord c − ord '0') ⟨$⟩ '0' ⟨..⟩ '9'*

The parser recognises the letter 'B' as a *Bin* alternative and a single digit as a *Leaf*.
Fig. 2 gives an overview of the parser combinators which are used [38]. The parser is
invoked from an alternative implementation of *main*:

*main :: IO ()*
*main =* **do** *tr ← parseIOMessage show pRepmin "B3B45"*
          *print tr*

We will not discuss this alternative further nor will we discuss this particular variant of
parser combinators. However, this approach is taken in the rest of these notes wherever
parsing is required.

| Combinator | Meaning | Result |
|---|---|---|
| *p* ⟨*⟩ *q* | *p* followed by *q* | result of *p* applied to result of *q* |
| *p* ⟨|⟩ *q* | *p* or *q* | result of *p* or result of *q* |
| *pSucceed r* | empty input ε | *r* |
| *f* ⟨$⟩ *p* | ≡ *pSucceed f* ⟨*⟩ *p* | |
| *pKey "x"* | symbol/keyword x | *"x"* |
| *p* ⟨**⟩ *q* | *p* followed by *q* | result of *q* applied to result of *p* |
| *p* 'opt' *r* | ≡ *p* ⟨|⟩ *pSucceed r* | |
| *p* ⟨??⟩ *q* | ≡ *p* ⟨**⟩ *q* 'opt' *id* | |
| *p* ⟨* *q, p* *⟩ *q, f* ⟨$ *p* | variants throwing away result of angle missing side | |
| *pFoldr listAlg p* | sequence of *p*'s | *foldr c n* (result of all *p*'s) |
| *pList p* | *pFoldr ((:), [ ]) p* | |
| *pChainr s p* | *p*'s (>1) separated by *s*'s | result of *s*'s applied to results of *p*'s aside |

**Fig. 2.** Parser combinators

*More features and typical usage: a pocket calculator.* We will continue with looking at
a more complex example, a pocket calculator which accepts expressions. The calculator
prints a pretty printed version of the entered expression, its computed value and some
statistics (the number of additions performed). An interactive terminal session of the
pocket calculator looks as follows:

```
$ build/bin/expr
Enter expression: 3+4
Expr='3+4', val=7, add count thus far=1
Enter expression: [a=3+4:a+a]
Expr='[a=3+4:a+a]', val=14, add count thus far=3
Enter expression: ^Cexpr: interrupted
$
```

This rudimentary calculator allows integer values, their addition and binding to identifiers. Parsing is character based, no scanner is used to transform raw text into tokens. No whitespace is allowed and a **let** expression is syntactically denoted by [<nm>=<expr>:<expr>].

The example will allow us to discuss more AG features as well as typical use of AG. We start with integer constants, addition followed by an attribute computation for the pretty printing:

**DATA** *AGItf*
  | *AGItf  expr* : *Expr*
**DATA** *Expr*
  | *IConst int*   : {*Int*}
  | *Add    e1*   : *Expr   e2* : *Expr*
**SET** *AllNT* = *AGItf  Expr*

The root of the tree is now called *AGItf* to indicate (as a naming convention) that this is the place where interfacing between the Haskell world and the AG world takes place.

The definition demonstrates the use of the **SET** keyword which allows the naming of a group of nodes. This name can later be used to declare attributes for all the named group of nodes at once.

The computation of a pretty printed representation follows the same pattern as the computation of *min* and *tree* in the *repmin* example, because of its compositional and bottom-up nature. The synthesized attribute *pp* is synthesized from the values of the *pp* attribute of the children of a node:

**ATTR** *AllNT* [∥ *pp* : *PP_Doc*]
**SEM** *Expr*
  | *IConst* **lhs**.*pp* = *pp* @*int*
  | *Add*    **lhs**.*pp* = @*e1.pp* ⊁ "+" ⊁ @*e2.pp*

The pretty printing uses a pretty printing library with combinators for values of type *PP_Doc* representing pretty printed documents. The library is not further discussed here; an overview of some of the available combinators can be found in Fig. 3.

As a next step we add **let** expressions and use of identifiers in expressions. This demonstrates an important feature of the AG system: we may introduce new alternatives for a ⟨*node*⟩ as well as may introduce new attribute computations in a separate piece of program text. We first add new AST alternatives for *Expr*:

| Combinator | Result |
|---|---|
| $p_1 \gg\!\!\mid\!\!< p_2$ | $p_1$ besides $p_2$, $p_2$ at the right |
| $p_1 \gg\!\!\#\!\!< p_2$ | same as $\gg\!\!\mid\!\!<$ but with an additional space in between |
| $p_1 \succ\!\!< p_2$ | $p_1$ above $p_2$ |
| *pp_parens p* | *p* inside parentheses |
| *text s* | string *s* as *PP_Doc* |
| *pp x* | pretty print *x* (assuming instance *PP x*) resulting in a *PP_Doc* |

**Fig. 3.** Pretty printing combinators

**DATA** *Expr*
   | *Let nm* : {*String*}    *val* : *Expr*    *body* : *Expr*
   | *Var nm* : {*String*}

One should keep in mind that the exensibility offered is simplistic of nature, but surprisingly flexible at the same time. The idea is that node variants, attribute declarations and attribute rules for node variants can all occur textually separated. The AG compiler gathers all definitions, combines, performs several checks (e.g. are attribute rules missing), and generates the corresponding Haskell code. All kinds of declarations can be distributed over several text files to be included with a **INCLUDE** directive (not discussed any further).

Any addition of new node variants requires also the corresponding definitions of already introduced attributes:

**SEM** *Expr*
   | *Let* **lhs**.*pp* = "[" $\gg\!\!\mid\!\!<$ @*nm* $\gg\!\!\mid\!\!<$ "=" $\gg\!\!\mid\!\!<$ @*val.pp* $\gg\!\!\mid\!\!<$ ":" $\gg\!\!\mid\!\!<$ @*body.pp* $\gg\!\!\mid\!\!<$ "]"
   | *Var* **lhs**.*pp* = *pp* @*nm*

The use of variables in the pocket calculator requires us to keep an administration of values bound to variables. An association list is used to provide this environmental and scoped information:

**ATTR** *Expr* [*env* : {[ (*String*, *Int*) ]} ‖]
**SEM** *Expr*
   | *Let*    *body.env* = (@*nm*, @*val.val*) : @**lhs**.*env*
**SEM** *AGItf*
   | *AGItf expr*.*env* = [ ]

The scope is enforced by extending the inherited attribute *env* top-down in the AST. Note that there is no need to specify a value for @*val.env* because of the copy rules discussed later. In the *Let* variant the inherited environment, which is used for evaluating the right hand sided of the bound expression, is extended with the new binding, before being used as the inherited *env* attribute of the body. The environment *env* is queried when the value of an expression is to be computed:

**ATTR** *AllNT* $[\|\ val : Int]$

**SEM** *Expr*

| *Var*    **lhs**.*val* = *maybe* 0 *id* (*lookup* @*nm* @**lhs**.*env*)
| *Add*    **lhs**.*val* = @*e1*.*val* + @*e2*.*val*
| *Let*    **lhs**.*val* = @*body*.*val*
| *IConst* **lhs**.*val* = @*int*

The attribute *val* holds this computed value. Because its value is needed in the 'outside' Haskell world it is passed through *AGItf* (as part of **SET** *AllNT*) as a synthesized attribute. This is also the case for the previously introduced *pp* attribute as well as the following *count* attribute used to keep track of the number of additions performed. However, the *count* attribute is also passed as an inherited attribute. Being both inherited and synthesized it is defined between the two vertical bars in the **ATTR** declaration for *count*:

**ATTR** *AllNT* $[|\ count : Int\ |]$

**SEM** *Expr*

| *Add* **lhs**.*count* = @*e2*.*count* + 1

The attribute *count* is said to be *threaded* through the AST, the AG solution to a global variable or the use of state monad. This is a result of the attribute being inherited as well as synthesized and the copy rules. Its effect is an automatic copying of the attribute in a preorder traversal of the AST.

*Copy rules* are attribute rules inserted by the AG system if a rule for an attribute ⟨*attr*⟩ in a production of ⟨*node*⟩ is missing. AG tries to insert a rule that copies the value of another attribute with the same name, searching in the following order:

1. Local attributes.
2. The synthesized attribute of the children to the left of the child for which an inherited ⟨*attr*⟩ definition is missing, with priority given to the nearest child fulfilling the condition. A synthesized ⟨*attr*⟩ of a parent is considered to be at the right of any child's ⟨*attr′*⟩.
3. Inherited attributes (of the parent).

In our example the effect is that for the *Let* variant of *Expr*

– (inherited) @**lhs**.*count* is copied to (inherited) @*val*.*count*,
– (synthesized) @*val*.*count* is copied to (inherited) @*body*.*count*,
– (synthesized) @*body*.*count* is copied to (synthesized) @**lhs**.*count*.

Similar copy rules are inserted for the other variants. Only for variant *Add* of *Expr* a different rule for  @**lhs**.*count* is explicitly specified, since here we have a non-trivial piece of semantics: i.e. we actually want to count something.

Automatic copy rule insertion can be both a blessing and curse. A blessing because it takes away a lot of tedious work and minimises clutter in the AG source text. On the other hand it can be a curse, because a programmer may have forgotten an otherwise required rule. If a copy rule can be inserted the AG compiler will silently do so, and the programmer will not be warned.

As with our previous example we can let a parser map input text to the invocations of semantic functions. For completeness this source text has been included in Fig. 4. The result of parsing combined with the invocation of semantic functions will be a function taking inherited attributes to a tuple holding all synthesized attributes. Even though the order of the attributes in the result tuple is specified, its extraction via pattern matching should be avoided. The AG system can be instructed to create a wrapper function which knows how to extract the attributes out of the result tuple:

**WRAPPER** *AGItf*

The attribute values are stored in a data type with labeled fields for each attribute. The attributes can be accessed with labels of the form ⟨*attr*⟩_*Syn*_⟨*node*⟩. The name of the wrapper is of the form *wrap*_⟨*node*⟩; the wrapper function is passed the result of the semantic function and a data type holding inherited attributes:

```
run :: Int → IO ()
run   count
   = do hPutStr stdout "Enter expression: "
        hFlush stdout
        l ← getLine
        r ← parseIOMessage show pAGItf l
        let r′ = wrap_AGItf r (Inh_AGItf{count_Inh_AGItf = count})
        putStrLn ("Expr='"                    ++ disp (pp_Syn_AGItf r′) 40 "" ++
                  "', val="                   ++ show (val_Syn_AGItf r′)      ++
                  ", add count thus far=" ++ show (count_Syn_AGItf r′)
                 )
        run (count_Syn_AGItf r′)
main :: IO ()
main = run 0
```

We face a similar problem with the passing of inherited attributes to the semantic function. Hence inherited attributes are passed to the wrapper function via a data type with name *Inh*_⟨*node*⟩ and a constructor with the same name, with fields having labels of the form ⟨*attr*⟩_*Inh*_⟨*node*⟩. The *count* attribute is an example of an attribute which must be passed as an inherited attribute as well as extracted as a synthesized attribute.

This concludes our introduction to the AG system. Some topics have either not been mentioned at all or only shortly touched upon. We provide a list of those topics together with a reference to the first use of the features which are actually used later in these notes. Each of these items is marked with 𝒜𝒢 to indicate that it is about the AG system.

- Type synonym, only for lists (see section 14).
- Left hand side patterns for simultaneous definition of rules (see section 42).
- Set notation for variant names in rules (see section 31).

- Local attributes (see section 31).
- Additional copy rule via **USE** (see section 3.2).
- Additional copy rule via **SELF** (see section 3.2).
- Rule redefinition via := (see section 3.3).
- Cycle detection and other (experimental) features, commandline invocation, etc.

We will come back to the AG system itself in our conclusion.

```
instance Symbol Char
pAGItf :: IsParser p Char ⇒ p T_AGItf
pAGItf = pRoot
    where pRoot      = sem_AGItf_AGItf ⟨$⟩ pExpr
          pExpr      = pChainr (sem_Expr_Add ⟨$ pSym '+') pExprBase
          pExprBase  = (sem_Expr_IConst.foldl (λl r → l ∗ 10 + r) 0)
                         ⟨$⟩ pList1 ((λc → ord c − ord '0') ⟨$⟩ '0' ⟨..⟩ '9')
                       ⟨|⟩ sem_Expr_Let
                         ⟨$ pSym '[' ⟨∗⟩ pNm ⟨∗ pSym '=' ⟨∗⟩ pExpr
                         ⟨∗ pSym ':' ⟨∗⟩                    pExpr
                         ⟨∗ pSym ']'
                       ⟨|⟩ sem_Expr_Var ⟨$⟩ pNm
          pNm        = (:"") ⟨$⟩ 'a' ⟨..⟩ 'z'
```

**Fig. 4.** Parser for calculator example

## 2   EH 1: Typed λ-Calculus

In this section we build the first version of our series of compilers: the typed $\lambda$-calculus packaged in Haskell syntax in which all values need to explicitly be given a type. The compiler checks if the specified types are in agreement with actual value definitions. For example

**let** $i :: Int$
　　$i = 5$
**in** $i$

is accepted, whereas

**let** $i :: Char$
　　$i = 5$
**in** $i$

produces a pretty printed version of the erroneous program, annotated with errors:

```
let i :: Char
    i = 5
    {- ***ERROR(S):
         In '5':
           Type clash:
             failed to fit: Int <= Char
             problem with : Int <= Char -}
    {- [ i:Char ] -}
in i
```

Type signatures have to be specified for identifiers bound in a **let** expression. For $\lambda$-expressions the type of the parameter can be extracted from these type signatures unless a $\lambda$-expression occurs at the position of an applied function. In that case a type signature for the $\lambda$-expression is required in the expression itself. This program will not typecheck because this EH version does not allow polymorphic types in general and on higher ranked (that is, parameter) positions in particular.

> **let** $v$ :: $(Int, Char)$
> $\quad v = ( (\lambda f \rightarrow (f\ 3, f\ \mathbf{'x'}))$
> $\qquad\qquad :: (Char \rightarrow Char) \rightarrow (Int, Char)$
> $\qquad ) (\lambda x \rightarrow x)$
> **in** $v$

The implementation of a type system will be the main focus of this and following sections. As a consequence the full environment/framework needed to build a compiler will not be discussed. This means in particular that error reporting, generation of a pretty printed annotated output, parsing and the compiler driver are not described.

We start with the definition of the AST and how it relates to concrete syntax, followed by the introduction of several attributes required for the implementation of the type system.

## 2.1   Concrete and Abstract Syntax

The *concrete syntax* of a (programming) language describes the structure of acceptable sentences for that language, or more down to earth, it describes what a compiler for that language accepts with respect to the textual structure. On the other hand, *abstract syntax* describes the structure used by the compiler itself for analysis and code generation. Translation from the more user friendly concrete syntax to the machine friendly abstract syntax is done by a parser; from the abstract to the concrete representation is done by a pretty printer.

Let us focus our attention first on the abstract syntax for EH1, in particular the part defining the structure for expressions (the remaining syntax can be found in Fig. 5).

**DATA** *Expr*
```
| IConst  int      : {Int}
| CConst char      : {Char}
| Con     nm       : {HsName}
| Var     nm       : {HsName}
| App     func     : Expr
          arg      : Expr
| Let     decls    : Decls
          body     : Expr
| Lam     arg      : PatExpr
          body     : Expr
| AppTop  expr     : Expr
| Parens  expr     : Expr
| TypeAs  tyExpr   : TyExpr
          expr     : Expr
```

Integer constants are represented by *IConst*, lowercase (uppercase) identifier occurrences by *Var* (*Con*), an *App* represents the application of a function to its argument, *Lam* and *Let* represent lambda expressions and let expressions.

𝒜𝒢: **Type synonyms (for lists).** The AG notation allows type synomyms for one special case, AG's equivalent of a list. It is an often occurring idiom to encode a list of nodes, say **DATA** *L* with elements ⟨*node*⟩ as:

**DATA** *L*
```
| Cons hd : ⟨node⟩
       tl  : L
| Nil
```

AG allows the following notation as a shorthand:

**TYPE** $L = [\langle node \rangle]$

The EH fragment (which is incorrect for this version of because type signatures are missing)

**let** *ic* @ $(i, c) = (5, \text{'}\mathbf{x}\text{'})$
      *id*        $= \lambda x \rightarrow x$
**in**  *id i*

is represented by the following piece of abstract syntax tree:

```
AGItf_AGItf
   Expr_Let
      Decls_Cons
```

```
          Decl_Val
        PatExpr_VarAs "ic"
           PatExpr_AppTop
             PatExpr_App
               PatExpr_App
                 PatExpr_Con ",2"
                 PatExpr_Var "i"
               PatExpr_Var "c"
          Expr_AppTop
            Expr_App
              Expr_App
                Expr_Con ",2"
                Expr_IConst 5
              Expr_CConst 'x'
        Decls_Cons
          Decl_Val
            PatExpr_Var "id"
            Expr_Lam
              PatExpr_Var "x"
              Expr_Var "x"
          Decls_Nil
      Expr_AppTop
        Expr_App
          Expr_Var "id"
          Expr_Var "i"
```

The example also demonstrates the use of patterns, which is almost the same as in Haskell: EH does not allow a type signature for the elements of a tuple.

Looking at this example and the rest of the abstract syntax in Fig. 5 we can make several observations of what one is allowed to write in EH and what can be expected from the implementation.

- There is a striking similarity between the structure of expressions *Expr* and patterns *PatExpr* (and as we will see later type expressions *TyExpr*): they all contain *App* and *Con* variants. This similarity will sometimes be exploited to factor out common code, and, if factoring out cannot be done, leads to similarities between pieces of code. This is the case with pretty printing(not included in these notes), which is quite similar for the different kinds of constructs.
- Type signatures (*Decl_TySig*) and value definitions (*Decl_Val*) may be freely mixed. However, type signatures and value definitions for the same identifier are still related.
- Because of the textual decoupling of value definitions and type signatures, a type signature may specify the type for an identifier occurring inside a pattern:

$$\textbf{let } a \qquad :: Int$$
$$(a, b) = (3, 4)$$
$$\textbf{in } \quad ...$$

Currently we do not allow this, but the following however is:

$$\textbf{let } ab \qquad :: (Int, Int)$$
$$ab @ (a, b) = (3, 4)$$
$$\textbf{in } \quad ...$$

because the specified type for *ab* corresponds to the top of a pattern of a value definition.

---

| **DATA** *AGItf* | | |
|---|---|---|
| \| *AGItf* | *expr* | : *Expr* |
| **DATA** *Decl* | | |
| \| *TySig* | *nm* | : {*HsName*} |
| | *tyExpr* | : *TyExpr* |
| \| *Val* | *patExpr* | : *PatExpr* |
| | *expr* | : *Expr* |
| **TYPE** *Decls* | = [*Decl*] | |
| **SET** *AllDecl* | = *Decl Decls* | |
| **DATA** *PatExpr* | | |
| \| *IConst* | *int* | : {*Int*} |
| \| *CConst* | *char* | : {*Char*} |
| \| *Con* | *nm* | : {*HsName*} |
| \| *Var* | *nm* | : {*HsName*} |
| \| *VarAs* | *nm* | : {*HsName*} |
| | *patExpr* | : *PatExpr* |
| \| *App* | *func* | : *PatExpr* |
| | *arg* | : *PatExpr* |
| \| *AppTop* | *patExpr* | : *PatExpr* |
| \| *Parens* | *patExpr* | : *PatExpr* |
| **SET** *AllPatExpr* = *PatExpr* | | |
| **DATA** *TyExpr* | | |
| \| *Con* | *nm* | : {*HsName*} |
| \| *App* | *func* | : *TyExpr* |
| | *arg* | : *TyExpr* |
| \| *AppTop* | *tyExpr* | : *TyExpr* |
| \| *Parens* | *tyExpr* | : *TyExpr* |
| **SET** *AllTyExpr* | = *TyExpr* | |
| **SET** *AllExpr* | = *Expr* | |
| **SET** *AllNT* | = *AllTyExpr AllDecl AllPatExpr AllExpr* | |

---

**Fig. 5.** Abstract syntax for EH (without Expr)

- In EH composite values are created by tupling, denoted by $(..,..)$. The same notation is also used for patterns (for unpacking a composite value) and types (describing the structure of the composite). In all these cases the corresponding AST consists of a *Con* applied to the elements of the tuple. For example, the value $(2, 3)$ corresponds to

$$Expr\_App \; (Expr\_App \; (Expr\_Con \; ",2") \; (Expr\_IConst \; 2)) \; (Expr\_IConst \; 3)$$

- For now there is only one value constructor: for tuples. The EH constructor for tuples also is the one which needs special treatment because it actually stands for a infinite family of constructors. This can be seen in the encoding of the name of the constructor which is composed of a ", " together with the arity of the constructor. For example, the expression $(3, 4)$ is encoded as an application *App* of *Con* ",2" to the two *Int* arguments: (,2 3 4). In our examples we will follow the Haskell convention, in which we write (,) instead of ',2'. By using this encoding we also get the unit type () as it is encoded by the name ",0".
- The naming convention for tuples and other naming conventions are available through the following definitions for Haskell names *HsName*.

```
data HsName = HNm String
            deriving (Eq, Ord)
instance Show HsName where
   show (HNm s) = s
hsnArrow, hsnUnknown, hsnInt, hsnChar, hsnWild :: HsName
hsnArrow                      = HNm "->"
hsnUnknown                    = HNm "??"
hsnInt                        = HNm "Int"
hsnChar                       = HNm "Char"
hsnWild                       = HNm "_"

hsnProd                       :: Int → HsName
hsnProd     i                 = HNm (',' : show i)

hsnIsArrow, hsnIsProd         :: HsName → Bool
hsnIsArrow   hsn              = hsn ≡ hsnArrow
hsnIsProd    (HNm (',' : _))  = True
hsnIsProd    _                = False

hsnProdArity                  :: HsName → Int
hsnProdArity (HNm (_ : ar))   = read ar
```

- Each application is wrapped on top with an *AppTop*. This has no meaning in itself but it simplifies the pretty printing of expressions[3]. We need *AppTop* for patterns, but for the rest it can be ignored.
- The location of parentheses around an expression is remembered by a *Parens* alternative. We need this for the reconstruction of the parenthesis in the input.

---

[3] As it also complicates parsing it may disappear in future versions of EH.

– *AGItf* is the top of a complete abstract syntax tree. As noted in the AG primer this is the place where interfacing with the 'outside' Haskell world takes place. It is a convention in these notes to give all nonterminals in the abstract syntax a name with *AGItf* in it, if it plays a similar role.

## 2.2   Types

We will now turn our attention to the way the type system is incorporated into EH1. We focus on the pragmatics of the implementation and less on the corresponding type theory.

**What is a type.** Compiler builders consider a *type* to be a description of the interpretation of a value whereas a value is to be understood as a bitpattern. This means in particular that machine operations such as integer addition, are only applied to patterns that are to be interpreted as integers. More generally, we want to prevent unintended interpretations of bitpatterns, which might likely lead to the crash of a program.

The flow of values, that is, the copying between memory locations, through the execution of a program may only be such that a copy is allowed only if the corresponding types relate to each other in some proper fashion. A compiler uses a type system to analyse this flow and to make sure that built-in functions are only applied to patterns that they are intended to work on. The idea is that if a compiler cannot find an erroneous flow of values, with the notion of erroneous defined by the type system, the program is guaranteed not to crash because of unintended use of bitpatterns.

In this section we start by introducing a type language in a more formal setting as well as a more practical setting. The formal setting uses typing rules to specify the static semantics of EH whereas in the practical setting the AG system is used, providing an implementation. In the following section we discuss the typing rules, the mechanism for enforcing the equality of types (called *fitting*) and the checking itself. Types will be introduced informally, instead of taking a more formal approach [40,41,34,2].

Types are described by a type language. The type language for EH1 allows some basic types and two forms of composite types, functions and tuples, and is described by the following grammar:

$$\sigma = Int \mid Char$$
$$\mid (\sigma, ..., \sigma)$$
$$\mid \sigma \to \sigma$$

The following definition however is closer to the one used in our implementation:

$$\sigma = Int \mid Char \mid \to \mid , \mid ,, \mid ...$$
$$\mid \sigma\,\sigma$$

The latter definition also introduces the possibility of describing types like *Int Int*. We nevertheless use this one since it is used in the implementation of later versions of EH where it will prove useful in expressing the application of type constructors to types. Here we just have to make sure no types like *Int Int* will be created; in a (omitted) later version of EH we perform kind inferencing/checking to prevent the creation of such types from showing up.

The corresponding encoding using AG notation differs in the presence of an *Any* type, also denoted by □. In section 2.3 we will say more about this. It is used to smoothen the type checking by (e.g.) limiting the propagation of erroneous types:

**DATA** *TyAGItf*
  | *AGItf ty*   : *Ty*

**DATA** *Ty*
  | *Con*   *nm*  : {*HsName*}
  | *App*   *func* : *Ty*
          *arg*  : *Ty*
  | *Any*

The formal system and implementation of this system use different symbols to refer to the same concept. For example, *Any* in the implementation is the same as □ in the typing rules. Not always is such a similarity pointed out explicitly but instead a notation *name₁*//*name₂* is used to simultaneously refer to both symbols $name_1$ and $name_2$, for example *Any*//□. The notation also implies that the identifiers and symbols separated by '//' are referring to the same concept.

The definition of *Ty* will be used in both the Haskell world and the AG world. In Haskell we use the corresponding **data** type generated by the AG compiler, for example in the derived type *TyL*:

**type** *TyL* = [*Ty*]

The data type is used to construct type representations. In the AG world we define computations over the type structure in terms of attributes. The corresponding semantic functions generated by the AG system can then be applied to Haskell values.

### 2.3 Checking Types

The type system of a programming language is described by typing rules. A *typing rule*

– Relates language constructs to types.
– Constrains the types of these language constructs.

**Type rules.** For example, the following is the typing rule (taken from Fig. 6) for function application

$$\frac{\Gamma \overset{expr}{\vdash} e_2 : \sigma^a \qquad \Gamma \overset{expr}{\vdash} e_1 : \sigma^a \to \sigma}{\Gamma \overset{expr}{\vdash} e_1\ e_2 : \sigma} \quad \text{(e-app1)}$$

It states that an application of $e_1$ to $e_2$ has type $\sigma$ provided that the argument has type $\sigma^a$ and the function has a type $\sigma^a \to \sigma$.

---

$$\boxed{\Gamma \overset{expr}{\vdash} e : \sigma}$$

$$\frac{\begin{array}{c} \Gamma \overset{expr}{\vdash} e_2 : \sigma^a \\ \Gamma \overset{expr}{\vdash} e_1 : \sigma^a \to \sigma \end{array}}{\Gamma \overset{expr}{\vdash} e_1\, e_2 : \sigma} \text{ (e-app1)} \qquad \frac{i \mapsto \sigma^i, \Gamma \overset{expr}{\vdash} e : \sigma^e}{\Gamma \overset{expr}{\vdash} \lambda i \to e : \sigma^i \to \sigma^e} \text{ (e-lam1)}$$

$$\frac{\begin{array}{c} \Gamma \overset{expr}{\vdash} e_2 : \sigma_2 \\ \Gamma \overset{expr}{\vdash} e_1 : \sigma_1 \end{array}}{\Gamma \overset{expr}{\vdash} (e_1, e_2) : (\sigma_1, \sigma_2)} \text{ (e-prod1)} \qquad \frac{\begin{array}{c} i \mapsto \sigma^i, \Gamma \overset{expr}{\vdash} e^i : \sigma^i \\ i \mapsto \sigma^i, \Gamma \overset{expr}{\vdash} e : \sigma^e \end{array}}{\Gamma \overset{expr}{\vdash} \textbf{let } i :: \sigma^i; i = e^i \textbf{in } e : \sigma^e} \text{ (e-let1)}$$

$$\frac{(i \mapsto \sigma) \in \Gamma}{\Gamma \overset{expr}{\vdash} i : \sigma} \text{ (e-ident1)} \qquad \frac{}{\Gamma \overset{expr}{\vdash} \textit{minint} .. \textit{maxint} : \textit{Int}} \text{ (e-int1)}$$

**Fig. 6.** Type rules for expressions

---

All rules we will use are of the form

$$\frac{\begin{array}{c} prerequisite_1 \\ prerequisite_2 \\ \cdots \end{array}}{consequence} \text{ (rule-name)}$$

with the meaning that if all $prerequisite_i$ can be proven we may conclude the *consequence*.

A *prerequisite* can take the form of any logical predicate or has a more structured form, usually called a *judgement*:

$$context \overset{judgetype}{\vdash} construct : property \rightsquigarrow more\ results$$

The part "$\rightsquigarrow$ *more results*" needs not always be present if there are no more results for a judgement. The notation reads as

In the interpretation *judgetype* the *construct* has property *property* assuming *context* and with optional additional *more results*.

If the *context* or *more results* itself consists of multiple parts, these parts are separated by a semicolon ';'. An underscore '_' has a similar role as in Haskell to indicate a property is not relevant for a type rule (see rule **e-app1B**, Fig. 7)

Although a rule formally is to be interpreted purely equational, it may help to realise that from an implementors point of view this (more or less) corresponds to an implementation template, either in the form of a function *judgetype*:

$$judgetype = \lambda construct \rightarrow$$
$$\lambda context \rightarrow ...(property, more\_results)$$

or a piece of AG:

$$\textbf{ATTR } judgetype \; [context : ... \; \|$$
$$property : ...more\_results : ...]$$

**SEM** *judgetype*
| *construct*
$$\textbf{lhs}.(property, more\_results) = ... \; @\textbf{lhs}.context ...$$

Typing rules and implementation templates differ in that the latter prescribes the order in which the computation of a property takes place, whereas the former simply postulates relationships between parts of a rule. In general typing rules presented throughout these notes will be rather explicit in the flow of information and thus be close to the actual implementation.

**Environment.** The rules in Fig. 6 refer to $\Gamma$, which is often called *assumptions*, *environment* or *context* because it provides information about what may be assumed about identifiers. Identifiers $\xi$ are distinguished on the case of the first character, capitalized $I$'s starting with an uppercase, uncapitalized $i$'s otherwise

$$\xi = i$$
$$| \; I$$

For type constants we will use capitalized identifiers $I$, whereas for identifiers bound to an expression in a **let**-expression we will use lower case identifiers $(i, j, ...)$.

An environment $\Gamma$ is a vector of bindings, a partial finite map from identifiers to types:

$$\Gamma = \overline{\xi \mapsto \sigma}$$

Concatenation of such collections as well as scrutinizing a collection is denoted with a comma ','. For example, '$i \mapsto \sigma, \Gamma$' represents a concatenation as well as a pattern match. For rules this does not make a difference, for the implementation there is a direction involved as we either construct from smaller parts or deconstruct (pattern match) into smaller parts.

If shadowing is involved, that is duplicate entries are added, left/first (w.r.t. to the comma ',') entries shadow right/later entries. In particular, when we locate some variable in a $\Gamma$ the first occurrence will be taken.

If convenient we will also use a list notation:

$$\Gamma = [\xi \mapsto \sigma]$$

This will be done if specific properties of a list are used or if we borrow from Haskell's repertoire of list functions. For simplicity we also use (assocation) lists in our implementation.

A list structure suffices to encode the presence of an identifier in a $\Gamma$, but it cannot be used to detect multiple occurrences caused by duplicate introductions. Thus in our implementation we use a stack of lists instead:

```
type AssocL k v = [(k, v)]
```

```
newtype Gam k v = Gam [AssocL k v] deriving Show
emptyGam       :: Gam k v
gamUnit        :: k → v      → Gam k v
gamLookup      :: Eq k ⇒ k → Gam k v → Maybe v
gamToAssocL    :: Gam k v   → AssocL k v
gamPushNew     :: Gam k v   → Gam k v
gamPushGam     :: Gam k v   → Gam k v → Gam k v
gamAddGam      :: Gam k v   → Gam k v → Gam k v
gamAdd         :: k → v      → Gam k v → Gam k v

emptyGam                          = Gam [[]]
gamUnit        k v                = Gam [[(k, v)]]
gamLookup      k (Gam ll)         = foldr (λl mv → maybe mv Just (lookup k l))
                                        Nothing ll
gamToAssocL    (Gam ll)           = concat ll
gamPushNew     (Gam ll)           = Gam ([] : ll)
gamPushGam g1 (Gam ll2)           = Gam (gamToAssocL g1 : ll2)
gamAddGam      g1 (Gam (l2 : ll2)) = Gam ((gamToAssocL g1 ++ l2) : ll2)
gamAdd         k v                = gamAddGam (k ↦ v)
```

Entering and leaving a scope is implemented by means of pushing and popping a $\Gamma$. Extending an environment $\Gamma$ will take place on the top of the stack only. A *gamUnit* used as an infix operator will print as $\mapsto$.

A specialization *ValGam* of *Gam* is used to store and lookup the type of value identifiers.

**data** *ValGamInfo* = *ValGamInfo*{*vgiTy* :: *Ty*} **deriving** *Show*
**type** *ValGam* = *Gam HsName ValGamInfo*

The type is wrapped in a *ValGamInfo*. Later versions of EH can add additional fields to this data type.

*valGamLookup* :: *HsName* → *ValGam* → *Maybe ValGamInfo*
*valGamLookup* = *gamLookup*

*valGamLookupTy* :: *HsName* → *ValGam* → (*Ty, ErrL*)
*valGamLookupTy n g*
  = **case** *valGamLookup n g* **of**
      *Nothing* → (*Ty_Any*, [*Err_NamesNotIntrod* [*n*]])
      *Just vgi* → (*vgiTy vgi*, [ ])

Later the variant *valGamLookup* will do additional work, but for now it does not differ from *gamLookup*. The additional variant *valGamLookupTy* is specialized further to produce an error message in case the identifier is missing from the environment.

**Checking Expr.** The rules in Fig. 6 do not provide much information about how the type $\sigma$ in the consequence of a rule is to be computed; it is just stated that it should relate in some way to other types. However, type information can be made available to parts of the abstract syntax tree, either because the programmer has supplied it somewhere or because the compiler can reconstruct it. For types given by a programmer the compiler has to check if such a type correctly describes the value of an expression for which the type is given. This is called *type checking*. If no type information has been given for a value, the compiler needs to reconstruct or infer this type based on the structure of the abstract syntax tree and the semantics of the language as defined by the typing rules. This is called *type inferencing*. In EH1 we exclusively deal with type checking.

We now can tailor the type rules in Fig. 6 towards an implementation which performs type checking, in Fig. 7. We also start with the discussion of the corresponding AG implementation. The rules now take an additional context, the expected (or known) type $\sigma^k$ (attribute *knTy*, simultaneously referred to by $\sigma^k /\!/ knTy$) as specified by the programmer, defined in terms of AG as follows:

  **ATTR** *AllExpr* [*knTy* : *Ty* ‖]

The basic idea underlying this implementation for type checking, as well as in later versions of EH also for type inferencing, is that

– A *known* (or *expected*) type $\sigma^k /\!/ knTy$ is passed top-down through the syntax tree of an expression, representing the maximal type (in terms of $\leqslant$, see Fig. 8 and discus-

$$\boxed{\Gamma; \sigma^k \overset{expr}{\vdash} e : \sigma}$$

$$\frac{\begin{array}{c}\Gamma; \sigma^a \overset{expr}{\vdash} e_2 : \_\\[2pt]\Gamma; \square \to \sigma^k \overset{expr}{\vdash} e_1 : \sigma^a \to \sigma\end{array}}{\Gamma; \sigma^k \overset{expr}{\vdash} e_1\, e_2 : \sigma} \text{ (e-app1B)} \qquad \frac{i \mapsto \sigma^i, \Gamma; \sigma^r \overset{expr}{\vdash} e : \sigma^e}{\Gamma; \sigma^i \to \sigma^r \overset{expr}{\vdash} \lambda i \to e : \sigma^i \to \sigma^e} \text{ (e-lam1B)}$$

$$\frac{\begin{array}{c}\Gamma; \sigma_2^k \overset{expr}{\vdash} e_2 : \sigma_2\\[2pt]\Gamma; \sigma_1^k \overset{expr}{\vdash} e_1 : \sigma_1\end{array}}{\Gamma; (\sigma_1^k, \sigma_2^k) \overset{expr}{\vdash} (e_1, e_2) : (\sigma_1, \sigma_2)} \text{ (e-prod1B)} \qquad \frac{\begin{array}{c}i \mapsto \sigma^i, \Gamma; \sigma^i \overset{expr}{\vdash} e^i : \_\\[2pt]i \mapsto \sigma^i, \Gamma; \sigma^k \overset{expr}{\vdash} e : \sigma^e\end{array}}{\Gamma; \sigma^k \overset{expr}{\vdash} \mathbf{let}\, i :: \sigma^i; i = e^i \mathbf{in}\, e : \sigma^e} \text{ (e-let1B)}$$

$$\frac{\begin{array}{c}(i \mapsto \sigma^i) \in \Gamma\\[2pt]\overset{fit}{\vdash} \sigma^i \leqslant \sigma^k : \sigma\end{array}}{\Gamma; \sigma^k \overset{expr}{\vdash} i : \sigma} \text{ (e-ident1B)} \qquad \frac{\overset{fit}{\vdash} Int \leqslant \sigma^k : \sigma}{\Gamma; \sigma^k \overset{expr}{\vdash} minint .. maxint : \sigma} \text{ (e-int1B)}$$

**Fig. 7.** Type checking for expression (checking variant)

sion below) the type of an expression can be. At all places where this expression is used it also is assumed that the type of this expression equals $\sigma^k$.

- A result type $\sigma /\!/ ty$ is computed bottom-up for each expression, representing the minimal type (in terms of $\leqslant$) the expression can have.
- At each node in the abstract syntax tree it is checked whether $\sigma \leqslant \sigma^k$ holds. The result of $lhs \leqslant rhs$ is $rhs$ which is subsequently used by the type checker, for example to simply return or use in constructing another, usually composite, type.
- In general, for $lhs \leqslant rhs$ the $rhs$ is an expected type whereas $lhs$ is the bottom-up computed result type.

An additional judgement type named *fit* (Fig. 8) is needed to check an actual type against an expected (known) type. The judgement specifies the matching $\sigma_1 \leqslant \sigma_2$ of two types $\sigma_1$ and $\sigma_2$. The meaning of $\leqslant$ is that the left hand side (lhs) type $\sigma_1$ of $\leqslant$ can be used where the right hand side (rhs) type $\sigma_2$ is expected. Expressed differently, $\leqslant$ checks whether a value of type $\sigma_1$ can flow (that is, be stored) into a memory location of type $\sigma_2$. This is an asymmetric relation because "a value flowing into a location" does not imply that it can flow the other way, so $\leqslant$ conceptually has a direction, even though in the rules in Fig. 8 $\leqslant$ is a test on equality of the two type arguments.

$$\boxed{\overset{fit}{\vdash} \sigma^l \leqslant \sigma^r : \sigma}$$

$$\frac{\overset{fit}{\vdash} \sigma_2^a \leqslant \sigma_1^a : \sigma^a \quad \overset{fit}{\vdash} \sigma_1^r \leqslant \sigma_2^r : \sigma^r}{\overset{fit}{\vdash} \sigma_1^a \to \sigma_1^r \leqslant \sigma_2^a \to \sigma_2^r : \sigma^a \to \sigma^r} \quad \text{(f-arrow1)}$$

$$\frac{\overset{fit}{\vdash} \sigma_1^l \leqslant \sigma_2^l : \sigma^l \quad \overset{fit}{\vdash} \sigma_1^r \leqslant \sigma_2^r : \sigma^r}{\overset{fit}{\vdash} (\sigma_1^l, \sigma_1^r) \leqslant (\sigma_2^l, \sigma_2^r) : (\sigma^l, \sigma^r)} \quad \text{(f-prod1)} \qquad \frac{I_1 \equiv I_2}{\overset{fit}{\vdash} I_1 \leqslant I_2 : I_2} \quad \text{(f-con1)}$$

$$\frac{}{\overset{fit}{\vdash} \square \leqslant \sigma : \sigma} \quad \text{(f-anyl1)} \qquad \frac{}{\overset{fit}{\vdash} \sigma \leqslant \square : \sigma} \quad \text{(f-anyr1)}$$

**Fig. 8.** Rules for fit

The rules for $\leqslant$ also specify a result type. Strictly this result is not required for the *fit* judgement to hold but in the implementation it is convenient to have the implementation *fitsIn* of $\leqslant$ return the smallest type $\sigma$ for which of $\sigma_1 \leqslant \sigma$ and $\sigma_2 \leqslant \sigma$ hold. This is useful in particular in relation to the use of $\square$ in in rule f-anyl1 and rule f-anyr1; we will come back to this later.

For example, $\leqslant$ is used in rule e-int1B which checks that its actual *Int* type matches the known type $\sigma^k$. The implementation of the type rule e-int1B performs this check and returns the type $\sigma$ in attribute *ty*:

**ATTR** *AllExpr* $[\| \ ty : Ty]$
**SEM** *Expr*
    | *CConst* **loc**.*fTy* = *tyChar*
    | *IConst*  **loc**.*fTy* = *tyInt*
    | *IConst CConst*
         **loc**.*fo*  = @*fTy* $\leqslant$ @**lhs**.*knTy*
         .*ty*  = *foTy* @*fo*

$\mathcal{AG}$: **Set notation for variants.** The rule for (e.g.) attribute *fo* is specified for *IConst* and *CConst* together. Instead of specifying only one variant a whitespace separated list of variant names may be specified after the vertical bar '|'. It is also allowed to specify this list relative to all declared variants by specifying for which variants the rule should *not* be declared. For example: $* - IConst\ CConst$ if the rule was to be defined for all variants except *IConst* and *CConst*.

$\mathcal{AG}$: **Local attributes.** The attribute *fTy* is declared locally. In this context 'local' means that the scope is limited to the variant of a node. Attribute *fTy* defined for variant *IConst* is available only for other attribute rules for variant *IConst* of *Expr*. Note that no explicit rule for synthesized attribute *ty* is required; a copy rule is inserted to use the value of the locally declared attribute *ty*. This is a common AG idiom when a value is required for later use as well or needs to be redefined in later versions of EH.

Some additional constants representing built-in types are also required:

$$tyInt\ \ = Ty\_Con\ hsnInt$$
$$tyChar = Ty\_Con\ hsnChar$$

The local attribute *fTy* (by convention) holds the type as computed on the basis of the abstract syntax tree. This type *fTy* is subsequently compared to the expected type **lhs**.*knTy* via the implementation *fitsIn* of the rules for *fit* $/\!/$ $\leqslant$. In infix notation *fitsIn* prints as $\leqslant$. The function *fitsIn* returns a *FIOut* (**fitsIn out**put) data structure in attribute *fo*. *FIOut* consists of a record containing amongst other things field *foTy*:

$$\mathbf{data}\ FIOut = FIOut\{foTy :: Ty \quad ,foErrL :: ErrL\}$$
$$emptyFO \ \ = FIOut\{foTy = Ty\_Any, foErrL = [\,] \quad \}$$

$$foHasErrs :: FIOut \to Bool$$
$$foHasErrs = \neg.null.foErrL$$

Using a separate attribute *fTy* instead of using its value directly has been done in order to prepare for a redefinition of *fTy* in later versions[4].

$Ty\_Any /\!/ Any /\!/ \square$ plays a special role. This type appears at two places in the implementation of the type system as a solution to the following problems:

– Invariant to our implementation is the top-down passing of an expected type. However, this type is not always fully known in a top-down order. For example, in rule **e-app1B** (Fig. 7) the argument of the expected function type $\square \to \sigma^k$ is not known because this information is only available from the environment $\Gamma$ which is used further down in the AST via rule **e-ident1B**. In this use of $\square$ it represents a "dont't know" of the type system implementation. As such $\square$ has the role of a type variable (as introduced for type inferencing in section 3).

---

[4] This will happen with other attributes as well.

– An error occurs at a place where the implementation of the type system needs a type to continue (type checking) with. In that case □ is used to prevent further errors from occurring. In this use of □ it represents a "dont't care" of the type system implementation. As such □ will be replaced by more a more specific type as soon as it matches (via $\leqslant$) such a type.

In both cases □ is a type exclusively used by the implementation to smoothen type checking. The rules for $\leqslant$ for □ in Fig. 8 state that □ is equal to any type. The effect is that the result of $\leqslant$ is a more specific type. This suits our "dont't know" and "dont't care" use. Later, when discussing the AG implementation for these rules this issue reappears. In later EH versions we will split the use of □ into the proper use of a type lattice, and will it thus disappear.

The role of □ may appear to be similar to $\top$ and $\bot$ known from type theory. However, □ is used only as a mechanism for the type system implementation. It is not offered as a feature to the user (i.e. the EH programmer) of the type system.

$Ty\_Any /\!/ Any /\!/ \square$ is also used at the top level where the actual expected type of the expression neither is specified nor matters because it is not used:

**SEM** *AGItf*
  | *AGItf expr.knTy* = *Ty\_Any*

The rule f-arrow1 in Fig. 8 for comparing function types compares the types for arguments in the opposite direction. Only in later versions of EH when $\leqslant$ really behaves asymmetrically we will discuss this aspect of the rules which is named *contravariance*. In the rules in Fig. 8 the direction makes no difference; the correct use of the direction for now only anticipates issues yet to come.

The Haskell counterpart of $\vdash^{fit} \sigma_1 \leqslant \sigma_2 : \sigma$ is implemented by *fitsIn*:

```
fitsIn :: Ty → Ty → FIOut
fitsIn ty₁ ty₂
    =  f ty₁ ty₂
  where
    res t            = emptyFO{foTy = t}
    f Ty_Any t₂     = res t₂
    f t₁      Ty_Any = res t₁
    f t₁ @ (Ty_Con s1)
      t₂ @ (Ty_Con s2)
        | s1 ≡ s2    = res t₂

    f t₁ @ (Ty_App (Ty_App (Ty_Con c1) ta₁) tr₁)
      t₂ @ (Ty_App (Ty_App (Ty_Con c2) ta₂) tr₂)
        | hsnIsArrow c1 ∧ c1 ≡ c2
        = comp ta₂ tr₁ ta₁ tr₂ (λa r → [a] 'mkTyArrow' r)
```

$$f\ t_1\ @\,(Ty\_App\ tf_1\ ta_1)$$
$$t_2\ @\,(Ty\_App\ tf_2\ ta_2)$$
$$= comp\ tf_1\ ta_1\ tf_2\ ta_2\ Ty\_App$$
$$f\ t_1 \qquad t_2 \qquad = err\,[Err\_UnifyClash\ ty_1\ ty_2\ t_1\ t_2]$$
$$err\ e \qquad\qquad = emptyFO\{foErrL = e\}$$
$$comp\ tf_1\ ta_1\ tf_2\ ta_2\ mkComp$$
$$= foldr1\ (\lambda fo_1\ fo_2 \rightarrow \textbf{if}\ foHasErrs\ fo_1\ \textbf{then}\ fo_1\ \textbf{else}\ fo_2)$$
$$[\textit{ffo}, afo, res\ rt]$$
$$\textbf{where}\ \textit{ffo} = f\ tf_1\ tf_2$$
$$afo = f\ ta_1\ ta_2$$
$$rt\ = mkComp\ (foTy\ \textit{ffo})\ (foTy\ afo)$$

The function *fitsIn* checks whether the *Ty\_App* structure and all type constants *Ty\_Con* are equal. If not, a non-empty list of errors is returned as well as type $Ty\_Any /\!/ Any /\!/ \square$. Matching a composite type is split in two cases for *Ty\_App*, one for function types (the first case), and one for the remaining type applications (the second case). For the current EH version the second case only concerns tuple types. Both matches for composite types use *comp* wich performs multiple $\leqslant$'s and combines the results. The difference lies in the treatment of contravariant behavior as discussed earlier.

The type rules leave in the open how to handle a situation when a required constraint is broken. For a compiler this is not good enough, being the reason *fitsIn* gives a "will-do" type *Ty\_Any* back together with an error for later processing. Errors themselves are also described via AG:

**DATA** *Err*
  | *UnifyClash ty1*    : {*Ty*} *ty2*    : {*Ty*}
                *ty1detail* : {*Ty*} *ty2detail* : {*Ty*}

**DATA** *Err*
  | *NamesNotIntrod nmL* : {[*HsName*]}

The *Err* datatype is available as a datatype in the same way *Ty* is. The error datatype is also used for signalling undeclared identifiers:

**SEM** *Expr*
  | *Var* **loc.**(*gTy, nmErrs*)
            = *valGamLookupTy* @*nm* @**lhs.**valGam*
    .*fTy* = @*gTy*
    .*fo*  = @*fTy* $\leqslant$ @**lhs.**knTy*
    .*ty*  = *foTy* @*fo*

𝒜𝒢: **Left hand side patterns.** The simplest way to define a value for an attribute is to define one value for one attribute at a time. However, if this value is a tuple, its fields are to be extracted and assigned to individual attributes (as in *tyArrowArgRes*). AG allows a pattern notation of the form(s) to make the notation for this situation more concise:

$$| \ \langle variant \rangle \quad \langle node \rangle.(\langle attr_1 \rangle \ , \langle attr_2 \rangle \qquad \ , ...) \ =$$
$$| \ \langle variant \rangle \quad (\langle node_1 \rangle.\langle attr_1 \rangle, \langle node_1 \rangle.\langle attr_2 \rangle, ...) \ =$$

Again, the error condition is signalled by a non empty list of errors if a lookup in $\Gamma$ fails. These errors are gathered so they can be incorporated into an annotated pretty printed version of the program.

Typing rule **e-ident1B** uses the environment $\Gamma$ to retrieve the type of an identifier. This environment *valGam* for types of identifiers simply is declared as an inherited attribute, initialized at the top of the abstrcat syntax tree. It is only extended with new bindings for identifiers at a declaration of an identifier.

**ATTR** *AllDecl AllExpr* $[valGam : ValGam \ ||]$
**SEM** *AGItf*
  | *AGItf expr.valGam* = *emptyGam*

One may wonder why the judgement $\overset{fit}{\vdash} \ \sigma_1 \leqslant \sigma_2 : \sigma$ and its implementation *fitsIn* returns a type at all; the idea of checking was to only pass explicit type information $\sigma^k$ (or *knTy*) from the top of the abstract syntax tree to the leaf nodes. Note that this idea breaks when we try to check the expression *id* 3 in

**let** *id* :: *Int* → *Int*
    *id* = $\lambda x \to x$
**in** *id* 3

What is the *knTy* against which 3 will be checked? It is the argument type of the type of *id*. However, in rule **e-app1B** and its AG implementation, the type of *id* is not the (top-to-bottom travelling) $\sigma^k // knTy$, but it will be the argument part of the (bottom-to-top travelling) resulting function type of $e_1 // func.ty$:

**SEM** *Expr*
  | *App* **loc** *.knFunTy*    = $[Ty\_Any]$ '*mkTyArrow*' @**lhs**.*knTy*
      *func.knTy*      = @*knFunTy*
      (*arg.knTy*, **loc**.*fTy*) = *tyArrowArgRes* @*func.ty*
      **loc** *.ty*        = @*fTy*

The idea here is to encode the partially known function type as $\square \ \to \ \sigma^k$ (passed to *fun.knTy*) and let *fitsIn* fill in the missing details, that is to find a type for $\square$. This is the place where it is convenient to have *fitsIn* return a type in which $\square // Ty\_Any$'s are replaced by a more concrete type. From that result the known/expected type of the argument can be extracted.

Note that we are already performing a little bit of type inferencing. This is however only done locally to *App* as the $\square$ in $\square \ \to \ \sigma^k$ is guaranteed to have disappeared in the result type of *fitsIn*. If this is not the case, the EH program contains an error. This is a mechanism we repeatedly use, so we summarize it here:

- Generally, the semantics of the language requires a type $\sigma$ to be of a specific form. Here $\sigma$ equals the type of the function (not known at the *App* location in the AST) which should have the form $\square \to \sigma^k$.
- The specific form may contain types about which we know nothing, here encoded by $\square$, in later EH versions by type variables.
- *fitsIn*$/\!/ \leqslant$ is used to enforce $\sigma$ to have the right form. Here this is done by pushing the form as $\sigma^k$ down the AST for the function (attribute *func.knTy*). The check $\sigma \leqslant \sigma^k$ is then performed in the *Var* variant of *Expr*.
- Enforcing may or may not succeed. In the latter case error messages are generated and the result of enforcing is $\square$.

The type construction and inspection done in the *App* variant of *Expr* requires some additional type construction functions, of which we only include *mkTyArrow*:

```
algTy       :: MkConApp Ty
algTy       = (Ty_Con, Ty_App, id, id)
mkTyArrow :: TyL → Ty → Ty
mkTyArrow = flip (foldr (mkArrow algTy))
```

The function is derived from a more general function *mkArrow*:

```
type MkConApp t = (HsName → t, t → t → t, t, t → t → t)

mkArrow :: MkConApp t → t → t → t
mkArrow alg @ (con, _, _, _) a r = mkApp alg [con hsnArrow, a, r]

mkApp :: MkConApp t → [t] → t
mkApp (_, app, top, _) ts
  = case ts of
      [t] → t
      _   → top (foldl1 app ts)
```

A *MkConApp* contains four functions, for constructing a value similar to *Con*, *App*, *AppTop* and *IConst* respectively. These functions are used by *mkApp* to build an *App* like structure and by *mkArrow* to build function like structures. The code for (e.g.) parsers (omitted from these notes), uses these functions parameterized with the proper four semantics functions as generated by the AG system. So this additional layer of abstraction improves code reuse. Similarly, function *mkTyProdApp* constructs a tuple type out of types for the elements.

The functions used for scrutinizing a type are given names in which (by convention) the following is encoded:

- What is scrutinized.
- What is the result of scrutinizing.

For example, *tyArrowArgRes* dissects a function type into its argument and result type. If the scrutinized type is not a function, "will do" values are returned:

*tyArrowArgRes* :: $Ty \rightarrow (Ty, Ty)$

*tyArrowArgRes t*
  = **case** *t* **of**
      *Ty_App (Ty_App (Ty_Con nm) a) r*
        | *hsnIsArrow nm* $\rightarrow (a, r)$
      _                  $\rightarrow (Ty\_Any, t)$

Similarly *tyProdArgs* is defined to return the types of the elements of a tuple type. The code for this and other similar functions have been omitted for brevity.

*Constructor Con, tuples.* Apart from constructing function types only tupling allows us to build composite types. The rule **e-prod1B** for tupling has no immediate counterpart in the implementation because a tuple $(a, b)$ is encoded as the application $(, )$ $a$ $b$. The alternative *Con* takes care of producing a type $a \rightarrow b \rightarrow (a, b)$ for $(, )$.

**SEM** *Expr*
  | *Con* **loc**.*ty* = **let** *resTy* = *tyArrowRes* @**lhs**.*knTy*
                    **in** *tyProdArgs resTy* `mkTyArrow` *resTy*

This type can be constructed from *knTy* which by definition has the form $\square \rightarrow \square \rightarrow$ $(a, b)$ (for this example). The result type of this function type is taken apart and used to produce the desired type. Also by definition (via construction by the parser) we know the arity is correct.

   Note that, despite the fact that the cartesian product constructors are essentially polymorphic, we do not have to do any kind of unification here, since they either appear in the right hand side of declaration where the type is given by an explcit type declaration, or they occur at an argument position where the type has been implicitly specified by the function type. Therefore we indeed can use the *a* and *b* from type $\square \rightarrow \square \rightarrow (a, b)$ to construct the type $a \rightarrow b \rightarrow (a, b)$ for the constructor $(, )$.

*λ-expression Lam.* For rule **e-lam1B** the check whether *knTy* has the form $\sigma_1 \rightarrow \sigma_2$ is done by letting *fitsIn* match the *knTy* with $\square \rightarrow \square$. The result (forced to be a function type) is split up by *tyArrowArgRes* into argument and result type. The function *gamPushNew* opens a new scope on top of *valGam* so as to be able to check duplicate names introduced by the pattern *arg*:

**SEM** *Expr*
  | *Lam* **loc**.*funTy*          = $[Ty\_Any]$ `mkTyArrow` *Ty_Any*
        .*foKnFun*           = @*funTy* $\leqslant$ @**lhs**.*knTy*
        (*arg.knTy, body.knTy*) = *tyArrowArgRes (foTy* @*foKnFun*)
        *arg.valGam*          = *gamPushNew* @**lhs**.*valGam*
        **loc**.*ty*              = @**lhs**.*knTy*

*Type annotations (for $\lambda$-expression).* In order to make $\lambda$-expressions typecheck correctly it is the responsibility of the EH programmer to supply the correct type signature. The *TypeAs* variant of *Expr* takes care of this by simply passing the type signature as the expected type:

**SEM** *Expr*
  | *TypeAs* **loc** .*fo*   = @*tyExpr.ty* ⩽ @**lhs**.*knTy*
        *expr.knTy* = @*tyExpr.ty*

The obligation for the EH programmer to specify a type is dropped in later versions of EH.

**Checking PatExpr.** Before we can look into more detail at the way new identifiers are introduced in **let**- and $\lambda$-expressions we take a look at patterns. The rule e-let1B is too restrictive for the actual language construct supported by EH because the rule only allows a single identifier to be introduced. The following program allows inspection of parts of a composite value by naming its components through pattern matching:

**let** $p :: (Int, Int)$
    $p @ (a, b) = (3, 4)$
  **in** $a$

The rule e-let1C from Fig. 9 together with the rules for patterns from Fig. 10 reflects the desired behaviour. These rules differ from those in Fig. 7 in that a pattern instead of a single identifier is allowed in a value definition and the parameter position of a $\lambda$-expression.

$$\boxed{\Gamma; \sigma^k \overset{expr}{\vdash} e : \sigma}$$

$$
\frac{
\begin{array}{c}
\Gamma^p, \Gamma; \sigma^i \overset{expr}{\vdash} e^i : \_\\[4pt]
\Gamma^p, \Gamma; \sigma^k \overset{expr}{\vdash} e : \sigma^e\\[4pt]
\sigma^i \overset{pat}{\vdash} p : \Gamma^p\\[4pt]
p \equiv i \vee p \equiv i @ ...
\end{array}
}{
\Gamma; \sigma^k \overset{expr}{\vdash} \textbf{let } i :: \sigma^i; p = e^i \textbf{in } e : \sigma^e
}
\quad \text{(e-let1C)}
$$

$$
\frac{
\begin{array}{c}
\Gamma^p, \Gamma; \sigma^r \overset{expr}{\vdash} e : \sigma^e\\[4pt]
\sigma^p \overset{pat}{\vdash} p : \Gamma^p
\end{array}
}{
\Gamma; \sigma^p \to \sigma^r \overset{expr}{\vdash} \lambda p \to e : \sigma^p \to \sigma^e
}
\quad \text{(e-lam1C)}
$$

**Fig. 9.** Type checking for let-expression with pattern

Again the idea is to distribute a known type over the pattern by dissecting it into its constituents. However, patterns do not return a type but type bindings for the identifiers inside a pattern instead. The new bindings are subsequently used in **let**- and $\lambda$-expressions bodies.

A tuple pattern with rule **p-prod1** is encoded in the same way as tuple expressions; that is, pattern $(a, b)$ is encoded as an application $(a,b)$ with an *AppTop* on top of it. We

---

$$\boxed{\sigma^k \overset{pat}{\vdash} p : \Gamma^p}$$

$$
\cfrac{}{\sigma^k \overset{pat}{\vdash} i : [i \mapsto \sigma^k]} \; \text{(p-var1)}
\qquad
\cfrac{
\begin{array}{c}
dom\,(\Gamma_1^p) \cap dom\,(\Gamma_2^p) = \emptyset \\
\sigma_2^k \overset{pat}{\vdash} p_2 : \Gamma_2^p \\
\sigma_1^k \overset{pat}{\vdash} p_1 : \Gamma_1^p
\end{array}
}{
(\sigma_1^k, \sigma_2^k) \overset{pat}{\vdash} (p_1, p_2) : \Gamma_1^p, \Gamma_2^p
} \; \text{(p-prod1)}
$$

**Fig. 10.** Building environments from patterns

---

dissect the known type of a tuple in rule **p-prod1** into its element types at *AppTop* using function *tyProdArgs*. For this version of EH we only have tuple patterns; we can indeed assume that we are dealing with a tuple type.

**ATTR** *AllPatExpr* $[knTy : Ty \parallel]$
**ATTR** *PatExpr* $[knTyL : TyL \parallel]$

**SEM** *PatExpr*
  | *AppTop* **loc** .*knProdTy*
                = @**lhs**.*knTy*
           .(*knTyL*, *aErrs*)
                = **case** *tyProdArgs* @*knProdTy* **of**
                   *tL* | @*patExpr*.*arity* $\equiv$ *length tL*
                     $\rightarrow$ (*reverse tL*, [ ])
                 _ $\rightarrow$ (*repeat Ty_Any*
                     , [*Err_PatArity*
                         @*knProdTy* @*patExpr*.*arity*])
  | *App*     **loc** .(*knArgTy*, *knTyL*)
                = *hdAndTl* @**lhs**.*knTyL*
         *arg*.*knTy* = @*knArgTy*

The list of these elements is passed through attribute *knTyL* to all *App*'s of the pattern. At each *App* one element of this list is taken as the *knTy* of the element AST.

The complexity in the *AppTop* alternative of *PatExpr* arises from repair actions in case the arity of the pattern and its known type do not match. In that case the subpatterns are given as many □'s as known type as necessary.

Finally, for the distribution of the known type throughout a pattern we need to properly initialize *knTyL*:

**SEM** *Decl*
  | *Val   patExpr.knTyL* = [ ]
**SEM** *Expr*
  | *Lam arg      .knTyL* = [ ]

The arity of the patterns is needed as well:

**ATTR** *PatExpr* [‖ *arity* : *Int*]
**SEM** *PatExpr*
  | *App* **lhs**.*arity* = @*func*.*arity* + 1
  | *Con Var AppTop IConst CConst*
      **lhs**.*arity* = 0

As a result of this unpacking, at a *Var* alternative attribute *knTy* holds the type of the variable name introduced. The type is added to attribute *valGam* that is threaded through the pattern for gathering all introduced bindings:

**ATTR** *AllPatExpr* [| *valGam* : *ValGam* |]
**SEM** *PatExpr*
  | *Var VarAs* **loc**.*ty*      = @**lhs**.*knTy*
              .*varTy*      = @*ty*
              .*addToGam* = **if** @**lhs**.*inclVarBind* ∧  @*nm* ≢ *hsnWild*
                          **then** *gamAdd* @*nm*
                                  (*ValGamInfo* @*varTy*)
                          **else** *id*
  | *Var*     **lhs**.*valGam* = @*addToGam* @**lhs**.*valGam*
  | *VarAs*   **lhs**.*valGam* = @*addToGam* @*patExpr*.*valGam*

The addition to *valGam* is encoded in the attribute *addToGam*, a function which only adds a new entry if the variable name is not equal to an underscore '_' and has not been added previously via a type signature for the variable name, signalled by attribute *inclVarBind* (defined later).

**Checking declarations.** In a **let**-expression type signatures, patterns and expressions do meet. Rule e-let1C from Fig. 9 shows that the idea is straightforward: take the type signature, distribute it over a pattern to extract bindings for identifiers and pass both type signature (as *knTy*) and bindings (as *valGam*) to the expression. This works fine for single combinations of type signature and the corresponding value definition for a pattern. However, it does not work for:

– Mutually recursive value definitions.

> **let** $f :: ...$
> $\quad f = \lambda x \rightarrow ...g ...$
> $\quad g :: ...$
> $\quad g = \lambda x \rightarrow ...f ...$
> **in**   ...

In the body of $f$ the type $g$ must be known and vice-versa. There is no ordering of what can be defined and checked first. In Haskell $f$ and $g$ together would be in the same binding group.

– Textually separated signatures and value definitions.

> **let** $f :: ...$
> $\quad ...$
> $\quad f = \lambda x \rightarrow ...$
> **in**   ...

Syntactically the signature and value definition for an identifier need not be defined adjacently or in any specific order.

In Haskell dependency analysis determines that $f$ and $g$ form a so-called *binding group*, which contains declarations that have to be subjected to type analysis together. However, due to the obligatory presence of the type signatures in this version of EH it is possible to first gather all signatures and only then type check the value definitions. Therefore, for this version of EH it is not really an issue as we always require a signature to be defined. For later versions of EH it actually will become an issue, so for simplicity all bindings in a **let**-expression are analysed together as a single (binding) group.

   Though only stating something about one combination of type signature and value definition, rule **e-let1C** still describes the basic strategy. First extract all type signatures, then distribute those signatures over patterns followed by expressions. The difference lies in doing it simultaneously for all declarations in a **let**-expression. So, first all signatures are collected:

**ATTR** *AllDecl* $[|\ gathTySigGam : ValGam\ |]$
**SEM** *Decl*
  | *TySig* **loc**  *.gamSigTy*         $= @tyExpr.ty$
              *.gathTySigGam*  $= gamAdd$
                               $@nm\ (ValGamInfo\ @gamSigTy)$
                               $@\mathbf{lhs}.gathTySigGam$

**SEM** *Expr*
  | *Let*   *decls.gathTySigGam*  $= emptyGam$

Attribute *gathTySigGam* is used to gather type signatures. The gathered signatures are then passed back into the declarations. Attribute *tySigGam* is used to distribute the gathered type signatures over the declarations.

**ATTR** *AllDecl* [*tySigGam* : *ValGam* ‖]
**SEM** *Expr*
  | *Let*  *decls.tySigGam*        = @*decls.gathTySigGam*

At a value declaration we extract the the type signature from *tySigGam* and use it to check whether a pattern has a type signature:

**SEM** *Decl*
  | *Val*  **loc**  .(*sigTy*, *hasTySig*) = **case** @*patExpr.mbTopNm* **of**
                                   *Nothing*
                                       → (*Ty_Any*, *False*)
                                 *Just nm*
                                     → **case** *gamLookup nm* @**lhs**.*tySigGam* **of**
                                            *Nothing* → (*Ty_Any*, *False*)
                                            *Just vgi* → (*vgiTy vgi*, *True*)

This type signature is then used as the known type of the pattern and the expression.

**SEM** *Decl*
  | *Val* **loc**.*knTy* = @*sigTy*

The flag *hasTySig* is used to signal the presence of a type signature for a value and a correct form of the pattern. We allow patterns of the form '*ab* @(*a*, *b*)' to have a type signature associated with *ab*. No type signatures are allowed for '(*a*, *b*)' without the '*ab* @' alias (because there is no way to refer to the anonymous tuple) nor is it allowed to specify type signature for the fields of the tuple (because of simplicity, additional plumbing would be required).

**ATTR** *PatExpr* [‖ *mbTopNm* : {*Maybe HsName*}]
**SEM** *PatExpr*
  | *Var VarAs* **loc**.*mbTopNm* = **if** @*nm* ≡ *hsnWild* **then** *Nothing* **else** *Just* @*nm*
  | ∗ − *Var VarAs*
              **loc**.*mbTopNm* = *Nothing*

The value of *hasTySig* is also used to decide on the binding of the top level identifier of a pattern, via *inclVarBind*.

**ATTR** *PatExpr* [*inclVarBind* : *Bool* ‖]
**SEM** *PatExpr*
  | *AppTop patExpr.inclVarBind* = *True*
**SEM** *Decl*
  | *Val*    *patExpr.inclVarBind* = ¬ @*hasTySig*
**SEM** *Expr*
  | *Lam*   *arg*    .*inclVarBind* = *True*

If a type signature for an identifier is already defined there is no need to rebind the identifier by adding one more binding to *valGam*.

New bindings are not immediately added to *valGam* but are first gathered in a separately threaded attribute *patValGam*, much in the same way as *gathTySigGam* is used.

**ATTR** *AllDecl* [| *patValGam* : *ValGam* |]

**SEM** *Decl*

| Val patExpr.valGam | = @**lhs**.patValGam |
| --- | --- |
| **lhs**   .patValGam | = @patExpr.valGam |
| expr   .valGam | = @**lhs**.valGam |

**SEM** *Expr*

| Let decls.patValGam | = @decls.gathTySigGam |
| --- | --- |
|  | 'gamPushGam' @**lhs**.valGam |
| **loc**  .(lValGam, gValGam) | = gamPop @decls.patValGam |
| decls.valGam | = @decls.patValGam |
| body.valGam | = @decls.patValGam |

Newly gathered bindings are stacked on top of the inherited *valGam* before passing them on to both declarations and body.

Some additional functionality for pushing and popping the stack *valGam* is also needed:

$$gamPop \quad :: Gam\ k\ v \quad \to (Gam\ k\ v, Gam\ k\ v)$$
$$assocLToGam :: AssocL\ k\ v \to Gam\ k\ v$$

$$gamPop \quad (Gam\ (l:ll)) = (Gam\ [l], Gam\ ll)$$
$$assocLToGam\ l \qquad\qquad = Gam\ [l]$$

Extracting the top of the stack *patValGam* gives all the locally introduced bindings in *lValGam*. An additional error message is produced if any duplicate bindings are present in *lValGam*.

**Checking TyExpr.** All that is left to do now is to use the type expressions to extract type signatures. This is straightforward as type expressions (abstract syntax for what the programmer specified) and types (as internally used by the compiler) have almost the same structure:

**ATTR** *TyExpr* [|| *ty* : *Ty*]

**SEM** *TyExpr*

| Con **lhs**.ty = Ty_Con @nm
| App **lhs**.ty = Ty_App @func.ty @arg.ty

Actually, we need to do more because we also have to check whether a type is defined. A variant of *Gam* is used to hold type constants:

**data** *TyGamInfo* = *TyGamInfo*{ *tgiTy* :: *Ty*} **deriving** *Show*

**type** *TyGam* = *Gam HsName TyGamInfo*

*tyGamLookup* :: *HsName* → *TyGam* → *Maybe TyGamInfo*
*tyGamLookup nm g*
    = **case** *gamLookup nm g* **of**
        *Nothing* | *hsnIsProd nm* → *Just* (*TyGamInfo* (*Ty_Con nm*))
        *Just tgi*                    → *Just tgi*
        _                             → *Nothing*

This Γ is threaded through *TyExpr*:

**ATTR** *AllTyExpr* [| *tyGam* : *TyGam* |]

At the root of the AST *tyGam* is initialized with the fixed set of types available in this version of the compiler:

**SEM** *AGItf*
    | *AGItf* **loc**.*tyGam* = *assocLToGam*
                            [ (*hsnArrow*, *TyGamInfo* (*Ty_Con hsnArrow*))
                            , (*hsnInt*,    *TyGamInfo tyInt*)
                            , (*hsnChar*,   *TyGamInfo tyChar*)
                            ]

Finally, at the *Con* alternative of *TyExpr* we need to check if a type is defined:

**SEM** *TyExpr*
    | *Con* **loc**.(*tgi*, *nmErrs*) = **case** *tyGamLookup* @*nm* @**lhs**.*tyGam* **of**
                            *Nothing* → (*TyGamInfo Ty_Any*
                                        , [*Err_NamesNotIntrod* [@*nm*]])
                            *Just tgi* → (*tgi*, [])

## 3   EH 2: Monomorphic Type Inferencing

The next version of EH drops the requirement that all value definitions need to be accompanied by an explicit type signature. For example, the example from the introduction:

**let** *i* = 5
**in** *i*

is accepted by this version of EH:

```
let i = 5
    {- [ i:Int ] -}
in i
```

The idea is that the type system implementation has an internal representation for "knowing it is a type, but not yet which one" which can be replaced by a more specific type if that becomes known. The internal representation for a yet unknown type is called a *type variable*, similar to mutable variables for (runtime) values.

The implementation attempts to gather as much information as possible from a program to reconstruct (or infer) types for type variables. However, the types it can reconstruct are limited to those allowed by the used type language, that is, basic types, tuples and functions. All types are assumed to be monomorphic, that is, polymorphism is not yet allowed. The next version of EH deals with polymorphism.

So

> **let** $id = \lambda x \rightarrow x$
> **in let** $v = id\ 3$
>   **in** $id$

will give

```
let id = \x -> x
     {- [ id:Int -> Int ] -}
in let v = id 3
        {- [ v:Int ] -}
     in id
```

If the use of *id* to define *v* is omitted, less information (namely the argument of *id* is an int) to infer a type for *id* is available. Because no more specific type information for the argument (and result) of *id* could be retrieved the representation for "not knowing which type", that is, a type variable, is shown:

```
let id = \x -> x
     {- [ id:v_1_1 -> v_1_1 ] -}
in id
```

On the other hand, if contradictory information is found we will have

```
let id = \x -> x
     {- [ id:Int -> Int ] -}
in let v = (id 3,id 'x')
        {- ***ERROR(S):
             In '(id 3,id 'x')':
                ... In ''x'':
                    Type clash:
                        failed to fit: Char <= Int
                        problem with : Char <= Int -}
        {- [ v:(Int,Int) ] -}
     in v
```

However, the next version of EH dealing with Haskell style polymorphism (section 4 ) accepts this program.

Partial type signatures are also allowed. A partial type signature specifies a type only for a part, allowing a coöperation between the programmer who specifies what is (e.g.) already known about a type signature and the type inferencer filling in the unspecified details. For example:

$$
\begin{aligned}
&\textbf{let } id :: \ldots \rightarrow \ldots \\
&\quad id = \lambda x \rightarrow x \\
&\textbf{in let } f :: (Int \rightarrow Int) \rightarrow \ldots \\
&\quad\quad f = \lambda i \rightarrow \lambda v \rightarrow i\ v \\
&\quad\quad v = f\ id\ 3 \\
&\quad\textbf{in let } v = f\ id\ 3 \\
&\quad\quad\textbf{in } v
\end{aligned}
$$

The type inferencer pretty prints the inferred type instead of the explicity type signature:

```
let id :: Int -> Int
    id = \x -> x
    {- [ id:Int -> Int ] -}
in let f :: (Int -> Int) -> Int -> Int
        f = \i -> \v -> i v
        v = f id 3
        {- [ v:Int, f:(Int -> Int) -> Int -> Int ] -}
    in let v = f id 3
            {- [ v:Int ] -}
        in v
```

The discussion of the implementation of this feature is postponed until section 3.6 in order to demonstrate the effects of an additional feature on the compiler implementation in isolation.

## 3.1  Type Variables

In order to be able to represent yet unknown types the type language needs *type variables* to represent this:

$$
\begin{aligned}
\sigma = &\ Int \mid Char \\
\mid &\ (\sigma, \ldots, \sigma) \\
\mid &\ \sigma \rightarrow \sigma \\
\mid &\ v
\end{aligned}
$$

The corresponding type structure *Ty* needs to be extended with an alternative for a variable:

**DATA** *Ty*
    | *Var tv* : {*TyVarId*}

A type variable is identified by a unique identifier, a *UID*:

**newtype** *UID* = *UID* [*Int*] **deriving** (*Eq*, *Ord*)

**type** *UIDL* = [*UID*]

**instance** *Show UID* **where**
　　*show* (*UID ls*) = *concat.intersperse* "_".*map show.reverse* $ *ls*

**type** *TyVarId* = *UID*

**type** *TyVarIdL* = [*TyVarId*]

The idea is to thread a counter as global variable through the AST, incrementing it whenever a new unique value is required. The implementation used throughout all EH compiler versions is more complex because an *UID* actually is a hierarchy of counters, each level counting in the context of an outer level. This is not discussed any further; we will ignore this aspect and just assume a unique *UID* can be obtained. However, a bit of its implementation is visible in the pretty printed representation as a underscore separated list of integer values, occasionaly visible in sample output of the compiler.

## 3.2   Constraints

Although the typing rules at Fig. 9 still hold we need to look at the meaning of $\leqslant$ (or *fitsIn*) in the presence of type variables. The idea here is that what is unknown may be replaced by that which is known. For example, when the check $v \leqslant \sigma$ is encountered, the easiest way to make $v \leqslant \sigma$ true is to state that the (previously) unknown type $v$ equals $\sigma$. An alternative way to look at this is that $v \leqslant \sigma$ is true under the constraint that $v$ equals $\sigma$.

**Remembering and applying constraints.** Next we can observe that once a certain type $v$ is declared to be equal to a type $\sigma$ this fact has to be remembered.

$$C = [v \mapsto \sigma]$$

A set of *constraints* $C$ (appearing in its non pretty printed form as Cnstr in the source text) is a set of bindings for type variables, represented as an association list:

**newtype** *C* = *C* (*AssocL TyVarId Ty*) **deriving** *Show*
*cnstrTyLookup* :: *TyVarId* → *C* → *Maybe Ty*
*cnstrTyLookup tv* (*C s*) = *lookup tv s*

*emptyCnstr* :: *C*
*emptyCnstr* = *C* []

*cnstrTyUnit* :: *TyVarId* → *Ty* → *C*
*cnstrTyUnit tv t* = *C* [(*tv*, *t*)]

If *cnstrTyUnit* is used as an infix operator it is printed as $\mapsto$ in the same way as used in type rules.

Different strategies can be used to cope with constraints [17,29]. Here constraints $C$ are used to replace all other references to $v$ by $\sigma$, for this reason often named a *substitution*. In this version of EH the replacement of type variables with newly types is done immediately after constraints are obtained as to avoid finding a new and probably conflicting constraint for a type variable. Applying constraints means substituting type variables with the bindings in the constraints, hence the class *Substitutable* for those structures which have references to type variables hidden inside and can replace, or substitute those type variables:

**infixr** 6 $\succ$

**class** *Substitutable s* **where**
$\quad$ $(\succ) :: C \to s \to s$
$\quad$ *ftv* $:: s \to TyVarIdL$

The operator $\succ$ applies constraints $C$ to a *Substitutable*. Function *ftv* extracts the free type variable references as a set of *TVarId*'s.

A $C$ can be applied to a type:

**instance** *Substitutable Ty* **where**
$\quad$ $(\succ) = tyAppCnstr$
$\quad$ *ftv* $= tyFtv$

This is another place where we use the AG notation and the automatic propagation of values as attributes throughout the type representation to make the description of the application of a $C$ to a $Ty$ easier. The function *tyAppCnstr* is defined in terms of the following AG. The plumbing required to provide the value of attribute *repl* (*tvs*) available as the result of Haskell function *tyAppCnstr* (*tyFtv*) has been omitted:

**ATTR** *TyAGItf AllTy* [*cnstr* : $C$ ||                ]
**ATTR** *AllAllTy*        [         || *repl* : **SELF**]
**ATTR** *TyAGItf*         [         || *repl* : *Ty*    ]
**SEM** *Ty*
$\quad$ | *Var*                    **lhs**.*repl* = *maybe* @*repl* *id* (*cnstrTyLookup* @*tv* @**lhs**.*cnstr*)

**ATTR** *TyAGItf AllTy* [|| *tvs* **USE**{$\cup$}{[ ]} : *TyVarIdL*]
**SEM** *Ty*
$\quad$ | *Var*                    **lhs**.*tvs* = [@*tv*]

$\mathcal{AG}$**: Attribute of type SELF.** The type of an attribute of type **SELF** depends on the node in which a rule is defined for the attribute. The generated type of an attribute ⟨*attr*⟩ for ⟨*node*⟩ is equal to the generated Haskell datatype of the same name ⟨*node*⟩. The AG compiler inserts code for building ⟨*node*⟩'s from the ⟨*attr*⟩ of the children and other fields. Insertion of this code can be overridden by providing a definition ourselves. In this way a complete copy of the AST can be built as a Haskell value. For example, via attribute *repl* a copy of the type is built which only differs (or, may differ) in the original in the value for the type variable.

$\mathcal{AG}$: **Attribute together with USE.** A synthesized attribute $\langle attr \rangle$ may be declared together with **USE**$\{\langle op \rangle\}\{\langle zero \rangle\}$. The $\langle op \rangle$ and $\langle zero \rangle$ allow the insertion of copy rules which behave similar to Haskell's *foldr*. The first piece of text $\langle op \rangle$ is used to combine the attribute values of two children by textually placing this text as an operator between references to the attributes of the children. If no child has an $\langle attr \rangle$, the second piece of text $\langle zero \rangle$ is used as a default value for $\langle attr \rangle$. For example, tvs USE {'union'} {[]} (appearing in pretty printed form as *tvs* **USE**$\{\cup\}\{[\,]\}$) gathers bottom-up the free type variables of a type.

The application of a $C$ is straightforwardly lifted to lists:

**instance** *Substitutable a* $\Rightarrow$ *Substitutable* $[a]$ **where**
   $s \succ l = map \ (s \succ) \ l$
   *ftv* $l = unionL.map \ ftv \ \$ \ l$

*unionL* :: *Eq a* $\Rightarrow$ $[[a]] \rightarrow [a]$
*unionL* = *foldr union* $[\,]$

A $C$ can also be applied to another $C$:

**instance** *Substitutable C* **where**
   $s1 \ @ \ (C \ sl_1) \succ s2 \ @ \ (C \ sl_2)$
      $= C \ (sl_1 \ +\!\!+ \ map \ (\lambda(v,t) \rightarrow (v, s1 \succ t)) \ sl'_2)$

      **where** $sl'_2 = deleteFirstsBy \ (\lambda(v1,\_) \ (v2,\_) \rightarrow v1 \equiv v2) \ sl_2 \ sl_1$
   *ftv* $(C \ sl)$
      $= ftv.map \ snd \ \$ \ sl$

Substituting a substitution is non-commutative as constraints $s_1$ in $s_1 \succ s_2$ take precedence over $s_2$. To make this even clearer all constraints for type variables in $s_1$ are removed from $s_2$, even though for a list implementation this would not be required.

**Computing constraints.** The only source of constraints is the check *fitsIn* which determines whether one type can flow into another one. The previous version of EH could only do one thing in case a type could not fit in another: report an error. Now, if one of the types is unknown, which means that it is a type variable, we have the additional possibility of returning a constraint on that type variable. The implementation *fitsIn* of $\leqslant$ additionaly has to return constraints:

**data** *FIOut* = *FIOut*{*foTy* :: *Ty*     ,*foErrL* :: *ErrL*, *foCnstr* :: *C*          }

*emptyFO*    = *FIOut*{*foTy* = *Ty_Any*, *foErrL* = $[\,]$     ,*foCnstr* = *emptyCnstr*}

Computation and proper combination of constraints necessitates *fitsIn* to be rewritten:

$$fitsIn :: Ty \rightarrow Ty \rightarrow FIOut$$
$$fitsIn \; ty_1 \; ty_2$$
$$= \; f \; ty_1 \; ty_2$$
**where**

| | |
|---|---|
| *res t* | $= emptyFO\{foTy = t\}$ |
| | |
| *bind tv t* | $= (res \; t)\{foCnstr = tv \mapsto t\}$ |
| *occurBind v t* $\mid v \in ftv \; t$ | $= err \; [Err\_UnifyOccurs \; ty_1 \; ty_2 \; v \; t]$ |
| $\mid otherwise$ | $= bind \; v \; t$ |

$$comp \; tf_1 \; ta_1 \; tf_2 \; ta_2 \; mkComp$$
$$= foldr1 \; (\lambda fo_1 \; fo_2 \rightarrow \textbf{if} \; foHasErrs \; fo_1 \; \textbf{then} \; fo_1 \; \textbf{else} \; fo_2)$$
$$[ffo, afo, rfo]$$
$$\textbf{where} \; ffo \; = f \; tf_1 \; tf_2$$
$$fs \; = foCnstr \; ffo$$
$$afo = f \; (fs \succ ta_1) \; (fs \succ ta_2)$$
$$as \; = foCnstr \; afo$$
$$rt \; = mkComp \; (as \succ foTy \; ffo) \; (foTy \; afo)$$
$$rfo = emptyFO\{foTy = rt, foCnstr = as \succ fs\}$$

| | | |
|---|---|---|
| *f Ty_Any* | $t_2$ | $= res \; t_2$ |
| $f \; t_1$ | *Ty_Any* | $= res \; t_1$ |
| $f \; t_1 \; @(Ty\_Con \; s1)$ | | |
| $t_2 \; @(Ty\_Con \; s2)$ | | |
| $\mid s1 \equiv s2$ | | $= res \; t_2$ |
| | | |
| $f \; t_1 \; @(Ty\_Var \; v1) \; (Ty\_Var \; v2)$ | | |
| $\mid v1 \equiv v2$ | | $= res \; t_1$ |
| | | |
| $f \; t_1 \; @(Ty\_Var \; v1) \; t_2$ | | $= occurBind \; v1 \; t_2$ |
| $f \; t_1$ | $t_2 \; @(Ty\_Var \; v2)$ | $= occurBind \; v2 \; t_1$ |

$$f \; t_1 \; @(Ty\_App \; (Ty\_App \; (Ty\_Con \; c1) \; ta_1) \; tr_1)$$
$$t_2 \; @(Ty\_App \; (Ty\_App \; (Ty\_Con \; c2) \; ta_2) \; tr_2)$$
$$\mid hsnIsArrow \; c1 \wedge c1 \equiv c2$$
$$= comp \; ta_2 \; tr_1 \; ta_1 \; tr_2 \; (\lambda a \; r \rightarrow [a] \; `mkTyArrow` \; r)$$
$$f \; t_1 \; @(Ty\_App \; tf_1 \; ta_1)$$
$$t_2 \; @(Ty\_App \; tf_2 \; ta_2)$$
$$= comp \; tf_1 \; ta_1 \; tf_2 \; ta_2 \; Ty\_App$$

| | | |
|---|---|---|
| $f \; t_1$ | $t_2$ | $= err \; [Err\_UnifyClash \; ty_1 \; ty_2 \; t_1 \; t_2]$ |
| *err e* | | $= emptyFO\{foErrL = e\}$ |

Although this version of the implementation of *fitsIn* resembles the previous one it differs in the following aspects:

– The datatype *FIOut* returned by *fitsIn* has an additional field *foCnstr* holding found constraints. This requires constraints to be combined for composite types like the *App* variant of *Ty*.

- The function *bind* creates a binding for a type variable to a type. The use of *bind* is shielded by *occurBind* which checks if the type variable for which a binding is created does not occur free in the bound type too. This is to prevent (e.g.) $a \leqslant a \rightarrow a$ to succeed. This is because it is not clear if $a \mapsto a \rightarrow a$ should be the resulting constraint or $a \mapsto (a \rightarrow a) \rightarrow (a \rightarrow a)$ or one of infinitely many other possible solutions. A so called *infinite type* like this is inhibited by the so called *occurs check*.

- An application *App* recursively fits its components with components of another *App*. The constraints from the first fit *ffo* are applied immediately to the following component before fitting that one. This is to prevent $a \rightarrow a \leqslant Int \rightarrow Char$ from finding two conflicting constraints $[a \mapsto Int, a \mapsto Char]$ instead of properly reporting an error.

## 3.3  Reconstructing Types for Expr

Constraints are used to make knowledge found about previously unknown types explicit. The typing rules in Fig. 6 (and Fig. 7, Fig. 9) in principle do not need to be changed. The only reason to adapt some of the rules to the variant in Fig. 11 is to clarify the way constraints are used.

$$\boxed{\Gamma;\sigma^k \overset{expr}{\vdash} e : \sigma \rightsquigarrow C}$$

$$\frac{\begin{array}{c}\Gamma;\sigma^a \overset{expr}{\vdash} e_2 : \_ \rightsquigarrow C_2 \\ \Gamma;v \rightarrow \sigma^k \overset{expr}{\vdash} e_1 : \sigma^a \rightarrow \sigma \rightsquigarrow C_1 \\ v \text{ fresh}\end{array}}{\Gamma;\sigma^k \overset{expr}{\vdash} e_1\, e_2 : C_2\sigma \rightsquigarrow C_{2..1}} \text{(e-app2)}$$

$$\frac{\begin{array}{c}\Gamma^p,\Gamma;\sigma^r \overset{expr}{\vdash} e : \sigma^e \rightsquigarrow C_3 \\ \sigma^p \overset{pat}{\vdash} p : \_ ; \Gamma^p \rightsquigarrow C_2 \\ \overset{fit}{\vdash} v_1 \rightarrow v_2 \leqslant \sigma^k : \sigma^p \rightarrow \sigma^r \rightsquigarrow C_1 \\ v_i \text{ fresh}\end{array}}{\Gamma;\sigma^k \overset{expr}{\vdash} \lambda p \rightarrow e : C_3\sigma^p \rightarrow \sigma^e \rightsquigarrow C_{3..1}} \text{(e-lam2)}$$

$$\frac{\begin{array}{c}(i \mapsto \sigma^i) \in \Gamma \\ \overset{fit}{\vdash} \sigma^i \leqslant \sigma^k : \sigma \rightsquigarrow C\end{array}}{\Gamma;\sigma^k \overset{expr}{\vdash} i : \sigma \rightsquigarrow C} \text{(e-ident2)}$$

$$\frac{\begin{array}{c}\overset{fit}{\vdash} (v_1, v_2, ..., v_n) \leqslant \sigma^r : (\sigma_1, \sigma_2, ..., \sigma_n) \rightsquigarrow C \\ \_ \rightarrow ... \rightarrow \sigma^r \equiv \sigma^k \\ v_i \text{ fresh}\end{array}}{\Gamma;\sigma^k \overset{expr}{\vdash} ,n : \sigma_1 \rightarrow ... \rightarrow \sigma_n \rightarrow (\sigma_1, \sigma_2, ..., \sigma_n) \rightsquigarrow C} \text{(e-con2)}$$

$$\frac{\overset{fit}{\vdash} Int \leqslant \sigma^k : \sigma \rightsquigarrow C}{\Gamma;\sigma^k \overset{expr}{\vdash} minint..maxint : \sigma \rightsquigarrow C} \text{(e-int2)}$$

**Fig. 11.** Type inferencing for expressions (using constraints)

The type rules in Fig. 11 enforce an order in which checking and inferring types has to be done.

Actually, the rules in Fig. 11 should be even more specific in how constraints flow around if we want to be closer to the corresponding AG description. The AG specifies a $C$ to be threaded instead of just returned bottom-up:

**ATTR** *AllExpr* $[|\ tyCnstr : C\ |]$

Its use in an expression application is as follows:

**SEM** *Expr*
  | *App* **loc**.*knFunTy* := $[mkNewTyVar\ @lUniq]$ '*mkTyArrow*' @**lhs**.*knTy*
       .*ty*     := $@arg.tyCnstr \succ @fTy$

$\mathcal{AG}$: **Redefining an attribute value.** Normally a value for an attribute may be associated with an attribute only once, using = in a rule. It is an error if multiple rules for an attribute are present. If := is used instead, any previous definition is overridden and no error message is generated. In this context previous means "textually occurring earlier". Because the AG system's flexibility finds its origin in the independence of textual locations of declarations and definitions, := should be used with care. For these notes the order in which redefinitions appear is the same as their textual appearance in these notes, which again is the same as the sequence of versions of EH.

This definition builds on top of the previous version by redefining some attributes (indicated by := instead of =). If this happens a reference to the location (in these notes) of the code on top of which the new code is added can be found[5].

To correspond better with the related AG code the rule **e-app2** should be:

$$\frac{\begin{array}{c} C_1; \Gamma; \sigma^a \overset{expr}{\vdash} e_2 : \_ \leadsto C_2 \\ C^k; \Gamma; v \to C^k \sigma^k \overset{expr}{\vdash} e_1 : \sigma^a \to \sigma \leadsto C_1 \\ v\ fresh \end{array}}{C^k; \Gamma; \sigma^k \overset{expr}{\vdash} e_1\ e_2 : C_2 \sigma \leadsto C_2} \quad \text{(e-app2B)}$$

The flow of constraints is made explicit as they are passed through the rules, from the context (left of $\vdash$) to a result (right of $\leadsto$). We feel this does not benefit clarity, even though it is correct. It is our opinion that typing rules serve their purpose best by providing a basis for proof as well as understanding and discussion. An AG description serves its purpose best by showing how it really is implemented. Used in tandem they strengthen each other.

---

[5] This is not an ideal solution to display combined fragments. A special purpose editor would probably do a better job of browsing textually separated but logically related pieces of code.

An implementation by necessity imposes additional choices, in order to make a typing rule into an algorithmic solution. For example, our AG description preserves the following invariant:

- A resulting type has all known constraints applied to it, here *ty*.

but as this invariant is not kept for *knTy* and *valGam* it requires to

- Explicitly apply known constraints to the inherited known type *knTy*.
- Explicitly apply known constraints to types from a Γ, here *valGam*.

The type rules in Fig. 11 do not mention the last two constraint applications (rule e-app2B does), and this will also be omitted for later typing rules. However, the constraint applications are shown by the AG code for the *App* alternative and the following *Var* alternative:

$$
\begin{aligned}
&\textbf{SEM } \textit{Expr} \\
&\quad | \textit{ Var } \textbf{loc}.\textit{fTy} \quad := @\textbf{lhs}.\textit{tyCnstr} \succ @\textit{gTy} \\
&\qquad\qquad .\textit{fo} \quad := @\textit{fTy} \leqslant (@\textbf{lhs}.\textit{tyCnstr} \succ @\textbf{lhs}.\textit{knTy}) \\
&\qquad \textbf{lhs}.\textit{tyCnstr} = \textit{foCnstr} @\textit{fo} \succ @\textbf{lhs}.\textit{tyCnstr}
\end{aligned}
$$

The rules for constants all resemble the one for *Int*, rule e-int2. Their implementation additionaly takes care of constraint handling:

$$
\begin{aligned}
&\textbf{SEM } \textit{Expr} \\
&\quad | \textit{ IConst CConst} \\
&\qquad \textbf{loc}.\textit{fo} \quad := @\textit{fTy} \leqslant (@\textbf{lhs}.\textit{tyCnstr} \succ @\textbf{lhs}.\textit{knTy}) \\
&\qquad \textbf{lhs}.\textit{tyCnstr} = \textit{foCnstr} @\textit{fo} \succ @\textbf{lhs}.\textit{tyCnstr}
\end{aligned}
$$

The handling of products does not differ much from the previous implementation. A rule e-con2 has been included in the typing rules, as a replacement for rule e-prod1B (Fig. 7) better resembling its implementation. Again the idea is to exploit that in this version of EH tupling is the only way to construct an aggregrate value. A proper structure for its type is (again) enforced by *fitsIn*.

$$
\begin{aligned}
&\textbf{SEM } \textit{Expr} \\
&\quad | \textit{ Con } \textbf{loc}.\textit{fo} \quad = \textbf{let } \textit{gTy} \quad = \textit{mkTyFreshProdFrom} @\textit{lUniq} \ (\textit{hsnProdArity} @\textit{nm}) \\
&\qquad\qquad\qquad\qquad \textit{foKnRes} = \textit{gTy} \leqslant (@\textbf{lhs}.\textit{tyCnstr} \succ \textit{tyArrowRes} @\textbf{lhs}.\textit{knTy}) \\
&\qquad\qquad\qquad \textbf{in } \textit{foKnRes}\{\textit{foTy} = \textit{tyProdArgs} \ (\textit{foTy foKnRes}) \\
&\qquad\qquad\qquad\qquad\qquad\qquad `\textit{mkTyArrow}` \ (\textit{foTy foKnRes})\} \\
&\qquad\qquad .\textit{ty} \quad := \textit{foTy} @\textit{fo} \\
&\qquad \textbf{lhs}.\textit{tyCnstr} = \textit{foCnstr} @\textit{fo} \succ @\textbf{lhs}.\textit{tyCnstr}
\end{aligned}
$$

Finally,

**SEM** *Expr*
| *Lam* **loc** .(*argTy*, *resTy*, *funTy*)
$\qquad\qquad\qquad$ := **let** $[a, r]$ = *mkNewTyVarL* 2 *@lUniq*
$\qquad\qquad\qquad\quad$ **in** $(a, r, [a]$ '*mkTyArrow*' $r)$
$\qquad$ .*foKnFun* $\quad$ := *@funTy* ⩽ (*@***lhs**.*tyCnstr* ≻ *@***lhs**.*knTy*)
$\quad$ *arg* .*knTy* $\qquad$ := *@argTy*
$\qquad$ .*tyCnstr* $\qquad$ = *foCnstr @foKnFun* ≻ *@***lhs**.*tyCnstr*
$\quad$ *body*.*knTy* $\qquad$ := *@resTy*
$\quad$ **loc** .*bodyTyCnstr* = *@body*.*tyCnstr*
$\qquad$ .*ty* $\qquad\quad$ := $[$*@bodyTyCnstr* ≻ *@arg*.*ty*$]$ '*mkTyArrow*' *@body*.*ty*

which uses some additional functions for creating type variables

*mkNewTyVar* :: *UID* → *Ty*
*mkNewTyVar u* = **let** $(\_, v)$ = *mkNewUID u* **in** *mkTyVar v*

*mkNewUIDTyVarL* :: *Int* → *UID* → $([UID], TyL)$
*mkNewUIDTyVarL sz u* = **let** *vs* = *mkNewUIDL sz u* **in** $(vs, map\ mkTyVar\ vs)$

*mkNewTyVarL* :: *Int* → *UID* → *TyL*
*mkNewTyVarL sz u* = *snd* (*mkNewUIDTyVarL sz u*)

Some observations are in place:

- The main difference with the previous implementation is the use of type variables to represent unknown knowledge. Previously □ was used for that purpose, for example, the rule **e-lam2** and its implementation show that fresh type variables $v_i$ in $v_1 → v_2$ are used instead of □ → □ to enforce a .. → .. structure. If □ still would be used, for example in:

  **let** *id* = $\lambda x → x$
  **in** *id* 3

  the conclusion would be drawn that *id* :: □ → □, whereas *id* :: $v → v$ would later on have bound $v ↦ Int$ (at the application *id* 3). So, □ represents "unknown knowledge", a type variable $v$ represents "not yet known knowledge" to which the inferencing process later has to refer to make it "known knowledge".
- Type variables are introduced under the condition that they are "fresh". For a typing rule this means that these type variables are not in use elsewhere, often more concretely specified with a condition $v \notin ftv\ (\Gamma)$. Freshness in the implementation is implemented via unique identifiers UID.

## 3.4　Reconstructing Types for PatExpr

In the previous version of EH we were only interested in bindings for identifiers in a pattern. The type of a pattern was already known via a corresponding type signature.

For this version this is no longer the case so the structure of a pattern reveals already some type structure. Hence we compute types for patterns too and use this type as the known type if no type signature is available.

Computation of the type of a pattern is similar to and yet more straightforward than for expressions. The rule e-pat2 from Fig. 12 binds the identifier to the known type and if no such known type is available it invents a fresh one, by means of *tyEnsureNonAny*:

**ATTR** *AllPatExpr* $[\,|\ tyCnstr : C \mid ty : Ty\,]$

**SEM** *PatExpr*
    | *Var VarAs* **loc**    .*ty*    := *tyEnsureNonAny* @*lUniq* @**lhs** *knTy*
    | *VarAs*    *patExpr.knTy* = @*ty*

*tyEnsureNonAny* :: *UID* → *Ty* → *Ty*
*tyEnsureNonAny* $u\ t =$ **if** $t \not\equiv Ty\_Any$ **then** $t$ **else** *mkNewTyVar u*

$$\boxed{\sigma^k \overset{pat}{\vdash} p : \sigma; \Gamma^p \leadsto C}$$

$$\frac{\begin{array}{c} \overset{fit}{\vdash} C_1 \sigma^k \leqslant \sigma^d : \sigma \leadsto C_2 \\ \sigma^d \to () \equiv \sigma^p \\ \_ \overset{pat}{\vdash} p : \sigma^p; \Gamma^p \leadsto C_1 \\ p \equiv p_1\, p_2 \dots p_n, n \geqslant 1 \end{array}}{\sigma^k \overset{pat}{\vdash} p : \sigma; \Gamma^p \leadsto C_{2..1}} \text{(p-apptop2)}$$

$$\frac{\begin{array}{c} dom\,(\Gamma_1^p) \cap dom\,(\Gamma_2^p) = \emptyset \\ \sigma_1^a \overset{pat}{\vdash} p_2 : \_; \Gamma_2^p \leadsto C_2 \\ \_ \overset{pat}{\vdash} p_1 : \sigma^d \to (\sigma_1^a, \sigma_2^a, ..., \sigma_n^a); \Gamma_1^p \leadsto C_1 \end{array}}{\_ \overset{pat}{\vdash} p_1\, p_2 : C_2(\sigma^d \to (\sigma_2^a, ..., \sigma_n^a)); \Gamma_1^p, \Gamma_2^p \leadsto C_{2..1}} \text{(p-app2)}$$

$$\frac{\sigma^k \not\equiv \Box}{\sigma^k \overset{pat}{\vdash} i : \sigma^k; [i \mapsto \sigma^k] \leadsto [\,]} \text{(p-var2)} \qquad \frac{v_i \text{ fresh}}{\_ \overset{pat}{\vdash} I : \sigma; (v_1, v_2, ..., v_n) \to (v_1, v_2, ..., v_n) \leadsto [\,]} \text{(p-con2)}$$

**Fig. 12.** Type inferencing for pattern (using constraints)

For tuples we again make use of the fact that the *Con* alternative will always represent a tuple. When datatypes are introduced (not part of these notes) this will no longer be the case. Here, we already make the required rule p-con2 more general than is required here because we already prepare for datatypes.

A pattern (in essence) can be represented by a function $\sigma \to (\sigma_1, ...)$ taking a value of some type $\sigma$ and dissecting it into a tuple $(\sigma_1, ...)$ containing all its constituents. For now, because we have only tuples to dissect, the function returned by the *Con* alternative is just the identity on tuples of the correct size. The application rule p-app2 consumes an element of this tuple representing the dissected value and uses it for checking and inferring the constituent.

The implementation of this representation convention returns the dissecting function type in *patFunTy*:

**ATTR** *PatExpr* $[\| patFunTy : Ty]$

**SEM** *PatExpr*
  | *Con* **loc**.*patFunTy* = **let** *prTy* = *mkTyFreshProdFrom* @*lUniq* (*hsnProdArity* @*nm*)
                    **in** ([*prTy*] '*mkTyArrow*' *prTy*)
  | *App* **lhs**.*patFunTy* = @*func.patFunTy*
  | * – *App Con*
        **lhs**.*patFunTy* = *Ty_Any*

The dissecting function type *patFunTy* is constructed from fresh type variables. Each occurrence of a tuple pattern deals with different unknown types and hence fresh type variables are needed. The availability of polymorphism in later versions of EH allows us to describe this in a more general way.

At *AppTop* of *PatExpr* the function type $\sigma \to (\sigma_1, ...)$ describing the dissection is split into the type $\sigma$ (attribute *knResTy*) of the pattern and the tuple type $(\sigma_1, ...)$ (attribute *knProdTy*) holding its constituents. The distribution of the types of the fields of *knProdTy* was described in the previous version of EH.

**SEM** *PatExpr*
  | *AppTop* **loc**.*patFunTy*         = @*patExpr.patFunTy*
        .(*knResTy*, *knProdTy*) := *tyArrowArgRes* @*patFunTy*

Finally, the type itself and additional constraints are returned:

**SEM** *PatExpr*
  | *IConst* **loc**   .*ty*     = *tyInt*
  | *CConst* **loc**   .*ty*     = *tyChar*
  | *AppTop* **loc**   .*fo*     = @**lhs**.*knTy* ⩽ @*knResTy*
                 .*ty*     = *foTy* @*fo*
        *patExpr.tyCnstr* = *foCnstr* @*fo* ≻ @**lhs**.*tyCnstr*
        **lhs**   .*ty*     = @*patExpr.tyCnstr* ≻ @*ty*
  | *App*   *arg*   .*knTy*  := @*func.tyCnstr* ≻ @*knArgTy*
  | *Con*   **loc**   .*ty*     = *Ty_Any*

The careful reader may have observed that the direction of $\leqslant$ for fitting actual (synthesized, bottom-up) and known type (inherited, top-down) is the opposite of the direction used for expressions. This is a result of a difference in the meaning of an expression and a pattern. An expression builds a value from bottom to top as seen in the context of an abstract syntax tree. A pattern dissects a value from top to bottom. The flow of data is opposite, hence the direction of $\leqslant$ too.

## 3.5   Declarations

Again, at the level of declarations all is tied together. Because we first gather information about patterns and then about expressions two separate threads for gathering constraints are used, *patTyCnstr* and *tyCnstr* respectively.

```
SEM Expr
  | Let decls.patTyCnstr = @lhs.tyCnstr
         .tyCnstr        = @decls.patTyCnstr
```

```
ATTR AllDecl [| tyCnstr : C   patTyCnstr : C |]
SEM Decl
  | Val   patExpr.tyCnstr    = @lhs.patTyCnstr
          lhs    .patTyCnstr = @patExpr.tyCnstr
          expr   .tyCnstr    = @lhs.tyCnstr
SEM AGItf
  | AGItf expr    .tyCnstr    = emptyCnstr
```

If a type signature has been given it is used as the known type for both expression and pattern. If not, the type of a pattern is used as the known type for an expression.

```
SEM Decl
  | Val expr.knTy = if @hasTySig then @knTy else @patExpr.ty
```

## 3.6   Partial Type Signatures: A Test Case for Extendibility

Partial type signatures allow the programmer to specify only a part of a type in a type signature. The description of the implementation of this feature is separated from the discussion of other features to show the effects of an additional feature on the compiler. In other words, the following is an impact analysis.

First, both abstract syntax and the parser (not included in these notes) contain an additional alternative for parsing the ". . ." notation chosen for unspecified type information designated by *Wild* for wildcard:

```
DATA TyExpr
  | Wild
```

A wildcard type is treated in the same way as a type variable as it also represents unknown type information:

**SEM** *TyExpr*
    | *Wild* **loc.***tyVarId* = @*lUniq*
                .*tgi*      = *TyGamInfo* (*mkNewTyVar* @*tyVarId*)

**SEM** *TyExpr*
    | *Wild* **lhs.***ty* = *tgiTy* @*tgi*

Changes also have to be made to the omitted parts of the implementation, in particular the pretty printing of the AST and generation of unique identifiers. We mention the necessity of this but omit the relevant code.

The pretty printing of a type signature is enhanced a bit further by either printing the type signature (if no wildcard types are present in it) or by printing the type of the type signature combined with all found constraints. The decision is based on the presence of wildcard type variables in the type signature:

**ATTR** *TyExpr* [|| *tyVarWildL* **USE**{ ++ }{ [ ] } : *TyVarIdL*]

**SEM** *TyExpr*
    | *Wild* **lhs.***tyVarWildL* = [ @*tyVarId* ]

The set of all constraints is retrieved at the root of the AST and passed back into the tree:

**ATTR** *AllDecl* [*finValGam* : *ValGam* ||]
**ATTR** *AllNT* [*finTyCnstr* : *C* ||]

**SEM** *Expr*
    | *Let*     *decls.finValGam* = @**lhs.***finTyCnstr* ≻ @*lValGam*

**SEM** *Decl*
    | *TySig* **loc**  .*finalTy*     = *vgiTy.fromJust.valGamLookup* @*nm*
                                     $ @**lhs.***finValGam*

**SEM** *AGItf*
    | *AGItf expr* .*finTyCnstr* = @*expr.tyCnstr*

## 4    EH 3: Polymorphic Type Inferencing

The third version of EH adds polymorphism, in particular so-called parametric polymorphism which allows functions to be used on arguments of differing types. For example

    **let** *id* :: *a* → *a*
        *id* = λ*x* → *x*
        *v*  = (*id* 3, *id* '**x**')
    **in** *v*

gives *v* :: (*Int*, *Char*) and *id* :: ∀ *a.a* → *a*. The polymorphic identity function *id* accepts a value of any type *a*, giving back a value of the same type *a*. Type variables in the type signature are used to specify polymorphic types. Polymorphism of a type variable in a type is made explicit in the type by the use of a universal quantifier forall, or ∀. The meaning of this quantifier is that a value with a universally quantified type can be used with different types for the quantified type variables.

The type signature may be omitted, and in that case the same type will still be inferred. However, the reconstruction of the type of a value for which the type signature is omitted has its limitations, the same as for Haskell98 [31]. Haskell98 also restricts what can be described by type signatures.

Polymorphism is allowed for identifiers bound by a **let**-expression, not for identifiers bound by another mechanism such as parameters of a lambda expression. The following variant of the previous example is therefore not to be considered correct:

$$
\begin{aligned}
&\textbf{let } f :: (a \rightarrow a) \rightarrow Int \\
&\quad f = \lambda i \rightarrow i\ 3 \\
&\quad id :: a \rightarrow a \\
&\quad id = \lambda x \rightarrow x \\
&\textbf{in } f\ id
\end{aligned}
$$

It will give the following output:

```
let f :: (a -> a) -> Int
    f = \i -> i 3
    {- ***ERROR(S):
           In '\i -> i 3':
             ... In 'i':
                    Type clash:
                        failed to fit: c_2_0 -> c_2_0 <= v_7_0 -> Int
                        problem with : c_2_0 <= Int -}
    id :: a -> a
    id = \x -> x
    {- [ id:forall a . a -> a, f:forall a . (a -> a) -> Int ] -}
in f id
```

The problem here is that the polymorphism of $f$ in $a$ means that the caller of $f$ can freely choose what this $a$ is for a particular call. However, from the viewpoint of the body of $f$ this limits the choice of $a$ to no choice at all. If the caller has all the freedom to make the choice, the callee has none. In our implementation this is encoded as a type constant $c\_$ chosen for $a$ during type checking the body of $f$. This type constant by definition is a type a programmer can never define or denote. The consequence is that an attempt to use $i$ in the body of $f$, which has type $c\_..\rightarrow c\_..$ cannot be used with an *Int*. The use of type constants will be explained later.

Another example of the limitations of polymorphism in this version of EH is the following variation:

**let** $f = \lambda i \rightarrow i\ 3$
  $id :: a \rightarrow a$
**in let** $v = f\ id$
  **in** $f$

for which the compiler will infer the following types:

```
let f = \i -> i 3
    id :: a -> a
    {- [ f:forall a . (Int -> a) -> a, id:forall a . a -> a ] -}
in let v = f id
        {- [ v:Int ] -}
    in f
```

EH version 3 allows parametric polymorphism but not yet polymorphic parameters. The parameter $i$ has a monomorphic type, which is made even more clear when we make an attempt to use this $i$ polymorphically in:

**let** $f = \lambda i \rightarrow (i\ 3, i\ \texttt{'x'})$
  $id = \lambda x \rightarrow x$
**in let** $v = f\ id$
  **in** $v$

about which the compiler will complain:

```
let f = \i -> (i 3,i 'x')
    {- ***ERROR(S):
        In '\i -> (i 3,i 'x')':
            ... In ''x'':
                Type clash:
                    failed to fit: Char <= Int
                    problem with : Char <= Int -}
    id = \x -> x
    {- [ id:forall a . a -> a, f:forall a . (Int -> a) -> (a,a) ] -}
in let v = f id
        {- [ v:(Int,Int) ] -}
    in v
```

Because $i$ is not allowed to be polymorphic it can either be used on *Int* or *Char*, but not both.

These problems can be overcome by allowing higher ranked polymorphism in type signatures. Later versions of EH deal with this problem, but this is not included in these notes. This version of EH resembles Haskell98 in these restrictions.

The reason not to allow explicit types to be of assistance to the type inferencer is that Haskell98 and this version of EH have as a design principle that all explicitly specified types in a program are redundant. That is, after removal of explicit type signatures, the type inferencer can still reconstruct all types. It is guaranteed that all reconstructed types are the same as the removed signatures or more general, that is, the type signatures are a special case of the inferred types. This guarantee is called the principal type property [9,26,18]. However, type inferencing also has its limits. In fact, the richer a type system becomes, the more difficult it is for a type inferencing algorithm to make the right choice for a type without the programmer specifying additional helpful type information.

## 4.1  Type Language

The type language for this version of EH adds quantification by means of the universal quantifier $\forall$:

$$
\begin{aligned}
\sigma = \ & Int \mid Char \\
\mid \ & (\sigma, ..., \sigma) \\
\mid \ & \sigma \rightarrow \sigma \\
\mid \ & v \mid f \\
\mid \ & \forall \alpha.\sigma
\end{aligned}
$$

A $f$ stands for a fixed type variable, a type variable which may not be constrained but still stands for an unknown type. A $v$ stands for a plain type variable as used in the previous EH version. A series of consecutive quantifiers in $\forall \alpha_1.\forall \alpha_2. ... \sigma$ is abbreviated to $\forall \overline{\alpha}.\sigma$.

The type language suggests that a quantifier may occur anywhere in a type. This is not the case, quantifiers may only be on the top of a type; this version of EH takes care to ensure this. A second restriction is that quantified types are present only in a $\Gamma$ whereas no $\forall$'s are present in types used throughout type inferencing expressions and patterns. This is to guarantee the principle type property.

The corresponding abstract syntax for a type needs additional alternative to represent a quantified type. For a type variable we also have to remember to which category it belongs, either *plain* or *fixed*:

**DATA** *Ty*
   | *Var tv*    : {*TyVarId*}
            *categ* : *TyVarCateg*
**DATA** *TyVarCateg*
   | *Plain*
   | *Fixed*

**DATA** *Ty*
   | *Quant tv* : {*TyVarId*}
           *ty* : *Ty*

**SET** *AllTyTy* = *Ty*

**SET** *AllTy*    = *AllTyTy*
**SET** *AllAllTy* = *AllTy TyVarCateg*

together with convenience functions for constructing these types:

*mkTyVar* :: *TyVarId* → *Ty*
*mkTyVar tv* = *Ty_Var tv TyVarCateg_Plain*

*mkTyQu* :: *TyVarIdL* → *Ty* → *Ty*
*mkTyQu tvL t* = *foldr* (*λtv t* → *Ty_Quant tv t*) *t tvL*

We will postpone the discussion of type variable categories until section 91.

The syntax of this version of EH only allows type variables to be specified as part of a type signature. The quantifier ∀ cannot be explicitly denoted. We only need to extend the abstract syntax for types with an alternative for type variables:

**DATA** *TyExpr*
  | *Var nm* : {*HsName*}


## 4.2   Type Inferencing

Compared to the previous version the type inferencing process does not change much. Because types used throughout the type inferencing of expressions and patterns do not contain ∀ quantifiers, nothing has to be changed there.

Changes have to be made to the handling of declarations and identifiers though. This is because polymorphism is tied up with the way identifiers for values are introduced and used.

A quantified type, also often named *type scheme*, is introduced in rule e-let3 and rule e-let-tysig3 and instantiated in rule e-ident3, see Fig. 13. We will first look at the instantiation.

**Instantiation.** A quantified type is introduced in the type inferencing process whenever a value identifier having that type is occurs in an expression:

**SEM** *Expr*
  | *Var* **loc**.*fTy* := @**lhs**.*tyCnstr* ≻ *tyInst* @*lUniq* @*gTy*

We may freely decide what type the quantified type variables may have as long as each type variable stands for a monomorphic type. However, at this point it is not known which type a type variable stands for, so fresh type variables are used instead. This is called *instantiation*, or specialization. The resulting instantiated type partakes in the inference process as usual.

The removal of the quantifier and replacement of all quantified type variables with fresh type variables is done by *tyInst*:

$$\boxed{\Gamma; \sigma^k \overset{expr}{\vdash} e : \sigma \rightsquigarrow C}$$

$$\dfrac{\begin{array}{c} \Gamma^q, \Gamma; \sigma^k \overset{expr}{\vdash} e : \sigma^e \rightsquigarrow C_3 \\ \Gamma^q \equiv [(i \mapsto \forall \overline{\alpha}.\sigma) \mid (i \mapsto \sigma) \leftarrow C_{2..1} \Gamma^p, \overline{\alpha} \equiv ftv\,(\sigma) - ftv\,(C_{2..1}\Gamma)] \\ \Gamma^p, \Gamma; \sigma^p \overset{expr}{\vdash} e^i : \_ \rightsquigarrow C_2 \\ \square \overset{pat}{\vdash} p : \sigma^p; 1^p \rightsquigarrow \hat{C}_1 \end{array}}{\Gamma; \sigma^k \overset{expr}{\vdash} \textbf{let}\ p = e^i \textbf{in}\ e : \sigma^e \rightsquigarrow C_{3..1}} \quad \text{(e-let3)}$$

$$\dfrac{\begin{array}{c} (\Gamma^q - [i \mapsto \_] + [i \mapsto \sigma^q]) + \Gamma; \sigma^k \overset{expr}{\vdash} e : \sigma^e \rightsquigarrow C_3 \\ \Gamma^q \equiv [(i \mapsto \forall \overline{\alpha}.\sigma) \mid (i \mapsto \sigma) \leftarrow C_{2..1} \Gamma^p, \overline{\alpha} \equiv ftv\,(\sigma) - ftv\,(C_{2..1}\Gamma)] \\ (\Gamma^p - [i \mapsto \_] + [i \mapsto \sigma^q]) + \Gamma; \sigma^j \overset{expr}{\vdash} e^i : \_ \rightsquigarrow C_2 \\ \sigma^q \equiv \forall \overline{\alpha}.\sigma^i \\ \sigma^j \equiv [\alpha_j \mapsto f_j]\,\sigma^i, f_j\ \text{fresh} \\ \overline{\alpha} \equiv ftv\,(\sigma^i) \\ p \equiv i \vee p \equiv i\,@... \\ \sigma^i \overset{pat}{\vdash} p : \_; \Gamma^p \rightsquigarrow C_1 \end{array}}{\Gamma; \sigma^k \overset{expr}{\vdash} \textbf{let}\ i :: \sigma^i; p = e^i \textbf{in}\ e : \sigma^e \rightsquigarrow C_{3..1}} \quad \text{(e-let-tysig3)}$$

$$\dfrac{\begin{array}{c} (i \mapsto \forall [\alpha_j].\sigma^i) \in \Gamma \\ \overset{fit}{\vdash} [\alpha_j \mapsto v_j]\,\sigma^i \leqslant \sigma^k : \sigma \rightsquigarrow C \\ v_j\ \text{fresh} \end{array}}{\Gamma; \sigma^k \overset{expr}{\vdash} i : \sigma \rightsquigarrow C} \quad \text{(e-ident3)}$$

**Fig. 13.** Type inferencing for expressions with quantifier $\forall$

```
tyInst' :: (TyVarId → Ty) → UID → Ty → Ty
tyInst' mkFreshTy uniq ty
  = s ≻ ty'
 where i u (Ty_Quant v t) = let (u',v') = mkNewUID u
                                (s,t') = i u' t
                            in ((v ↦ (mkFreshTy v')) ≻ s, t')
       i _ t             = (emptyCnstr, t)
       (s,ty')           = i uniq ty
tyInst :: UID → Ty → Ty
tyInst = tyInst' mkTyVar
```

Function *tyInst* strips all quantifiers and substitutes the quantified type variables with fresh ones. It is assumed that quantifiers occur only at the top of a type.

**Quantification.** The other way around, quantifying a type, happens when a type is bound to a value identifier and added to a $\Gamma$. The way this is done varies with the presence of a type signature. Rule e-let3 and rule e-let-tysig3 (Fig. 13) specify the respective variations.

A type signature itself is specified without explicit use of quantifiers. These need to be added for all introduced type variables, except the ones specified by means of '. . .' in a partial type signature:

**SEM** *Decl*
   | *TySig* **loc**.*sigTy*     = *tyQuantify* ($\in$ @*tyExpr.tyVarWildL*) @*tyExpr.ty*
                  .*gamSigTy* := @*sigTy*

A type signature simply is quantified over all free type variables in the type using

*tyQuantify* :: (*TyVarId* $\rightarrow$ *Bool*) $\rightarrow$ *Ty* $\rightarrow$ *Ty*
*tyQuantify tvIsBound ty* = *mkTyQu* (*filter* ($\neg$.*tvIsBound*) (*ftv ty*)) *ty*

Type variables introduced by a wildcard may not be quantified over because the type inferencer will fill in the type for those type variables.

We now run into a problem which will be solved no sooner than the next version of EH. In a declaration of a value (variant *Val* of *Decl*) the type signature acts as a known type *knTy* against which checking of the value expression takes place. Which type do we use for that purpose, the quantified *sigTy* or the unquantified *tyExpr.ty*?

– Suppose the *tyExpr.ty* is used. Then, for the erroneous

   **let** *id* :: $a \rightarrow a$
      *id* = $\lambda x \rightarrow 3$
   **in**  ...

we end up with fitting $v_1 \rightarrow Int \leqslant a \rightarrow a$. This can be accomplished via constraints $[v_1 \mapsto Int, a \mapsto Int]$. However, $a$ was supposed to be chosen by the caller of *id*. Now it is constrained by the body of *id* to be an *Int*. Somehow constraining $a$ whilst being used as part of a known type for the body of *id* must be inhibited.
– Alternatively, *sigTy* may be used. However, the inferencing process and the fitting done by *fitsIn* cannot (yet) handle types with quantifiers.

For now, this can be solved by replacing all quantified type variables of a known type with type constants:

**SEM** *Decl*
   | *Val* **loc**.*knTy* := *tyInstKnown* @*lUniq* @*sigTy*

by using a variant of *tyInst*:

$tyInstKnown :: UID \rightarrow Ty \rightarrow Ty$
$tyInstKnown = tyInst' \ (\lambda tv \rightarrow Ty\_Var \ tv \ TyVarCateg\_Fixed)$

This changes the category of the fresh type variable replacing the quantified type variable to 'fixed'. A *fixed type variable* is like a plain type variable but may not be constrained, that is, bound to another type. This means that *fitsIn* has to be adapted to prevent this from happening. The difference with the previous version only lies in the handling of type variables. Type variables now may be bound if not fixed, and to be equal only if their categories match too. For brevity the new version of *fitsIn* is omitted.

**Generalization/quantification of inferred types.** How do we determine if a type for some expression bound to an identifier in a value declaration is polymorphic? If a (non partial) type signature is given, the signature itself describes the polymorphism via type variables explicitly. However, if for a value definition a corresponding type signature is missing, the value definition itself gives us all the information we need. We make use of the observation that a binding for a value identifier acts as a kind of boundary for that expression.

**let** $id = \lambda x \rightarrow x$
**in**  ...

The only way the value associated with *id* ever will be used outside the expression bound to *id*, is via the identifier *id*. So, if the inferred type $v_1 \rightarrow v_1$ for the expression $\lambda x \rightarrow x$ has free type variables (here: $[v_1]$) and these type variables are not used in the types of other bindings, in particular those in the global $\Gamma$, we know that the expression $\lambda x \rightarrow x$ nor any other type will constrain those free type variables. The type for such a type variable apparently can be freely chosen by the expression using *id*, which is exactly the meaning of the universal quantifier. These free type variables are the candidate type variables over which quantification can take place, as described by the typing rules for **let**-expressions in Fig. 13 and its implementation:

```
SEM Expr
  | Let loc  .lSubsValGam  = @decls.tyCnstr ≻ @lValGam
           .gSubsValGam = @decls.tyCnstr ≻ @gValGam
           .gTyTvL      = ftv @gSubsValGam
           .lQuValGam   = valGamQuantify @gTyTvL @lSubsValGam
      body.valGam      := @lQuValGam
                        'gamPushGam' @gSubsValGam
```

All available constraints in the form of *decls.tyCnstr* are applied to both global (*gValGam*) and local (*lValGam*) $\Gamma$. All types in the resulting local *lSubsValGam* are then quantified over their free type variables, with the exception of those referred to more globally, the *gTyTvL*. We use *valGamQuantify* to accomplish this:

$valGamQuantify :: TyVarIdL \rightarrow ValGam \rightarrow ValGam$
$valGamQuantify\ globTvL = valGamMapTy\ (\lambda t \rightarrow tyQuantify\ (\in globTvL)\ t)$

$valGamMapTy :: (Ty \rightarrow Ty) \rightarrow ValGam \rightarrow ValGam$
$valGamMapTy\ f = gamMapElts\ (\lambda vgi \rightarrow vgi\{vgiTy = f\ (vgiTy\ vgi)\})$

$gamMap :: ((k,v) \rightarrow (k',v')) \rightarrow Gam\ k\ v \rightarrow Gam\ k'\ v'$
$gamMap\ f\ (Gam\ ll) = Gam\ (map\ (map\ f)\ ll)$
$gamMapElts :: (v \rightarrow v') \rightarrow Gam\ k\ v \rightarrow Gam\ k\ v'$
$gamMapElts\ f = gamMap\ (\lambda(n,v) \rightarrow (n,f\ v))$

The condition that quantification only may be done for type variables not occurring in the global $\Gamma$ is a necessary one. For example:

**let** $h :: a \rightarrow a \rightarrow a$
$\quad f = \lambda x \rightarrow$ **let** $g = \lambda y \rightarrow (h\ x\ y, y)$
$\qquad\qquad$ **in** $g\ 3$
**in** $f$ **'x'**

If the type $g :: a \rightarrow (a,a)$ would be concluded, $g$ can be used with $y$ an *Int* parameter, as in the example. Function $f$ can then be used with $x$ a *Char* parameter. This would go wrong because $h$ assumes the types of its parameters $x$ and $y$ are equal. So, this justifies the error given by the compiler for this version of EH:

```
let h :: a -> a -> a
    f = \x -> let g = \y -> (h x y,y)
                    {- [ g:Int -> (Int,Int) ] -}
                in g 3
    {- [ f:Int -> (Int,Int), h:forall a . a -> a -> a ] -}
in f 'x'
{- ***ERROR(S):
     In 'f 'x'':
        ... In ''x'':
              Type clash:
                failed to fit: Char <= Int
                problem with : Char <= Int -}
```

All declarations in a **let**-expression together form what in Haskell is called a binding group. Inference for these declarations is done together and all the types of all identifiers are quantified together. The consequence is that a declaration that on its own would be polymorphic, may not be so in conjunction with an additional declaration which uses the previous declaration:

**let** $id1 = \lambda x \rightarrow x$
$\quad id2 = \lambda x \rightarrow x$
$\quad v_1 = id1\ 3$
**in let** $v_2 = id2\ 3$
$\quad$ **in** $v_2$

The types of the function *id1* and value $v_1$ are inferred in the same binding group. However, in this binding group the type for *id1* is $v_1 \rightarrow v_1$ for some type variable $v_1$, without any quantifier around the type. The application *id1* 3 therefore infers an additional constraint $v_1 \mapsto Int$, resulting in type $Int \rightarrow Int$ for *id1*

```
let id1 = \x -> x
    id2 = \x -> x
    v1 = id1 3
    {- [ v1:Int, id2:forall a . a -> a, id1:Int -> Int ] -}
in let v2 = id2 3
        {- [ v2:Int ] -}
    in v2
```

On the other hand, *id2* is used after quantification, outside the binding group, with type $\forall\, a.a \rightarrow a$. The application *id2* 3 will not constrain *id2*.

In Haskell binding group analysis will find groups of mutually dependent definitions, each of these called a binding group. These groups are then ordered according to "define before use" order. Here, for EH, all declarations in a **let**-expression automatically form a binding group, the ordering of two binding groups $d_1$ and $d_2$ has to be done explicitly using sequences of **let** expressions: **let** $d_1$ **in let** $d_2$ **in**....

Being together in a binding group can create a problem for inferencing mutually recursive definitions, for example:

$$\textbf{let } f_1 = \lambda x \rightarrow g_1\ x$$
$$g_1 = \lambda y \rightarrow f_1\ y$$
$$f_2 :: a \rightarrow a$$
$$f_2 = \lambda x \rightarrow g_2\ x$$
$$g_2 = \lambda y \rightarrow f_2\ y$$
$$\textbf{in } 3$$

This results in

```
let f1 = \x -> g1 x
    g1 = \y -> f1 y
    f2 :: a -> a
    f2 = \x -> g2 x
    g2 = \y -> f2 y
    {- [ g2:forall a . a -> a, g1:forall a . forall b . a -> b
       , f1:forall a . forall b . a -> b, f2:forall a . a -> a ] -}
in 3
```

For $f_1$ it is only known that its type is $v_1 \rightarrow v_2$. Similarly $g_1$ has a type $v_3 \rightarrow v_4$. More type information cannot be constructed unless more information is given as is done for $f_2$. Then also for $g_2$ may the type $\forall\, a.a \rightarrow a$ be reconstructed.

**Type expressions.** Finally, type expressions need to return a type where all occurrences of type variable names (of type *HsName*) coincide with type variables (of type *TyVarId*). Type variable names are identifiers just as well so a *TyGam* similar to *ValGam* is used to map type variable names to freshly created type variables.

**SEM** *TyExpr*
   | *Var* (**loc**.*tgi*, **lhs**.*tyGam*) = **case** *tyGamLookup* @*nm* @**lhs**.*tyGam* **of**
                        *Nothing* → **let** *t*  = *mkNewTyVar* @*lUniq*
                                    *tgi* = *TyGamInfo* *t*
                                **in** (*tgi*, *gamAdd* @*nm* *tgi* @**lhs**.*tyGam*)
                        *Just tgi* → (*tgi*, @**lhs**.*tyGam*)

**SEM** *TyExpr*
   | *Var* **lhs**.*ty* = *tgiTy* @*tgi*

Either a type variable is defined in *tyGam*, in that case the type bound to the identifier is used, otherwise a new type variable is created.

## 5   Remarks, Experiences and Conclusion

*AG system.* At the start of these notes we did make a claim that our "describe separately" approach contributes to a better understood implementation of a compiler, in particular a Haskell compiler. Is this true? We feel that this is the case, and thus the benefits outweigh the drawbacks, based on some observations made during this project:

The AG system provides mechanisms to split a description into smaller fragments, combine those fragments and redefine part of those fragments. An additional fragment management system did allow us to do the same with Haskell fragments. Both are essential in the sense that the simultaneous 'existence' of a sequence of compiler versions, all in working order when compiled, with all aspects described with the least amount of duplication, presentable in a consistent form in these notes could not have been achieved without these mechanisms and supporting tools.

The AG system allows focusing on the places where something unusual needs to be done, similar to other approaches [24]. In particular, copy rules allow us to forget about a large amount of plumbing.

The complexity of the language Haskell, its semantics, and the interaction between features is not reduced. However, it becomes manageable and explainable when divided into small fragments. Features which are indeed independent can also be described independently of each other by different attributes. Features which evolve through different versions, like the type system, can also be described separately, but can still be looked upon as a group of fragments. This makes the variation in the solutions explicit and hence increases the understanding of what really makes the difference between two subsequent versions.

On the downside, fragments for one aspect but for different compiler versions end up in different sections of these notes. This makes their understanding more difficult because one now has to jump between pages. This is a consequence of the multiple dimensions we describe: variation in language elements (new AST), additional semantics (new attributes) and variation in the implementation. Paper, on the other hand, provides by definition a linear, one dimensional rendering of this multidimensional view. We can only expect this to be remedied by the use of proper tool support (like a fragment editor or browser). On paper, proper cross referencing, colors, indexing or accumulative merging of text are most likely to be helpful.

The AG system, though in its simplicity surprisingly usable and helpful, could be improved in many areas. For example, no type checking related to Haskell code for attribute definitions is performed, nor will the generated Haskell code when compiled by a Haskell compiler produce sensible error messages in terms of the original AG code. The AG system also lacks features necessary for programming in the large. For example, all attributes for a node live in a global namespace for that node instead of being packaged in some form of module.

Performance is expected to give problems for large systems. This seems to be primarily caused by the simple translation scheme in which all attributes together live in a tuple just until the program completes. This inhibits garbage collection of intermediate attributes that are no longer required. It also stops GHC from performing optimizations; informal experimentation with a large AG program resulted in GHC taking approximately 10 times more time with optimization flags on. The resulting program only ran approximately 15% faster. The next version of the AG system will be improved in this area [35].

*AG vs Haskell.* Is the AG system a better way to do Haskell programming? In general, no, but for Haskell programs which can be described by a catamorphism the answer is yes (see also section 1.4). In general, if the choices made by a function are mainly driven by some datastructure, it is likely that this datastructure can be described by an AST and the function can be described by the AG's attribution. This is the case for an abstract syntax tree or analysis of a single type. It is not the case for a function like *fitsIn* (section 35) in which decisions are made based on the combination of two (instead of just one) type.

*About these notes EH and its code.* The linear presentation of code and explanation might suggest that this is also the order in which the code and these notes came into existence. This is not the case. A starting point was created by programming a final version (at that time EH version 6, not included in these notes). From this version the earlier versions were constructed. After that, later versions were added. However, these later versions usually needed some tweaking of earlier versions. The consequence of this approach is that the rationale for design decisions in earlier versions become clear only in later versions. For example, an attribute is introduced only so later versions only need to redefine the rule for this single attribute. However, the initial rule for such an attribute often just is the value of another attribute. At such a place the reader is left wondering. This problem could be remedied by completely redefining larger program fragments. This in turn decreases code reuse. Reuse, that is, sharing of common code turned out to be beneficial for the development process as the use of different contexts provides more opportunities to test for correctness. No conclusion is attached to this observation, other than being another example of the tension between clarity of explanation and the logistics of compiler code management.

*Combining theory and practice.* Others have described type systems in a practical setting as well. For example, Jones [21] describes the core of Haskell98 by a monadic style type inferencer. Pierce [34] explains type theory and provides many small implementations performing (mainly) type checking for the described type systems in his book. On the other hand, only recently the static semantics of Haskell has been described formally [14]. Extensions to Haskell usually are formally described but once they find their way into a production compiler the interaction with other parts of Haskell is left in the open or is at best described in the manual.

The conclusion of these observations might be that a combined description of a language, its semantics, its formal analysis (like the type system), and its implementation is not feasible. Whatever the cause of this is, certainly one contributing factor is the sheer size of all these aspects in combination. We feel that our approach contributes towards a completer description of Haskell, or any other language if described by the AG system. Our angle of approach is to keep the implementation and its explanation consistent and understandable at the same time. However, this document clearly is not complete either. Formal aspects are present, let alone a proof that the implementation is sound and complete with respect to the formal semantics. Of course one may wonder if this is at all possible; in that case our approach may well be a feasible second best way of describing a compiler implementation.

*EH vs Haskell.* The claim of our title also is that we provide an implementation of Haskell, thereby implying recent versions of Haskell, or at least Haskell98. However, these notes does not include the description of (e.g.) a class system; the full version of EH however does.

**Acknowledgements.** We thank both (anonymous) reviewers for their extremely valuable and helpful comments.

# References

1. The Glasgow Haskell Compiler. http://www.haskell.org/ghc/, 2004.
2. Martin Abadi and Luca Cardelli. *A Theory of Objects.* Springer, 1996.
3. Arthur Baars. Attribute Grammar System. http://www.cs.uu.nl/groups/ST/twiki/bin/view/Center/AttributeGrammarSystem, 2004.

4. Richard S. Bird. Using Circular Programs to Eliminate Multiple Traversals of Data. *Acta Informatica*, 21:239–250, 1984.
5. Urban Boquist. *Code Optimisation Techniques for Lazy Functional Languages, PhD Thesis.* Chalmers University of Technology, 1999.
6. Urban Boquist and Thomas Johnsson. The GRIN Project: A Highly Optimising Back End For Lazy Functional Languages. In *Selected papers from the 8th International Workshop on Implementation of Functional Languages*, 1996.
7. Didier Botlan, Le and Didier Remy. ML-F, Raising ML to the Power of System F. In *ICFP*, 2003.
8. Luis Damas and Robin Milner. Principal type-schemes for functional programs. In *Proceedings of Principles of Programming Languages (POPL)*, pages 207–212. ACM, ACM, 1982.
9. Luis Damas and Robin Milner. Principal type-schemes for functional programs. In *9th symposium Principles of Programming Languages*, pages 207–212. ACM Press, 1982.
10. Iavor S. Diatchki, Mark P. Jones, and Thomas Hallgren. A Formal Specification of the Haskell 98 Module System. In *Haskell Workshop*, pages 17–29, 2002.
11. Atze Dijkstra. EHC Web. http://www.cs.uu.nl/groups/ST/Ehc/WebHome, 2004.
12. Atze Dijkstra and Doaitse Swierstra. Explicit implicit parameters. Technical Report UU-CS-2004-059, Institute of Information and Computing Science, 2004.
13. Atze Dijkstra and Doaitse Swierstra. Typing Haskell with an Attribute Grammar (Part I). Technical Report UU-CS-2004-037, Department of Computer Science, Utrecht University, 2004.
14. Karl-Filip Faxen. A Static Semantics for Haskell. *Journal of Functional Programming*, 12(4):295, 2002.
15. Benedict R. Gaster and Mark P. Jones. A Polymorphic Type System for Extensible Records and Variants. Technical Report NOTTCS-TR-96-3, Languages and Programming Group, Department of Computer Science, Nottingham, November 1996.
16. Cordelia Hall, Kevin Hammond, Simon Peyton Jones, and Philip Wadler. Type Classes in Haskell. *ACM TOPLAS*, 18(2):109–138, March 1996.
17. Bastiaan Heeren, Jurriaan Hage, and S. Doaitse Swierstra. Generalizing Hindley-Milner Type Inference Algorithms. Technical Report UU-CS-2002-031, Institute of Information and Computing Science, University Utrecht, Netherlands, 2002.
18. J.R. Hindley. The principal type-scheme of an object in combinatory logic. *Transactions of the American Mathematical Society*, 146:29–60, December 1969.
19. Thomas Johnsson. Attribute grammars as a functional programming paradigm. In *Functional Programming Languages and Computer Architecture*, pages 154–173, 1987.
20. Mark P. Jones. Typing Haskell in Haskell. In *Haskell Workshop*, 1999.
21. Mark P. Jones. Typing Haskell in Haskell. http://www.cse.ogi.edu/ mpj/thih/, 2000.
22. Mark P. Jones and Simon Peyton Jones. Lightweight Extensible Records for Haskell. In *Haskell Workshop*, number UU-CS-1999-28. Utrecht University, Institute of Information and Computing Sciences, 1999.
23. M.F. Kuiper and S.D. Swierstra. Using Attribute Grammars to Derive Efficient Functional Programs. In *Computing Science in the Netherlands CSN'87*, November 1987.
24. Ralf Lämmel and Simon Peyton Jones. Scrap your boilerplate: a practical design pattern for generic programming. In *Types In Languages Design And Implementation*, pages 26–37, 2003.

25. Konstantin Laufer and Martin Odersky. Polymorphic Type Inference and Abstract Data Types. Technical Report LUC-001, Loyola University of Chicago, 1994.
26. R. Milner. A theory of type polymorphism in programming. *Journal of Computer and System Sciences*, 17(3), 1978.
27. John C. Mitchell and Gordon D. Plotkin. Abstract Types Have Existential Type. *ACM TOPLAS*, 10(3):470–502, July 1988.
28. Martin Odersky and Konstantin Laufer. Putting Type Annotations to Work. In *Principles of Programming Languages*, pages 54–67, 1996.
29. Martin Odersky, Martin Sulzmann, and Martin Wehr. Type Inference with Constrained Types. In *Fourth International Workshop on Foundations of Object-Oriented Programming (FOOL 4)*, 1997.
30. Nigel Perry. The Implementation of Practical Functional Programming Languages, 1991.
31. Simon Peyton Jones. *Haskell 98, Language and Libraries, The Revised Report*. Cambridge Univ. Press, 2003.
32. Simon Peyton Jones and Mark Shields. Practical type inference for arbitrary-rank types. `http://research.microsoft.com/Users/simonpj/papers/putting/index.htm`, 2004.
33. Simon L. Peyton Jones. *The Implementation of Functional Programming Languages*. Prentice Hall, 1987.
34. Benjamin C. Pierce. *Types and Programming Languages*. MIT Press, 2002.
35. Joao Saraiva. *Purely Functional Implementation of Attribute Grammars*. PhD thesis, Utrecht University, 1999.
36. Chung-chieh Shan. Sexy types in action. *ACM SIGPLAN Notices*, 39(5):15–22, May 2004.
37. Mark Shields and Simon Peyton Jones. First-class Modules for Haskell. In *Ninth International Conference on Foundations of Object-Oriented Languages (FOOL 9), Portland, Oregon*, December 2001.
38. Utrecht University Software Technology Group. UUST library. `http://cvs.cs.uu.nl/cgi-bin/cvsweb.cgi/uust/`, 2004.
39. S.D. Swierstra, P.R. Azero Alocer, and J. Saraiava. Designing and Implementing Combinator Languages. In Doaitse Swierstra, Pedro Henriques, and José Oliveira, editors, *Advanced Functional Programming, Third International School, AFP'98*, number 1608 in LNCS, pages 150–206. Springer-Verlag, 1999.
40. Simon Thompson. *Type Theory and Functional Programming*. Addison-Wesley, 1991.
41. Phil Wadler. Theorems for free! In *4'th International Conference on Functional Programming and Computer Architecture*, September 1989.
42. Philip Wadler. Deforestation: transforming programs to eliminate trees. In *Theoretical Computer Science, (Special issue of selected papers from 2'nd European Symposium on Programming)*, number 73, pages 231–248, 1990.

# Programming with Arrows

John Hughes

Department of Computer Science and Engineering,
Chalmers University of Technology,
S-41296 Göteborg, Sweden
rjmh@cs.chalmers.se

## 1 Introduction

### 1.1 Point-Free Programming

Consider this simple Haskell definition, of a function which counts the number of occurrences of a given word w in a string:

```
count w = length . filter (==w) . words
```

This is an example of "point-free" programming style, where we build a function by composing others, and make heavy use of higher-order functions such as filter. Point-free programming is rightly popular: used appropriately, it makes for concise and readable definitions, which are well suited to equational reasoning in the style of Bird and Meertens [2]. It's also a natural way to assemble programs from components, and closely related to connecting programs via pipes in the UNIX shell.

Now suppose we want to modify count so that it counts the number of occurrences of a word in a *file*, rather than in a string, and moreover prints the result. Following the point-free style, we might try to rewrite it as

```
count w = print . length . filter (==w) . words . readFile
```

But this is rejected by the Haskell type-checker! The problem is that readFile and print have side-effects, and thus their types involve the IO monad:

```
readFile :: String -> IO String
print :: Show a => a -> IO ()
```

Of course, it is one of the *advantages* of Haskell that the type-checker can distinguish expressions with side effects from those without, but in this case we pay a price. These functions simply have the wrong types to compose with the others in a point-free style.

Now, we can write a point-free definition of this function using combinators from the standard Monad library. It becomes:

```
count w = (>>=print) .
          liftM (length . filter (==w) . words) .
          readFile
```

But this is no longer really perspicuous. Let us see if we can do better.

V. Varmo and T. Uustalu (Eds.): AFP 2004, LNCS 3622, pp. 73–129, 2005.

In Haskell, functions with side-effects have types of the form a -> IO b. Let us introduce a type synonym for this:

```
type Kleisli m a b = a -> m b
```

So now we can write the types of readFile and print as

```
readFile :: Kleisli IO String String
print :: Show a => Kleisli IO a ()
```

We parameterise Kleisli over the IO monad because the same idea can be used with any other one, and we call this type Kleisli because functions with this type are arrows in the Kleisli category of the monad m.

Now, given two such functions, one from a to b, and one from b to c, we can "compose" them into a Kleisli arrow from a to c, combining their side effects in sequence. Let us define a variant composition operator to do so. We choose to define "reverse composition", which takes its arguments in the opposite order to (.), so that the order in which we write the arrows in a composition corresponds to the order in which their side effects occur.

```
(>>>) :: Monad m =>
            Kleisli m a b -> Kleisli m b c -> Kleisli m a c
(f >>> g) a = do b <- f a
                 g b
```

We can use this composition operator to define functions with side-effects in a point-free style — for example, the following function to print the contents of a file:

```
printFile = readFile >>> print
```

Returning to our original example, we cannot yet reprogram it in terms of (>>>) because it also involves functions *without* side-effects, and these have the wrong type to be composed by (>>>). Fortunately, we can easily convert a pure function of type a -> b into a Kleisli arrow with no side-effects. We define a combinator to do so, and we call it arr.

```
arr :: Monad m => (a->b) -> Kleisli m a b
arr f = return . f
```

Using this combinator, we can now combine side-effecting and pure functions in the same point-free definition, and solve our original problem in the following rather clear way:

```
count w = readFile >>>
            arr words >>> arr (filter (==w)) >>> arr length >>>
            print
```

## 1.2   The Arrow Class

Now we have two ways to write point-free definitions: using functions and composition, or Kleisli arrows and arrow composition. We can unify them by *overloading* the arrow operators, so that the same operations can be used with both. To do so, we introduce an **Arrow** class with **arr** and (>>>) as methods:

```
class Arrow arr where
  arr :: (a -> b) -> arr a b
  (>>>) :: arr a b -> arr b c -> arr a c
```

It is trivial to define an instance for the function type:

```
instance Arrow (->) where
  arr = id
  (>>>) = flip (.)
```

But in order to make Kleisli arrows an instance, we have to make `Kleisli` a new type rather than a type synonym:

```
newtype Kleisli m a b = Kleisli {runKleisli :: a -> m b}
```

We can now declare

```
instance Monad m => Arrow (Kleisli m) where ...
```

where the method definitions are those we have already seen, modified to add and remove the `Kleisli` constructor appropriately.

The extra constructor clutters our definitions a little. We must now redefine `count` as

```
count w = Kleisli readFile >>>
          arr words >>> arr (filter (==w)) >>> arr length >>>
          Kleisli print
```

and invoke it via

```
runKleisli (count w) filename
```

rather than simply `count w filename`, but this is a small price to pay for a uniform notation. Indeed, Jansson and Jeuring used arrows in the derivation of matched parsers and prettyprinters *purely* for the notational benefits in equational proofs [11]. This notation is available in any Haskell program just by importing the hierarchical library `Control.Arrow`, which defines `Arrow`, `Kleisli`, and a number of other useful classes.

Now that we have defined an **Arrow** class, it's natural to ask if we can find other interesting instances — and indeed we can. Here, for example, is the arrow of *stream functions*:

```
newtype SF a b = SF {runSF :: [a] -> [b]}
```

The arrow operations are defined as follows:

```
instance Arrow SF where
  arr f = SF (map f)
  SF f >>> SF g = SF (f >>> g)
```

and might be used like this:

```
StreamFns> runSF (arr (+1)) [1..5]
[2,3,4,5,6]
```

Just like monads, arrow types are useful for the *additional* operations they support, over and above those that every arrow provides. In the case of stream functions, one very useful operation is to *delay* the stream by one element, adding a new element at the beginning of the stream:

```
delay x = SF (x:)
```

The `delay` arrow might be used like this:

```
StreamFns> runSF (delay 0) [1..5]
[0,1,2,3,4,5]
```

It will appear many times in examples below.

Most applications of arrows do not, in fact, use the function or Kleisli arrows — they use other instances of the `Arrow` class, which enables us to program in the same, point-free way with other kinds of objects. In real applications an arrow often represents some kind of a *process*, with an input channel of type a, and an output channel of type b. The stream functions example above is perhaps the simplest case of this sort, and will be developed in some detail.

## 1.3   Arrows as Computations

We are used to thinking of monads as modelling computations, but monads are used in two distinct ways in Haskell. On the one hand, the IO and ST monads provide a referentially transparent interface to imperative operations at a lower level. On the other hand, monads used in libraries of parsing combinators, for example, help to structure purely functional code, with not an imperative operation in sight. In this second kind of example, the `Monad` class is used as a *shared interface* that many different combinator libraries can provide.

Why bother to share the same interface between many combinator libraries? There are several important reasons:

- We know from experience that the `Monad` interface is a good one. The library designer who chooses to use it knows that it will provide users with a powerful tool.
- The library designer can exploit tools for implementing the interface systematically — monad transformers nowadays make it easy to construct complex implementations of class `Monad` [13], thus reducing the library author's work.

- We can write overloaded code that works with many different libraries — the functions in the standard Monad library are good examples. Such code provides free functionality that the library author need neither design nor implement.
- When a shared interface is sufficiently widely used, it can even be worthwhile to add specific language support for using it. Haskell's do syntax does just this for monads.
- Library users need learn less to use a new library, if a part of its interface is already familiar.

These are compelling advantages — and yet, the monadic interface suffers a rather severe restriction. While a monadic program can produce its *output* in many different ways — perhaps not at all (the Maybe monad), perhaps many times (the list monad), perhaps by passing it to a continuation — it takes its *input* in just one way: via the parameters of a function.

We can think of arrows as computations, too. The Arrow class we have defined is clearly analogous to the usual Monad class — we have a way of creating a pure computation without effects (arr/return), and a way of sequencing computations ((>>>)/(>>=)). But whereas monadic computations are parameterised over the type of their output, but not their input, arrow computations are parameterised over both. The way monadic programs take input cannot be varied by varying the monad, but arrow programs, in contrast, can take their input in many different ways depending on the particular arrow used. The stream function example above illustrates an arrow which takes its input in a different way, as a stream of values rather than a single value, so this is an example of a kind of computation which cannot be represented as a monad.

Arrows thus offer a competing way to represent computations in Haskell. But their purpose is not to replace monads, it is to bring the benefits of a shared interface, discussed above, to a wider class of computations than monads can accomodate. And in practice, this often means computations that represent processes.

## 1.4   Arrow Laws

One aspect of monads we have not touched on so far, is that they satisfy the so-called *monad laws* [26]. These laws play a rather unobtrusive rôle in practice — since they do not appear explicitly in the code, many programmers hardly think about them, much less prove that they hold for the monads they define. Yet they are important: it is the monad laws that allow us to write a sequence of operations in a **do** block, without worrying about how the sequence will be bracketed when it is translated into binary applications of the monadic bind operator. Compare with the associative law for addition, which is virtually never explicitly used in a proof, yet underlies our notation every time we write $a+b+c$ without asking ourselves what it means.

Arrows satisfy similar laws, and indeed, we have already implicitly assumed the associativity of (>>>), by writing arrow compositions without brackets!

Other laws tell us, for example, that `arr` distributes over (>>>), and so the definition of `count` we saw above,

```
count w = Kleisli readFile >>>
          arr words >>> arr (filter (==w)) >>> arr length >>>
          Kleisli print
```

is equivalent to

```
count w = Kleisli readFile >>>
          arr (words >>> filter (==w) >>> length) >>>
          Kleisli print
```

Now, it would be very surprising if this were *not* the case, and that illustrates another purpose of such laws: they help us avoid "surprises", where a slight modification of a definition, that a programmer would reasonably expect to be equivalent to the original, leads to a different behaviour. In this way laws provide a touchstone for the implementor of an arrow or monad, helping to avoid the creation of a design with subtle traps for the user. An example of such a design would be a "monad" which measures the cost of a computation, by counting the number of times bind is used. It is better to define a separate operation for consuming a unit of resource, and let bind just combine these costs, because then the monad laws are satisfied, and cosmetic changes to a monadic program will not change its cost.

Nevertheless, programmers do sometimes use monads which do *not* satisfy the stated laws. Wadler's original paper [26] introduced the "strictness monad" whose only effect is to force sequencing to be strict, but (as Wadler himself points out), the laws are not satisfied. Another example is the random generation "monad" used in our QuickCheck [4] testing tool, with which terms equivalent by the monad laws may generate different random values — but with the same distribution. There is a sense in which both these examples "morally" satisfy the laws, so that programmers are not unpleasantly surprised by using them, but strictly speaking the laws do not hold.

In the same way, some useful arrow instances may fail to satisfy the arrow laws. In fact, the stream functions we are using as our main example fail to do so, without restrictions that we shall introduce below. In this case, if we drop the restrictions then we may well get unpleasant surprises when we use stream function operations later.

Despite the importance of the arrow laws, in these notes I have chosen to de-emphasize them. The reason is simple: while monads can be characterised by a set of three laws, the original arrows paper states twenty [10], and Paterson's tutorial adds at least seven more [18]. It is simply harder to characterise the expected behaviour of arrows equationally. I have therefore chosen to focus on understanding, using, and implementing the arrow interface, leaving a study of the laws for further reading. Either of the papers cited in this paragraph is a good source.

## 2    The Arrow Classes

As we already noted, the monadic interface is a powerful one, which enables programmers to build a rich library of operations which work with any monad. There is an important difference between the monadic interface, and the `Arrow` class that we have seen so far, that has a major impact on how arrows can be implemented and used. Compare the types of the sequencing operators for monads and arrows:

```
class Monad m where
   (>>=) :: m b -> (b -> m c) -> m c
   ...
class Arrow arr where
   (>>>) :: arr a b -> arr b c -> arr a c
   ...
```

In the case of monads, the second argument of (>>=) is a Haskell function, which permits the user of this interface to use all of Haskell to map the result of the first computation to the computation to be performed next. Every time we sequence two monadic computations, we have an opportunity to run arbitrary Haskell code in between them. But in the case of arrows, in contrast, the second argument of (>>>) is just an arrow, an element of an abstract datatype, and the only things we can do in that arrow are things that the abstract data type interface provides. Certainly, the `arr` combinator enables us to have the output of the first arrow passed to a Haskell function — but this function is a *pure* function, with the type b -> c, which thus has no opportunity to perform further effects. If we want the *effects* of the second arrow to depend on the output of the first, then we must construct it using operations other than `arr` and (>>>).

Thus the simple `Arrow` class that we have already seen is *not* sufficiently powerful to allow much in the way of useful overloaded code to be written. Indeed, we will need to add a plethora of other operations to the arrow interface, divided into a number of different classes, because not all useful arrow types can support all of them. Implementing all of these operations makes defining a new arrow type considerably more laborious than defining a new monad — but there is another side to this coin, as we shall see later. In the remainder of this section, we will gradually extend the arrow interface until it *is* as powerful as the monadic one.

### 2.1    Arrows and Pairs

Suppose we want to sequence two computations delivering integers, and add their results together. This is simple enough to do with a monad:

```
addM a b = do x <- a
              y <- b
              return (x+y)
```

But the arrow interface we have seen so far is not even powerful enough to do this!

Suppose we are given two arrows f and g, which output integers from the same input. If we could make a pair of their outputs, then we could supply that to arr (uncurry (+)) to sum the components, and define

```
addA :: Arrow arr => arr a Int -> arr a Int -> arr a Int
addA f g = f_and_g >>> arr (uncurry (+))
```

But clearly, there is no way to define f_and_g just in terms of f, g, (>>>) and arr. Any composition of the form ... >>> f >>> ... loses all information other than f's output after the appearance of f, and so neither g's output nor the input needed to compute it can be available afterwards.

We therefore add an operator to construct f_and_g to the arrow interface:

```
class Arrow arr where
    ...
    (&&&) :: arr a b -> arr a c -> arr a (b,c)
```

which enables us to define addA by

```
addA f g = f &&& g >>> arr (uncurry (+))
```

(The composition operator binds less tightly than the other arrow operators).

The new operator is simple to implement for functions and Kleisli arrows:

```
instance Arrow (->) where
    ...
    (f &&& g) a = (f a, g a)

instance Monad m => Arrow (Kleisli m) where
    ...
    Kleisli f &&& Kleisli g = Kleisli $ \a -> do b <- f a
                                                 c <- g a
                                                 return (b,c)
```

For stream functions, we just zip the output streams of f and g together. We can conveniently use the arrow operators on *functions* to give a concise point-free definition!

```
instance Arrow SF where
    ...
    SF f &&& SF g = SF (f &&& g >>> uncurry zip)
```

As an example, here is a stream function which maps a stream to a stream of pairs, by pairing together each input value and its predecessor:

```
pairPred = arr id &&& delay 0
```

Running `pairPred` on an example gives

```
StreamFns> runSF (arr id &&& delay 0) [1..5]
[(1,0),(2,1),(3,2),(4,3),(5,4)]
```

The (`&&&`) operator is convenient to use, but it is not the simplest way to add this functionality to the arrow interface. Arrow types can be complex to implement, and as we observed above, there are many operations that need to be defined. To make implementing arrows as lightweight as possible, it is important to dissect each combinator into parts which are the same for each arrow type, and so can be implemented once and for all, and the minimal functionality that must be reimplemented for each new `Arrow` instance. In this case, the (`&&&`) operator, among other things, duplicates the input so it can be fed to both arguments. Duplication can be performed using `arr (\x->(x,x))`, so we factor this out and define (`&&&`) in terms of a simpler operator (`***`):

```
f &&& g = arr (\x->(x,x)) >>> f *** g
```

The new operator in turn is added to the `Arrow` class:

```
class Arrow arr where
  ...
  (***) :: arr a b -> arr c d -> arr (a,c) (b,d)
```

The combination `f *** g` constructs an arrow from pairs to pairs, that passes the first components through `f`, and the second components through `g`.

Now, (`***`) turns out not to be the simplest way to provide this functionality either. It combines *two* arrows into an arrow on pairs, but we can obtain the same functionality using a combinator that just lifts *one* arrow to an arrow on pairs. We therefore introduce the combinator `first`, which lifts an arrow to operate on pairs by feeding just the first components through the given arrow, and leaving the second components untouched. Its type is

```
class Arrow arr where
  ...
  first :: arr a b -> arr (a,c) (b,c)
```

Its implementations for functions, Kleisli arrows, and stream functions are:

```
instance Arrow (->) where
  ...
  first f (a,c) = (f a,c)

instance Monad m => Arrow (Kleisli m) where
  ...
  first (Kleisli f) = Kleisli (\(a,c) -> do b <- f a
                                            return (b,c))

instance Arrow SF where
  first (SF f) = SF (unzip >>> first f >>> uncurry zip)
```

If we had taken (***) as primitive, then we could have defined `first` by

```
first f = f *** arr id
```

But we can instead define (***) in terms of `first`, by first defining

```
second :: Arrow arr => arr a b -> arr (c,a) (c,b)
second f = arr swap >>> first f >>> arr swap
  where swap (x,y) = (y,x)
```

which lifts an arrow to work on the second components of pairs, and then defining

```
f *** g = first f >>> second g
```

This definition also has the advantage that it clarifies that the effects of `f` come before the effects of `g`, something that up to this point has been unspecified.

The `Arrow` class defined in `Control.Arrow` includes all of these combinators as methods, with the definitions given here as defaults. That permits an implementor to declare an instance of this just be defining `arr`, (`>>>`) and `first`. It also permits implementors to give specialised definitions of *all* the arrow operations, which in general will be more efficient. In that case, the specialised definitions should, of course, respect the semantics of those given here. An implementation of `first` is often only half the size of a corresponding implementation of (***) or (&&&), and so, at least in the earlier stages of development, the simplification made here is well worth while.

## 2.2    Arrows and Conditionals

The combinators in the previous section allow us to combine the results from several arrows. But suppose we want to make a choice between two arrows, on the basis of a previous result? With the combinators we have seen so far, every arrow in a combination is always "invoked" — we cannot make any arrow conditional on the output of another. We will need to introduce further combinators to make this possible.

At first sight, one might expect to introduce a combinator modelling an "if-then-else" construct, perhaps

```
ifte :: Arrow arr => arr a Bool -> arr a b -> arr a b -> arr a b
```

where `ifte p f g` uses p to compute a boolean, and then chooses between f and g on the basis of its output. But once again, we can simplify this combinator considerably.

First of all, we can easily factor out p by computing its result *before* the choice: we can do so with p &&& arr id, which outputs a pair of the boolean and the original input. We would then define `ifte` by

```
ifte p f g = p &&& arr id >>> f ||| g
```

where `f ||| g` chooses between f and g on the basis of the first component of the pair in its input, passing the second component on to f or g. But we can

do better than this: note that the input type of f ||| g here, (Bool,a), carries
the same information as Either a a, where (True,a) corresponds to Left a,
and (False,a) to Right a. If we use an Either type as the input to the choice
operator, rather than a pair, then the Left and Right values can carry *different*
types of data, which is usefully more general. We therefore define

```
class Arrow arr => ArrowChoice arr where
    (|||) :: arr a c -> arr b c -> arr (Either a b) c
```

Note the duality between (|||) and (&&&) — if we reverse the order of the
parameters of arr in the type above, and replace Either a b by the pair type
(a,b), then we obtain the type of (&&&)! This duality between choice and pairs
recurs throughout this section. As we will see later, not all useful arrow types
can support the choice operator; we therefore place it in a new subclass of Arrow,
so that we can distinguish between arrows with and without a choice operator.

As an example of using conditionals, let us see how to define a map function
for arrows:

```
mapA :: ArrowChoice arr => arr a b -> arr [a] [b]
```

The definition of mapA requires choice, because we must choose between the base
and recursive cases on the basis of the input list. We shall express mapA as *base-
case* ||| *recursive-case*, but first we must convert the input into an Either type.
We do so using

```
listcase []     = Left ()
listcase (x:xs) = Right (x,xs)
```

and define mapA by

```
mapA f = arr listcase >>>
         arr (const []) ||| (f *** mapA f >>> arr (uncurry (:)))
```

where we choose between immediately returning [], and processing the head
and tail, then consing them together. We will see examples of using mapA once
we have shown how to implement (|||).

Notice first that f ||| g requires that f and g have the same output type,
which is a little restrictive. Another possibility is to allow for different output
types, and combine them into an Either type by tagging f's output with Left,
and g's output with Right. We call the operator that does this (+++):

```
class Arrow arr => ArrowChoice arr where
    ...
    (+++) :: arr a b -> arr c d -> arr (Either a c) (Either b d)
```

Now observe that (+++) is to (|||) as (***) is to (&&&): in other words, we
can easily define the latter in terms of the former, and the former is (marginally)
simpler to implement. Moreover, it is dual to (***) — just replace Either types
by pairs again, and swap the parameters of arr. In this case the definition of
(|||) becomes

```
f ||| g = f +++ g >>> arr join
   where join (Left b)  = b
         join (Right b) = b
```

Now, just as (***) combined two arrows into an arrow on pairs, and could be defined in terms of a simpler combinator which lifted *one* arrow to the first components of pairs, so (+++) can be defined in terms of a simpler operator which just lifts an arrow to the *left* summand of an Either type. Therefore we introduce

```
class Arrow arr => ArrowChoice arr where
   . . .
   left :: arr a b -> arr (Either a c) (Either b c)
```

The idea is that left f passes inputs tagged Left to f, passes inputs tagged Right straight through, and tags outputs from f with Left. Given left, we can then define an analogous combinator

```
right f = arr mirror >>> left f >>> arr mirror
   where mirror (Left a)  = Right a
         mirror (Right a) = Left a
```

and combine them to give a definition of (+++) in terms of simpler combinators:

```
f +++ g = left f >>> right g
```

Just as in the previous section, the definition of the ArrowChoice class in Control.Arrow includes all of these combinators (except ifte), with the definitions given here as defaults. Thus one can make an arrow an instance of ArrowChoice just by implementing left, or alternatively give specialised definitions of all the combinators for greater efficiency.

Choice is easy to implement for functions and Kleisli arrows:

```
instance ArrowChoice (->) where
   left f (Left a) = Left (f a)
   left f (Right b) = Right b

instance Monad m => ArrowChoice (Kleisli m) where
   left (Kleisli f) = Kleisli (\x ->
      case x of
        Left a -> do b <- f a
                     return (Left b)
        Right b -> return (Right b))
```

With these definitions, mapA behaves like map for functions, and mapM for Kleisli arrows[1]:

```
StreamFns> mapA (arr (+1)) [1..5]
[2,3,4,5,6]
StreamFns> runKleisli (mapA (Kleisli print) >>> Kleisli print)
                      [1..5]
1
2
3
4
5
[(),(),(),(),()]
```

But what about stream functions?

Implementing left for stream functions is a little trickier. First of all, it is clear that the input xs is a list of tagged values, from which all those tagged with Left should be extracted and passed to the argument stream function, whose outputs should be retagged with Left:

```
map Left (f [a | Left a <- xs])
```

Moreover, all the elements of xs tagged Right should be copied to the output. *But how should the Left and Right values be merged into the final output stream?*

There is no single "right answer" to this question. We shall choose to restrict our attention to synchronous stream functions, which produce exactly one output per input[2]. With this assumption, we can implement left by including one element of f's output in the combined output stream every time an element tagged Left appears in the input. Thus:

```
instance ArrowChoice SF where
  left (SF f) = SF (\xs -> combine xs (f [y | Left y <- xs]))
    where combine (Left y:xs) (z:zs) = Left z: combine xs zs
          combine (Right y:xs) zs = Right y: combine xs zs
          combine [] zs = []
```

In fact, the restriction we have just made, to length-preserving stream functions, turns out to be necessary not only to define left, but also to ensure the good behaviour of first. The definition of first we gave in the previous section does not in general satisfy the "arrow laws" formulated in [10], which means that it occasionally behaves in surprising ways — but the laws *are* satisfied under the restriction to length-preserving functions.

---

[1] Here the second expression to be evaluated is split across several lines for readability, which is of course not allowed by Hugs or GHCi.

[2] The delay arrow is clearly problematic, but don't worry! We shall see how to fix this shortly.

The only stream function arrow we have seen so far which does *not* preserve the length of its argument is `delay` — the delayed stream has one more element than the input stream. Recall the definition we saw earlier:

```
delay x = SF (x:)
```

In order to meet our new restriction, we redefine `delay` as

```
delay x = SF (init . (x:))
```

This does not change the behaviour of the examples we saw above.

As an example of using choice for stream functions, let us explore how `mapA` behaves for this arrow type. It is interesting to map the `delay` arrow over a stream of lists:

```
StreamFns> runSF (mapA (delay 0)) [[1,2,3],[4,5,6],[7,8,9]]
[[0,0,0],[1,2,3],[4,5,6]]
```

Even more interesting is a stream of lists of different lengths:

```
StreamFns> runSF (mapA (delay 0))
            [[1,2,3],[4,5],[6],[7,8],[9,10,11],[12,13,14,15]]
[[0,0,0],[1,2],[4],[6,5],[7,8,3],[9,10,11,0]]
```

If we arrange the input and output streams as tables,

| 1 2 3 | | 0 0 0 |
|-------|---|-------|
| 4 5 | | 1 2 |
| 6 | | 4 |
| 7 8 | | 6 5 |
| 9 10 11 | | 7 8 3 |
| 12 13 14 15 | | 9 10 11 0 |

then we can see that the *shape* of the table output correponds to the shape of the input, but the elements in each column form a stream delayed by one step, where the gaps in the columns are ignored.

As another example, consider the following arrow which delays a list by passing the head straight through, and recursively delaying the tail by one more step.

```
delaysA = arr listcase >>>
             arr (const []) |||
             (arr id *** (delaysA >>> delay [])) >>>
             arr (uncurry (:)))
```

Running this on an example gives

```
StreamFns> runSF delaysA [[1,2,3],[4,5,6],[7,8,9],[10,11,12]]
[[1],[4,2],[7,5,3],[10,8,6]]
```

or, laid out as tables,

| 1 | 2 | 3 |
|---|---|---|
| 4 | 5 | 6 |
| 7 | 8 | 9 |
| 10 | 11 | 12 |

| 1 | | |
|---|---|---|
| 4 | 2 | |
| 7 | 5 | 3 |
| 10 | 8 | 6 |

We can see that each column is delayed by a different amount, with missing entries represented by the empty list.

## 2.3   Arrows and Feedback

Stream functions are useful for simulating synchronous circuits. For example, we could represent a NOR-gate by the arrow

```
nor :: SF (Bool,Bool) Bool
nor = arr (not.uncurry (||))
```

and simulate it by using runSF to apply it to a list of pairs of booleans. In this section we shall visualise such lists by drawing signals as they might appear on an oscilloscope, so a test of nor might produce this output:

Here the top two signals are the input, and the bottom one the output. As we would expect, the output is high only when both inputs are low. (The ASCII graphics are ugly, but easily produced by portable Haskell code: a function which does so is included in the appendix).

Synchronous circuits contain delays, which we can simulate with the delay arrow. For example, a rising edge detector can be modelled by comparing the input with the same signal delayed one step.

```
edge :: SF Bool Bool
edge = arr id &&& delay False >>> arr detect
  where detect (a,b) = a && not b
```

Testing this arrow might produce

where a pulse appears in the output at each rising edge of the input.

Now, by connecting two NOR-gates together, one can build a flip-flop (see Figure 1). A flip-flop takes two inputs, SET and RESET, and produces two outputs, one of which is the negation of the other. As long as both inputs remain low, the outputs remain stable, but when the SET input goes high, then the first output does also, and when the RESET input goes high, then the first output goes low. If SET and RESET are high simultaneously, then the flip-flop becomes unstable. A flip-flop is made by connecting the output of each NOR-gate to one input of the other; the remaining two inputs of the NOR-gates are the inputs of the flip-flop, and their outputs are the outputs of the flip-flop.

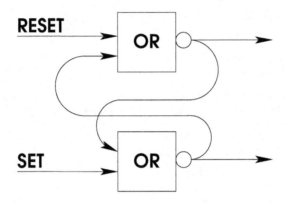

**Fig. 1.** A flip-flop built from two NOR-gates

To represent the flip-flop as an arrow, we need to *feed back* the outputs of the NOR-gates to their inputs. To make this possible, we introduce a new arrow class with a feedback combinator:

```
class Arrow arr => ArrowLoop arr where
  loop :: arr (a,c) (b,c) -> arr a b
```

The intention is that the component of type c in the output of the argument arrow is fed back to become the second component of its input. For example, for ordinary functions loop just creates a simple recursive definition:

```
instance ArrowLoop (->) where
  loop f a = b
    where (b,c) = f (a,c)
```

Feedback can also be implemented for Kleisli arrows over monads which are instances of the MonadFix class, but we omit the details here. Instead, let us implement feedback for stream functions. We might expect to use the following definition:

```
instance ArrowLoop SF where
  loop (SF f) = SF $ \as ->
      let (bs,cs) = unzip (f (zip as cs)) in bs
```

which closely resembles the definition for functions, making a recursive definition of the feedback stream cs. However, this is just a little too strict. We would of course expect loop (arr id) to behave as arr id (with an undefined feedback stream), and the same is true of loop (arr swap), which feeds its input through the feedback stream to its output. But with the definition above, both these loops are undefined. The problem is the recursive definition of (bs,cs) above: the functions unzip and zip are both strict — they must evaluate their arguments before they can return a result — and so are arr id and arr swap, the two functions we are considering passing as the parameter f, with the result that the value to be bound to the pattern (bs,cs) cannot be computed until the value of cs is known! Another way to see this is to remember that the semantics of a recursive definition is the limit of a sequence of approximations starting with the undefined value, $\perp$, and with each subsequent approximation constructed by evaluating the right hand side of the definition, with the left hand side bound to the previous one. In this case, when we initially bind (bs,cs) to $\perp$ then both bs and cs are bound to $\perp$, but now because zip is strict then zip as $\perp=\perp$, because f is strict then f $\perp=\perp$, and because unzip is strict then unzip $\perp=\perp$. So the second approximation, unzip (f (zip as $\perp$ )), is also $\perp$, and by the same argument so are all of the others. Thus the limit of the approximations is undefined, and the definition creates a "black hole".

To avoid this, we must ensure that cs is *not* undefined, although it may be a stream of undefined elements. We modify the definition as follows:

```
instance ArrowLoop SF where
  loop (SF f) = SF $ \as ->
      let (bs,cs) = unzip (f (zip as (stream cs))) in bs
    where stream ~(x:xs) = x:stream xs
```

The ~ in the definition of stream indicates Haskell's *lazy pattern matching* — it delays matching the argument of stream against the pattern (x:xs) until the bound variables x and xs are actually used. Thus stream returns an infinite list *without* evaluating its argument — it is only when the *elements* of the result are needed that the argument is evaluated. Semantically, stream $\perp=\perp:\perp:\perp:$ …. As a result, provided as is defined, then so is zip as (stream $\perp$) — it is a list of pairs with undefined second components. Since neither f nor unzip needs these components to deliver a defined result, we now obtain defined values for bs and cs in the second approximation, and indeed the limit of the approximations is the result we expect. The reader who finds this argument difficult should work out the sequence of approximations in the call runSF (loop (arr swap)) [1,2,3] — it is quite instructive to do so.

Note that stream itself is not a length-preserving stream function: its result is always infinite, no matter what its argument is. But loop respects our restriction to synchronous stream functions, because zip always returns a list as long as its *shorter* argument, which in this case is as, so the lists bound to bs and cs always have the same length as as.

Returning to the flip-flop, we must pair two NOR-gates, take their outputs and duplicate them, feeding back one copy, and supplying each NOR-gate with one input and the output of the other NOR-gate as inputs. Here is a first attempt:

```
flipflop =
  loop (arr (\((reset,set),(c,d)) -> ((set,d),(reset,c))) >>>
        nor *** nor >>>
        arr id &&& arr id)
```

The first line takes the external inputs and fed-back outputs and constructs the inputs for each NOR-gate. The second line invokes the two NOR-gates, and the third line duplicates their outputs.

Unfortunately, this definition is circular: the $i$th output depends on itself. To make a working model of a flip-flop, we must add a delay. We do so as follows:

```
flipflop =
  loop (arr (\((reset,set),~(c,d)) -> ((set,d),(reset,c))) >>>
        nor *** nor >>>
        delay (False,True) >>>
        arr id &&& arr id)
```

which initialises the flip-flop with the first output low. We must also ensure that the loop body is not strict in the loop state, which explains the lazy pattern matching on the first line. Note that the **delay** in the code delays a *pair* of bits, and so corresponds to *two* single-bit delays in the hardware, and the feedback path in this example passes through both of them (refer to Figure 1). This makes the behaviour a little less responsive, and we must now trigger the flip-flop with pulses lasting at least two cycles. For example, one test of the flip-flop produces this output:

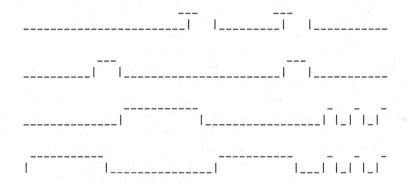

Here the first two traces are the RESET and SET inputs, and the bottom two are the outputs from the flip-flop. Initially the first output is low, but when the SET input goes high then so does the output. It goes low again when the RESET input goes high, then when both inputs go high, the flip-flop becomes unstable.

The **ArrowLoop** class, together with instances for functions and Kleisli arrows, is included in **Control.Arrow**. Ross Paterson has also suggested overloading delay, and placing it in an `ArrowCircuit` class, but this has not (yet) found its way into the standard hierarchical libraries.

## 2.4 Higher-Order Arrows

What about higher-order programming with arrows? Can we construct arrows which receive other arrows in their input, and invoke them? We cannot, using the combinators we have already seen, but we can, of course, add a new class to make this possible. We introduce an arrow analogue of the "apply" function:

```
class Arrow arr => ArrowApply arr where
  app :: arr (arr a b, a) b
```

Instances for functions and Kleisli arrows are easy to define:

```
instance ArrowApply (->) where
  app (f,x) = f x
```

```
instance Monad m => ArrowApply (Kleisli m) where
  app = Kleisli (\(Kleisli f,x) -> f x)
```

but there is no reasonable implementation for stream functions. We shall see why shortly.

First of all, note that both `first` and `left` are easy to implement in terms of `app` (the details are left as an exercise). So `app` is a strictly more powerful operator to provide. We have also seen that we can base a Kleisli arrow on *any* monad, and we can implement all of `first`, `left` and `app` for such a type. In fact, `app` is so powerful that we can reconstruct a monad from any arrow type which supports it! We represent a computation of an `a` as an arrow from the empty tuple to `a`:

```
newtype ArrowMonad arr a = ArrowMonad (arr () a)
```

We can now define `return` and (`>>=`) as follows:

```
instance ArrowApply a => Monad (ArrowMonad a) where
  return x = ArrowMonad (arr (const x))
  ArrowMonad m >>= f =
    ArrowMonad (m >>>
                arr (\x-> let ArrowMonad h = f x in (h, ())) >>>
                app)
```

The second argument of (`>>=`) is a function returning an arrow, which we turn into an arrow outputting an arrow (`h`) using `arr`; we then need `app` to invoke the result.

Thus we have finally fulfilled our promise at the beginning of this section, to extend the arrow interface until it is as powerful as — indeed, equivalent to — the monadic one. We can now do everything with arrows that can be done with monads — if need be, by converting our arrow type into a monad. Yet this is only a Pyrrhic victory. If we want to do "monadic" things, it is much simpler to define a monad directly, than to first define all the arrow operations, and then build a monad on top of them.

The conclusion we draw is that arrows that support app are of relatively little interest! Apart from the benefits of point-free notation, we might as well use a monad instead. The truly *interesting* arrow types are those which do *not* correspond to a monad, because it is here that arrows give us real extra generality. Since we know that stream functions cannot be represented as a monad, then they are one of these "interesting" arrow types. So are the arrows used for functional reactive programming, for building GUIs, and the arrows for discrete event simulation we present in Section 5. And since these arrows cannot be represented by a monad, we know that they cannot support a sensible definition of app either.

## 2.5   Exercises

1. **Filtering.** Define

   ```
   filterA :: ArrowChoice arr => arr a Bool -> arr [a] [a]
   ```

   to behave as filter on functions, and like filterM on Kleisli arrows. Experiment with running

   ```
   filterA (arr even >>> delay True)
   ```

   on streams of lists of varying lengths, and understand its behaviour.
2. **Stream processors.** Another way to represent stream processors is using the datatype

   ```
   data SP a b = Put b (SP a b) | Get (a -> SP a b)
   ```

   where Put b f represents a stream processor that is ready to output b and continue with f, and Get k represents a stream processor waiting for an input a, which will continue by passing it to k. Stream processors can be interpreted as stream functions by the function

   ```
   runSP (Put b s) as = b:runSP s as
   runSP (Get k) (a:as) = runSP (k a) as
   runSP (Get k) [] = []
   ```

   Construct instances of the classes Arrow, ArrowChoice, ArrowLoop, and ArrowCircuit for the type SP.
   - You are provided with the module Circuits, which defines the class ArrowCircuit.
   - You should find that you can drop the restriction we imposed on stream functions, that one output is produced per input — so SP arrows can represent *asynchronous* processes.
   - On the other hand, you will encounter a tricky point in defining first. How will you resolve it?

– Check that your implementation of `loop` has the property that the arrows
`loop (arr id)` and `loop (arr swap)` behave as `arr id`:

```
SP> runSP (loop (arr id)) [1..10]
[1,2,3,4,5,6,7,8,9,10]
SP> runSP (loop (arr swap)) [1..10]
[1,2,3,4,5,6,7,8,9,10]
```

Module `Circuits` also exports the definition `flipflop` above, together
with sample input `flipflopInput` and a function `showSignal` which
visualises tuples of lists of booleans as the "oscilloscope traces" we saw
above.

```
SP> putStr$ showSignal$ flipflopInput
```

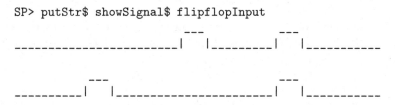

Use these functions to test a flipflop using your stream processors as the
underlying arrow type. The behaviour should be the same as we saw
above.

# 3 Pointed Arrow Programming

We began these notes by arguing the merits of a point-free programming style.
Yet although point-free programming is often concise and readable, it is not
*always* appropriate. In many cases it is clearer to give names to the values being
manipulated, and in ordinary Haskell programs we do not hesitate to do so. This
"pointed" style is also well-supported in monadic programs, by the do notation.
But what if we want to use a pointed style in an arrow-based program? With
the combinators we have seen so far, it is quite impossible to do so.

In fact, an extension to the language is needed to make pointed arrow programming possible. Ross Paterson designed such an extension [17], and implemented it using a preprocessor, and it was built into GHC in version 6.2. Paterson's extension is comparable to the do notation for monads — it is quite
possible to program without it, but some programs are much nicer with it. But
just as arrows have a more complex interface than do monads, so Paterson's notation is more complex than the do, and its translation much more complicated.
The complexity of the translation, of course, makes the notation all the more
valuable. In this section we will explain how to use this extension.

## 3.1 Arrow Abstractions

Paterson's extension adds a new form of expression to Haskell: the *arrow abstraction*, of the form `proc pat -> body`. Arrow abstractions are analogous to

$\lambda$-expressions: they denote an arrow, and bind a name (or, in general, a pattern) to the arrow input, which may then be used in the body of the abstraction.

However, the body of an arrow abstraction is not an expression: it is of a new syntactic category called a *command*. Commands are designed to help us construct just those arrows that can be built using the arrow combinators — but in a sometimes more convenient notation.

The simplest form of command, `f -< exp`, can be thought of as a form of "arrow application" — it feeds the value of the expression `exp` to the arrow `f`. (The choice of notation will make more sense shortly). Thus, for example, an AND-gate with a delay of one step could be expressed by

```
proc (x,y) -> delay False -< x && y
```

This is equivalent to `arr (\(x,y) -> x&&y) >>> delay False`. Arrow abstractions with a simple command as their body are translated as follows,

$$\texttt{proc pat -> a -< e} \longrightarrow \texttt{arr (\textbackslash pat -> e) >>> a}$$

and as this translation suggests, arrow-bound variables (such as `x` and `y` in the AND-gate example above) are *not in scope* to the left of the `-<`. This is an easy way to see that `proc` could not possibly be implemented by a combinator taking a $\lambda$-expression as an argument: the scopes of arrow-bound variables do not correspond to the scopes of $\lambda$-bound variables.

This scope rule rules out arrow abstractions such as

```
proc (f,x) -> f -< x
```

which is rejected, because it translates to `arr (\(f,x)->x) >>> f`, in which `f` is used outside its scope. As usual, if we want to apply an arrow received as input, we must use `app`:

```
proc (f,x) -> app -< (f,x)
```

The arrow notation does offer syntactic sugar for this as well:

```
proc (f,x) -> f -<< x
```

However, this is of little importance, since there is little reason to use arrows with `app` — one might as well use the equivalent monad instead.

Pointed arrow notation really comes into its own when we start to form *compound commands* from simpler ones. For example, suppose we want to feed inputs to either the arrow `f` or `g`, depending on the value of a predicate `p`. Using the arrow combinators, we would need to encode the choice using `Left` and `Right`, in order to use the choice combinator (`|||`):

```
arr (\x -> if p x then Left x else Right x) >>> f ||| g
```

Using the pointed arrow notation, we can simply write

```
proc x -> if p x then f -< x else g -< x
```

Here the `if...then...else...` is a *conditional command*, which is translated as follows:

```
proc pat -> if e then c1 else c2
⟶
arr (\pat -> if e then Left pat else Right pat) >>>
(proc pat -> c1 ||| proc pat -> c2)}
```

Note that the scope of x in the example now has *two* holes: the arrow-valued expressions before each arrow application.

Even in the simple example above, the pointed notation is more concise than the point-free. When we extend this idea to `case` commands, its advantage is even greater. Recall the definition of `mapA` from section 2.2:

```
mapA f = arr listcase >>>
           arr (const []) ||| (f *** mapA f >>> arr (uncurry (:)))
  where listcase [] = Left ()
        listcase (x:xs) = Right (x,xs)
```

We were obliged to introduce an encoding function `listcase` to convert the case analysis into a choice between `Left` and `Right`. Clearly, a case analysis with more cases would require an encoding into nested `Either` types, which would be tedious in the extreme to program. But all these encodings are generated automatically from `case`-commands in the pointed arrow notation. We can reexpress `mapA` as

```
mapA f = proc xs ->
  case xs of
    [] -> returnA -< []
    x:xs' -> (f *** mapA f >>> uncurry (:)) -< (x,xs')
```

which is certainly more readable.

Just as in the monadic notation, we need a way to express just delivering a result without any effects: this is the rôle of `returnA -< []` above, which corresponds to `arr (const [])` in the point-free code. In fact, `returnA` *is* just an arrow, but a trivial arrow with no effects: it is defined to be `arr id`. We could have written this `case` branch as `arr (const []) -< xs`, which would correspond exactly to the point-free code, but it is clearer to introduce `returnA` instead.

## 3.2   Naming Intermediate Values

Just as in monadic programs, it is convenient to be able to name intermediate values in arrow programs. This is the primary function of Haskell's do notation for monads, and it is provided for arrows by a similar do notation. However, while a monadic do block is an expression, an arrow do block is a command, and can thus only appear inside an arrow abstraction. Likewise, while the statements x <- e in a monadic do bind a name to the result of an expression e, the arrow form binds a name to the output of a command. As a simple example, we can reexpress the `printFile` arrow of the introduction as

```
printFile = proc name ->
  do s <- Kleisli readFile -< name
     Kleisli print -< s
```

in which we name the string read by `readFile` as `s`. And now at last the choice of `-<` as the arrow application operator makes sense — it is the tail feathers of an arrow! A binding of the form `x <- f -< e` looks suggestively as though `e` is being fed through an arrow labelled with `f` to be bound to `x`!

As another example, recall the rising edge detector from section 2.3:

```
edge :: SF Bool Bool
edge = arr id &&& delay False >>> arr detect
  where detect (a,b) = a && not b
```

We can give a name to the intermediate, delayed value by using a `do` block:

```
edge = proc a -> do
          b <- delay False -< a
          returnA -< a && not b
```

Notice that both `a` and `b` are in scope after the binding of `b`, although they are bound at different places. Thus a binding is translated into an arrow that *extends the environment*, by pairing the bound value with the environment received as input. The translation rule is

$$
\begin{array}{ccc}
\texttt{proc pat -> do x <- c1} & \longrightarrow & \texttt{(arr id \&\&\& proc pat -> c1) >>>} \\
\texttt{c2} & & \texttt{proc (pat,x) -> c2}
\end{array}
$$

where we see clearly which variables are in scope in each command. Applying the rule to this example, the translation of the pointed definition of `edge` is

```
edge = (arr id &&& (arr (\a->a) >>> delay False)) >>>
       (arr (\(a,b) -> a && not b) >>> returnA)
```

which can be simplified by the arrow laws to the point-free definition we started with, bearing in mind that `arr (\a->a)` and `returnA` are both the identity arrow, and thus can be dropped from compositions. In practice, GHC can and does optimise these translations, discarding unused variables from environments, for example. But the principle is the one illustrated here.

Note that the same variable occupies different positions in the environment in different commands, and so different occurrences must be translated differently. The arrow notation lets us use the *same* name for the *same value*, no matter where it occurs, which is a major advantage.

We can use the `do` notation to rewrite `mapA` in an even more pointed form. Recall that in the last section we redefined it as

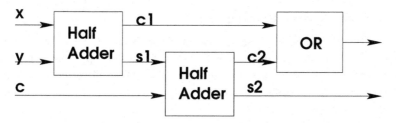

**Fig. 2.** A full adder built from half-adders

```
mapA f = proc xs ->
  case xs of
    [] -> returnA -< []
    x:xs' -> (f *** mapA f >>> uncurry (:)) -< (x,xs')
```

Here the second branch of the case is still expressed in a point-free form. Let us use do to name the intermediate results:

```
mapA f = proc xs ->
  case xs of
    [] -> returnA -< []
    x:xs' -> do y <- f -< x
                ys' <- mapA f -< xs'
                returnA -< y:ys
```

We are left with a definition in a style which closely resembles ordinary monadic programming.

When used with the stream functions arrow, the pointed notation can be used to express circuit diagrams with named signals very directly. For example, suppose that a half-adder block is available, simulated by

```
halfAdd :: Arrow arr => arr (Bool,Bool) (Bool,Bool)
halfAdd = proc (x,y) -> returnA -< (x&&y, x/=y)
```

A full adder can be constructed from a half adder using the circuit diagram in Figure 2. From the diagram, we can read off how each component maps input signals to output signals, and simply write this down in a do block.

```
fullAdd :: Arrow arr => arr (Bool,Bool,Bool) (Bool,Bool)
fullAdd = proc (x,y,c) -> do
            (c1,s1) <- halfAdd -< (x,y)
            (c2,s2) <- halfAdd -< (s1,c)
            returnA -< (c1||c2,s2)
```

The arrow code is essentially a net-list for the circuit. Without the pointed arrow notation, we would have needed to pass c past the first half adder, and c1 past the second, explicitly, which would have made the dataflow much less obvious.

### 3.3   Recursive Arrow Bindings

Of course, this simple scheme doesn't work if the circuit involves feedback. We have already seen an example of such a circuit: the flipflop of section 2.3. We repeat its circuit diagram again in Figure 3. In section 2.3 we represented this diagram as an arrow as follows:

```
flipflop =
  loop (arr (\((reset,set),~(c,d)) -> ((set,d),(reset,c))) >>>
        nor *** nor >>>
        delay (False,True) >>>
        arr id &&& arr id)
```

The arrow do syntax provides syntactic sugar for an application of loop: a group of bindings can be preceded by rec to make them recursive using loop. In this example, we can define flipflop instead by

```
flipflop :: ArrowCircuit arr => arr (Bool,Bool) (Bool,Bool)
flipflop = proc (reset,set) -> do
             rec c <- delay False -< nor reset d
                 d <- delay True -< nor set c
             returnA -< (c,d)
  where nor a b = not (a || b)
```

As always with stream functions, we must insert enough delays to ensure that each stream element is well-defined (in this example, one delay would actually suffice). In this case also, the pointed definition is more straightforward than the point-free one. Its relationship to the circuit diagram is much more obvious.

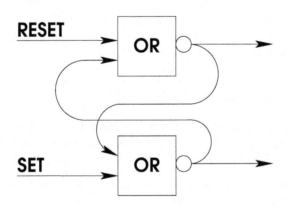

**Fig. 3.** The flip-flop, again

### 3.4   Command Combinators

Of course, once we have introduced commands, it is natural to want to define *command combinators*. But since commands are not first-class expressions, it appears at first that we cannot define combinators that take commands as arguments. However, commands *do* denote arrows from environments to outputs, and these are first-class values. The pointed arrow notation therefore provides a mechanism for using *arrow combinators* as command combinators.

However, we cannot use just any arrow combinator as a command combinator. The commands that appear in pointed arrow notation denote arrows with types of the form `arr env a`, where `env` is the type of the environment that the command appears in, and `a` is the type of its output. Now, when we apply a command combinator, then all of the commands we pass to it naturally occur in the *same* environment, which is moreover the same environment that the combinator itself appears in. Thus the type of a command combinator should have the form

$$\text{arr env a -> arr env b -> ... -> arr env c}$$

That is, all the arrows passed to it as arguments should have the *same* input type, which moreover should be the same input type as the arrow produced.

For example, the pairing combinator

```
(&&&) :: Arrow arr => arr a b -> arr a c -> arr a (b,c)
```

has just such a type (where `a` is the type of the environment), while in contrast

```
(|||) :: Arrow arr => arr a c -> arr b c -> arr (Either a b) c
```

does not. We can indeed use (&&&) as an operator on commands:

```
example = proc x ->
                do returnA -< x
            &&& do delay 0 -< x
```

is equivalent to `returnA &&& delay 0`. Running the example gives

```
Main> runSF example [1..5]
[(1,0),(2,1),(3,2),(4,3),(5,4)]
```

(One trap for the unwary is that this syntax is ambiguous: in the example above, &&& could be misinterpreted as a part of the expression following `returnA -<`. The dos in the example are there to prevent this. Because of the layout rule, it is clear in the example above that &&& is not a part of the preceding command.)

When a command combinator is not an infix operator, then applications are enclosed in banana brackets to distinguish them from ordinary function calls. Thus (since (&&&) is not an infix operator), we could also write the example above as

```
example = proc x -> (| (&&&) (returnA -< x) (delay 0 -< x) |)
```

The translation of banana brackets is just

```
proc pat -> (| e c1...cn |) ⟶ e (proc pat->c1)...(proc pat->cn)
```

Lovers of higher-order programming (such as ourselves!) will of course wish to define combinators which not only accept and return commands, but *parameterised* commands, or "functions returning commands", if you will. The pointed arrow notation supports this too. Parameterised commands are represented as arrows with types of the form `arr (env, a) b`, where `env` is the type of the environment and the `b` the type of the result, as usual, but `a` is the type of the parameter. Such parameterised commands can be constructed using lambda-notation: the command `\x -> cmd` is translated into an arrow taking a pair of the current environment and a value for `x`, to the output of `cmd`. The translation rule is (roughly)

$$\text{proc pat -> \x -> c} \longrightarrow \text{proc (pat,x) -> c}$$

Likewise the command `cmd e` can be thought of as supplying such a parameter: `cmd` is expected to be a command taking a pair of an environment and value as input, and `cmd e` is a command which just takes the environment as input, and extends the environment with the output of `e` before passing it to `cmd`. The translation rule is (roughly)

$$\text{proc pat -> c e} \longrightarrow \text{arr (\pat -> (pat,e)) >>> proc pat -> c}$$

See the GHC documentation for more details on the translation.

As an example, let us define a command combinator corresponding to `map`. The arrow map we have already defined,

```
mapA :: ArrowChoice arr => arr a b -> arr [a] [b]
```

is not suitable, because it changes the type of the input in a way which is not allowable. Let us instead pair the input of both the argument and result arrow with the environment:

```
mapC :: ArrowChoice arr => arr (env,a) b -> arr (env,[a]) [b]
mapC c = proc (env,xs) ->
  case xs of
    [] -> returnA -< []
    x:xs' -> do y <- c -< (env,x)
                ys <- mapC c -< (env,xs')
                returnA -< y:ys
```

With this type, `mapC` can be used as a command combinator. To apply it, we have to first apply the command combinator `mapC` to a command abstraction (inside banana brackets), and then apply the resulting command to a suitable list (no banana brackets). For example,

```
example2 = proc (n,xs) ->
  (| mapC (\x-> do delay 0 -< n
            &&& do returnA -< x) |) xs
```

is a stream function whose input stream contains pairs of numbers and lists, and which pairs each element of such a list (using `mapC`) with a *delayed* number from the foregoing input stream element. It can be run as follows:

```
Main> runSF example2 [(1,[1,2]),(3,[4]),(5,[6,7])]
[[(0,1),(0,2)],[(1,4)],[(3,6),(3,7)]]
```

The example may seem a little contrived, but its purpose is to illustrate the behaviour when the argument of mapC refers *both* to its parameter and a free variable (n). A much more useful example of this can be found in Exercise 4d below.

Taken together, these extensions provide us with a comprehensive notation for pointed programming with arrows, which leads to programs which, superficially at least, resemble monadic programs very closely.

### 3.5   Exercises

1. **Adder.** An $n$-bit adder can be built out of full adders using the design shown in Figure 4, which adds two numbers represented by lists of booleans, and delivers a sum represented in the same way, and a carry bit. Simulate this design by defining

   ```
   adder :: Arrow arr => Int ->
               arr ([Bool],[Bool]) ([Bool],Bool)
   ```

   Represent the inputs and the sum with the *most* significant bit first in the list.

2. **Bit serial adder.** A bit-serial adder can be constructed from a full adder using feedback, by the circuit in Figure 5. The inputs are supplied to such an adder one bit at a time, starting with the least significant bit, and the sum is output in the same way. Model this circuit with an arrow

   ```
   bsadd :: ArrowCircuit arr => arr (Bool,Bool) Bool
   ```

   Use the rec arrow notation to obtain feedback. The showSignal function from module Circuits may be useful again for visualising the inputs and outputs.

3. **Filter.**
   (a) Define

   ```
   filterA :: ArrowChoice arr => arr a Bool -> arr [a] [a]
   ```

   again (as in exercise 1 in section 2.5), but this time use the pointed arrow notation.

   (b) Now define a *command combinator* filterC:

   ```
   filterC :: ArrowChoice arr =>
                 arr (env,a) Bool -> arr (env,[a]) [a]
   ```

   and test it using the following example:

   ```
   test :: Show a => Kleisli IO [a] [a]
   test = proc xs -> (|filterC (\x->Kleisli keep-<x)|) xs
     where keep x = do putStr (show x++"? ")
                       s <- getLine
                       return (take 1 s == "y")
   ```

   Running this example might yield:

   ```
   Main> runKleisli (test3 >>> Kleisli print) [1..3]
   1? y
   2? n
   3? y
   [1,3]
   ```

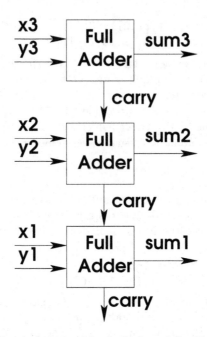

Fig. 4. A 3-bit adder built from full adders

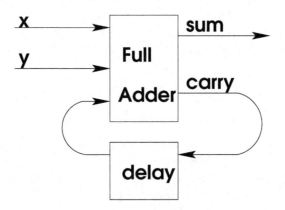

Fig. 5. A bit-serial adder

4. **Counters.**

(a) One of the useful circuit combinators used in the Lava hardware description environment [15] is row, illustrated in Figure 6. Let us represent f by an arrow from pairs to pairs,

    f :: arr (a,b) (c,d)

with the components representing inputs and outputs as shown:

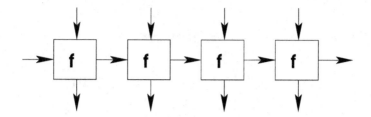

**Fig. 6.** A row of f

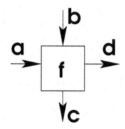

Define a command combinator

```
rowC :: Arrow arr =>
            Int ->
                arr (env,(a,b)) (c,a) ->
                    arr (env,(a,[b])) ([c],a)
```

to implement the connection pattern in the Figure.

(b) A one-bit counter can be constructed using the circuit diagram in Figure 7. Implement this as an arrow using the pointed arrow notation:

```
counter1bit :: ArrowCircuit arr => arr Bool (Bool,Bool)
```

(c) An $n$-bit counter can be built by connecting $n$ 1-bit counters in a row, with the carry output of each counter connected to the input of the next. (Note that, in this case, the vertical input of the row is unused). Implement an $n$-bit counter using your rowC command combinator.

(d) In practice, it must be possible to *reset* a counter to zero. Modify your one bit counter so that its state can be reset, changing its type to

```
counter1bit :: ArrowCircuit arr =>
                    arr (Bool,Bool) (Bool,Bool)
```

to accomodate a reset input. Now modify your $n$-bit counter to be resettable also. This kind of modification, which requires feeding a new signal to every part of a circuit description, would be rather more difficult without the arrow notation.

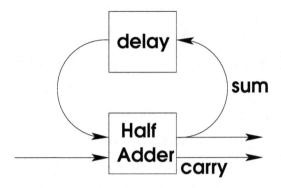

**Fig. 7.** A 1-bit counter

## 4    Implementing Arrows

We began section 2 by comparing the types of the sequencing operators for monads and arrows respectively:

```
class Monad m where
  (>>=) :: m b -> (b -> m c) -> m c
  ...
class Arrow arr where
  (>>>) :: arr a b -> arr b c -> arr a c
  ...
```

As we observed then, the fact that the second argument of (>>=) is a Haskell function gives the user a great deal of expressivity "for free" — to obtain similar expressivity with the arrows interface, we have to introduce a large number of further operations on the arrow types. However, there is another side to this coin. When we *implement* a monad, the (>>=) can do nothing with its second argument except apply it — the (>>=) operator is forced to treat its second operand as abstract. When we implement an arrow, on the other hand, the (>>>) can inspect the representation of its second operand and make choices based on what it finds. Arrows can carry *static information*, which is available to the arrow combinators, and can be used to implement them more efficiently.

This was, in fact, the original motivation for developing arrows. Swierstra and Duponcheel had developed a parsing library, in which the representation of parsers included a list of starting symbols, and the choice combinator made use of this information to avoid backtracking (which can incur a heavy space penalty by saving previous states in case it is necessary to backtrack to them) [24]. Their parsing library, in contrast to many others, did not — indeed, could not — support a monadic interface, precisely because the starting symbols of f >>= g cannot be determined in general without knowing the starting symbols of both f *and* g, and the latter are not available to (>>=). It was the search for an interface with similar generality to the monadic one, which *could* be supported by Swierstra and Duponcheel's library, which led to my proposal to use arrows.

However, since parsing arrows have been discussed in several papers already, we will take other examples in these notes.

## 4.1    Optimising Composition

For some arrow types (such as stream transformers), composition is quite expensive. Yet in some cases it can be avoided, by applying arrow laws. For example, one law states that

```
arr f >>> arr g = arr (f >>> g)
```

but whereas the left hand side involves composition of arrows, the right hand side involves only composition of functions. Replacing the left hand side by the right may thus be an optimisation — in the case of stream functions, it corresponds to optimising map f.map g to map (f.g).

Suppose, now, that we represent arrows constructed by arr specially, so that the implementation of (>>>) can recognise them. Then we can apply this optimisation dynamically, every time a composition of two such pure arrows is constructed!

To implement this optimisation in as general a form as possible, we define a new arrow type Opt arrow, based on an underlying arrow type arrow, which represents arrows of the form arr f specially.

```
data Opt arrow a b = Arr (a->b)
                   | Lift (arrow a b)
```

Thus an Opt arrow arrow is either the special case arr f, or just contains an arrow of the underlying type. We can recover an underlying arrow from an Opt arrow arrow using the function

```
runOpt (Arr f)  = arr f
runOpt (Lift f) = f
```

Now we implement the Arrow operations as follows:

```
instance Arrow arrow => Arrow (Opt arrow) where
  arr = Arr
  Arr f >>> Arr g = Arr (f>>>g)
  f >>> g = Lift (runOpt f>>>runOpt g)
  first (Arr f) = Arr (first f)
  first (Lift f) = Lift (first f)
```

We implement arr just by building the special case representation, and each of the other operations by first testing for the special case and optimising if possible, then falling through into a general case which just converts to the underlying arrow type and applies the same operation there. The other arrow classes can be implemented in a similar way. Yampa [8], perhaps the most extensive application of arrows, makes use of just such an optimisation — with the addition of another special form for constant arrows (of the form arr (const k)).

This is an example of an *arrow transformer* or *functor*, analogous to a monad transformer. In his experimental arrow library [16], Paterson defines a class of arrow transformers:

```
class (Arrow a, Arrow (f a)) => ArrowTransformer f a where
  lift :: a b c -> f a b c
```

(The library contains a number of useful transformers, corresponding to many of the well-known monad transformers, plus several which make sense only for arrows). We can declare Opt to be an arrow transformer very simply:

```
instance Arrow arrow => ArrowTransformer Opt arrow where
  lift = Lift
```

This idea can be taken further, of course. As it stands, the optimisation of composition is applied only if compositions are bracketed correctly — a term such as (Lift f >>> arr g) >>> arr h would not be optimised, because the leftmost composition constructs the arrow Lift (f >>> arr g), which cannot be optimised by the rightmost composition.

Let us see how to improve this, by taking advantage of the associativity of composition. Rather than representing optimised arrows as one of the forms arr f or lift g, let us use the forms arr f and arr f >>> lift g >>> arr h. The advantage of this latter form is that we can keep the "pure part" of each arrow separate on both the left and the right, thus making it possible to optimise compositions with pure arrows on both sides.

We need existential types to represent these forms in a data structure, because in the form arr f >>> lift g >>> arr h then the arrow g may have any type at all. The Opt type becomes

```
data Opt arrow a b = Arr (a->b)
                   | forall c d. ALA (a->c) (arrow c d) (d->b)
```

(where ALA stands for arr-lift-arr: a value of the form ALA f g h represents arr f >>> lift g >>> arr h). We lift underlying arrows to this type by pre- and post-composing with the identity arrow:

```
instance ArrowTransformer Opt arrow where
  lift f = ALA id f id
```

We convert back to the underlying arrow type in the obvious way:

```
runOpt :: Arrow arrow => Opt arrow a b -> arrow a b
runOpt (Arr f) = arr f
runOpt (ALA pre f post) = arr pre >>> f >>> arr post
```

The implementations of the arrow operations just take advantage of the known pure parts to construct compositions of *functions*, rather than the underlying arrow type, wherever possible.

```
instance Arrow arrow => Arrow (Opt arrow) where
  arr = Arr

  Arr f >>> Arr g = Arr (f>>>g)
  Arr f >>> ALA pre g post = ALA (f >>> pre) g post
  ALA pre f post >>> Arr g = ALA pre f (post >>> g)
  ALA pre f post >>> ALA pre' g post' =
    ALA pre (f >>> arr (post>>>pre')) >>> g) post'

  first (Arr f) = Arr (first f)
  first (ALA pre f post) =
    ALA (first pre) (first f) (first post)
```

In the code above, the *only* composition at the underlying arrow type takes place in the last equation defining (>>>), when two impure arrows are composed. Writing out the left and right hand sides as their interpretations, this equation reads

```
arr pre >>> f >>> arr post >>> arr pre' >>> g >>> arr post'
=
arr pre >>> (f >>> arr (post >>> pre') >>> g) >>> arr post'
```

and we see that, even in this case, one arrow composition is converted into a composition of functions (post and pre').

However, as it stands this implementation is not a good one, because every time we lift an underlying arrow to the Opt type, we insert two identity functions, which must later be composed with the underlying arrow. Lifting an arrow f and then running it actually introduces two new arrow compositions:

```
runOpt (lift f) = runOpt (ALA id f id)
                = arr id >>> f >>> arr id
```

Thus lifting computations into the "optimised" arrow type might well make them run slower. But we can avoid this overhead, in either of two different ways:

- We can introduce new constructors in the Opt type, to represent arrows of the form lift f, lift f>>>arr g, and arr f>>>lift g. With these additional constructors, no identity functions need be introduced, and so no spurious compositions are necessary.
- We can change the representation of the pre and post functions to make the identity function recognisable, so we can treat it as a special case.

The first solution is straightforward but slightly inelegant, since it leads to rather long and repetetive code. The second solution gives us an opportunity to define another arrow transformer, which optimises composition with the identity, using the same approach as in this section. One can go on to build optimising arrow transformers that implement more and more algebraic laws; we skip the details here. We remark only that the generalised algebraic data types recently added to GHC [20] are invaluable here, allowing us to define constructors such as

```
First :: Opt arrow a b -> Opt arrow (a,c) (b,c)
```

whose result type is not of the usual form, so that we can pattern match on, and thus optimise, arrows built using the `first` combinator.

## 5    Arrows for Simulation

In the last section of these notes, we will carry through an extended example of defining a prototype arrow library with richer functionality. Staying with the application area of circuit simulation, we will construct a library which can perform more accurate timing simulations. The stream functions we used earlier perform a synchronous, or "cycle based" simulation, which proceeds in discrete steps, and computes the value of every signal at every step. This is why, when we defined the arrow operations, we could assume that each stream functions produced one output for each input. This kind of simulation is costly if the time represented by each step is short (because there must be many steps), and inaccurate if it is long (because potentially many changes in a signal *during one step* must be approximated by a single value). In contrast, our new library will track *every* change in a signal's value, no matter how often they occur, but incur costs only when signals actually do change. It will implement a form of *discrete event* simulation.

To give a flavour of the library, here is how we might use it to simulate a flip-flop, in which the two NOR-gates have slightly different gate delays. The description of the flip-flop itself is not unlike those we have already seen — we shall see the details later. When we run the simulation, we provide a list of all the changes in the value of the input, with the times at which they occur:

```
Sim> runSim (printA "input " >>>
            cutoff 6.5 flipflop >>>
            printA "output")
        (False,False)
        [Event 1 (False,True), Event 2 (False,False), ...]
```

The arrow we are simulating contains "probes" of the form `printA s`, which behave as identity arrows but also print the values which pass through them. We also specify a time at which simulation should end. The output of the simulation tells us how the probed signals changed over time:

```
input : (False,False)@init
output: (False,True)@init
input : (False,True)@1.0
output: (False,False)@1.1
output: (True,False)@1.2100000000000002
input : (False,False)@2.0
input : (True,False)@3.0
output: (False,False)@3.11
output: (False,True)@3.21
```

```
input : (False,False)@4.0
input : (True,True)@5.0
output: (False,False)@5.1
input : (False,False)@6.0
output: (False,True)@6.1
output: (True,True)@6.109999999999999
output: (False,True)@6.209999999999999
output: (False,False)@6.209999999999999
output: (False,True)@6.309999999999999
output: (True,True)@6.319999999999985
output: (False,True)@6.419999999999998
output: (False,False)@6.419999999999998
```

We can see that when the set or reset input goes high, the flip-flop responds by quickly setting the appropriate output high, after a brief moment in which both outputs are low. When both inputs go low, the output does not change, and no event appears in the trace above. If both inputs are high simultaneously, and then drop, then the flip-flop becomes unstable and begins to oscillate, generating many output events although no further events appear in the input.

One application for this more accurate kind of simulation is power estimation for integrated circuits. Although the *behaviour* of such a circuit can be simulated by a synchronous simulation which just computes the *final* value of each signal on each clock cycle, the power consumption depends also on how many times each signal changes its value *during* a clock cycle. This is because much of the power in such a circuit is consumed charging and discharging wires, and if this happens several times during one clock cycle, the power consumed is correspondingly higher.

Like the stream functions arrow, our new simulation arrows represent a kind of process, transforming input events to output events. They are thus a rather typical kind of application for arrows, and useful to study for that reason. Moreover, this library (although much smaller) is closely related to the Yampa simulation library [8] — many design decisions are resolved in the same way, and the reader who also studies the internals of Yampa will find much that is familiar. However, there is also much that is different, since Yampa is not a discrete event simulator: Yampa simulations proceed in steps in which every signal is calculated, although the "sampling interval" between steps can vary.

## 5.1   Signals and Events

Abstractly, we think of the inputs and outputs of simulation arrows as *signals*, which are piecewise constant functions from time to values. Times may be any real number:

```
type Time = Double
```

and we explicitly allow negative times. We refer to a change in a signal's value as an *event*, and require the event times for each signal to form a (possibly infinite)

increasing sequence. That is, each signal must have a first event before which it
has a constant value no matter how far back in time we go, and after each event
there must be a *next* event. We can thus represent a signal by its initial value,
and the events at which its value changes[3]. We shall represent events by the type

```
data Event a = Event {time::Time, value::a}
```

The value of a signal at time t will be the initial value, if t is before the time of
the first event, or the value of the last event at a time less than or equal to t.

This abstract view of signals fits our intended application domain well, but
it is worth noting that we are ruling out at least one useful kind of signal: those
which take a different value at a single point only. Consider an edge detector for
example: when the input signal changes from False to True, we might expect
the output signal to be True at the time of the change, but False immediately
before and after. We cannot represent this: if the output signal takes the value
True at all, then it must remain True throughout some non-zero interval — it
would be non-sensical to say that the output signal has *both* a rising and a falling
event at the same time.

Of course, a hardware edge detector must *also* keep its output high for a
non-zero period, so our abstraction is realistic, but nevertheless in some types of
simulation we might find it useful to allow instantaneously different signal values.
For example, if we were simulating a car wash, we might want to represent the
arrival of a car as something that takes place at a particular instant, rather
than something that extends over a short period. What Yampa calls "events"
are in fact precisely such signals: they are signals of a Maybe type whose value is
Nothing except at the single instant where an event occurs. We could incorporate
such signals into our model by associating *two* values with each event, the value
at the instant of the event itself, and the value at later times, but for simplicity
we have not pursued this approach.

## 5.2   Simulation Arrows

We might expect a simulation arrow just to be a function from a list of input
events to a list of output events, rather like the stream function arrows of Section 1.2. Unfortunately, this simple approach does not work at all. To see why
not, consider a simulated adder, which combines two input integer signals to
an output integer signal. Clearly, whenever an event occurs on *either* input, the
adder must produce an event on its output with the new sum. So, to decide
which output event to produce next, the adder must choose the *earliest* event
from its next two input events. If these are supplied as lists of events, then this
cannot be done without inspecting, and thus computing, *both* of them — and

---

[3] The reader might be tempted to treat the initial value as an event at time "minus
infinity", to avoid introducing a special case. It is tempting, but it does not work
well: at a number of places in the simulation code, the initial value of a signal *must*
be treated differently from the later ones. Exactly the same design choice is made in
Yampa, so there is safety in numbers!

one of them may lie far in the simulated future. In the presence of feedback, it is disastrous if we cannot compute present simulated events without knowing future ones, since then events may depend on themselves and simulation may be impossible. Hence this approach fails. We will use an approach related to the *stream processors* of Exercise 2 instead.

Abstractly, though, we will think of a simulation arrow as a function from an input signal to an output signal. (In practice, we shall parameterise simulation arrows on a monad, but we ignore that for the time being). But we place two restrictions on these functions: they should respect *causality*, and be *time-invariant*.

Causality means that the output of an arrow at time t should not be affected by the value of its input at later times: the future may not affect the past. Causality is a vital property: it makes it possible to run a simulation from earlier times to later ones, without the need to return to earlier times and revise the values of prescient signals when later events are discovered.

Time-invariance means that shifting the input signal of an arrow backwards or forwards in time should shift the output signal in the same way: the behaviour should not depend on the *absolute* time at which events occur. One important consequence is that the output of an arrow cannot change from its initial value until the input has (since any such event can depend only on the constant part of the input by causality, and so can by shifted arbitrarily later in time by time invariance). This relieves the simulator of the need to simulate all of history, from the beginning of time until the first input event, since we know that all signals must retain their initial values until that point.

We shall represent simulation arrows by functions from the initial input value, to the initial output value and a simulation state:

```
newtype Sim m a b = Sim (a -> m (b, State m a b))
```

This state will then evolve as the simulation proceeds, and (in general) it depends on the initial input value. We parameterise simulation arrows on a monad m (in our examples, the IO monad), so that it is possible to define probes such as printA, which we saw in the introduction to this section.

A running simulation can be in one of three states, which we represent using the following type:

```
data State m a b =
    Ready (Event b) (State m a b)
  | Lift (m (State m a b))
  | Wait Time (State m a b) (Event a -> State m a b)
```

Here

- **Ready e s** represents a simulation that is ready to output **e**, then behave like **s**,
- **Lift m** represents a simulation that is ready to perform a computation m in the underlying monad, then continue in the state that m delivers,

- `Wait t s k` represents a simulation that is waiting for an input event until time `t`: if an input arrives *before* time `t`, then it is passed to the continuation `k`, and if no input arrives before simulated time reaches `t` then the simulation changes to the "timeout" state `s`.

Conveniently, Haskell's `Double` type includes the value infinity,

```
infinity = 1/0
```

which behaves as a real number greater than all others. We can thus represent a simulation state which is waiting for ever using `Wait infinity`.

Given an initial input value and a list of input events, we run a simulation simply by supplying the inputs at the right simulated times and performing the underlying monadic actions, in simulated time order. We can discard the outputs, since simulations are observed by inserting probes. Thus:

```
runSim (Sim f) a as = do
  (b,r) <- f a
  runState r as

runState (Ready b s) as = runState s as
runState (Lift m) as = do s <- m
                          runState s as
runState (Wait t s k) []                -- no further inputs
  | t==infinity = return ()             -- infinity never comes
  | otherwise   = runState s []         -- timeout
runState (Wait t s k) (a:as)            -- inputs waiting
  | t <= time a = runState s (a:as)     -- timeout
  | otherwise   = runState (k a) as     -- supply event
```

Simulation states should satisfy a number of invariants, of course. Since they represent signal functions, no output events should be generated before the first input, and output events should not depend on later inputs. To ensure the latter property, we require that output events generated after an input is received carry the same or a later time. Moreover, output events must be generated in time order.

Since simulation states are in general infinite, we cannot *check* whether or not these invariants are satisfied, but we can guarantee them by construction. We therefore define "smart constructors" for the `Sim` and `State` types, which check that the values they are constructing satisfy the invariants, and raise an exception if an invariant would be broken. We ensure that simulation states are initially quiescent by constructing them with

```
sim f = Sim $ \a -> do
  (b,s) <- f a
  return (b,quiescent s)

quiescent (Lift m) = Lift (liftM quiescent m)
quiescent (Wait t s k) = wait t (quiescent s) k
```

which fails if the constructed state is ready to output before the first input, and we ensure the other invariants hold by constructing simulation states using

```
ready e r = Ready e (causal (time e) r)
lift m = Lift m
wait t f k = Wait t (causal t f)
                (\e -> causal (time e) (k e))

causal t (Ready e f) | t <= time e = Ready e f
causal t (Lift m) = Lift (liftM (causal t) m)
causal t (Wait t' s k) = Wait t' (causal t s) (causal t.k)
```

Here causal t s raises an exception if the *first* event output by s precedes time t; provided s itself satisfied the invariants then this is enough to ensure that the states constructed using causal also do so. It is used in ready to ensure that output events occur in increasing time order, and in wait to ensure that output events do not precede inputs which have been received, or timeouts which have passed. The alert reader will notice that causal does not prevent successive output events occurring at the *same* time, and this is because such "glitches" do seem occasionally to be unavoidable (we will return to this point).

Using these smart constructors, we can now define primitive arrows with confidence that mistakes that break the invariants will not go undiscovered, at least not if they would affect the results of simulation. For example, we can define the printA arrow that we saw above as follows:

```
printA name = sim $ \a -> do
  message (show a++"@init")
  return (a,s)
  where s = waitInput $ \a -> lift $ do
                message (show a)
                return (ready a s)
        message a = putStrLn (name++": "++a)
```

(The show method for events is defined to display the value along with the time, in the format we saw earlier). Typically the simulation state is defined recursively, as we see here, in order to respond to any number of input events. The waitInput function is just a useful shorthand for a wait with an infinite timeout:

```
waitInput k = wait infinity undefined k
```

Of course, it is not necessary to define smart constructors as we have done: we could simply replace them with the real ones, and provided we make no mistakes, our simulations would behave identically. However, the smart constructors have proven to be invaluable while debugging the library. Indeed, the real code contains a more elaborate version of causal, which collects and reports a trace of the events leading up to a violation, which is invaluable information when a bug is discovered.

Note, however, that these smart constructors do not ensure time invariance in the arrows we write, because we write code which manipulates absolute times. It would be possible to build a further layer of abstraction on top of them, in which we would program with relative times only (except in monadic actions which do not affect future output, such as printing the simulated time in printA). For this prototype library, however, this degree of safety seems like overkill: we rely on writing correct code instead.

## 5.3   Implementing the Arrow Operations

In this section, we shall see how to implement the arrow operations for this type. Of course, we must require the underlying monad to be a monad:

```
instance Monad m => Arrow (Sim m) where
   ...
```

The arr operation is rather simple to define: arr f just applies f to the initial input value, and to the value in every subsequent input event. Computing a new output takes no simulated time.

```
arr f = sim $ \a -> return (f a, s)
   where s = waitInput (\a ->
                ready (Event (time a) (f (value a))) s)
```

Note, however, that the output events generated may well be redundant. For example, if we simulate an AND-gate as follows:

```
Main> runSim (arr (uncurry (&&)) >>> printA "out") (False,False)
         [Event 1 (False,True),
          Event 2 (True,False),
          Event 3 (True,True)]
out: False@init
out: False@1.0
out: False@2.0
out: True@3.0
```

then we see that the output signal carries three events, even though the value only changes once.

Redundant events are undesirable, even if they seem semantically harmless, because they cause unnecessary computation as later parts of the simulation react to the "change" of value. Our approach to avoiding the problem is to define an arrow nubA which represents the identity function on signals, but drops redundant events. Inserting nubA into the example above, we now see the output we would expect:

```
Main> runSim (arr (uncurry (&&)) >>> nubA >>> printA "out")
         (False,False)
         [Event 1 (False,True),
```

```
            Event 2 (True,False),
            Event 3 (True,True)]
out: False@init
out: True@3.0
```

Defining `nubA` just involves some simple programming with our smart constructors:

```
nubA :: (Eq a, Monad m) => Sim m a a
nubA = sim $ \a -> return (a,loop a)
  where loop a = waitInput $ \(Event t a') ->
                   if a==a' then loop a
                   else ready (Event t a') (loop a')
```

Why not just include this in the definition of `arr`? Or why not rename the old definition of `arr` to `protoArr` and redefine `arr` as follows?

```
arr f = protoArr f >>> nubA
```

The reason is *types*: we are constrained by the type stated for `arr` in the `Arrow` class. The definition above does not have that type — it has the type

```
arr :: (Arrow arr, Eq b) => (a->b) -> arr a b
```

with the extra constraint that the output type must support equality, so that `nubA` can discard events with values equal to previous one. Of course, we could just define `arr'` as above, and use that instead, but any overloaded arrow functions which we use with simulation arrows, and the code generated from the pointed arrow notation, will still use the class method `arr`. For this reason we make `nubA` explicit as an arrow, and simply expect to use it often[4].

Composing simulation arrows is easy — we just have to compute the initial output — but the real work is in composing simulation states.

```
Sim f >>> Sim g = sim $ \a -> do
  (b,sf) <- f a
  (c,sg) <- g b
  return (c,sf `stateComp` sg)
```

When we compose simulation states, we must be careful to respect our invariants. Since all the outputs of a composition are generated by a single arrow (the second operand), which should itself fulfill the invariants, we can expect them to be correctly ordered at least. However, we must see to it that no output is delayed until after a *later* input is received by the first operand, which would violate

---

[4] It is interesting to note that the same problem arose in a different context in the first arrow paper [10]. I have proposed a language extension that would solve the problem, by allowing parameterised types to restrict their parameters to instances of certain classes only [9]. With this extension, simulation arrows could require that their output type be in class `Eq`, making equality usable on the output even though no such constraint appears in the `Arrow` class itself.

causality. To ensure this, we always produce outputs (and perform monadic actions) as early as possible. Thus, if the second operand of a composition is ready to output an event or perform a monadic computation, then so is the composition.

```
sf `stateComp` Ready c sg = ready c (sf `stateComp` sg)
sf `stateComp` Lift m = lift (liftM (sf`stateComp`) m)
```

If neither of these equations applies, then the second operand must be of the form Wait .... We assume this in the equations that follow — thanks to Haskell's top-to-bottom strategy, the equations above take precedence over (apparently overlapping) equations below.

Given that the second operand is waiting, then if the first is ready to output or perform a computation, then we allow it to proceed, in the hope that it will wake up the second operand, and enable us to generate an event from the composition without needing to wait for an input. When the first operand outputs an event, then we must of course feed it into the second. This is the purpose of the operator `after`, which computes the state of sg *after* it has received the event b. Thus `after` is the state transition function for simulation states.

```
Ready b sf `stateComp` sg = sf `stateComp` (sg `after` b)
Lift m `stateComp` sg = lift (liftM (`stateComp` sg) m)
```

When *both* operands of a composition are waiting, then the composition must also wait — but only until the earlier of the deadlines of its operands. When that simulated time is reached, the operand with the earlier deadline times out and may continue computing. If an input event is received in the meantime, it is sent (of course) to the first operand of the composition.

```
Wait tf sf kf `stateComp` Wait tg sg kg =
  wait (min tf tg)
       timeout
       (\a -> kf a `stateComp` Wait tg sg kg)
  where timeout | tf<tg  = sf `stateComp` Wait tg sg kg
                | tf==tg = sf `stateComp` sg
                | tf>tg  = Wait tf sf kf `stateComp` sg
```

Note that this code behaves correctly even if one or both deadlines is infinity.

To complete the definition of composition, we must implement the state transition function after. But this is easy: an input event is received by the first Wait whose deadline is after the event itself:

```
Ready b s  `after` a = ready b (s `after` a)
Lift m     `after` a = lift (liftM (`after` a) m)
Wait t s k `after` a
  | t <= time a = s `after` a
  | otherwise   = k a
```

Moving on to the first combinator, once again computing the initial output is easy, but adapting the simulation state much more complex.

```
simFirst (Sim f) = sim $ \(a,c) -> do
  (b,s) <- f a
  return ((b,c), stateFirst b c s)
```

When does the output of `first f` change? Well, clearly, if the output of `f`
changes, then so does the output of `first f`. But the output of `first f` may also
change if its *input* changes, since the change may affect the second component of
the pair, which is fed directly through to the output. Moreover, when the output
of `f` changes, then we need to know the current value of the second component
of the input, so we can construct the new pair of output values. Likewise, when
the input to `first f` changes, and we have a new second component for the
output pair, then we need to know the current value of the first component of
the output to construct the new output pair. For this reason, the `stateFirst`
function is parameterised not only on the state of `f`, but also on the current
values of the components of the output.

In the light of this discussion, we can see that if `f` is waiting, then `first f`
should also wait: no change to the output can occur until either the deadline
is reached, or an input is received. If an input is received before the deadline,
then `first f` is immediately ready to output a new pair containing an updated
second component.

```
stateFirst b c (Wait t s k) =
  wait t (stateFirst b c s) $ \(Event t' (a,c')) ->
    ready (Event t' (b,c')) (stateFirst b c' (k (Event t' a)))
```

As before, if `f` is ready to perform a monadic action, then so is `first f`:

```
stateFirst b c (Lift m) = lift (liftM (stateFirst b c) m)
```

The trickiest case is when `f` is ready to output an event. Before we can actually
output the corresponding event from `first f`, we must ensure that there are
no remaining inputs at earlier times, which would cause changes to the output
of `first f` that should precede the event we are about to generate. The only
way to ensure this is to wait until the simulated time at which the event should
occur, and see whether we timeout or receive an input. Thus we define:

```
stateFirst b c (Ready b' s) =
  wait (time b')
       (ready (Event (time b') (value b',c))
              (stateFirst (value b') c s))
       (\(Event t' (a,c')) ->
         ready (Event t' (b,c'))
               (stateFirst b c'
                     (ready b' (s `after` (Event t' a)))))
```

After waiting without seeing an input until the time of the new event, we can
generate a new output immediately. If an input is received in the meantime, we
generate a corresponding output event and continue waiting, but in the state

we reach by feeding the first component of the input just received into the state of **f**.

This definition seems very natural, but it does exhibit a surprising behaviour which we can illustrate with the following example:

```
Sim> runSim (first (arr (+1)) >>> printA "out") (0,0)
          [Event 1 (1,1)]
out:  (1,0)@init
out:  (1,1)@1.0
out:  (2,1)@1.0
```

Although there is only one input event, **first** generates *two* output events, one generated by the change of the input, and the other by the change in the output of **arr (+1)**. Moreover, both output events occur *at the same simulated time* — and how should we interpret that? Our solution is to declare that when several events appear at the same simulated time, then the last one to be generated gives the true value of the output signal at that time. The previous events we call "glitches", and they represent steps towards the correct value. Glitches arise, as in this example, when two parts of the simulation produce output events at exactly the same time, and they are then combined into the same signal. A glitch results because we make no attempt to identify such simultaneous events and combine them into a single one.

We put up with glitches, because of our design decision to produce output events as soon as possible. To eliminate them, we would, among other things, need to change the semantics of **Wait**. At present, **Wait** times out if no input event arrives *before* the deadline; we would need to change this to time out only if the next input event is *after* the deadline, thus allowing inputs that arrive exactly on the deadline to be received, possibly affecting the output at the same simulated time. The danger would be that some arrows would then be unable to produce their output at time **t**, without seeing a *later* input event — which would make feedback impossible to implement. However, it is not obvious that this would be inevitable, and a glitch-free version of this library would be worth investigating. For the purpose of these notes, though, we stick with the glitches.

We will, however, introduce an arrow to filter them out: an arrow which copies its input to its output, but whose output is glitch-free even when its input contains glitches. To filter out glitches in the input at time **t**, we must wait until we can be certain that all inputs at time **t** have been received — which we can only be *after* time **t** has passed! It follows that a glitch-remover *must* introduce a delay: it must wait until some time **t'** later than **t**, before it can output a copy of the input at time **t**. We therefore build glitch removal into our delay arrow, which we call **delay1**, because there is at most one event at each simulated time in its output.

In contrast to the **delay** arrow we saw earlier, in this case we do not need to supply an initial value for the output. The stream function **delay**, for use in synchronous simulation, delays its output by one step with respect to its input, and needs an initial value to insert in the output at the first simulation step. In contrast, our signals all have an initial value "since time immemorial", and the output of delay1 just has the same initial value as its input.

We define delay1 as follows:

```
delay1 d = sim (\a -> return (a,r))
  where r = waitInput loop
          loop (Event t a) =
            wait (t+d) (ready (Event (t+d) a) r) $
              \(Event t' a') ->
                if t==t'
                  then loop (Event t' a')
                  else ready (Event (t+d) a) (loop (Event t' a'))
```

It delays its input signal by time d, which permits it to wait until time t+d to be sure that the input at time t is stable.

## 5.4  Implementing Feedback

Just as with the other arrow combinators, implementing feedback requires two stages: first we define loop for simulation arrows, constructing the initial values, then we implement looping for simulation states. Now, recall that the argument of loop is an arrow of type arr (a,c) (b,c), where c is the type of the loop state. Clearly the initial output of this arrow will depend on its initial input, which in turn depends on its initial output! Thus the initial output of a loop must be recursively defined. Since simulation arrows are based on an underlying monad, we need a fixpoint operator for that monad. Such a fixpoint operator is provided by the class

```
class (Monad m) => MonadFix m where
  mfix :: (a -> m a) -> m a
```

and there are instances for IO and many other monads.

Using this operator, we can now define loop for simulation arrows:

```
instance MonadFix m => ArrowLoop (Sim m) where
  loop (Sim f) = sim $ \a-> do
    ((b,c),s) <- mfix (\(~((b,c),s)) -> f (a,c))
    return (b,stateLoop a c [] s)
```

We just recursively construct the initial output from the parameter arrow f, and return its first component as the initial output of the loop. Obviously, the function we pass to mfix must not be strict, and so the lazy pattern matching (indicated by ~) in the definition above is essential.

As simulation proceeds, the loop body f will periodically produce new outputs, whose second components must be fed back as changes to the input. But those input changes must be *merged* with changes to the input of the loop as a whole. We handle this by passing stateLoop a *queue* of pending changes to the loop state, to be merged with changes to the loop input as those arrive. We must also track the current values of the loop input and the loop state, so as to be able to construct a new input pair for the loop body when either one changes.

After this discussion, we can present the code of stateLoop. If the loop body is ready to output, the loop as a whole does so, and the change to the loop state is added to the pending queue.

```
stateLoop a c q (Ready (Event t (b,c'))) s =
   ready (Event t b) (stateLoop a c (q++[(t,c')]) s)
```

If the loop body is ready to perform a monadic action, then we do so.

```
stateLoop a c q (Lift m) = lift $ liftM (stateLoop a c q) m
```

If the loop body is waiting, and there are *no* pending state changes, then the loop as a whole waits. If a new input is received, then it is passed together with the current loop state to the loop body, and the current input value is updated.

```
stateLoop a c [] (Wait t s k) =
   wait t (stateLoop a c [] s) $ \(Event t' a') ->
      stateLoop a' c [] (k (Event t' (a',c)))
```

Finally, if the loop body is waiting and there *are* pending state changes, then we must wait and see whether any input event arrives before the first of them. If so, we process the input event, and if not, we make the state change.

```
stateLoop a c ((t',c'):q) (Wait t s k) =
   wait (min t t') timeout $ \(Event t'' a') ->
      stateLoop a' c ((t',c'):q) (k (Event t'' (a',c)))
   where timeout
            | t'<t = stateLoop a c' q (k (Event t' (a,c')))
            | t'>t = stateLoop a c ((t',c'):q) s
            | t'==t= stateLoop a c' q (s `after` Event t (a,c'))
```

As a simple example, let us simulate a loop which simply copies its input to its output — a loop in which the feedback is irrelevant.

```
Sim> runSim (loop (arr id) >>> printA "out") 0
           [Event 1 1, Event 2 2]
out: 0@init
out: 1@1.0
out: 1@1.0
out: 1@1.0
out: 1@1.0
out: 1@1.0
 ...
```

It doesn't work! The simulation produces an infinite number of glitch events, as soon as the input changes. The reason is that the first input change generates an output from the loop body including a "new" (but unchanged) loop state.

This state change is fed back to the loop body, and generates another new (and also unchanged) state, and so on. To avoid this, we must *discard* state "changes" which do not actually change the state, by inserting a nubA arrow into the loop body.

```
Sim> runSim (loop nubA >>> printA "out")
            0
            [Event 1 1, Event 2 2]
out: 0@init
out: 1@1.0
*** Exception: <<loop>>
```

This does not work either! In this case, the exception "<<loop>>" is generated when a value depends on itself, and it is fairly clear which value that is — it is, of course, the loop state, whose initial value is undefined[5]. Indeed, since the initial value of the loop state cannot be determined from the input, there is no alternative to specifying it explicitly. We therefore define a new combinator, which provides the initial output value for an arrow explicitly:

```
initially x (Sim f) = Sim $ \a -> do (_,s) <- f a
                                     return (x,s)
```

Now we can revisit our example and initialise the loop state as follows:

```
Sim> runSim (loop (initially (0,0) nubA) >>> printA "out") 0
            [Event 1 1, Event 2 2]
out: 0@init
out: 1@1.0
out: 2@2.0
```

At last, it works as expected.

Now, although this example was very trivial, the difficulties that arose will be with us every time we use loop: the loop state must (almost) always be initialised, and we must always discard redundant state changes, to avoid generating an infinite number of events. This means that we will always need to include nubA in a loop body. This is not an artefact of our particular library, but a fundamental property of simulation with feedback: after an input change, a number of state changes may result, but eventually (we hope) the state will stabilise. A simulator *must* continue simulating until the state reaches a fixed point, and that is exactly what loop with nubA does.

It would be natural, now, to include nubA in the definition of loop, since it will always be required, but once again the type stated for loop in the class ArrowLoop prevents us from doing so. Instead, we define a new looping combinator just for simulations, which combines loop with nubA. We give it a type analogous to mfix:

---

[5] The generation of loop exceptions is somewhat variable between one GHC version and another. The output shown here was generated using version 6.2.1, but other versions might actually loop infinitely rather than raise an exception.

```
afix :: (MonadFix m, Eq b) => Sim m (a,b) b -> Sim m a b
afix f = loop (f >>> nubA >>> arr id &&& arr id) >>> nubA
```

Because we cannot define loop to discard redundant state changes, we will not
be able to use the rec syntax in the pointed arrow notation — it is simply
impossible to insert nubA in the source code, so that it appears in the correct
place in the translation. But afix is a good alternative: it can be used as a
command combinator to good effect, as we will see in the next section.

## 5.5    Examples

In this section we will give just a few simple examples to show how the simulation
arrows can be used to simulate small circuits. First let us revisit the nor gate:
we can now make our simulation more realistic, by including a gate delay.

```
nor = proc (a,b) -> do
         (a',b') <- delay1 0.1 -< (a,b)
         returnA -< not (a'||b')
```

A nor gate can be used to construct an oscillator, which generates an oscillating
signal as long as its input is low:

```
oscillator = proc disable ->
  (|afix (\x -> nor -< (disable,x))|)
```

Here the output of the nor gate is fed back, using afix, to one of its inputs.
While disable is low, the nor gate simply inverts its other input, and so the
circuit acts as an inverter with its output coupled to its input, and oscillates.
When disable is high, then the output of the nor gate is always held low.
Running a simulation, we see that the oscillator behaves as expected:

```
Sim> runSim (oscillator >>> printA "out") True
          [Event 1 False, Event 2 True]
 out: False@init
 out: True@1.1
 out: False@1.2000000000000002
 out: True@1.3000000000000003
 out: False@1.4000000000000004
 out: True@1.5000000000000004
 out: False@1.600000000000005
 out: True@1.7000000000000006
 out: False@1.8000000000000007
 out: True@1.9000000000000008
 out: False@2.000000000000001
```

Of course, it is important to initialise the input signal to True, since otherwise
the oscillator should oscillate "since time immemorial", and we cannot represent
that. If we try, we find that the output of the oscillator is undefined.

It is interesting that in this example, we did *not* need to initialise the oscillator
state. This is because the initial state is the solution to the equation

```
x = not (True || x)
```

and this is equal to `False`, because Haskell's "or" operator (`||`) is not strict in its second input, when the first one is `True`.

Finally, let us see how we can use `afix` to define a flip-flop:

```
flipflop = proc (reset,set) ->
  (|afix (\ ~(x,y)->do
      x' <- initially False nor -< (reset,y)
      y' <- initially True nor -< (set,x)
      returnA -< (x',y'))|)
```

Although this is not quite as notationally elegant as the `rec` syntax, we can see that `afix` does let us emulate recursive definitions rather nicely, and that we are able to describe the flip-flop in a natural way. As usual, the argument of a fix-point combinator cannot be strict, so we must match on the argument pair lazily. Simulating this flip-flop, we obtain the results presented in the introduction to this section.

## 5.6   Exercises

1. **Circuit simulation.** Revisit exercises 1, 2, and 4 of Section 3.5, and simulate the adder, bit serial adder, and $n$-bit counter using the new simulation arrows.

2. **Choice.** In this section, we implemented the operations in class `Arrow`, but we did not implement those in `ArrowChoice`. Can you construct an implementation of `left` for simulation arrows?

   The input signal to `left` is of type `Either a c`, which we can think of as *two* signals, one of type `a`, and one of type `c`, multiplexed onto one channel. It is the signal of type `a` that must be provided as the input to `left`'s argument, but `left f` receives this signal only incompletely — at times when the input signal is carrying a `Right` value, then the value of the input to `f` is unknown. You will need to *complete* this partially known input signal to construct an input signal for `f`, which can be done by assuming that the signal remains constant during the periods when it is unknown.

   If the initial value of the input signal is a `Right` value, then we must initialise `left f` without knowing the initial value of `f`'s input! Fortunately, we *do* know the initial value of `left f`'s *output* — it is just the same as the input in this case. We are left with the problem of initialising the arrow `f`. This cannot be done at this time, because its initial input is unknown. However, if we assume that the initial value of the `Left` input is the *same* as the first value we see, then we can initialise `f` when the first event of the form `Left a` is received.

   The output from `left f` can *also* be thought of as two signals multiplexed onto one channel, but in this case these signals are the `Right` input signal to `left f`, and the output signal from `f` itself. How should these be multiplexed? That is, when should the output signal be taken from the `Right` input, and when should it be taken from f? It seems natural to take the Right input when it is present, and the output from f when it is not, with the result that the multiplexing of the output channel is the same as the multiplexing of the input.

Implement left according to the ideas in this discussion, and experiment with the if-then-else pointed arrow notation (which uses it) to investigate its usefulness.

## 6   Arrows in Perspective

Arrows in Haskell are directly inspired by category theory, which in turn is just the theory of arrows — a category is no more than a collection of arrows with certain properties. Thus every time we define a new instance of class Arrow, we construct a category! However, categorical arrows are more general than their Haskell namesakes, in two important ways. Firstly, the "source" and "target" of Haskell arrows, that is the types of their inputs and outputs, are just Haskell types. The source and target of a categorical arrow can be anything at all — natural numbers, for example, or pet poodles. In the general case, most of the operations we have considered make no sense — what would the target of f &&& g be, in a category where the targets of arrows are natural numbers? Secondly, Haskell arrows support many more operations than categorical arrows do. In fact, categorical arrows need only support composition and identity arrows (which we constructed as arr id). In general, categories have no equivalent even of our arr operator, let alone all the others we have considered. Thus even Haskell arrows which are only instances of class Arrow have much more structure than categorical arrows do in general.

However, as we saw in the introduction, there is little interesting that can be done without more operations on arrows than just composition. The same is true in category theory, and mathematicians have explored an extensive flora of additional operations that some categories have. Of particular interest to programming language semanticists are *cartesian closed* categories, which have just the right structure to model λ-calculus. In such models, the meaning of a λ-expression is an arrow of the category, from the types of its free variables (the context), to the type of its value — compare with the translations of Paterson's arrow notation. The advantage of working categorically is that one can study the properties of *all* semantic models at once, without cluttering one's work with the details of any particular one. Pierce's book is an excellent introduction to category theory from the programming language semantics perspective [21].

One may wonder, then, whether the structure provided by Haskell arrows has been studied by theoreticians? The answer turns out to be "yes". Monads, which were invented by category theorists for quite different purposes, were first connected with computational effects by Moggi [14], who used them to structure denotational semantic descriptions, and his work was the direct inspiration for Wadler to introduce monads in Haskell [26]. But Power and Robinson were dissatisfied with Moggi's approach to modelling effects, because the semantics of terms was no longer a simple arrow in a category, but rather a combination of an arrow and a monad. They asked the question: what properties should a category have for its arrows to *directly* model computations with effects? Their answer was to introduce "premonoidal" categories [22], now called Freyd categories, which correspond closely to instances of class `Arrow`. Later, Power and Thielecke studied the command abstractions and applications that we saw in Paterson's arrow notation, under the name *closed κ-categories* [23]. Feedback operators, which are called *trace* operators by category theorists, have been studied in this setting by Benton and Hyland [1]. This latter paper morcover makes the connection back to Haskell programs, which can otherwise be somewhat obscured by notational and terminological differences.

The use of arrows in programming was introduced in my paper from the year 2000 [10]. That paper introduced the arrow classes presented here (with the exception of `ArrowLoop`), arrow transformers, and a number of applications. The direct inspiration was Swierstra and Duponcheel's non-monadic parser library [24], which collected static information about parsers to optimise them during their construction. My paper showed that their library *could* be given an arrow interface. While doing so, I also introduced two classes for arrows that can fail: `ArrowZero` and `ArrowPlus`, which provide operations for failure and failure-handling respectively. My paper also discussed stream processors, and showed that the Fudgets GUI library [3], which is based on a kind of abstract stream processor, can be given an arrow interface. Finally, I presented a small library for CGI programming.

CGI scripts are small programs that run on web servers to generate dynamic web pages. Typically, when a user fills in an HTML form in a browser, the form data is sent to a CGI script on the server which generates the next web page the user sees. CGI programming is awkward, because the script which generates a form is not usually the script that processes the user's reply. This leads to all sorts of complication, software engineering problems, and bugs.

The key idea behind my library was for a CGI script generating a form to *suspend its own state*, embed that state in a hidden field of the form (where it is sent to the client browser and returned with the other form data once the form is filled in), and then *restart* from the same state when the client's reply is received. That permits CGI programs to be written like ordinary interactive programs, where communication with the client appears as a simple function call, delivering the client's answer as a result. My implementation was based on an arrow type with a suspend operator. On suspension, the arrow combinators constructed a kind of "program counter" for the arrow, where the program counter for a composition, for example, recorded whether the suspension point was in the first or second operand, and the program counter within that operand. The program counter could then be shipped to and from the client browser, and used to restart in the same state. This idea turns out to be useful outside the world of arrows: Peter Thiemann realised that the same behaviour can be achieved elegantly using a monad, and this insight lies behind his Wash/CGI library [25].

Ross Paterson developed the pointed arrow notation presented in these notes [17], collaborated with Peyton-Jones on its implementation in GHC, and is one of the people behind the arrows web page [6]. Paterson introduced the `ArrowLoop` class, and has developed an extensive experimental arrow library containing many arrow transformers, and classes to make arrows constructed using many transformers easy to use. Paterson applied arrows to circuit simulation, and made an arrowized version of Launchbury et als. architecture description language Hawk [12]. A good description of this work can be found in Paterson's excellent tutoral on arrows [18].

Patrik Jansson and Johan Jeuring used arrows to develop polytypic data conversion algorithms [11]. Their development is by equational reasoning, and the advantage of arrows in this setting is just the point-free notation — Jansson and Jeuring could have worked with monads instead, but their proofs would have been much clumsier.

Joe English uses arrows in his library for parsing and manipulating XML [7]. Inspired by Wallace and Runciman's HaxML [27], XML is manipulated by composing *filters*, which are almost, but not quite, functions from an a to a list of bs. Filters are defined as an arrow type, and the advantage of using arrows rather than a monad in this case is that the composition operator can be very slightly stricter, which improves memory use when the filters are run.

Courney and Elliott developed an arrow-based GUI library called Fruit [5], based on functional reactive programming. Fruit considers a GUI to be a mapping between the entire history of the user's input (mouse motion, button presses, etc), and the history of the appearance of the screen — from a user input signal to a screen output signal. The GUIs are implemented as arrows, which leads to a very attractive programming style.

Indeed, arrows have been adopted comprehensively in recent work on functional reactive programming, now using a system called Yampa [8]. Yampa programs define arrows from input signals to output signals, where a signal, just as in these notes, is a function from time to a value. Functional reactive programming is older than arrows, of course, and in its original version programmers wrote real functions from input signals to output signals. The disadvantage of doing so is that signals become real Haskell values, and are passed around in FRP programs. Since a signal represents the entire history of a value, and in principle a program might ask for the signal's value at any time, it is difficult for the garbage collector to recover any memory. In the arrowized version, in contrast, signals are not first-class values, and the arrow combinators can be implemented to make garbage collection possible. As a result, Yampa has much better memory behaviour than the original versions of FRP.

Finally, arrows have been used recently by the Clean group to develop graphical editor components [19]. Here a GUI is seen as a kind of editor for an underlying data structure — but the data structure is subject to constraints. Whenever the user interacts with the interface, thus editing the underlying data, the editor reacts by modifying other parts, and possibly performing actions on the real world, to reestablish the constraints. Editors are constructed as arrows from the underlying datatype to itself: invoking the arrow maps the data modified by the user to data in which the constraints are reestablished. This work will be presented at this very summer school.

If these applications have something in common, it is perhaps that arrows are used to combine an attractive programming style with optimisations that would be hard or impossible to implement under a monadic interface. Arrows have certainly proved to be very useful, in applications I never suspected. I hope that these notes will help you, the reader, to use them too.

# References

1. Nick Benton and Martin Hyland. Traced premonoidal categories. *ITA*, 37(4):273–299, 2003.
2. R. S. Bird. A calculus of functions for program derivation. In D. Turner, editor, *Research Topics in Functional Programming*. Addison-Wesley, 1990.
3. M. Carlsson and T. Hallgren. FUDGETS - A graphical user interface in a lazy functional language. In *Proceedings of the ACM Conference on Functional Programming and Computer Architecture*, Copenhagen, 1993. ACM.
4. Koen Claessen and John Hughes. Quickcheck: A lightweight tool for random testing of Haskell programs. In *International Conference on Functional Programming (ICFP)*. ACM SIGPLAN, 2000.
5. Anthony Courtney and Conal Elliott. Genuinely functional user interfaces. In *Haskell Workshop*, pages 41–69, Firenze, Italy, 2001.
6. Antony Courtney, Henrik Nilsson, and Ross Paterson. Arrows: A general interface to computation. http://www.haskell.org/arrows/.
7. Joe English. Hxml. http://www.flightlab.com/~joe/hxml/.
8. Paul Hudak, Antony Courtney, Henrik Nilsson, and John Peterson. Arrows, robots, and functional reactive programming. In *Summer School on Advanced Functional Programming 2002, Oxford University*, volume 2638 of *Lecture Notes in Computer Science*, pages 159–187. Springer-Verlag, 2003.
9. J. Hughes. Restricted Datatypes in Haskell. In *Third Haskell Workshop*. Utrecht University technical report, 1999.
10. John Hughes. Generalising monads to arrows. *Science of Computer Programming*, 37(1–3):67–111, 2000.
11. Patrik Jansson and Johan Jeuring. Polytypic data conversion programs. *Science of Computer Programming*, 43(1):35–75, 2002.
12. John Launchbury, Jeffrey R. Lewis, and Byron Cook. On embedding a microarchitectural design language within Haskell. In *ICFP*, pages 60–69, Paris, 1999. ACM Press.
13. Sheng Liang, Paul Hudak, and Mark P. Jones. Monad transformers and modular interpreters. In *Symposium on Principles of Programming Languages*, San Francisco, January 1995. ACM SIGPLAN-SIGACT.
14. Eugenio Moggi. Computational lambda-calculus and monads. In *Proceedings 4th Annual IEEE Symp. on Logic in Computer Science, LICS'89, Pacific Grove, CA, USA, 5–8 June 1989*, pages 14–23. IEEE Computer Society Press, Washington, DC, 1989.
15. M. Sheeran P. Bjesse, K. Claessen and S. Singh. Lava: Hardware design in Haskell. In *ICFP*. ACM Press, 1998.

16. Ross Paterson.   Arrow transformer library. http://www.haskell.org/arrows/download.html.

17. Ross Paterson. A new notation for arrows. In *ICFP*, Firenze, Italy, 2001. ACM.

18. Ross Paterson. Arrows and computation. In Jeremy Gibbons and Oege De Moor, editors, *The Fun of Programming*. Palgrave, 2003.

19. Rinus Plasmijer Peter Achten, Marko van Eekelen. Arrows for generic graphical editor components. Technical Report NIII-R0416, Nijmegen Institute for Computing and Information Sciences, University of Nijmegen, 2004.

20. Simon Peyton-Jones, Geoffrey Washburn, and Stephanie Weirich.   Wobbly types: type inference for generalised algebraic data types. http://research.microsoft.com/Users/simonpj/papers/gadt/index.htm, July 2004.

21. Benjamin C. Pierce. *Basic Category Theory for Computer Scientists*. MIT Press, 1991.

22. John Power and Edmund Robinson. Premonoidal categories and notions of computation. *Mathematical Structures in Computer Science*, 7(5):453–468, 1997.

23. John Power and Hayo Thielecke. Closed Freyd- and κ-categories. In J. Wiedermann, P. van Emde Boas, and M. Nielsen, editors, *Proceedings 26th Int. Coll. on Automata, Languages and Programming, ICALP'99, Prague, Czech Rep., 11–15 July 1999*, volume 1644, pages 625–634. Springer-Verlag, Berlin, 1999.

24. D. S. Swierstra and L. Duponcheel. Deterministic, error-correcting combinator parsers. In John Launchbury, Erik Meijer, and Tim Sheard, editors, *Advanced Functional Programming*, volume 1129 of *Lecture Notes in Computer Science*, pages 184–207. Springer, 1996.

25. Peter Thiemann. WASH/CGI: Server-side web scripting with sessions and typed, compositional forms. In *Practical Aspects of Declarative Languages*, pages 192–208, 2002.

26. P. L. Wadler. Comprehending monads. In *Proceedings of the 1990 ACM Conference on LISP and Functional Programming, Nice*, pages 61–78, New York, NY, 1990. ACM.

27. Malcolm Wallace and Colin Runciman. Haskell and XML: Generic combinators or type-based translation? In *International Conference on Functional Programming*, pages 148–159. ACM Press, 1999.

# Appendix: The Module `Circuits.hs`

```haskell
module Circuits where

import Control.Arrow
import List

class ArrowLoop a => ArrowCircuit a where
  delay :: b -> a b b

nor :: Arrow a => a (Bool,Bool) Bool
nor = arr (not.uncurry (||))

flipflop :: ArrowCircuit a => a (Bool,Bool) (Bool,Bool)
flipflop = loop (arr (\((a,b),~(c,d)) -> ((a,d),(b,c))) >>>
                nor *** nor >>>
                delay (False,True) >>>
                arr id &&& arr id)

class Signal a where
  showSignal :: [a] -> String

instance Signal Bool where
  showSignal bs = concat top++"\n"++concat bot++"\n"
    where (top,bot) = unzip (zipWith sh (False:bs) bs)
          sh True True  = ("__","  ")
          sh True False = ("  ","|_")
          sh False True = (" _","| ")
          sh False False = ("  ","__")

instance (Signal a,Signal b) => Signal (a,b) where
  showSignal xys = showSignal (map fst xys) ++
                   showSignal (map snd xys)

instance Signal a => Signal [a] where
  showSignal = concat . map showSignal . transpose

sig = concat . map (uncurry replicate)

flipflopInput = sig
        [(5,(False,False)),(2,(False,True)),(5,(False,False)),
         (2,(True,False)),(5,(False,False)),(2,(True,True)),
         (6,(False,False))]
```

# Epigram: Practical Programming
# with Dependent Types

Conor McBride

School of Computer Science and Information Technology,
University of Nottingham, Jubilee Campus,
Wollaton Road, Nottingham NG8 1BB, United Kingdom
ctm@cs.nott.ac.uk

## 1   Motivation

Find the type error in the following Haskell expression:

```
if null xs then tail xs else xs
```

You can't, of course: this program is obviously nonsense unless you're a type-checker. The trouble is that only certain computations make sense if the `null xs` test is `True`, whilst others make sense if it is `False`. However, as far as the type system is concerned, the type of the `then` branch is the type of the `else` branch is the type of the entire conditional. Statically, the test is irrelevant. Which is odd, because if the test really were irrelevant, we wouldn't do it. Of course, `tail []` doesn't go wrong—well-typed programs don't go wrong—so we'd better pick a different word for the way they do go.

Abstraction and application, tupling and projection: these provide the 'software engineering' superstructure for programs, and our familiar type systems ensure that these operations are used compatibly. However, sooner or later, most programs inspect data and make a choice—at that point our familiar type systems fall silent. They simply can't talk about specific data. All this time, we thought our *programming* was strongly typed, when it was just our *software engineering*. In order to do better, we need a static language capable of expressing the significance of particular values in legitimizing some computations rather than others. We should not give up on programming.

James McKinna and I designed Epigram [27,26] to support a way of programming which builds more of the intended meaning of functions and data into their types. Its *style* draws heavily from the Alf system [13,21]; its *substance* from my to Randy Pollack's Lego system [20,23] Epigram is in its infancy and its implementation is somewhat primitive. We certainly haven't got everything right, nor have we yet implemented the whole design. We hope we've got *something* right. In these notes, I hope to demonstrate that such nonsense as we have seen above is not inevitable in real life, and that the extra articulacy which dependent types offer is both useful and *usable*. In doing so, I seek to stretch your imaginations towards what programming can be if we choose to make it so.

V. Varmo and T. Uustalu (Eds.): AFP 2004, LNCS 3622, pp. 130–170, 2005.

## 1.1  What Are Dependent Types?

Dependent type systems, invented by Per Martin-Löf [22] generalize the usual function types $S \rightarrow T$ to dependent function types $\forall x : S \Rightarrow T$, where $T$ may mention—hence *depend* on—$x$. We still write $S \rightarrow T$ when $T$ doesn't depend on $x$. For example, matrix multiplication may be typed[1]

$$\text{mult} : \forall i, j, k : \text{Nat} \Rightarrow \text{Matrix } i\, j \ \rightarrow \ \text{Matrix } j\, k \ \rightarrow \ \text{Matrix } i\, k$$

Datatypes like $\text{Matrix } i\, j$ may depend on values fixing some particular property of their elements—a natural number indicating size is but one example. A function can specialize its return type to suit each argument. The typing rules for abstraction and application show how:

$$\frac{x : S \vdash t : T}{\lambda x \Rightarrow t : \forall x : S \Rightarrow T} \qquad \frac{f : \forall x : S \Rightarrow T \quad s : S}{f\, s : [s/x]T}$$

Correspondingly, $\text{mult}\, 2\, 3\, 1 : \text{Matrix}\, 2\, 3 \ \rightarrow \ \text{Matrix}\, 3\, 1 \ \rightarrow \ \text{Matrix}\, 2\, 1$ is the specialized multiplier for matrices of the given sizes.

We're used to universal quantification expressing *polymorphism*, but the quantification is usually over types. Now we can quantify over all values, and these include the types, which are values in $\star$. Our $\forall$ captures many forms of abstraction uniformly. We can also see $\forall x : S \Rightarrow T$ as a logical formula and its inhabitants as a function which computes a *proof* of $[s/x]T$ given a particular value $s$ in $S$. It's this correspondence between programs and proofs, the *Curry-Howard Isomorphism*, with the slogan 'Propositions-as-Types', which makes dependent type systems particularly suitable for representing computational logics.

However, if you want to check dependent types, be careful! Look again at the application rule; watch $s$ hopping over the copula,[2] from the term side in the argument hypothesis (eg., our specific dimensions) to the type side in the conclusion (eg., our specific matrix types). With expressions in types, we must think again about when types are equal. Good old syntactic equality won't do: $\text{mult}\, (1{+}1)$ should have the same type as $\text{mult}\, 2$, so $\text{Matrix}\, (1{+}1)\, 1$ should *be* the same type as $\text{Matrix}\, 2\, 1$! If we want computation to preserve types, we need at least to identify types with the same *normal forms*. Typechecking requires the *evaluation* of previously typechecked expressions—the phase distinction is still there, but it's slipperier.

What I like about dependent types is their precise language of data structures. In Haskell, we could define a sequence of types for lists of fixed lengths

```
data List0 x = Nil
data List1 x = Cons0 x (List0 x)
data List2 x = Cons1 x (List1 x)
```

---

[1] We may write $\forall x : X; y : Y \Rightarrow T$ for $\forall x : X \Rightarrow \forall y : Y \Rightarrow T$ and $\forall x_1, x_2 : X \Rightarrow T$ for $\forall x_1 : X; x_2 : X \Rightarrow T$. We may drop the type annotation where inferrable.

[2] By *copula*, I mean the ':' which in these notes is used to link a term to its typing: Haskell uses '::', and the bold use the set-theoretic '$\in$'.

but we'd have to stop sooner or later, and we'd have difficulty abstracting over either the whole collection, or specific subcollections like lists of even length. In Epigram, we can express the lot in one go, giving us the family of *vector* types with indices from Nat representing length. Nat is just an ordinary datatype.

$$\underline{\text{data}} \left( \frac{}{\text{Nat} \; : \; \star} \right) \; \underline{\text{where}} \; \left( \frac{}{\text{zero} \; : \; \text{Nat}} \right) \; ; \; \left( \frac{n \; : \; \text{Nat}}{\text{suc } n \; : \; \text{Nat}} \right)$$

$$\underline{\text{data}} \left( \frac{n \; : \; \text{Nat} \; ; \quad X \; : \; \star}{\text{Vec } n \; X \; : \; \star} \right) \; \underline{\text{where}} \; \left( \frac{}{\text{vnil} \; : \; \text{Vec zero } X} \right)$$

$$\left( \frac{x \; : \; X \; ; \quad xs \; : \; \text{Vec } n \; X}{\text{vcons } x \; xs \; : \; \text{Vec (suc } n) \; X} \right)$$

Inductive families [15], like Vec, are collections of datatypes, defined mutually and systematically, indexed by other data. Now we can use the dependent function space to give the 'tail' function a type which prevents criminal behaviour:

$$\text{vtail} \; : \; \forall n : \text{Nat} \Rightarrow \forall X : \star \Rightarrow \text{Vec (suc } n) \; X \; \rightarrow \; \text{Vec } n \; X$$

For no $n$ is **vtail $n$ $X$ vnil** well typed. Indexed types state properties of their data which functions can rely on. They are the building blocks of Epigram programming. Our Matrix $i$ $j$ can just be defined as a vector of columns, say:

$$\underline{\text{let}} \; \left( \frac{rows, cols \; : \; \text{Nat}}{\text{Matrix } rows \; cols \; : \; \star} \right) \; \text{Matrix } rows \; cols \; \Rightarrow \; \text{Vec } cols \; (\text{Vec } rows \; \text{Nat})$$

Already in Haskell, there are hooks available to crooks who want more control over data. One can exploit *non-uniform* polymorphism to enforce some kinds of structural invariant [31], like this

```
data Rect col x = Columns [col] | Longer (Rect (col, x))
type Rectangular = Rect ()
```

although this type merely enforces rectangularity, rather than a specific size. One can also collect into a Vec type class those functors which generate vector structures [24]. Matrix multiplication then acquires a type like

```
mult :: (Vec f,Vec g,Vec h)=> f (g Int) -> g (h Int) -> f (h Int)
```

Programming with these 'fake' dependent types is an entertaining challenge, but let's be clear: these techniques are cleverly dreadful, rather than dreadfully clever. Hideously complex dependent types certainly exist, but they express basic properties like size in a straightforward way—why should the length of a list be anything less ordinary than a *number*? In Epigram, it doesn't matter whether the size of a matrix is statically determined or dynamically supplied—the size invariants are enforced, maintained and exploited, regardless of phase.

## 1.2   What Is Epigram?

Epigram is a dependently typed functional programming language. On the surface, the system is an integrated editor-typechecker-interpreter for the language, owing a debt to the Alf [13,21] and Agda [12] family of proof editors. Underneath, Epigram has a tactic-driven proof engine, like those of Coq [11] and Epigram's immediate ancestor, the 'Oleg' variant of Lego [20,23]. The latter has proof tactics which mimic Alf's pattern matching style of proof in a more spartan type theory (Luo's UTT [19]); James McKinna and I designed Epigram [27] as a 'high-level programming' interface to this technology. An Epigram program is really a tree of proof tactics which drive the underlying construction in UTT.

But this doesn't answer the wider cultural question of what Epigram is. How it does it relate to functional languages like SML [29] and Haskell [32]? How does it relate to previous dependently typed languages like DML [39] and Cayenne [4]? How does it relate pragmatically to more conventional ways of working in type theory in the systems mentioned above? What's new?

I'll return to these questions at the end of these notes, when I've established more of the basis for a technical comparison, but I can say this much now: DML refines the ML type system with numerical indexing, but the programs remain the same—erase the indices and you have an ML program; Cayenne programs are LazyML programs with a more generous type system, including programs at the type level, but severely restricted support for inductive families. Epigram is not an attempt to strap a more powerful type system to standard functional programming constructs—it's rather an attempt to rethink what programming can become, given such a type system.

Dependent types can make explicit reference to programs and data. They can talk about program*ming* in a way that simple types can't. In particular, an *induction principle* is a dependent type. We learned this one as children:

$$
\begin{aligned}
\text{NatInd} \;:\; &\forall P : \text{Nat} \to \star \;\Rightarrow\\
&P \,\text{zero} \;\to\; (\forall n : \text{Nat} \Rightarrow P\,n \to P\,(\text{suc } n)) \;\to\;\\
&\forall n : \text{Nat} \Rightarrow P\,n
\end{aligned}
$$

It gives rise to a proof technique—to give a proof of a more general proposition $P\,n$, give proofs that $P$ holds for more specific *patterns* which $n$ can take. Now cross out 'proof' and write 'program'. The induction principle for Nat specifies a particular strategy of case analysis and recursion, and Epigram can read it as such. Moreover, we can readily execute 'proofs' by induction, recursively applying the step program to the base value, to build a proof for any specific $n$:

$$
\begin{aligned}
\text{NatInd } P \; mz \; ms \;\text{zero} \;&\leadsto\; mz\\
\text{NatInd } P \; mz \; ms \;(\text{suc } n) \;&\leadsto\; ms\,n\,(\text{NatInd } P \; mz \; ms \; n)
\end{aligned}
$$

Usually, functional languages have hard-wired constructs for constructor case analysis and general recursion; Epigram supports programming with *any* matching and recursion which you can specify as an induction principle and implement as a function. Epigram also supports a first-order method of implementing new induction principles—they too arise from inductive families.

It may surprise (if not comfort) functional programmers to learn that dependently typed programming seems odd to type theorists too. Type theory is usually seen either as the integration of 'ordinary' programming with a logical *superstructure*, or as a constructive logic which permits programs to be quietly extracted from proofs. Neither of these approaches really exploits dependent types in the programs and data themselves. At time of writing, neither Agda nor Coq offers substantial support for the kind of data structures and programs we shall develop in these notes, even though Alf and 'Oleg' did!

There is a tendency to see programming as a fixed notion, essentially untyped. In this view, we make sense of and organise programs by assigning types to them, the way a biologist classifies species, and in order to classify more the exotic creatures, like `printf` or the `zipWith` family, one requires more exotic types. This conception fails to engage with the full potential of types to make a positive contribution to program construction. Given what types can now express, let us open our minds afresh to the design of programming language *constructs*, and of programming *tools* and of the *programs* we choose to write anyway.

### 1.3    Overview of the Remaining Sections

1. **Warm Up;Add Up** tries to give an impression of Epigram's interactive style programming and the style of the programs via very simple examples—addition and the Fibonacci function. I expose the rôle of dependent types behind the scenes, even in simply typed programming.

2. **Vectors and Finite Sets** introduces some very basic datatype families and operations—I explore Vec and also the family Fin of finite enumeration types, which can be used to index vectors. I show how case analysis for dependent types can be more powerful and more subtle than its simply typed counterpart.

3. **Representing Syntax** illustrates the use of dependent types to enforce key invariants in expression syntax—in particular, the λ-calculus. I begin with untyped de Bruijn terms after the manner of Bird and Paterson [9] and end with simply typed de Bruijn terms in the manner of Altenkirch and Reus [2].[3] On the way, I'll examine some pragmatic issues in data structure design.

4. **Is Looking Seeing?** homes in on the crux of dependently typed programming—*evidence*. Programs over indexed datatypes may *enforce* invariants, but how do we *establish* them? This section explores our approach to data analysis [27], expressing inspection as a form of induction and deriving induction principles for old types by defining new families.

5. **Well Typed Programs which Don't Go Wrong** shows the development of two larger examples—a typechecker for simply typed λ-calculus which yields a typed version *of its input* or an informative diagnostic, and a tagless and total evaluator for the well typed terms so computed.

6. **Epilogue** reflects on the state of Epigram and its future in relation to what's happening more widely in type theory and functional programming.

---

[3] As I'm fond of pointing out, these papers were published almost simultaneously and have only one reference in common. I find that shocking!

I've dropped from these notes a more formal introduction to type theory: which introductory functional programming text explains how the typechecker works within the first forty pages? A precise understanding of type theory isn't necessary to engage with the ideas, get hold of the basics and start programming. I'll deal with technicalities as and when we encounter them. If you do feel the need to delve deeper into the background, there's plenty of useful literature out there—the next subsection gives a small selection.

## 1.4   Some Useful Reading

Scholars of functional programming and of type theory should rejoice that they now share much of the same ground. It would be terribly unfortunate for the two communities each to fail to appreciate the potential contribution of the other, through cultural ignorance. We must all complain less and read more!

For a formal presentation of the Epigram language, see '*The view from the left*' [27] For a deeper exploration of its underlying type theory—see '*Computation and Reasoning: A Type Theory for Computer Science*' [19] by Zhaohui Luo. User documentation, examples and solutions to exercises are available online [26].

Much of the impetus for Epigram comes from proof assistants. Proof and programming are similar activities, but the tools have a different feel. I can recommend '*Coq'Art*' [7] by Yves Bertot and Pierre Castéran as an excellent tutorial for this way of working, and for the Coq system in particular. The tactics of a theorem prover animate the rules of its underlying type theory, so this book also serves as a good practical introduction to the more formal aspects.

The seminal textbook on type theory as a programming language is '*Programming in Martin-Löf's type theory: an introduction*' [35] by Bengt Nordström, Kent Petersson and Jan Smith. It is now fifteen years old and readily available electronically, so there's no excuse to consider type theory a closed book.

Type theorists should get reading too! Modern functional programming uses richer type systems to express more of the structure of data and capture more patterns of computation. I learned a great deal from '*Algebra of Programming*' by Richard Bird and Oege de Moor [8]. It's a splendid and eye-opening introduction to a more categorical and calculational style of correct program construction. '*Purely Functional Data Structures*' by Chris Okasaki [30] is a delightful compendium of data structures and algorithms, clearly showing the advantages of fitting datatypes more closely to algorithms.

The literature on overloading, generic programming, monads, arrows, higher-order polymorphism is too rich to enumerate, but it raises important issues which type theorists must address if we want to make a useful contribution to functional programming in practice. I'd advise hungry readers to start with this very series of Advanced Functional Programming lecture notes.

## 1.5   For Those of You Watching in Black & White

Before we start in earnest, let's establish typographical conventions and relate the system's display with these notes. Epigram's syntax is two-dimensional: the buffer contains a *document* with a rectangular region selected—highlighted with a bright background. A *document* is a vertical sequence of lines; a *line* is a horizontal sequence of boxes; a *box* is either a character, or a bracket containing a document. A *bracket* is either a

*group,*  ( ! ⋯ ! ! ) , which has the usual functions of parenthesis, or a

*shed,*  [ ! ⋯ ! ! ] , where you can tinker with text as you please. An Epigram

line may thus occupy more than one ASCII line. If a bracket is opened on a physical line, it must either be closed on that line or *suspended* with a !, then *resumed* on the next physical line with another !. I hasten to add that the Epigram editor does all of this box-drawing for you. You can fit two Epigram lines onto one physical line by separating them with ;, and split one Epigram line into two physical lines by prefixing the second with %.

The Epigram document is a syntax tree in which leaves may be sheds—their contents are monochrome and belong to you. You can edit any shed without Epigram spying on you, but the rest of the document gets *elaborated*—managed, typechecked, translated to UTT, typeset, coloured in and generally abused by the system. In particular, Epigram colours recognized identifiers. There is only one namespace—this colour is just for show. If you can't see the colours in your copy of these notes, don't worry: I've adopted font and case conventions instead.

| Blue | sans serif, uppercase initial | type constructor |
|---|---|---|
| red | sans serif, lowercase initial | data constructor |
| green | serif, boldface | defined variable |
| *purple* | serif, italic | abstracted variable |
| black | serif, underlined | reserved word |

These conventions began in my handwritten slides—the colour choices are more or less an accident of the pens available, but they seem to have stuck. Epigram also has a convention for background colour, indicating the elaboration status of a block of source code.

**white**  (light green when selected) indicates successful elaboration

**yellow**  indicates that Epigram cannot yet see why a piece of code is good

**brown**  indicates that Epigram can see why a piece of code is bad

Yellow backgrounds come about when typing constraints cannot yet be solved, but it's still possible for the variables they involve to become more instantiated, allowing for a solution in the future.

There are some pieces of ASCII syntax which I cannot bring myself to uglify in LaTeX. I give here the translation table for tokens and for the extensible delimiters of two-dimensional syntax:

| ⋆ | ∀ | λ | → | ∧ | ⇒ | ⇐ | ( | ) | \| | \| | —— |
|---|---|---|---|---|---|---|---|---|---|---|---|
| * | all | lam | -> | /\ | => | <= | ( ! / ! ) | | [ ! / ! ] | | --- |

Moreover, to save space here, I adopt an end-of-line style with braces {}, where the system puts them at the beginning.

At the top level, the document is a vertical sequence of **declarations** delineated by *rules*. A *rule* is a sequence of at least three ---. The initial document has just one declaration, consisting of a shed, waiting for you to start work.

## 2   Warm Up; Add Up

Let's examine the new technology in the context of a simple and familiar problem: adding natural numbers. We have seen this Epigram definition:[4]

$$\underline{\text{data}} \ \left( \frac{\phantom{xxxx}}{\text{Nat} \ : \ \star} \right) \ \underline{\text{where}} \ \left( \frac{\phantom{xxx}}{\text{zero} \ : \ \text{Nat}} \right) \ ; \ \left( \frac{n \ : \ \text{Nat}}{\text{suc} \ n \ : \ \text{Nat}} \right)$$

We can equally well define the natural numbers in Epigram as follows:

$$\underline{\text{data}} \ \text{Nat} : \star \ \underline{\text{where}} \ \text{zero} : \text{Nat} \ ; \ \text{suc} : \text{Nat} \to \text{Nat}$$

In Haskell, we would write 'data Nat = Zero | Suc Nat'.

The 'two-dimensional' version is a first-order presentation in the style of natural deduction rules[5] [34]. Above the line go hypotheses typing the arguments; below, the conclusion typing a template for a value. The declarations 'zero is a Nat; if $n$ is a Nat, then so is suc $n$' tell us what Nats look like. We get the actual types of zero and suc implicitly, by discharging the hypotheses.

We may similarly declare our function in the natural deduction style:

$$\underline{\text{let}} \ \left( \frac{x, y \ : \ \text{Nat}}{\text{plus} \ x \ y \ : \ \text{Nat}} \right)$$

This signals our intention to define a function called plus which takes two natural numbers and returns a natural number. The machine responds

$$\text{plus} \ x \ y \quad []$$

by way of asking 'So plus has two arguments, $x$ and $y$. What should it do with them?'. Our type signature has become a *programming problem* to be solved interactively. The machine supplies a **left-hand side**, consisting of a function

---

[4] Unary numbers are not an essential design feature; rest assured that primitive binary numbers will be provided eventually [10].

[5] Isn't this a big step backwards for brevity? Or does Haskell's brevity depend on some implicit presumptions about what datatypes can possibly be?

symbol applied to **patterns**, binding **pattern variables**—initially, the left-hand side looks just like the typical application of plus which we declared and the pattern variables have the corresponding names. But they are binding occurrences, not references to the hypotheses. The scope of a rule's hypotheses extends only to its conclusion; each problem and subproblem has its own scope.

Sheds [] are where we develop solutions. The basic editing operation in Epigram is to expose the contents of a shed to the elaborator. We can write the whole program in one shed, then elaborate it; or we can work a little at a time. If we select a shed, Epigram will tell us what's in scope (here, $x, y$ in Nat), and what we're supposed to be doing with it (here, explaining how to compute plus $x$ $y$ in Nat). We may proceed by filling in a **right-hand side**, explaining how to reduce the current problem to zero or more subproblems.

I suggest that we seek to define plus by structural recursion on $x$, entering the right-hand side $\Leftarrow$ rec $x$. The '$\Leftarrow$' is pronounced 'by': it introduces right-hand sides which explain *by what means* to reduce the problem. Here we get

$$\text{plus } x\, y \;\Leftarrow\; \underline{\text{rec}}\; x \;\{$$
$$\text{plus } x\, y \;\;[]\;\}$$

Apparently, nothing has changed. There is no presumption that recursion on $x$ will be accompanied immediately (or ever) by case analysis on $x$. If you select the shed, you'll see that something has changed—the context of the problem has acquired an extra hypothesis, called a *memo-structure*. A precise explanation must wait, but the meaning of the problem is now 'construct plus $x$ $y$, given $x$, $y$ *and* the ability to call to plus on structural subterms of $x$'. So let us now analyse $x$, proceeding $\Leftarrow$ case $x$.

$$\text{plus } x\, y \;\Leftarrow\; \underline{\text{rec}}\; x \;\{$$
$$\text{plus } x\, y \;\Leftarrow\; \underline{\text{case}}\; x \;\{$$
$$\text{plus zero } y \;\;[]$$
$$\text{plus (suc } x)\, y \;\;[]\;\}\}$$

The two subproblems are precisely those corresponding to the two ways $x$ could have been made by constructors of Nat. We can certainly finish the first one off, entering $\Rightarrow y$. (The ' $\Rightarrow$ ' is 'return'.) We can make some progress on the second by deciding to return the successor of something, $\Rightarrow$ suc [] .

$$\text{plus } x\, y \;\Leftarrow\; \underline{\text{rec}}\; x \;\{$$
$$\text{plus } x\, y \;\Leftarrow\; \underline{\text{case}}\; x \;\{$$
$$\text{plus zero } y \;\Rightarrow\; y$$
$$\text{plus (suc } x)\, y \;\Rightarrow\; \text{suc } []\;\}\}$$

Select the remaining shed and you'll see that we have to fill in an element of Nat, given $x$, $y$ and a subtly different memo-structure. Case analysis has instantiated the original argument, so we now have the 'ability to make recursive calls to plus on structural subterms of (suc $x$)' which amounts to the more concrete and more useful 'ability to make recursive calls to plus on structural subterms of $x$, and on $x$ itself'. Good! We can finish off as follows:

$$\text{plus } x\, y \;\Leftarrow\; \underline{\text{rec }} x\; \{$$
$$\quad\text{plus } x\, y \;\Leftarrow\; \underline{\text{case }} x\; \{$$
$$\quad\quad\text{plus zero } y \;\Rightarrow\; y$$
$$\quad\quad\text{plus (suc } x)\, y \;\Rightarrow\; \text{suc (plus } x\, y)\; \}\}$$

## 2.1  Who Did the Work?

Two pages to add unary numbers? And that's a simple example? If it's that much like hard work, do we really want to know? Well, let's look at how much was work and how much was culture shock. We wrote the bits in the boxes:

$$\underline{\text{let}} \; \left( \frac{x, y \,:\, \mathsf{Nat}}{\text{plus } x\, y \,:\, \mathsf{Nat}} \right) \; ; \; \text{plus } x\, y \;\boxed{\Leftarrow\; \underline{\text{rec }} x}\; \{$$
$$\qquad\qquad \text{plus } x\, y \;\boxed{\Leftarrow\; \underline{\text{case }} x}\; \{$$
$$\qquad\qquad\quad \text{plus zero } y \;\boxed{\Rightarrow\; y}$$
$$\qquad\qquad\quad \text{plus (suc } x)\, y \;\boxed{\Rightarrow\; \text{suc (plus } x\, y)}\; \}\}$$

We wrote the type signature: we might have done that for virtue's sake, but virtue doesn't pay the rent. Here, we were repaid—we exchanged the usual hand-written left-hand sides for machine-generated patterns resulting from the conceptual step (usually present, seldom written) $\Leftarrow$ case $x$. This was only possible because the machine already knew the type of $x$. We also wrote the $\Leftarrow \underline{\text{rec}}\, x$, a real departure from conventional practice, but we got repaid for that too—we (humans and machines) know that plus is *total*.

Perhaps it's odd that the program's text is not entirely the programmer's work. It's the record of a partnership where we say what the plan is and the machine helps us carry it out. Contrast this with the 'type inference' model of programming, where we write down the details of the execution and the machine tries to guess the plan. In its pure form, this necessitates the restriction of plans to those which are blatant enough to be guessed. As we move beyond the Hindley-Milner system, we find ourselves writing down type information anyway.

'Type inference' thus has two aspects: 'top-level inference'—inferring type schemes, as with Hindley-Milner 'let'—and 'program inference given types'—inferring details when a scheme is instantiated, as with Hindley-Milner variables. Epigram rejects the former, but takes the latter further than ever. As types represent a higher-level design statement than programs, we should prefer to write types if they make programs cheaper.

Despite its interactive mode of construction, Epigram is fully compliant with the convention that a file of source code, however manufactured, contains all that's required for its recognition as a program. The bare text, without colour or other markup, is what gets elaborated. The elaboration process for a large code fragment just reconstructs a suitable interactive development offstage, cued by the program text—this is how we reload programs. You are free to negotiate your own compromise between incremental and batch-mode programming.

## 2.2    Where Are the Dependent Types?

The type of plus is unremarkably simple, but if you were watching closely, you'll have noticed that the *machine* was using dependent types the whole time. Let's take a closer look. Firstly, a thought experiment—define a primitive recursion operator for Nat in Haskell as follows:

```
primRec{-p-} :: Nat -> p -> (Nat -> p -> p) -> p
primRec{-p-} Zero    mz ms = mz
primRec{-p-} (Suc n) mz ms = ms n (primRec{-p-} n mz ms)
```

I've made primRec's type parameter explicit in a comment so we can follow what happens as we put it to work. How might we write plus? Try applying primRec to the first argument, then checking what's left to do:

```
plus :: Nat -> Nat -> Nat
plus = \ x -> primRec{-Nat -> Nat-} x mz ms where
  mz :: Nat -> Nat                         -- fill this in
  ms :: Nat -> (Nat -> Nat) -> Nat -> Nat  -- fill this in
```

Now we must fill in the *methods* mz and ms, but do their types show what rôle they play? There are seven occurrences[6] of Nat in their types—which is which? Perhaps *you* can tell, because you understand primRec, but how would a machine guess? And if we were defining a more complex function this way, we might easily get lost—try defining equality for lists using foldr.

However, recall our NatInd principle with operational behaviour just like primRec but a type which makes clear the relationship between the methods and the patterns for which they apply. If we're careful, we can use that extra information to light our way. Where primRec takes a constant type parameter, NatInd takes a *function* $P$ : Nat $\to \star$. If we take $P\,x \rightsquigarrow$ Nat $\to$ Nat, we get the primRec situation. How might we use $P$'s argument to our advantage? Internally, Epigram doesn't build plus : Nat $\to$ Nat $\to$ Nat but rather a *proof*

$$\lozenge \text{plus} : \forall x, y \!:\! \text{Nat} \Rightarrow \langle \text{plus}\,x\,y : \text{Nat} \rangle$$

We can interpret $\langle \text{plus}\,x\,y : \text{Nat} \rangle$ as the property of $x$ and $y$ that 'plus $x\,y$ is a *computable* element of Nat'. This type is equipped with a constructor which packs up values and a function which runs computations

$$\frac{n \,:\, \text{Nat}}{\text{return} \langle \text{plus}\,x\,y \rangle\, n \,:\, \langle \text{plus}\,x\,y : \text{Nat} \rangle} \qquad \frac{c \,:\, \langle \text{plus}\,x\,y : \text{Nat} \rangle}{\text{call} \langle \text{plus}\,x\,y \rangle\, c \,:\, \text{Nat}}$$

---

[6] If I had chosen a first-order recursion, there would have been as few as four, but that would presume to fix the second argument through the course of the recursion.

such that
$$\text{call}\langle\,\text{plus}\ x\ y\,\rangle\ (\text{return}\langle\,\text{plus}\ x\ y\,\rangle\ n)\ \leadsto\ n$$

Given $\Diamond$plus, we may readily extract plus—apply and run!

$$\text{plus}\leadsto\lambda x,y\Rightarrow\text{call}\langle\,\text{plus}\ x\ y\,\rangle\ (\Diamond\text{plus}\ x\ y)\ :\ \mathsf{Nat}\to\mathsf{Nat}\to\mathsf{Nat}$$

Now, let's build $\Diamond$plus as a proof by **NatInd**:

$$\Diamond\text{plus}\leadsto\textbf{NatInd}\ (\lambda x\Rightarrow\forall y\!:\!\mathsf{Nat}\Rightarrow\langle\,\text{plus}\ x\ y\ :\ \mathsf{Nat}\,\rangle)\ \text{mz}\ \text{ms}$$
$$\text{where}\ \ \text{mz}\ :\ \forall y\!:\!\mathsf{Nat}\Rightarrow\langle\,\text{plus}\ \text{zero}\ y\ :\ \mathsf{Nat}\,\rangle$$
$$\text{ms}\ :\ \forall x\!\cdot\!\mathsf{Nat}\to(\forall y\!:\!\mathsf{Nat}\to\langle\,\text{plus}\ x\ y\ :\ \mathsf{Nat}\,\rangle)$$
$$\to\ \forall y\!:\!\mathsf{Nat}\Rightarrow\langle\,\text{plus}\ (\text{suc}\ x)\ y\ :\ \mathsf{Nat}\,\rangle$$

It's not hard to see how to generate the left-hand sides of the subproblems for each case—just read them off from their types! Likewise, it's not hard to see how to translate the right-hand sides we supplied into the proofs—pack them up with return$\langle\,\cdots\,\rangle$ translate recursive calls via call$\langle\,\cdots\,\rangle$:

$$\text{mz}\leadsto\lambda y\Rightarrow\text{return}\langle\,\text{plus}\ \text{zero}\ y\,\rangle\ \ y$$
$$\text{ms}\leadsto\lambda x\Rightarrow\lambda xhyp\Rightarrow\lambda y\Rightarrow$$
$$\text{return}\langle\,\text{plus}\ (\text{suc}\ x)\ y\,\rangle\ \ (\text{suc}\ (\text{call}\langle\,\text{plus}\ x\ y\,\rangle\ (xhyp\ y)))$$

From this proof, you can read off both the high-level program and the its low-level operational behaviour in terms of primitive recursion. And that's basically how Epigram works! Dependent types aren't just the basis of the Epigram *language*— the *system* uses them to organise even simply typed programming.

## 2.3    What Are <u>Case</u> and <u>Rec</u>?

In the plus we actually wrote, we didn't use induction—we used <u>case</u> $x$ and <u>rec</u> $x$. These separate induction into its aspects of distinguishing constructors and of justifying recursive calls. The keywords <u>case</u> and <u>rec</u> cannot stand alone, but <u>case</u> $e$ and <u>rec</u> $e$ are meaningful whenever $e$ belongs to a datatype—Epigram constructs their meaning from the structure of that datatype.

In our example, $x\ :\ \mathsf{Nat}$, and Epigram give us

$$\underline{\text{case}}\ x\ :\ \forall P\ :\ \mathsf{Nat}\to\star\ \Rightarrow$$
$$(P\ \text{zero})\ \to\ (\forall x'\!:\!\mathsf{Nat}\Rightarrow P\ (\text{suc}\ x'))\ \to\ P\ x$$

This is an induction principle instantiated at $x$ with its inductive hypotheses chopped off: it just says, 'to do $P$ with $x$, show how to do $P$ with each of these patterns'. The associated computational behaviour puts proof into practice:

$$(\underline{\text{case}}\ \text{zero})\ \ \ P\ mz\ ms\leadsto mz$$
$$(\underline{\text{case}}\ (\text{suc}\ x))\ P\ mz\ ms\leadsto ms\ x$$

There is nothing special about <u>case</u> $x$. When elaborating $\Leftarrow e$, it's the *type* of $e$ which specifies how to split a problem into subproblems. If, as above, we take

$$P\leadsto\lambda x\Rightarrow\forall y\!:\!\mathsf{Nat}\Rightarrow\langle\,\text{plus}\ x\ y\ :\ \mathsf{Nat}\,\rangle$$

then the types of $mz$ and $ms$ give us the split we saw when we wrote the program. What about <u>rec</u> $x$?

$$\underline{\text{rec}}\ x\ :\ \forall P : \mathsf{Nat} \to \star \Rightarrow$$
$$(\forall x : \mathsf{Nat} \Rightarrow (\underline{\text{memo}}\ x)\ P \to P\ x) \to$$
$$P\ x$$

This says 'if you want to do $P\ x$, show how to do it given access to $P$ for everything structurally smaller than $x$'. This $(\underline{\text{memo}}\ x)$ is another gadget generated by Epigram from the structure of $x$'s type—it uses the power of computation in types to capture the notion of 'structurally smaller':

$$(\underline{\text{memo}}\ \mathsf{zero})\qquad P \rightsquigarrow \mathsf{One}$$
$$(\underline{\text{memo}}\ (\mathsf{suc}\ n))\ P \rightsquigarrow (\underline{\text{memo}}\ n)\ P\ \wedge\ P\ n$$

That is $(\underline{\text{memo}}\ x)P$ is the type of a big tuple which memoizes $P$ for everything smaller than $x$. If we analyse $x$, the memo-structure computes,[7] giving us the trivial tuple for the zero case, but for $(\mathsf{suc}\ n)$, we gain access to $P\ n$. Let's watch the memo-structure unfolding in the inevitable Fibonacci example.

$$\underline{\text{let}}\quad \left(\frac{n\ :\ \mathsf{Nat}}{\mathsf{fib}\ n\ :\ \mathsf{Nat}}\right)\ ;\ \begin{array}{l}\mathsf{fib}\ n\ \Leftarrow\ \underline{\text{rec}}\ n\ \{\\ \quad\mathsf{fib}\ n\ \Leftarrow\ \underline{\text{case}}\ n\ \{\\ \quad\quad\mathsf{fib}\ \mathsf{zero}\ \Rightarrow\ \mathsf{zero}\\ \quad\quad\mathsf{fib}\ (\mathsf{suc}\ n)\ \Leftarrow\ \underline{\text{case}}\ n\ \{\\ \quad\quad\quad\mathsf{fib}\ (\mathsf{suc}\ \mathsf{zero})\ \Rightarrow\ \mathsf{suc}\ \mathsf{zero}\\ \quad\quad\quad\mathsf{fib}\ (\mathsf{suc}\ (\mathsf{suc}\ n))\ \Rightarrow\ [\,]\ \}\}\}\end{array}$$

If you select the remaining shed, you will see that the memo structure in the context has unfolded (modulo trivial algebra) to:

$$(\underline{\text{memo}}\ n)\ (\lambda x \Rightarrow \langle \mathsf{fib}\ x : \mathsf{Nat}\rangle)\ \wedge\ \langle \mathsf{fib}\ n : \mathsf{Nat}\rangle\ \wedge\ \langle \mathsf{fib}\ (\mathsf{suc}\ n) : \mathsf{Nat}\rangle$$

which is just as well, as we want to fill in $\mathsf{plus}\ (\mathsf{fib}\ n)\ (\mathsf{fib}\ (\mathsf{suc}\ n))$.

At this stage, the approach is more important than the details. The point is that programming with $\Leftarrow$ imposes *no fixed notion* of case analysis or recursion. Epigram does not have 'pattern matching'. Instead, $\Leftarrow$ admits whatever notion of problem decomposition is specified by the type of the expression (the *eliminator*) which follows it. The value of the eliminator gives the operational semantics to the program built from the solutions to the subproblems.

Of course, Epigram equips every datatype with <u>case</u> and <u>rec</u>, giving us the usual notions of *constructor* case analysis *structural* recursion. But we are free to make our own eliminators, capturing more sophisticated analyses or more powerful forms of recursion. By talking about *patterns*, dependent types give us the opportunity to specify and implement new ways of programming.

---

[7] Following a suggestion by Thierry Coquand, Eduardo Giménez shows how to separate induction into <u>case</u> and <u>rec</u> in [17]. He presents memo-structures inductively, to justify the *syntactic* check employed by Coq's `Fix` construct. The computational version is mine [23]; its unfolding memo-structures give you a *menu* of recursive calls.

## 2.4    Pause for Thought

Concretely, we have examined one datatype and two programs. Slightly more abstractly, we have seen the general shape of Epigram programs as **decision trees**. Each node has a left-hand side, stating a programming problem $p$, and a right-hand-side stating how to attack it. The leaves of the tree $p \Rightarrow t$ explain directly what value to return. The internal nodes $p \Leftarrow e$ use the type of the eliminator $e$ as a recipe for reducing the problem statement to subproblem statements, and the value of $e$ as a recipe for solving the whole problem, given the solutions to the subproblems. Every datatype is equipped with eliminators of form case $x$ for constructor case analysis and rec $x$ for structural recursion, allowing us to construct obviously total programs in a pattern matching style.

However, the $\Leftarrow$ construct is a more general tool than the `case` construct of conventional languages. We answer Wadler's question of how to combine data abstraction with notions of pattern matching [38] by making notions of pattern matching first-class values.

It's reasonable to ask 'Can't I write ordinary programs in an ordinary way? Must I build decision trees?'. I'm afraid the answer, for now, is 'yes', but it's just a matter of syntactic sugar. We're used to prioritized lists of patterns with a 'take the first match' semantics [28]. Lennart Augustsson showed us how to compile these into trees of `case`-on-variables [3]. Programming in Epigram is like being Augustsson's compiler—you choose the tree, and it shows you the patterns. The generalization lies in what may sit at the nodes. One could flatten those regions of the tree with nonempty $\Leftarrow$ case $x$ nodes and use Augustsson's algorithm to recover a decision tree, leaving $\Leftarrow$ explicit only at 'peculiar' nodes.

Of course, this still leaves us with explicit $\Leftarrow$ rec $x$ supporting structural recursion. Can we get rid of that? There are various methods of spotting safe recursive calls [17]; some even extend to tracking guardedness through mutual definitions [1]. We could use these to infer obvious appeals to rec, leaving only sophisticated recursions explicit. Again, it's a question of work. Personally, I want to write functions which are seen to be total.

Some might complain 'What's the point of a programming language that isn't Turing complete?', but I ask in return, 'Do you demand *compulsory ignorance* of totality?'. Let's guarantee totality explicitly whenever we can [37]. It's also possible, contrary to popular nonsense, to have dependent types and general recursive programs, preserving decidable typechecking: the cheapest way to do this is to work under an *assumed* eliminator with type

$$\forall P : \star \Rightarrow (P \to P) \ \to \ P$$

to which only the run time system gives a computational behaviour; a less drastic way is to treat general recursion as an impure monadic effect.

But in any case, you might be surprised how little you need general recursion. Dependent types make more programs structurally recursive, because dependent types have more structure. Inductive families with inductive indices support recursion on the data itself and recursion on the indices. For example, first-order unification [36] becomes structurally recursive when you index terms by the number of variables over which they are constructed—solving a variable may blow up the terms, but it decreases this index [25].

## 2.5   Some Familiar Datatypes

Just in time for the first set of exercises, let's declare some standard equipment. We shall need Bool, which can be declared like so:

$$\underline{\text{data}} \quad \text{Bool} : \star \quad \underline{\text{where}} \quad \text{true}, \text{false} : \text{Bool}$$

The standard Maybe type constructor is also useful:

$$\underline{\text{data}} \left( \frac{X : \star}{\text{Maybe } X : \star} \right) \quad \underline{\text{where}} \left( \frac{}{\text{nothing} : \text{Maybe } X} \right) ; \left( \frac{x : X}{\text{just } x : \text{Maybe } X} \right)$$

Note that I didn't declare $X$ in the rules for nothing and just. The hypotheses of a rule scope only over its conclusion, so it's not coming from the Maybe rule. Rather, in each rule Epigram can tell from the way $X$ is used that it must be a type, and it silently generalizes the constructors, just the way the Hindley-Milner system generalizes definitions.

It's the natural deduction notation which triggers this generalization. We were able to define Bool without it because there was nothing to generalize. Without the rule to 'catch' the $X$, plain

$$\text{nothing} \ : \ \text{Maybe} \ X$$

wouldn't exactly be an error. The out-of-scope $X$ is waiting to be explained by some *prior* definition: the nothing constructor would then be specific to that $X$.

Rule-induced generalization is also happening here, for polymorphic lists:

$$\underline{\text{data}} \left( \frac{X : \star}{\text{List } X : \star} \right) \quad \underline{\text{where}} \left( \frac{}{\text{nil} : \text{List } X} \right) ; \left( \frac{x : X ; \quad xs : \text{List } X}{\text{cons } x \ xs : \text{List } X} \right)$$

We also need the binary trees with $N$-labelled nodes and $L$-labelled leaves.

$$\underline{\text{data}} \left( \frac{N, L : \star}{\text{Tree } N \ L : \star} \right) \quad \underline{\text{where}} \left( \frac{l : L}{\text{leaf } l : \text{Tree } N \ L} \right) ; \left( \frac{n : N ; \quad s, t : \text{Tree } N \ L}{\text{node } n \ s \ t : \text{Tree } N \ L} \right)$$

## 2.6   Exercises: Structural Merge-Sort

To get used to the system, and to programming with structural recursion, try these exercises, which only involve the simple types above

**Exercise 1 (le).** *Define the 'less-or-equal' test:*

$$\underline{\text{let}} \quad \left( \frac{x, y \ : \ \text{Nat}}{\text{le } x \ y \ : \ \text{Bool}} \right)$$

*Does it matter which argument you do* <u>rec</u> *on?*

**Exercise 2** (cond). *Define the conditional expression:*

$$\text{let} \quad \left( \frac{b \; : \; \mathsf{Bool} \; ; \quad then, else \; : \; T}{\mathrm{cond} \; b \; then \; else \; : \; T} \right)$$

**Exercise 3** (merge). *Use the above to define the function which* merges *two lists, presumed already sorted into increasing order, into one sorted list containing the elements from both.*

$$\text{let} \quad \left( \frac{xs, ys \; : \; \mathsf{List \; Nat}}{\mathrm{merge} \; xs \; ys \; : \; \mathsf{List \; Nat}} \right)$$

*Is this function structurally recursive on just one of its arguments? Nested* recs *combine lexicographically.*

**Exercise 4** (flatten). *Use* merge *to implement a function* flatten*ing a tree which may have numbers at the leaves, to produce a sorted list of those numbers. Ignore the node labels.*

$$\text{let} \quad \left( \frac{t \; : \; \mathsf{Tree} \; N \; (\mathsf{Maybe \; Nat})}{\mathrm{flatten} \; t \; : \; \mathsf{List \; Nat}} \right)$$

We can have a structurally recursive $O(n \log n)$ sorting algorithm if we can share out the elements of a list into a *balanced* tree, then flatten it.

**Exercise 5** (insert). *Implement the* insert*ion of a number into a tree:*

$$\text{let} \quad \left( \frac{n \; : \; \mathsf{Nat} \; ; \quad t \; : \; \mathsf{Tree \; Bool} \; (\mathsf{Maybe \; Nat})}{\mathrm{insert} \; n \; t \; : \; \mathsf{Tree \; Bool} \; (\mathsf{Maybe \; Nat})} \right)$$

*Maintain this balancing invariant throughout: in* (node true $s$ $t$)*, $s$ and $t$ contain equally many numbers, whilst in* (node false $s$ $t$)*, $s$ contains exactly one more number than $t$.*

**Exercise 6** (share, sort). *Implement*

$$\text{let} \quad \left( \frac{ns \; : \; \mathsf{List \; Nat}}{\mathrm{share} \; ns \; : \; \mathsf{Tree \; Bool} \; (\mathsf{Maybe \; Nat})} \right)$$

$$\text{let} \quad \left( \frac{ns \; : \; \mathsf{List \; Nat}}{\mathrm{sort} \; ns \; : \; \mathsf{List \; Nat}} \right)$$

*so that* sort *sorts its input in* $O(n \log n)$ *time.*

# 3   Vectors and Finite Sets

Moving on to dependent data structures now, let's take a closer look at Vec:

$$\underline{\text{data}} \ \left( \frac{n \ : \ \mathsf{Nat} \ ; \ \ X \ : \ \star}{\mathsf{Vec} \ n \ X \ : \ \star} \right) \ \underline{\text{where}} \ \left( \frac{}{\mathsf{vnil} \ : \ \mathsf{Vec} \ \mathsf{zero} \ X} \right)$$

$$\left( \frac{x \ : \ X \ ; \ \ xs \ : \ \mathsf{Vec} \ n \ X}{\mathsf{vcons} \ x \ xs \ : \ \mathsf{Vec} \ (\mathsf{suc} \ n) \ X} \right)$$

The generalization mechanism ensures that all the previously undeclared variables arising inside each deduction rule are silently quantified in the resulting type, with the *implicit* $\forall_{\_}$ quantifier. Written out in full, we have declared

$$\begin{aligned}
&\underline{\text{data}} \quad \mathsf{Vec} : \mathsf{Nat} \ \rightarrow \ \star \ \rightarrow \ \star \\
&\underline{\text{where}} \quad \mathsf{vnil} : \forall_{\_}X : \star \Rightarrow \mathsf{Vec} \ \mathsf{zero} \ X \\
&\qquad\quad \mathsf{vcons} : \forall_{\_}X : \star \Rightarrow \forall_{\_}n : \mathsf{Nat} \Rightarrow X \ \rightarrow \ \mathsf{Vec} \ n \ X \ \rightarrow \ \mathsf{Vec} \ (\mathsf{suc} \ n) \ X
\end{aligned}$$

On usage, Epigram tries to infer arguments for expressions with implicitly quantified types, just the way the Hindley-Milner system specializes polymorphic things—by solving the equational constraints which arise in typechecking. However, Epigram needs and supports a 'manual override': the postfix $_{\_}$ operator inhibits inference and makes an implicit function explicit, so

$$\begin{aligned}
\mathsf{vnil}_{\_} &: \forall X : \star \Rightarrow \mathsf{Vec} \ \mathsf{zero} \ X \\
\mathsf{vnil}_{\_}\mathsf{Nat} &: \mathsf{Vec} \ \mathsf{zero} \ \mathsf{Nat}
\end{aligned}$$

To save space, I often write overridden arguments as subscripts—eg., $\mathsf{vnil}_{\mathsf{Nat}}$.
Given this definition, let's start to write some simple programs:

$$\underline{\text{let}} \ \left( \frac{ys \ : \ \mathsf{Vec} \ (\mathsf{suc} \ m) \ Y}{\mathsf{vhead} \ ys \ : \ Y} \right) \ ; \ \ \mathsf{vhead} \ ys \ [\ \texttt{<= case ys}\ ]$$

What happens when we elaborate? Well, consider which constructors can possibly have made $ys$. Certainly not $\mathsf{vnil}$, unless $\mathsf{zero} = \mathsf{suc} \ n$. We just get a $\mathsf{vcons}$ case—the one case we want, for 'head' and 'tail':

$$\underline{\text{let}} \ \left( \frac{ys \ : \ \mathsf{Vec} \ (\mathsf{suc} \ m) \ Y}{\mathsf{vhead} \ ys \ : \ Y} \right) \ ; \ \begin{aligned} \mathsf{vhead} \ ys \ &\Leftarrow \ \underline{\text{case}} \ ys \ \{ \\ \mathsf{vhead} \ (\mathsf{vcons} \ y \ ys) \ &\Rightarrow \ y \ \} \end{aligned}$$

$$\underline{\text{let}} \ \left( \frac{ys \ : \ \mathsf{Vec} \ (\mathsf{suc} \ m) \ Y}{\mathsf{vtail} \ ys \ : \ \mathsf{Vec} \ m \ Y} \right) \ ; \ \begin{aligned} \mathsf{vtail} \ ys \ &\Leftarrow \ \underline{\text{case}} \ ys \ \{ \\ \mathsf{vtail} \ (\mathsf{vcons} \ y \ ys) \ &\Rightarrow \ ys \ \} \end{aligned}$$

In the latter, not only do we get that it's $\mathsf{vcons}$ as opposed to $\mathsf{vnil}$: it's the particular $\mathsf{vcons}$ which extends vectors of the length we need. What's going on?

Much as Thierry Coquand proposed in [13], Epigram is *unifying* the scrutinee of the <u>case</u> with the possible constructor patterns, in both term and type:

| | unifier |
|---|---|
| $ys$ : Vec (suc $m$) $Y$ | |
| vnil$_X$ : Vec   zero   $X$ | impossible |
| vcons$_X$ $n$ $x$ $xs'$ : Vec (suc $n$) $X$ | $X = Y, n = m, xs = $ vcons$_Y$ $m$ $x$ $xs'$ |

Only the vcons case survives—Epigram then tries to choose names for the pattern variables which maintain a 'family resemblance' to the scrutinee, hence the (vcons $y$ $ys$) in the patterns.

This unification doesn't just rule cases in or out: it can also feed information to type-level computations. Here's how to append vectors:

$$\underline{\text{let}} \left( \frac{xs \ : \ \mathsf{Vec} \ m \ X \ ; \ \ ys \ : \ \mathsf{Vec} \ n \ X}{\mathbf{vappend}_m \ xs \ ys : \mathsf{Vec} \ (\mathsf{plus} \ m \ n) \ X} \right)$$

$$\begin{aligned}
&\mathbf{vappend}_m \ xs \ ys \ \Leftarrow \ \underline{\text{rec}} \ xs \ \{ \\
&\quad \mathbf{vappend}_m \ xs \ ys \ \Leftarrow \ \underline{\text{case}} \ xs \ \{ \\
&\quad\quad \mathbf{vappend}_{\mathsf{zero}} \ \mathsf{vnil} \ ys \ \Rightarrow \ ys \\
&\quad\quad \mathbf{vappend}_{(\mathsf{suc} \ m)} \ (\mathsf{vcons} \ x \ xs) \ ys \ \Rightarrow \ \mathsf{vcons} \ x \ (\mathbf{vappend}_m \ xs \ ys) \ \}\}
\end{aligned}$$

I've overridden the length arguments just to show what's happening—you can leave them implicit if you like. The point is that by looking at the first vector, we learn about its length. This lets plus compute exactly as we need for $ys$ : Vec (plus zero $n$) $X$ in the vnil case. For vcons, the return type is Vec (plus (suc $m$) $n$) $X \rightsquigarrow$ Vec (suc (plus $m$ $n$)) $X$, which is what we supply.

### 3.1 Finite Sets

Let's examine the consequences of dependent case analysis for a different family:

$$\underline{\text{data}} \left( \frac{n \ : \ \mathsf{Nat}}{\mathsf{Fin} \ n \ : \ \star} \right) \ \underline{\text{where}} \ \left( \frac{}{\mathsf{fz} \ : \ \mathsf{Fin} \ (\mathsf{suc} \ n)} \right) ; \left( \frac{i \ : \ \mathsf{Fin} \ n}{\mathsf{fs} \ i \ : \ \mathsf{Fin} \ (\mathsf{suc} \ n)} \right)$$

What happens when we elaborate this?

$$\underline{\text{let}} \left( \frac{i \ : \ \mathsf{Fin} \ \mathsf{zero}}{\mathbf{magic} \ i \ : \ X} \right) ; \quad \mathbf{magic} \ i \ [ \ \texttt{<= case i} \ ]$$

You've probably guessed, but let's just check:

| $i$ : Fin   zero | unifier |
|---|---|
| fz$_n$ : Fin (suc $n$) | impossible |
| fs$_n$ $j$ : Fin (suc $n$) | impossible |

So the finished product is just   $\mathbf{magic} \ i \ \Leftarrow \ \underline{\text{case}} \ i$

The idea is that $\mathsf{Fin}\ n$ is an enumeration type containing $n$ values. Let's tabulate the first few members of the family, just to see what's going on. (I'll show the implicit arguments as subscripts, but write in decimal to save space.)

| Fin 0 | Fin 1 | Fin 2 | Fin 3 | Fin 4 | $\cdots$ |
|---|---|---|---|---|---|
| | $\mathsf{fz}_0$ | $\mathsf{fz}_1$ | $\mathsf{fz}_2$ | $\mathsf{fz}_3$ | $\cdots$ |
| | | $\mathsf{fs}_1\ \mathsf{fz}_0$ | $\mathsf{fs}_2\ \mathsf{fz}_1$ | $\mathsf{fs}_3\ \mathsf{fz}_2$ | $\ddots$ |
| | | | $\mathsf{fs}_2\ (\mathsf{fs}_1\ \mathsf{fz}_0)$ | $\mathsf{fs}_3\ (\mathsf{fs}_2\ \mathsf{fz}_1)$ | $\ddots$ |
| | | | | $\mathsf{fs}_3\ (\mathsf{fs}_2\ (\mathsf{fs}_1\ \mathsf{fz}_0))$ | $\ddots$ |
| | | | | | $\ddots$ |

Fin zero is empty, and each $\mathsf{Fin}\ (\mathsf{suc}\ n)$ is made by embedding the $n$ 'old' elements of $\mathsf{Fin}\ n$, using $\mathsf{fs}_n$, and adding a 'new' element $\mathsf{fz}_n$. $\mathsf{Fin}\ n$ provides a representation of numbers *bounded by* $n$, which can be used as 'array subscripts':

$$\underline{\mathsf{let}}\ \left( \frac{xs\ :\ \mathsf{Vec}\ n\ X\ ;\quad i\ :\ \mathsf{Fin}\ n}{\mathbf{vproj}\ xs\ i\ :\ X} \right)\ ;\ \ \begin{aligned} &\mathbf{vproj}\ xs\ i\ \Leftarrow\ \underline{\mathsf{rec}}\ xs\ \{ \\ &\quad \mathbf{vproj}\ xs\ i\ \Leftarrow\ \underline{\mathsf{case}}\ xs\ \{ \\ &\qquad \mathbf{vproj}\ \mathsf{vnil}\ i\ \Leftarrow\ \underline{\mathsf{case}}\ i \\ &\qquad \mathbf{vproj}\ (\mathsf{vcons}\ x\ xs)\ i\ \Leftarrow\ \underline{\mathsf{case}}\ i\ \{ \\ &\qquad\quad \mathbf{vproj}\ (\mathsf{vcons}\ x\ xs)\ \mathsf{fz}\ \Rightarrow\ x \\ &\qquad\quad \mathbf{vproj}\ (\mathsf{vcons}\ x\ xs)\ (\mathsf{fs}\ i) \\ &\qquad\qquad \Rightarrow\ \mathbf{vproj}\ xs\ i\ \}\}\} \end{aligned}$$

We need not fear projection from $\mathsf{vnil}$, for we can dismiss $i\ :\ \mathsf{Fin}$ zero, as a harmless fiction. Of course, we could have analysed the arguments the other way around:

$$\begin{aligned} &\mathbf{vproj}\ xs\ i\ \Leftarrow\ \underline{\mathsf{rec}}\ xs\ \{ \\ &\quad \mathbf{vproj}\ xs\ i\ \Leftarrow\ \underline{\mathsf{case}}\ i\ \{ \\ &\qquad \mathbf{vproj}\ xs\ \mathsf{fz}\ \Leftarrow\ \underline{\mathsf{case}}\ xs\ \{ \\ &\qquad\quad \mathbf{vproj}\ (\mathsf{vcons}\ x\ xs)\ \mathsf{fz}\ \Rightarrow\ x\ \} \\ &\qquad \mathbf{vproj}\ xs\ (\mathsf{fs}\ i)\ \Leftarrow\ \underline{\mathsf{case}}\ xs\ \{ \\ &\qquad\quad \mathbf{vproj}\ (\mathsf{vcons}\ x\ xs)\ (\mathsf{fs}\ i)\ \Rightarrow\ \mathbf{vproj}\ xs\ i\ \}\}\} \end{aligned}$$

Here, inspecting $i$ forces $n$ to be non-zero in each case, so $xs$ can only be a $\mathsf{vcons}$. The same result is achieved either way, but in both definitions, we rely on the impact the first case analysis has on the possibilities for the second. It may seem a tautology that dependent case analyses are not independent, but its impact is profound. We should certainly ask whether the traditional **case** expression, only expressing the patterns of its scrutinee, is as appropriate as it was in the past.

## 3.2   Refining Programming Problems

Our unification tables give some intuition to what is happening with case analysis. In Thierry Coquand's presentation of dependent pattern matching [13], constructor case analysis is hard-wired and unification is built into the typing rules. In Epigram, we have the more generic notion of refining a programming problem by an *eliminator*, $\Leftarrow e$. If we take a closer look at the elaboration of this construct, we'll see how unification arises and is handled *inside* the type theory. I'll maintain both the general case and the vtail example side by side.

As we saw with plus, when we say[8]

$$\underline{\text{let}}\ \left(\frac{\Gamma}{\mathsf{f}\,\Gamma\ :\ R}\right) \quad \Bigg| \quad \underline{\text{let}}\ \left(\frac{ys\ :\ \mathsf{Vec}\,(\mathsf{suc}\,m)\ Y}{\mathsf{vtail}\ ys\ :\ \mathsf{Vec}\,m\ Y}\right)$$

Epigram initiates the development of a proof

$$\Diamond\mathsf{f}\ :\ \forall\Gamma \Rightarrow \langle\mathsf{f}\,\Gamma\ :\ R\rangle \quad \Big| \quad \Diamond\mathsf{vtail}\ :\ \forall m\!:\!\mathsf{Nat};\ Y\!:\!\star;\ ys\!:\!\mathsf{Vec}\,(\mathsf{suc}\,m)\ Y$$
$$\Rightarrow \langle\mathsf{vtail}_m\ Y\ ys\ :\ \mathsf{Vec}\,m\ Y\rangle$$

The general form of a subproblem in this development is

$$\Diamond\mathsf{fsub}\ :\ \forall\Delta \Rightarrow \langle\mathsf{f}\,\vec{p}\ :\ T\rangle \quad \Big| \quad \Diamond\mathsf{vtail}\ :\ \forall m\!:\!\mathsf{Nat};\ Y\!:\!\star;\ ys\!:\!\mathsf{Vec}\,(\mathsf{suc}\,m)\ Y$$
$$\Rightarrow \langle\mathsf{vtail}_m\ Y\ ys\ :\ \mathsf{Vec}\,m\ Y\rangle$$

where $\vec{p}$ are *patterns*—expressions over the variables in $\Delta$. In the example, I've chosen the initial patterns given by vtails formal parameters. Note that patterns in Epigram are *not* a special subclass of expression. Now let's proceed

$$\mathsf{f}\,\vec{p} \Leftarrow e \quad \Big| \quad \mathsf{vtail}\ ys \Leftarrow \underline{\text{case}}\ ys$$

$$e\ :\ \forall\ P\!:\!\forall\Theta \Rightarrow \star \quad \Big| \quad \underline{\text{case}}\ ys\ :\ \forall\ P\!:\!\forall n;\ X;\ xs\!:\!\mathsf{Vec}\,n\ X \Rightarrow \star$$
$$m_1\!:\!\forall\Delta_1 \Rightarrow P\,\vec{s}_1 \qquad\qquad m_1\!:\!\forall\_X\!:\!\star \Rightarrow P\ \mathsf{zero}\ X\ \mathsf{vnil}$$
$$\vdots \qquad\qquad\qquad m_2\!:\!\forall\_X\!:\!\star;\ \_n\!:\!\mathsf{Nat};$$
$$\qquad\qquad\qquad x\!:\!X;\ xs\!:\!\mathsf{Vec}\,n\ X$$
$$m_n\!:\!\forall\Delta_n \Rightarrow P\,\vec{s}_n \qquad\qquad \Rightarrow P\ (\mathsf{suc}\,n)\ X\ (\mathsf{vcons}\ x\ xs)$$
$$\Rightarrow P\,\vec{t} \qquad\qquad\qquad \Rightarrow P\ (\mathsf{suc}\,m)\ Y\ ys$$

We call $P$ the *motive*—it says what we gain from the elimination. In particular, we'll have a proof of $P$ for the $\vec{t}$. The $m_i$ are the *methods* by which the motive is to be achieved for each $\vec{s}_i$. James McKinna taught me to choose this motive:

$$P \rightsquigarrow \lambda\Theta \Rightarrow \quad \Big| \quad P \rightsquigarrow \lambda n;\ X;\ xs \Rightarrow$$
$$\forall\Delta \Rightarrow \Theta{=}\vec{t} \to \qquad \forall m\!:\!\mathsf{Nat};\ Y\!:\!\star;\ ys\!:\!\mathsf{Vec}\,(\mathsf{suc}\,m)\ Y$$
$$\langle\mathsf{f}\,\vec{p}\ :\ T\rangle \qquad\qquad \Rightarrow n{=}(\mathsf{suc}\,m) \to X{=}Y \to xs{=}ys \to$$
$$\langle\mathsf{vtail}_m\ Y\ ys\ :\ \mathsf{Vec}\,m\ Y\rangle$$

This is just Henry Ford's old joke. Our motive is to produce a proof of $\forall\Delta \Rightarrow \langle\mathsf{f}\,\vec{p}\ :\ T\rangle$, for 'any $\Theta$ we like as long as it's $\vec{t}$'—the $\vec{t}$ are the only $\Theta$ we keep in stock. For our example, that means 'any vector you like as long as it's

---

[8] I write Greek capitals for sequences of variables with type assignments in binders and also for their unannotated counterparts as argument sequences.

nonempty and its elements are from $Y'$. This $=$ is **heterogeneous equality**,[9] which allows any elements of arbitrary types to be proclaimed equal. Its one constructor, refl, says that a thing is equal to itself.

$$\frac{s \;:\; S \;; \;\; t \;:\; T}{s=t \;:\; \star} \qquad \overline{\text{refl} \;:\; t=t}$$

Above, the types of $xs$ and $ys$ are different, but they will unify if we can solve the prior equations. Hypothetical equations don't change the internal rules by which the typechecker compares types—this is lucky, as hypotheses can lie.

If we can construct the methods, $m_i$, then we're done:

$$\lozenge\text{fsub} \rightsquigarrow \lambda\Delta \Rightarrow e\,P\,m_1 \ldots m_n$$
$$\Delta\;\text{refl} \ldots \text{refl}$$
$$: \forall\Delta \Rightarrow \langle\,f\,\vec{p} \;:\; T\,\rangle$$

$$\lozenge\text{vtail} \rightsquigarrow \lambda m; \; Y; \; ys \Rightarrow (\underline{\text{case}}\;ys)\,P\,m_1\,m_2$$
$$m\;Y\;ys\;\text{refl}\;\text{refl}\;\text{refl}$$
$$: \forall m : \text{Nat}; \; Y : \star; \; ys : \text{Vec}\,(\text{suc}\,m)\,Y$$
$$\Rightarrow \langle\,\text{vtail}_m\;Y\;ys \;:\; \text{Vec}\,m\,Y\,\rangle$$

But what are the methods? We must find, for each $i$

$$m_i \;:\; \forall\Delta_i; \Delta \Rightarrow \vec{s}_i = \vec{t} \;\rightarrow\; \langle\,f\,\vec{p} \;:\; T\,\rangle$$

In our example, we need

$$m_1 \;:\; \forall\_X; \quad \_m; \_Y; ys : \text{Vec}\,(\text{suc}\,m)\,Y \Rightarrow$$
$$\text{zero}=(\text{suc}\,m) \;\rightarrow\; X=Y \;\rightarrow\; \text{vnil}=ys \;\rightarrow$$
$$\langle\,\text{vtail}_m\;Y\;ys \;:\; \text{Vec}\,m\,Y\,\rangle$$
$$m_2 \;:\; \forall\_X; \_n; x; xs : \text{Vec}\,n\,X; \quad \_m; \_Y; xs : \text{Vec}\,(\text{suc}\,m)\,Y \Rightarrow$$
$$(\text{suc}\,n)=(\text{suc}\,m) \;\rightarrow\; X=Y \;\rightarrow\; (\text{vcons}\,x\,xs)=ys \;\rightarrow$$
$$\langle\,\text{vtail}_m\;Y\;ys \;:\; \text{Vec}\,m\,Y\,\rangle$$

Look at the equations! They express exactly the unification problems for case analysis which we tabulated informally. Now to solve them: the rules of first-order unification for data constructors—see figure 1—are derivable in UTT. Each rule (read backwards) simplifies a problem with an equational hypothesis. We apply these simplifications to the method types. The **conflict** and **cycle** rules dispose of 'impossible case' subproblems. Meanwhile, the **substitution** rule instantiates pattern variables. In general, the equations $\vec{s}_i = \vec{t}$ will be reduced as far as possible by first-order unification, and either the subproblem will be dismissed, or it will yield some substitution, instantiating the patterns $\vec{p}$.

In our example, the vnil case goes by **conflict**, and the vcons case becomes:

$$\forall\_Y; \_m; x : Y; xs : \text{Vec}\,Y\,m \;\Rightarrow\; \langle\,\text{vtail}_{Y\,m}\,(\text{vcons}\,x\,xs) \;:\; \text{Vec}\,Y\,m\,\rangle$$

After 'cosmetic renaming' gives $x$ and $xs$ names more like the original $ys$, we get

$$\text{vtail}\,(\text{vcons}\,y\,ys)\;[\,]$$

---

[9] Also known as 'John Major' equality [23].

| deletion | $\dfrac{P \rightarrow}{x=x \rightarrow P}$ | |
|---|---|---|
| conflict | chalk $\vec{s}$=cheese $\vec{t} \rightarrow P$ | |
| injectivity | $\dfrac{(\vec{s}=\vec{t} \rightarrow P) \rightarrow}{\text{chalk } \vec{s}=\text{chalk } \vec{t} \rightarrow P}$ | |
| substitution | $\dfrac{P\ t \rightarrow}{x=t \rightarrow P\ x}$ | $x, t : T; x \notin FV(t)$ |
| cycle | $x=t \rightarrow P$ | $x$ constructor-guarded in $t$ |

**Fig. 1.** derivable unification rule schemes

To summarize, elaboration of $\Leftarrow e$ proceeds as follows:

(1) choose a motive with equational constraints;
(2) simplify the constraints in the methods by first-order unification;
(3) leave the residual methods as the subproblems to be solved by subprograms.

In the presence of defined functions and higher types, unification problems won't always be susceptible to first-order unification, but Epigram will make what progress it can and leave the remaining equations unsolved in the hypotheses of subproblems—later analyses may reduce them to a soluble form. Moreover, there is no reason in principle why we should not consider a constraint-solving procedure which can be customized by user-supplied rules.

### 3.3 Reflection on Inspection

We're not used to thinking about what functions really tell us, because simple types don't say much about values, statically. For example, we could write

$$\underline{\text{let}}\ \left( \frac{n\ :\ \mathsf{Nat}}{\mathsf{nonzero}\ n\ :\ \mathsf{Bool}} \right)\ ;\ \begin{array}{l} \mathsf{nonzero}\ n \Leftarrow \underline{\mathsf{case}}\ n\ \{ \\ \quad \mathsf{nonzero}\ \mathsf{zero} \Rightarrow \mathsf{false} \\ \quad \mathsf{nonzero}\ (\mathsf{suc}\ n) \Rightarrow \mathsf{true}\ \} \end{array}$$

but suppose we have $xs$ : $\mathsf{Vec}\ n\ X$—what do we learn by testing $\mathsf{nonzero}\ n$? All we get is a $\mathsf{Bool}$, with no direct implications for our understanding of $n$ or $xs$. We are in no better position to apply vtail to $xs$ after inspecting this $\mathsf{Bool}$ than before. Instead, if we do case analysis on $n$, we learn what $n$ is *statically* as well as dynamically, and in the $\mathsf{suc}$ case we can apply vtail to $xs$.

Of course, we could think of writing a **preVtail** function which operates on any vector but requires a precondition, like

$$\underline{\text{let}}\ \left( \frac{xs\ :\ \mathsf{Vec}\ n\ X\ ;\ \ q\ :\ \mathsf{nonzero}\ n=\mathsf{true}}{\mathbf{preVtail}\ xs\ q\ :\ \mathsf{Vec}\ [\,]\ X} \right)$$

I'm not quite sure what to write as the length of the returned vector, so I've left a shed: perhaps it needs some kind of predecessor function with a precondition. If we have $ys$ : Vec $(\text{suc } m)$ $Y$, then **preVtail** $ys$ refl will be well typed. We could even use this function with a more informative conditional expression:

$$\text{condInfo} \; : \; \forall P\!:\!\star; \; b\!:\!\mathsf{Bool} \Rightarrow (b\!=\!\mathsf{true} \rightarrow P) \; \rightarrow \; (b\!=\!\mathsf{false} \rightarrow P) \; \rightarrow \; P$$

However, this way of working is clearly troublesome.

Moreover, given a nonempty vector $xs$, there is more than just a stylistic difference between decomposing it with **vhead** and **vtail** and decomposing it with $(\underline{\text{case }} xs)$—the destructor functions give us an element and a shorter vector; the case analysis tells us that $xs$ is the **vcons** of them, and if any types depend on $xs$, that might just be important. Again, we can construct a proof of $xs=\mathsf{vcons}\,(\mathsf{vhead}\,xs)\,(\mathsf{vtail}\,xs)$, but this is much harder to work with.

In the main, selectors-and-destructors are poor tools for working with data on which types depend. We really need forms of inspection which yield static information. This is a new issue, so there's no good reason to believe that the old design choices remain appropriate. We need to think carefully about how to reflect data's new rôle as *evidence*.

## 3.4   Vectorized Applicative Programming

Now that we've seen how dependent case analysis is elaborated, let's do some more work with it. The next example shows a key difference between Epigram's implicit syntax and *parametric* polymorphism. The operation

$$\underline{\text{let}} \; \left( \frac{x \; : \; X}{\mathsf{vec}\; x \; : \; \mathsf{Vec}\; n\; X} \right)$$

makes a vector of copies of its argument. For any given *usage* of **vec**, the intended type determined the length, but how are we to *define* **vec**? We shall need to work by recursion on the intended length, hence we shall need to make this explicit at definition time. The following declaration achieves this:

$$\underline{\text{let}} \; \left( \frac{n \; : \; \mathsf{Nat}\,; \;\; x \; : \; X}{\mathsf{vec}_n\; x \; : \; \mathsf{Vec}\; n\; X} \right) \; ; \;\; \mathsf{vec}_n\, x \; \Leftarrow \; \underline{\text{rec}}\; n \; \{$$
$$\mathsf{vec}_n\, x \; \Leftarrow \; \underline{\text{case}}\; n \; \{$$
$$\mathsf{vec}_{\mathsf{zero}}\, x \; \Rightarrow \; \mathsf{vnil}$$
$$\mathsf{vec}_{(\mathsf{suc}\; n)}\, x \; \Rightarrow \; \mathsf{vcons}\, x\, (\mathsf{vec}_n\, x) \; \}\}$$

Note that in **vec**'s type signature, I explicitly declare $n$ first, thus making it the first implicit argument: otherwise, $X$ might happen to come first. By the way, we don't have to override the argument in the recursive call $\mathsf{vec}_n\, x$—it's got to be a Vec $n$ $X$—but it would perhaps be a little disconcerting to omit the $n$, especially as it's the key to **vec**'s structural recursion.

The following operation—vectorized application—turns out to be quite handy.

$$\underline{\text{let}} \left( \frac{fs \;:\; \mathsf{Vec}\; n\; (S \to T) \;;\;\; ss \;:\; \mathsf{Vec}\; n\; S}{\mathsf{va}\; fs\; ss \;:\; \mathsf{Vec}\; n\; T} \right)$$

va $fs$ $ss$ $\Leftarrow$ rec $fs$ {
  va $fs$ $ss$ $\Leftarrow$ case $fs$ {
    va vnil $ss$ $\Leftarrow$ case $ss$ {
      va vnil vnil $\Rightarrow$ vnil }
    va (vcons $f$ $fs$) $ss$ $\Leftarrow$ case $ss$ {
      va (vcons $f$ $fs$) (vcons $s$ $ss$) $\Rightarrow$ vcons ($f$ $s$) (va $fs$ $ss$) }}}

As it happens, the combination of vec and va equip us with 'vectorized applicative programming', with vec embedding the constants, and va providing application. Transposition is my favourite example of this:

$$\underline{\text{let}} \left( \frac{xij \;:\; \mathsf{Vec}\; i\; (\mathsf{Vec}\; j\; X)}{\text{transpose}\; xij \;:\; \mathsf{Vec}\; j\; (\mathsf{Vec}\; i\; X)} \right)$$

transpose $xij$ $\Leftarrow$ rec $xij$ {
  transpose $xij$ $\Leftarrow$ case $xij$ {
    transpose vnil $\Rightarrow$ vec vnil
    transpose (vcons $xj$ $xij$) $\Rightarrow$ va (va (vec vcons) $xj$) (transpose $xij$) }}

### 3.5   Exercises: Matrix Manipulation

**Exercise 7 (vmap, vZipWith).** *Show how vec and va can be used to generate the vector analogues of Haskell's* map, zipWith, *and the rest of the family. (A glance at [16] may help.)*

**Exercise 8 (vdot).** *Implement vdot, the scalar product of two vectors of* Nats.

Now, how about matrices? Recall the vector-of-columns representation:

$$\underline{\text{let}} \left( \frac{rows, cols \;:\; \mathsf{Nat}}{\mathsf{Matrix}\; rows\; cols \;:\; \star} \right) \quad \mathsf{Matrix}\; rows\; cols \;\Rightarrow\; \mathsf{Vec}\; cols\; (\mathsf{Vec}\; rows\; \mathsf{Nat})$$

**Exercise 9 (zero, identity).** *How would you compute the zero matrix of a given size? Also implement a function to compute any identity matrix.*

**Exercise 10 (matrix by vector).** *Implement matrix-times-vector multiplication. (ie, interpret a* Matrix $m$ $n$ *as a linear map* Vec $n$ Nat $\to$ Vec $m$ Nat.)

**Exercise 11 (matrix by matrix).** *Implement matrix-times-matrix multiplication. (ie, implement composition of linear maps.)*

**Exercise 12 (monad).** *(Mainly for Haskellers.) It turns out that for each* $n$, Vec $n$ *is a monad, with vec playing the part of* return. *What should the corresponding notion of* join *do? What plays the part of* ap?

## 3.6   Exercises: Finite Sets

**Exercise 13** (fmax, fweak). *Implement* fmax *(each nonempty set's maximum value) and* fweak *(the function preserving* fz *and* fs, *incrementing the index).*

$$\underline{\text{let}}\ \left(\frac{}{\text{fmax}_n\ :\ \text{Fin (suc } n)}\right)\ \Bigg|\ \underline{\text{let}}\ \left(\frac{i\ :\ \text{Fin } n}{\text{fweak } i\ :\ \text{Fin (suc } n)}\right)$$

You should find that fmax and fweak partition the finite sets, just as fz and fs do. Imagine how we might pretend they're an alternative set of constructors...

**Exercise 14** (vtab). *Implement* vtab, *the inverse of* vproj, *tabulating a function over finite sets as a vector.*

$$\underline{\text{let}}\ \left(\frac{n\ :\ \text{Nat}\ ;\ f\ :\ \text{Fin } n\ \to\ X}{\text{vtab}_n\ f\ :\ \text{Vec } n\ X}\right)$$

Note that vtab and vproj offer alternative definitions of matrix operations.

**Exercise 15** (OPF, opf). *Devise an inductive family,* OPF $m$ $n$ *which gives a unique first-order representation of exactly the* order-preserving *functions in* Fin $m\ \to$ Fin $n$. *Give your family a semantics by implementing*

$$\underline{\text{let}}\ \left(\frac{f\ :\ \text{OPF } m\ n\ ;\ \ i\ :\ \text{Fin } m}{\text{opf } f\ i\ :\ \text{Fin } n}\right)$$

**Exercise 16** (iOPF, cOPF). *Implement identity and composition:*

$$\underline{\text{let}}\ \left(\frac{}{\text{iOPF}_n\ :\ \text{OPF } n\ n}\right)\ \Bigg|\ \underline{\text{let}}\ \left(\frac{f\ \text{OPF } m\ n\ ;\ \ g\ \text{OPF } l\ m}{\text{cOPF} f\ g\ :\ \text{OPF } l\ n}\right)$$

Which laws should relate iOPF, cOPF and opf?

## 4   Representing Syntax

The Fin family can represent de Bruijn indices in nameless expressions [14]. As Françoise Bellegarde and James Hook observed in [6], and Richard Bird and Ross Paterson were able to implement in [9], you can do this in Haskell, up to a point—here are the λ-terms with *free* variables given by v:

```
data Term v = Var v
            | App (Term v) (Term v)
            | Lda (Term (Maybe v))
```

Under a Lda, we use (Maybe v) as the variable set for the body, with Nothing being the new free variable and Just embedding the old free variables. Renaming is just fmap, and substitution is just the monadic 'bind' operator >>=.

However, **Term** is a bit *too* polymorphic. We can't see the *finiteness* of the variable context over which a term is constructed. In Epigram, we can take the number of free variables to be a number $n$, and choose variables from Fin $n$.

$$\underline{\text{data}} \ \left( \frac{n \ : \ \text{Nat}}{\text{Tm } n \ : \ \star} \right)$$

$$\underline{\text{where}} \ \left( \frac{i \ : \ \text{Fin } n}{\text{var } i \ : \ \text{Tm } n} \right) \ ; \ \left( \frac{f, s \ : \ \text{Tm } n}{\text{app } f \ s \ : \ \text{Tm } n} \right) \ ; \ \left( \frac{t \ : \ \text{Tm (suc } n)}{\text{lda } t \ : \ \text{Tm } n} \right)$$

Tho $n$ in Term $n$ indicates the number of variables available for term formation: we can explain how to $\lambda$-lift a term, by abstracting over all the available variables:

$$\underline{\text{let}} \ \left( \frac{t \ : \ \text{Tm } n}{\text{ldaLift}_n \ t \ : \ \text{Tm zero}} \right) \ ; \ \begin{array}{l} \text{ldaLift}_n \ t \ \Leftarrow \ \underline{\text{rec}} \ n \ \{ \\ \quad \text{ldaLift}_n \ t \ \Leftarrow \ \underline{\text{case}} \ n \ \{ \\ \quad \quad \text{ldaLift}_{\text{zero}} \ t \ \Rightarrow \ t \\ \quad \quad \text{ldaLift}_{(\text{suc } n)} \ t \ \Rightarrow \ \text{ldaLift}_n \ (\text{lda } t) \ \}\} \end{array}$$

Not so long ago, we were quite excited about the power of non-uniform datatypes to capture useful structural invariants. Scoped de Bruijn terms gave a good example, but most of the others proved more awkward even than the 'fake' dependent types you can cook up using type classes [24].

Real dependent types achieve more with less fuss. This is mainly due to the flexibility of inductive families. For example, if you wanted to add 'weakening' to delay explicitly the shifting of a term as you push it under a binder—in Epigram, but not Haskell or Cayenne, you could add the constructor

$$\left( \frac{t \ : \ \text{Tm } n}{\text{weak } t \ : \ \text{Tm (suc } n)} \right)$$

## 4.1   Exercises: Renaming and Substitution

If Fin $m$ is a variable set, then some $\rho \ : \ \text{Fin } m \to \text{Fin } n$ is a *renaming*. If we want to apply a renaming to a term, we need to be able to push it under a lda. Hence we need to *weaken* the renaming, mapping the new source variable to the new target variable, and renaming as before on the old variables.[10]

$$\underline{\text{let}} \ \left( \frac{\rho \ : \ \text{Fin } m \to \text{Fin } n \ ; \ \ i \ : \ \text{Fin (suc } m)}{\text{wren } \rho \ i \ : \ \text{Fin (suc } n)} \right) \ \begin{array}{l} \text{wren } \rho \ i \ \Leftarrow \ \underline{\text{case}} \ i \ \{ \\ \quad \text{wren } \rho \ \text{fz} \ \Rightarrow \ \text{fz} \\ \quad \text{wren } \rho \ (\text{fs } i) \ \Rightarrow \ \text{fs} \ (\rho \ i) \ \} \end{array}$$

You get to finish the development.

---

[10] Categorists! Note wren makes suc a functor in the category of Fin-functions. What other structure can you sniff out here?

**Exercise 17** (ren). *Use* wren *to help you implement the renaming traversal*

$$\text{let} \ \left( \frac{\rho \ : \ \mathsf{Fin} \ m \ \to \ \mathsf{Fin} \ n \ ; \ \ t \ : \ \mathsf{Tm} \ m}{\mathsf{ren} \ \rho \ t \ : \ \mathsf{Tm} \ n} \right)$$

Now repeat the pattern for substitutions—functions from variables to terms.

**Exercise 18** (wsub, sub). *Develop weakening for substitutions, then use it to go under* lda *in the traversal:*

$$\text{let} \ \left( \frac{\sigma \ : \ \mathsf{Fin} \ m \ \to \ \mathsf{Tm} \ n \ ; \ \ i \ : \ \mathsf{Fin} \ (\mathsf{suc} \ m)}{\mathsf{wsub} \ \sigma \ i \ : \ \mathsf{Tm} \ (\mathsf{suc} \ n)} \right)$$

$$\text{let} \ \left( \frac{\sigma \ : \ \mathsf{Fin} \ m \ \to \ \mathsf{Tm} \ n \ ; \ \ t \ : \ \mathsf{Tm} \ m}{\mathsf{sub} \ \sigma \ t \ : \ \mathsf{Tm} \ n} \right)$$

**Exercise 19** (*For the brave*). *Refactor this development, abstracting the weakening-then-traversal pattern. If you need a hint, see chapter 7 of [23].*

## 4.2   Stop the World I Want to Get Off! (A First Try at Typed Syntax)

We've seen untyped $\lambda$-calculus: let's look at how to enforce stronger invariants, by representing a *typed* $\lambda$-calculus. Recall the rules of the simply typed $\lambda$-calculus:

$$\frac{}{\Gamma;x \in \sigma;\Gamma' \vdash x \in \sigma} \quad \frac{\Gamma;x \in \sigma \vdash t \in \tau}{\Gamma \vdash \lambda x \in \sigma.\,t \in \sigma \supset \tau} \quad \frac{\Gamma \vdash f \in \sigma \supset \tau \quad \Gamma \vdash s \in \sigma}{\Gamma \vdash f\,s \in \tau}$$

Well-typed terms are defined with respect to a context and a type. Let's just turn the rules into data! I add a base type, to make things more concrete.

$$\text{data} \ \left( \frac{}{\mathsf{SType} \ : \ \star} \right) \ \text{where} \ \left( \frac{}{\mathsf{sNat} \ : \ \mathsf{SType}} \right) \ ; \ \left( \frac{\sigma,\tau \ : \ \mathsf{SType}}{\mathsf{sFun} \ \sigma \ \tau \ : \ \mathsf{SType}} \right)$$

We could use Vec for contexts, but I prefer contexts which grow on the right.

$$\text{data} \ \left( \frac{n \ : \ \mathsf{Nat}}{\mathsf{SCtxt} \ n \ : \ \star} \right) \ \text{where} \ \left( \frac{}{\mathsf{empty} \ : \ \mathsf{SCtxt} \ \mathsf{zero}} \right)$$

$$\left( \frac{\Gamma \ : \ \mathsf{SCtxt} \ n \ ; \ \ \sigma \ : \ \mathsf{SType}}{\mathsf{bind} \ \Gamma \ \sigma \ : \ \mathsf{SCtxt} \ (\mathsf{suc} \ n)} \right)$$

Now, assuming we have a projection function **sproj**, defined in terms of SCtxt and Fin the way we defined **vproj**, we can just turn the inference rules of the typing relation into constructors:

$$\underline{\text{data}} \left( \frac{\Gamma \,:\, \mathsf{SCtxt}\, n \,;\quad \tau \,:\, \mathsf{SType}}{\mathsf{STm}\, \Gamma\, \tau \,:\, \star} \right)$$

$$\underline{\text{where}} \left( \frac{i \,:\, \mathsf{Fin}\, n}{\mathsf{svar}\, i \,:\, \mathsf{STm}\, \Gamma\, (\mathsf{sproj}\, \Gamma\, i)} \right) \;;\; \left( \frac{t \,:\, \mathsf{STm}\, (\mathsf{bind}\, \Gamma\, \sigma)\, \tau}{\mathsf{slda}\, t \,:\, \mathsf{STm}\, \Gamma\, (\mathsf{sFun}\, \sigma\, \tau)} \right)$$

$$\left( \frac{f \,:\, \mathsf{STm}\, \Gamma\, (\mathsf{sFun}\, \sigma\, \tau) \,;\quad s \,:\, \mathsf{STm}\, \Gamma\, \sigma}{\mathsf{sapp}\, f\, s \,:\, \mathsf{STm}\, \Gamma\, \tau} \right)$$

This is a precise definition of the simply-typed $\lambda$-terms. But is it any good? Well, just try writing programs with it.

How would you implement *renaming*? As before, we could represent a renaming as a function $\rho : \mathsf{Fin}\, m \to \mathsf{Fin}\, n$. Can we rename a term in $\mathsf{STm}\, \Gamma\, \tau$ to get a $\mathsf{STm}\, \Delta\, \tau$, where $\Gamma : \mathsf{SCtxt}\, m$ and $\Delta : \mathsf{SCtxt}\, n$? Here comes the crunch:

$$\cdots \quad \mathsf{ren}_n\, \Gamma\, \Delta\, \rho\, (\mathsf{svar}\, i) \;\Rightarrow\; \boxed{\mathsf{svar}\, (\rho\, i)}$$

The problem is that $\mathsf{svar}\, i \,:\, \mathsf{STm}\, \Gamma\, (\mathsf{sproj}\, \Gamma\, i)$, so we want a $\mathsf{STm}\, \Delta\, (\mathsf{sproj}\, \Gamma\, i)$ on the right, but we've got a $\mathsf{STm}\, \Delta\, (\mathsf{sproj}\, \Delta\, (\rho\, i))$. We need to know that $\rho$ is type-preserving! Our choice of variable representation prevents us from building this into the type of $\rho$. We are forced to state an extra condition:

$$\forall i : \mathsf{Fin}\, m \Rightarrow \mathsf{sproj}\, \Gamma\, i = \mathsf{sproj}\, \Delta\, (\rho\, i)$$

We'll need to repair our program by rewriting with this proof.[11] But it's worse than that! When we move under a slda, we'll lift the renaming, so we'll need a *different* property:

$$\forall i' : \mathsf{Fin}\, (\mathsf{suc}\, m) \Rightarrow \mathsf{sproj}\, (\mathsf{bind}\, \Gamma\, \sigma)\, i' = \mathsf{sproj}\, (\mathsf{bind}\, \Delta\, \sigma)\, (\mathsf{lift}\, \rho\, i')$$

This follows from the previous property, but it takes a little effort. My program has just filled up with ghastly theorem-proving. Don't dependent types make life a nightmare? Stop the world I want to get off!

If you're not afraid of hard work, you can carry on and make this program work. I think discretion is the better part of valour—let's solve the problem instead. We're working with *typed* terms but *untyped* variables, and our function which gives types to variables does not connect the variable clearly to the context. For all we know, sproj always returns sNat! No wonder we need 'logical superstructure' to recover the information we've thrown away.

## 4.3    Dependent Types to the Rescue

Instead of using a program to assign types to variables and then reasoning about it, let's just have *typed* variables, as Thorsten Altenkirch and Bernhard Reus [2].

$$\underline{\text{data}} \left( \frac{\Gamma \,:\, \mathsf{SCtxt}\, n \,;\quad \tau \,:\, \mathsf{SType}}{\mathsf{SVar}\, \Gamma\, \tau \,:\, \star} \right)$$

$$\underline{\text{where}} \left( \frac{}{\mathsf{vz} \,:\, \mathsf{SVar}\, (\mathsf{bind}\, \Gamma\, \sigma)\, \sigma} \right) \;;\; \left( \frac{i \,:\, \mathsf{SVar}\, \Gamma\, \tau}{\mathsf{vs}\, i \,:\, \mathsf{SVar}\, (\mathsf{bind}\, \Gamma\, \sigma)\, \tau} \right)$$

---

[11] I shan't show how to do this, as we shall shortly avoid the problem.

This family strongly resembles Fin. Its constructors target only nonempty contexts; it has one constructor which references the 'newest' variable; the other constructor embeds the 'older' variables. You may also recognize this family as an inductive definition of context *membership*. Being a variable *means* being a member of the context. Fin just gives a data representation for variables without their meaning. Now we can replace our awkward svar with

$$\left( \frac{i \; : \; \mathsf{SVar} \; \Gamma \; \tau}{\mathsf{svar} \; i \; : \; \mathsf{STm} \; \Gamma \; \tau} \right)$$

A renaming *from* $\Gamma$ *to* $\Delta$ becomes an element of

$$\forall \tau : \mathsf{SType} \Rightarrow \mathsf{SVar} \; \Gamma \; \tau \rightarrow \mathsf{SVar} \; \Delta \; \tau$$

Bad design makes for hard work, whether you're making can-openers, doing mathematics or writing programs. It's often tempting to imagine that once we've made our representation of data tight enough to rule out meaningless values, our job is done and things should just work out. This experience teaches us that more is required—we should use types to give meaningful values their meaning. Fin contains the right data, but SVar actually explains it.

**Exercise 20.** *Construct simultaneous renaming and simultaneous substitution for this revised definition of* STm. *Just lift the pattern from the untyped version!*

## 4.4   Is Looking Seeing?

It's one thing to define data structures which *enforce* invariants and to write programs which *respect* invariants, but how can we *establish* invariants?

We've seen how to use a finite set to index a vector, enforcing the appropriate bounds, but what if we only have a *number*, sent to us from the outside world? We've seen how to write down the STms, but what if we've read in a program from a file? How do we compute its type-safe representation if it has one?

If we want to index a Vec $n \; X$ by $m$ : Nat, it's no good testing the Boolean $m < n$. The value true or false won't explain whether $m$ can be represented by some $i$ : Fin $n$. If we have a $f$ : STm $\Gamma$ (sFun $\sigma \; \tau$) and some $a$ : STm $\Gamma \; \alpha$, we could check Boolean equality $\sigma == \alpha$, but true doesn't make $\alpha$ into $\sigma$, so we can't construct sapp $f \; a$.

Similar issues show up in the 'Scrap Your Boilerplate' library of dynamically typed traversal operators by Ralf Lämmel and Simon Peyton Jones [18]. The whole thing rests on a 'type safe cast' operator, comparing types at run time:

```
cast :: (Typeable a, Typeable b) => a -> Maybe b
cast x = r
        where
          r = if typeOf x == typeOf (get r)
              then Just (unsafeCoerce x)
              else Nothing
```

```
get :: Maybe a -> a
get x = undefined
```

This program does not, of itself, make sense. The best we can say is that *we* can make sense of it, provided `typeOf` has been correctly implemented. The machine *looks* at the types but does not *see* when they are the same, hence the `unsafeCoerce`. The significance of the test is obscure, so blind obedience is necessary. Of course, *I* trust them, but I think they could aspire for better.

The trouble is that representing the result of a computation is not enough: you need to know the *meaning* of the computation if you want to justify its consequences. A Boolean is a bit uninformative. To see when we look, we need a new way of looking. Take the vector indexing example. We can explain which number is represented by a given $i$ : Fin $n$ by *forgetting* its bound:

$$\underline{\text{let}} \ \left( \frac{i \ : \ \text{Fin } n}{\text{fFin } i \ : \ \text{Nat}} \right) \ ; \ \ \text{fFin } i \ \Leftarrow \ \underline{\text{rec}} \ i \ \{$$
$$\text{fFin } i \ \Leftarrow \ \underline{\text{case}} \ i \ \{$$
$$\text{fFin fz} \ \Rightarrow \ \text{zero}$$
$$\text{fFin (fs } i) \ \Rightarrow \ \text{suc (fFin } i) \ \}\}$$

Now, for a given $n$ and $m$, $m$ is either

- (fFin $i$)    for some $i$ : Fin $n$, or
- (plus $n$ $m'$)    for some $m'$ : Nat

Our types can talk about values—we can *say* that!

$$\text{checkBound } n \ m \ : \ \forall P \ : \ \text{Nat} \to \text{Nat} \to \star \ \Rightarrow$$
$$(\forall n : \text{Nat}; \ i : \text{Fin } n \Rightarrow P \ n \ (\text{fFin } i)) \ \to$$
$$(\forall n, m' : \text{Nat} \Rightarrow P \ n \ (\text{plus } n \ m')) \ \to$$
$$P \ n \ m$$

That's to say: 'whatever $P$ you want to do with $n$ and $m$, it's enough to explain $P$ for $n$ and (fFin $i$) and also for $n$ and (plus $n$ $m'$)'. Or 'you can match $n, m$ against the *patterns*, $n$, (fFin $i$) and $n$, (plus $n$ $m'$)'. I designed the above type to look like a <u>case</u> principle, so that I can program with it. Note that I don't just get an element either of (Fin $i$) or of Nat from an anonymous informant; it really is my very own $n$ and $m$ which get analysed—the type says so! If I have checkBound, then I can check $m$ like this:

$$\underline{\text{let}} \ \left( \frac{xs \ : \ \text{Vec } n \ X \ ; \ \ m \ : \ \text{Nat}}{\text{mayProj}_n \ xs \ m \ : \ \text{Maybe } X} \right)$$

$$\text{mayProj}_n \ xs \ m \ \Leftarrow \ \text{checkBound } n \ m \ \{$$
$$\text{mayProj}_n \ xs \ (\text{fFin } i) \ \Rightarrow \ \text{just } (\textbf{vproj } xs \ i)$$
$$\text{mayProj}_n \ xs \ (\text{plus } n \ m') \ \Rightarrow \ \text{nothing} \ \}$$

In one case, we get a bounded $i$, so we can apply bounds-safe projection. In the other, we clearly fail. Moreover, if the return type were to depend on $m$, that's fine: not only do *we* see what $m$ must be, Epigram sees it too! But checkBound has quite a complicated higher-order type. Do I really expect you to dump good old $m < n$ for some bizarre functional? Of course I don't: I'll now explain the straightforward first-order way to construct checkBound.

## 4.5    A Funny Way of Seeing Things

Constructor case analysis is the normal way of seeing things. Suppose I have a funny way of seeing things. We know that $\Leftarrow$ doesn't care—a 'way of seeing things' is expressed by a type and interpreted as a way of decomposing a programming problem into zero or more subproblems. But how do I establish that my funny way of seeing at things makes sense?

Given $n, m :$ Nat, we want to see $m$ as either (fFin $i$) for some $i :$ Fin $n$, or else some (plus $n$ $m'$). We can write a predicate which characterizes the $n$ and $m$ for which this is possible—it's possible for the very patterns we want.[12]

$$\underline{\text{data}} \left( \frac{n, m \ : \ \text{Nat}}{\text{BoundCheck } n \ m \ : \ \star} \right)$$

$$\underline{\text{where}} \left( \frac{i \ : \ \text{Fin } n}{\text{inBound } i \ : \ \text{BoundCheck } n \ (\text{fFin } i)} \right)$$

$$\left( \frac{m' \ : \ \text{Nat}}{\text{outOfBound } m' \ : \ \text{BoundCheck } n \ (\text{plus } n \ m')} \right)$$

A value $bc :$ BoundCheck $n$ $m$ tells us something about $n$ and $m$, and it's just $n$ and $m$ that we care about here—$bc$ is just a means to this end. The eliminator (case $bc$) expects a motive abstracting over $n$, $m$ and $bc$, allowing us to inspect $bc$ also. If we restrict the motive to see only $n$ and $m$, we get

$$\lambda P : \text{Nat} \to \text{Nat} \to \star \ \Rightarrow \ (\underline{\text{case}} \ bc) \ (\lambda \ n'; \ m'; \ bc' \Rightarrow P \ n' \ m')$$
$$: \ \forall P \ : \ \text{Nat} \to \text{Nat} \to \star \ \Rightarrow$$
$$(\forall n : \text{Nat}; \ i : \text{Fin } n \Rightarrow P \ n \ (\text{fFin } i)) \ \to$$
$$(\forall n, m' : \text{Nat} \Rightarrow P \ n \ (\text{plus } n \ m')) \ \to$$
$$P \ n \ m$$

and that's exactly the type of checkBound $n$ $m$. This construction on a predicate is sufficiently useful that Epigram gives it a special name, (view $bc$). That's to say, the machine-generated eliminator which just looks at BoundCheck's *indices* in terms of its constructors. Logically, view gives a datatype family its **relation induction** principle. But to use this 'view', we need $bc :$ BoundCheck $n$ $m$. That is, we must show that every $n$ and $m$ are checkable in this way:

---

[12] I forgot that I'm *programming*: of course, I mean 'datatype family'.

$$\underline{\text{let}} \left( \frac{}{\text{boundCheck } n\ m\ :\ \text{BoundCheck } n\ m} \right)$$

boundCheck $n\ m\ \Leftarrow\ \underline{\text{rec}}\ n\ \{$
  boundCheck $n\ m\ \Leftarrow\ \underline{\text{case}}\ n\ \{$
   boundCheck zero $m\ \Rightarrow\ $ outOfBound $m$
   boundCheck (suc $n$) $m\ \Leftarrow\ \underline{\text{case}}\ m\ \{$
    boundCheck (suc $n$) zero $\Rightarrow$ inBound fz
    boundCheck (suc $n$) (suc $m$) $\Leftarrow\ \underline{\text{view}}$ (boundCheck $n\ m$) $\{$
     boundCheck (suc $n$) (suc (**fFin** $i$)) $\Rightarrow$ inBound (fs $i$)
     boundCheck (suc $n$) (suc (**plus** $n\ m'$)) $\Rightarrow$ outOfBound $m'$ $\}\}\}\}$

There's no trouble using the view we're trying to establish: the recursive call is structural, but used in an eliminator rather than a return value. This function works much the way *subtraction* works. The only difference is that it has a type which establishes a connection between the output to the function and its inputs, shown directly in the patterns! We may now take

$$\text{checkBound } n\ m\ \rightsquigarrow\ \underline{\text{view}}\ (\text{boundCheck } n\ m)$$

### 4.6  Patterns Forget; Matching Is Remembering

What has 'pattern matching' become? In general, a pattern is a *forgetful* operation. Constructors like zero and suc forget *themselves*—you can't tell from the type Nat, which constructor you've got. Case analysis remembers what constructors forget. And so it is with our funny patterns: the fFin function forgets bounded whilst (plus $n\ m'$) forgets by how much its output exceeds $n$. Our view remembers what these patterns forget.

The difference between Epigram views and Phil Wadler's views [38] is that Epigram views cannot lie. Epigram views talk directly about the values being inspected in terms of the forgetful operations which generate them. Wadler's views ascribe that informative significance to an independent value, whether or not it's justified. We shouldn't criticize Wadler for this—dependent types can see where simple types can only look. Of course, to work with dependent types, we *need* to be able to see. If we want to generate values in types which enforce strong invariants, we need to see that those invariants hold.

**Exercise 21.** *Show that* fmax *and* fweak *cover* Fin *by constructing a view.*

## 5  Well Typed Programs which Don't Go Wrong

Let's have a larger example of derivable pattern matching—building simply-typed terms in the STm family by typechecking 'raw' untyped terms from

$$\underline{\text{data}} \left( \frac{n \ : \ \text{Nat}}{\text{RTm } n \ : \ \star} \right)$$

$$\underline{\text{where}} \left( \frac{i \ : \ \text{Fin } n}{\text{rvar } i \ : \ \text{RTm } n} \right) \ ; \ \left( \frac{f, s \ : \ \text{RTm } n}{\text{rapp } f \ s \ : \ \text{RTm } n} \right)$$

$$\left( \frac{\sigma \ : \ \text{SType} ; \quad b \ : \ \text{RTm (suc } n)}{\text{rlda } \sigma \ b \ : \ \text{RTm } n} \right)$$

Typechecking is a form of looking. It relies on two auxiliary forms of looking—looking up a variable in the context, and checking that two types are the same. Our svar constructor takes context-references expressed in terms of SVar, and our sapp constructor really needs the domain of the function to be the same as the type of the argument, so just looking is not enough. Let's see.

An SVar is a context-reference; a Fin is merely a context-pointer. We can clearly turn a reference into a pointer by forgetting what's referred to:

$$\underline{\text{let}} \left( \frac{\Gamma \ : \ \text{SCtxt } n ; \quad i \ : \ \text{SVar } \Gamma \ \tau}{\text{fV } \tau \ i \ : \ \text{Fin } n} \right) \ ; \ \begin{array}{l} \textbf{fV } \tau \ i \ \Leftarrow \ \underline{\text{rec}} \ i \ \{ \\ \quad \textbf{fV } \tau \ i \ \Leftarrow \ \underline{\text{case}} \ i \ \{ \\ \quad\quad \textbf{fV } \tau \ \text{vz} \ \Rightarrow \ \text{fz} \\ \quad\quad \textbf{fV } \tau \ (\text{vs } i) \ \Rightarrow \ \text{fs } (\textbf{fV } \tau \ i) \ \} \} \end{array}$$

Why is $\tau$ an explicit argument? Well, the point of writing this forgetful map is to define a notion of *pattern* for finite sets which characterizes projection. We need to see the information which the pattern throws away. Let's establish the view—it's just a more informative **vproj**, telling us not only the projected thing, but that it is indeed the projection we wanted.

$$\underline{\text{data}} \left( \frac{\Gamma \ : \ \text{SCtxt } n ; \quad i \ : \ \text{Fin } n}{\text{Find } \Gamma \ i \ : \ \star} \right) \quad \underline{\text{where}} \left( \frac{i \ : \ \text{SVar } \Gamma \ \tau}{\text{found } \tau \ i \ : \ \text{Find } \Gamma \ (\text{fV } \tau \ i)} \right)$$

$$\underline{\text{let}} \left( \frac{}{\text{find } \Gamma \ i \ : \ \text{Find } \Gamma \ i} \right)$$

$$\begin{array}{l} \text{find } \Gamma \ i \ \Leftarrow \ \underline{\text{rec}} \ \Gamma \ \{ \\ \quad \text{find } \Gamma \ i \ \Leftarrow \ \underline{\text{case}} \ i \ \{ \\ \quad\quad \text{find } \Gamma \ \text{fz} \ \Leftarrow \ \underline{\text{case}} \ \Gamma \ \{ \\ \quad\quad\quad \text{find } (\text{bind } \Gamma \ \sigma) \ \text{fz} \ \Rightarrow \ \text{found } \sigma \ \text{vz} \ \} \\ \quad\quad \text{find } \Gamma \ (\text{fs } i) \ \Leftarrow \ \underline{\text{case}} \ \Gamma \ \{ \\ \quad\quad\quad \text{find } (\text{bind } \Gamma \ \sigma) \ (\text{fs } i) \ \Leftarrow \ \underline{\text{view}} \ (\text{find } \Gamma \ i) \ \{ \\ \quad\quad\quad\quad \text{find } (\text{bind } \Gamma \ \sigma) \ (\text{fs } (\text{fV } \tau \ i)) \ \Rightarrow \ \text{found } \tau \ (\text{vs } i) \ \} \} \} \} \end{array}$$

## 5.1  Term and Terror

We can follow the same recipe for typechecking as we did for context lookup. Help me fill in the details:

**Exercise 22** (fTm). *Implement the forgetful map:*

$$\underline{\text{let}}\ \left(\frac{\varGamma\ \text{SCtxt}\ n\ ;\ \ t\ :\ \text{STm}\ \varGamma\ \tau}{\text{fTm}\ \tau\ t\ :\ \text{RTm}\ n}\right)$$

But not every raw term is the forgetful image of a well typed term. We'll need

$$\underline{\text{data}}\ \left(\frac{\varGamma\ :\ \text{SCtxt}\ n}{\text{TError}\ \varGamma\ :\ \star}\right)\ \underline{\text{where}}\ \cdots$$

$$\underline{\text{let}}\ \left(\frac{\varGamma\ :\ \text{SCtxt}\ n\ ;\ \ e\ :\ \text{TError}\ \varGamma}{\text{fTError}\ e\ :\ \text{RTm}\ n}\right)$$

**Exercise 24** (TError, fTError). *Fill out the definition of* TError *and implement* fTError. *(This will be easy, once you've done the missing exercise. The TErrors will jump out as we write the typechecker—they pack up the failure cases.)*

Let's start on the typechecking view. First, the checkability relation:

$$\underline{\text{data}}\ \left(\frac{\varGamma\ :\ \text{SCtxt}\ n : r\ :\ \text{RTm}\ n}{\text{Check}\ \varGamma\ r\ :\ \star}\right)$$

$$\underline{\text{where}}\ \left(\frac{t\ :\ \text{STm}\ \varGamma\ \tau}{\text{good}\ t\ :\ \text{Check}\ \varGamma\ (\text{fTm}\ \tau\ t)}\right)\ ;\ \left(\frac{e\ :\ \text{TError}\ \varGamma}{\text{bad}\ e\ :\ \text{Check}\ \varGamma\ (\text{fTError}\ e)}\right)$$

Next, let's start on the proof of checkability—sorry, the typechecker:

$$\underline{\text{let}}\ \left(\frac{}{\text{check}\ \varGamma\ r\ :\ \text{Check}\ \varGamma\ r}\right)$$

```
check Γ r ⇐ rec r {
  check Γ r ⇐ case r {
   check Γ (rvar i) ⇐ view (find Γ i) {
    check Γ (rvar (fV τ i)) ⇒ good (svar i) }
   check Γ (rapp f s) ⇐ view (check Γ f) {
    check Γ (rapp (fTm φ f) s) ⇐ case φ {
     check Γ (rapp (fTm sNat f) s) ⇒ bad []
     check Γ (rapp (fTm (sFun σ τ) f) s) ⇐ view (check Γ s) {
      check Γ (rapp (fTm (sFun σ τ) f) (fTm α s))  []
      check Γ (rapp (fTm (sFun σ τ) f) (fTError e)) ⇒ bad [] }}
    check Γ (rapp (fTError e) s) ⇒ bad [] }
   check Γ (rlda σ t) ⇐ view (check (bind Γ σ) t) {
    check Γ (rlda σ (fTm τ t)) ⇒ good (slda t)
    check Γ (rlda σ (fTError e)) ⇒ bad [] }}}
```

The story so far: we used find to check variables; we used check recursively to check the body of an rlda and packed up the successful outcome. Note that we don't need to write the types of the good terms—they're implicit in STm.

We also got some way with application: checking the function; checking that the function inhabits a function space; checking the argument. The only trouble is that our function expects a $\sigma$ and we've got an $\alpha$. We need to *see* if they're the same: that's the missing exercise.

**Exercise 23.** *Develop an equality* view *for* SType:

$$\underline{\text{data}} \left( \frac{\sigma, \tau \ : \ \text{SType}}{\text{Compare } \sigma \ \tau \ : \ \star} \right)$$

$$\underline{\text{where}} \left( \frac{}{\text{same} \ : \ \text{Compare } \tau \ \tau} \right) ; \left( \frac{\sigma' \ : \ \text{Diff } \sigma}{\text{diff } \sigma' \ : \ \text{Compare } \sigma \ (\text{fDiff } \sigma \ \sigma')} \right)$$

$$\underline{\text{let}} \left( \frac{}{\text{compare } \sigma \ \tau \ : \ \text{Compare } \sigma \ \tau \ : \ \star} \right)$$

*You'll need to define a representation of* STypes *which differ from a given* $\sigma$ *and a forgetful map* fDiff *which forgets this difference.*

How to go about it? Wait and see. Let's go back to application...

check $\Gamma$ (rapp (fTm (sFun $\sigma$ $\tau$) $f$) (fTm $\alpha$ $s$)) $\Leftarrow$ <u>view</u> (compare $\sigma$ $\alpha$) {
  check $\Gamma$ (rapp (fTm (sFun $\sigma$ $\tau$) $f$) (fTm $\sigma$ $s$)) $\Rightarrow$ good (sapp $f$ $s$)
  check $\Gamma$ (rapp (fTm (sFun $\sigma$ $\tau$) $f$) (fTm (fDiff $\sigma$ $\sigma'$) $s$)) $\Rightarrow$ bad [] }

If we use your compare view, we can see directly that the types match in one case and mismatch in the other. For the former, we can now return a well typed application. The latter is definitely wrong.

We've done all the good cases, and we're left with choosing inhabitants of TError $\Gamma$ for the bad cases. There's no reason why you shouldn't define TError $\Gamma$ to make this as easy as possible. Just pack up the information which is lying around! For the case we've just seen, you could have:[13]

$$\left( \frac{\sigma' \ : \ \text{Diff } \sigma \ ; \ \ f \ : \ \text{STm } \Gamma \ (\text{sFun } \sigma \ \tau) \ ; \ \ s \ : \ \text{STm } \Gamma \ (\text{fDiff } \sigma \ \sigma')}{\text{mismatchError } \sigma' \ f \ s \ : \ \text{TError } \Gamma} \right)$$

fTError (mismatchError $\sigma'$ $f$ $s$) $\Rightarrow$ rapp (fTm ? $f$) (fTm ? $s$)

This recipe gives one constructor for each bad case, and you don't have any choice about its declaration. There are two basic type errors—the above mismatch and the application of a non-function. The remaining three bad cases just propagate failure outwards: you get a type of located errors.

Of course, you'll need to develop comparable first. To define Diff, just play the same type-of-diagnostics game. Develop the equality test, much as you would

---

[13] The ? means 'please infer'—it's often useful when writing forgetful maps. Why?

with the Boolean version, but using the view recursively in order to see when the sources and targets of two sFuns are the same. If you need a hint, see [27].

What have we achieved? We've written a typechecker which not only returns *some* well typed term or error message, but, specifically, *the* well typed term or error message which corresponds to its input by fTm or fTError. That correspondance is directly expressed by a very high level derived form of pattern matching: not rvar, rapp or rlda, but 'well typed' or 'ill typed'.

## 5.2   A Typesafe and Total Interpreter

Once you have a well typed term, you can extract some operational benefit from its well-typedness—you can execute it without run-time checks. This example was inspired by Lennart Augustsson and Magnus Carlsson's interpreter for terms with a typing proof [5]. Epigram's inductive families allow us a more direct approach: we just write down a denotational semantics for well typed terms. Firstly, we must interpret SType:

$$\underline{\text{let}} \ \left( \frac{\tau \ : \ \text{SType}}{\text{Value} \ \tau \ : \ \star} \right) \ ; \ \begin{array}{l} \text{Value} \ \tau \ \Leftarrow \ \underline{\text{rec}} \ \tau \ \{ \\ \quad \text{Value} \ \tau \ \Leftarrow \ \underline{\text{case}} \ \tau \ \{ \\ \quad\quad \text{Value sNat} \ \Rightarrow \ \text{Nat} \\ \quad\quad \text{Value} \ (\text{sFun} \ \sigma \ \tau) \ \Rightarrow \ \text{Value} \ \sigma \rightarrow \text{Value} \ \tau \ \}\} \end{array}$$

Now we can explain how to interpret a context by an environment of values:

$$\underline{\text{data}} \ \left( \frac{\Gamma \ : \ \text{SCtxt} \ n}{\text{Env} \ \Gamma \ : \ \star} \right)$$

$$\underline{\text{where}} \ \left( \frac{}{\text{eempty} \ : \ \text{Env empty}} \right) \ ; \ \left( \frac{\gamma \ : \ \text{Env} \ \Gamma \ ; \ v \ : \ \text{Value} \ \sigma}{\text{ebind} \ \gamma \ \sigma \ : \ \text{Env} \ (\text{bind} \ \Gamma \ \sigma)} \right)$$

Next, interpret variables by looking them up:

$$\underline{\text{let}} \ \left( \frac{\gamma \ : \ \text{Env} \ \Gamma \ ; \ i \ : \ \text{SVar} \ \Gamma \ \tau}{\text{evar} \ \gamma \ i \ : \ \text{Value} \ \tau} \right) \ ; \ \begin{array}{l} \text{evar} \ \gamma \ i \ \Leftarrow \ \underline{\text{rec}} \ i \ \{ \\ \quad \text{evar} \ \gamma \ i \ \Leftarrow \ \underline{\text{case}} \ i \ \{ \\ \quad\quad \text{evar} \ \gamma \ \text{vz} \ \Leftarrow \ \underline{\text{case}} \ \gamma \ \{ \\ \quad\quad\quad \text{evar} \ (\text{ebind} \ \gamma \ v) \ \text{vz} \ \Rightarrow \ v \ \} \\ \quad\quad \text{evar} \ \gamma \ (\text{vs} \ i) \ \Leftarrow \ \underline{\text{case}} \ \gamma \ \{ \\ \quad\quad\quad \text{evar} \ (\text{ebind} \ \gamma \ v) \ (\text{vs} \ i) \ \Rightarrow \ \text{evar} \ \gamma \ i \ \}\}\} \end{array}$$

Finally, interpret the well typed terms:

$$\underline{\text{let}} \ \left( \frac{\gamma \ : \ \text{Env} \ \Gamma \ ; \ t \ : \ \text{STm} \ \Gamma \ \tau}{\text{eval} \ \gamma \ t \ : \ \text{Value} \ \tau} \right)$$

$$\begin{array}{l} \text{eval} \ \gamma \ t \ \Leftarrow \ \underline{\text{rec}} \ t \ \{ \\ \quad \text{eval} \ \gamma \ t \ \Leftarrow \ \underline{\text{case}} \ t \ \{ \\ \quad\quad \text{eval} \ \gamma \ (\text{svar} \ i) \ \Rightarrow \ \text{evar} \ \gamma \ i \\ \quad\quad \text{eval} \ \gamma \ (\text{sapp} \ f \ s) \ \Rightarrow \ \text{eval} \ \gamma \ f \ (\text{eval} \ \gamma \ s) \\ \quad\quad \text{eval} \ \gamma \ (\text{slda} \ t) \ \Rightarrow \ \lambda v \Rightarrow \text{eval} \ (\text{ebind} \ \gamma \ v) \ t \ \}\} \end{array}$$

**Exercise 25.** *Make an environment whose entries are the constructors for* Nat, *together with some kind of iterator. Add two and two.*

## 6   Epilogue

Well, we've learned to add two and two. It's true that Epigram is currently little more than a toy, but must it necessarily remain so? There is much work to do.

I hope I have shown that precise data structures can manipulated successfully and in a highly articulate manner. You don't have to be content with giving orders to the computer and keeping your ideas to yourself. What has become practical is a notion of program as *effective explanation*, rather than merely an effective procedure. Upon what does this practicality depend?

- *adapting the programming language to suit dependent types*
  Our conventional programming constructs are not well-suited either to cope with or to capitalize on the richness of dependent data structures. We have had to face up to the fact that inspecting one value can tell us more about types and about other values. And so it should: at long last, testing makes a difference! Moreover, the ability of types to talk about values gives us ready access to a new, more articulate way of programming with the high-level structure of values expressed directly as patterns.
- *using type information earlier in the programming process*
  With so much structure—and computation—at the type level, keeping yourself type correct is inevitably more difficult. But it isn't necessary! Machines can check types and run programs, so use them! Interactive programming shortens the feedback loop, and it makes types a positive input to the programming process, not just a means to police its output.
- *changing the programs we choose to write*
  We shouldn't expect dependently typed programming merely to extend the functional canon with new programs which could not be typed before. In order to exploit the power of dependent types to express and enforce stronger invariants, we need a new style of programming which explicitly *establishes* those invariants. We need to rework old programs, replacing uninformative types with informative ones.

### 6.1   Related Work

Epigram's elder siblings are DML [39] and Cayenne [4]. DML equips ML programs with types refined by linear integer constraints and equips the typechecker with a constraint-solver. Correspondingly, many basic invariants, especially those involving sizes and ranges, can be statically enforced—this significantly reduces the overhead of run time checking [40]. Epigram has no specialist constraint-solver for arithmetic, although such a thing is a possible and useful extension. Epigram's strength is in the diversity of its type-level language.

Cayenne is much more ambitious than DML and a lot closer to Epigram. It's notorious for its looping typechecker, although(contrary to popular misconception)this is not an inevitable consequence of mixing dependent types with general recursion—recursion is implemented via fixpoints, so even structurally recursive programs can loop—you can always expand a fixpoint.

Cayenne's main drawback is that it doesn't support the kind of inductive families which Epigram inherited from the Alf system [21,13]. It rules out those in which constructors only target *parts* of a family, the way vnil makes *empty* vectors and vcons makes *nonempty* vectors. This also rules out SVar, STm and all of our 'views'. All of these examples can be given a cumbersome encoding if you are willing to work hard enough: I for one am not.

The Agda proof assistant [12], like Epigram, is very much in the spirit of Alf, but it currently imposes the same restrictions on inductive definitions as Cayenne and hence would struggle to support the programs in these notes—this unfortunate situation is unlikely to continue. Meanwhile Coq [11] certainly accepts the inductive definitions in this paper: it just has no practical support for programming with them—there is no good reason for this to remain so.

In fact, the closest programming language to Epigram at time of writing is Haskell, with ghc's new 'generalised algebraic data types' [33]. These turn out to be, more or less, inductive families! Of course, in order to preserve the rigid separation of static types and dynamic terms, GADTs must be indexed by *type* expressions. It becomes quite easy to express examples like the type-safe interpreter, which exploit the invariants enforced by indexing. What is still far from obvious is how to *establish* invariants for run time data, as we did in our typechecker—this requires precisely the transfer of information from the dynamic to the static which is still excluded.

## 6.2 What Is to Be Done?

We have only the very basic apparatus of dependently typed programming in place at the moment. We certainly need some way to analyse the results of *intermediate* computations in a way which reflects their significance for the existing type and value information—I have studiously avoided this issue in these notes. In [27], we propose a construct which adds the result of an intermediate computation to the collection of values being scrutinized on the left-hand side, at the same time abstracting it from types. This is not yet implemented.

We shall certainly need coinductive data in order to develop interactive systems. Inspired by the success of monads in Haskell, we shall also need to investigate the enhanced potential for 'categorical packaging' of programming in a language where the notion of category can be made abstract. And of course, there are all the 'modern conveniences': infix operators, ad-hoc polymorphism, generics, and so forth. These require design effort: the underlying expressivity is available, but we need good choices for their high-level presentation.

Work has already begun on a compiler for Epigram [10]: we have barely started to exploit our new wealth of static information for performance. We have the benefit of a large total fragment, in which evaluation strategy is unimportant and program transformation is no longer troubled by $\bot$. The fact that partial evaluation is already a fact of life for us must surely help also.

We need a library, but it's not enough to import the standard presentation of standard functionality. Our library must support the idioms of dependently typed programming, which may well be different. Standardizing too early might be a mistake: we need to explore the design space for standard equipment.

But the greatest potential for change is in the tools of program development. Here, we have barely started. Refinement-style editing is great when you have a plan, but often we don't. We need to develop *refactoring* technology for Epigram, so that we can sharpen our definitions as we learn from experiments. It's seldom straight away that we happen upon exactly the indexed data structure we need.

Moreover, we need editing facilities that reflect the idioms of programming. Many data structures have a rationale behind them—they are intended to relate to other data structures in particular ways and support particular operations. At the moment we write none of this down. The well typed terms are supposed to be a more carefully indexed version of the raw terms—we should have been able to construct them explicitly as such. If only we could express our design principles then we could follow them deliberately. Currently, we engineer coincidences, dreaming up datatypes and operations as if from thin air.

But isn't this just wishful thinking? I claim not. Dependent types, seen through the Curry-Howard lens, can characterize types and programs in a way which editing technology can exploit. We've already seen one class of logical principle reified as a programming operation—the $\Leftarrow$ construct. We've been applying reasoning to the construction of programs on paper for years. We now have what we need to do the same effectively on a computer: a high-level programming language in which reasons and programs not merely coexist but coincide.

## Acknowledgements

I'd like to thank the editors, Tarmo Uustalu and Varmo Vene, and the anonymous referees, for their patience and guidance. I'd also like to thank my colleagues and friends, especially James McKinna, Thorsten Altenkirch, Zhaohui Luo, Paul Callaghan, Randy Pollack, Peter Hancock, Edwin Brady, James Chapman and Peter Morris. Sebastian Hanowski and Wouter Swierstra deserve special credit for the feedback they have given me. Finally, to those who were there in Tartu, thank you for making the experience one I shall always value.

This work was supported by EPSRC grants GR/R72259 and EP/C512022.

## References

1. Andreas Abel and Thorsten Altenkirch. A predicative analysis of structural recursion. *Journal of Functional Programming*, 2000.
2. Thorsten Altenkirch and Bernhard Reus. Monadic presentations of lambda-terms using generalized inductive types. In *Computer Science Logic 1999*, 1999.
3. Lennart Augustsson. Compiling Pattern Matching. In Jean-Pierre Jouannaud, editor, *Functional Programming Languages and Computer Architecture*, volume 201 of *LNCS*, pages 368–381. Springer-Verlag, 1985.

4. Lennart Augustsson. Cayenne—a language with dependent types. In *ACM International Conference on Functional Programming '98*. ACM, 1998.
5. Lennart Augustsson and Magnus Carlsson. An exercise in dependent types: A well-typed interpreter. Available at `http://www.cs.chalmers.se/ augustss/ cayenne/interp.ps`, 1999.
6. Françoise Bellegarde and James Hook. Substitution: A formal methods case study using monads and transformations. *Science of Computer Programming*, 1995.
7. Yves Bertot and Pierre Castéran. *Interactive Theorem Proving and Program Development, Coq'Art: The Calculus of Inductive Constructions*. Texts in Theoretical Computer Science. Springer-Verlag, 2004.
8. Richard Bird and Oege de Moor. *Algebra of Programming*. Prentice Hall, 1997.
9. Richard Bird and Ross Paterson. de Bruijn notation as a nested datatype. *Journal of Functional Programming*, 9(1):77–92, 1999.
10. Edwin Brady. *Practical Implementation of a Dependently Typed Functional Programming Language*. PhD thesis, University of Durham, 2005.
11. L'Équipe Coq. The Coq Proof Assistant Reference Manual. `http://pauillac.inria.fr/coq/doc/main.html`, 2001.
12. Catarina Coquand and Thierry Coquand. Structured Type Theory. In *Workshop on Logical Frameworks and Metalanguages*, 1999.
13. Thierry Coquand. Pattern Matching with Dependent Types. In Bengt Nordström, Kent Petersson, and Gordon Plotkin, editors, *Electronic Proceedings of the Third Annual BRA Workshop on Logical Frameworks (Båstad, Sweden)*, 1992.
14. Nicolas G. de Bruijn. Lambda Calculus notation with nameless dummies: a tool for automatic formula manipulation. *Indagationes Mathematicæ*, 34:381–392, 1972.
15. Peter Dybjer. Inductive Sets and Families in Martin-Löf's Type Theory. In Gérard Huet and Gordon Plotkin, editors, *Logical Frameworks*. CUP, 1991.
16. Daniel Fridlender and Mia Indrika. Do we need dependent types? *Journal of Functional Programming*, 10(4):409–415, 2000.
17. Eduardo Giménez. Codifying guarded definitions with recursive schemes. In Peter Dybjer, Bengt Nordström, and Jan Smith, editors, *Types for Proofs and Programs, '94*, volume 996 of *LNCS*, pages 39–59. Springer-Verlag, 1994.
18. Ralf Lämmel and Simon Peyton Jones. Scrap your boilerplate: a practical design pattern for generic programming. *ACM SIGPLAN Notices*, 38(3):26–37, March 2003. Proc. of the ACM SIGPLAN Workshop on Types in Language Design and Implementation (TLDI 2003).
19. Zhaohui Luo. *Computation and Reasoning: A Type Theory for Computer Science*. Oxford University Press, 1994.
20. Zhaohui Luo and Robert Pollack. LEGO Proof Development System: User's Manual. Technical Report ECS-LFCS-92-211, Laboratory for Foundations of Computer Science, University of Edinburgh, 1992.
21. Lena Magnusson and Bengt Nordström. The ALF proof editor and its proof engine. In Henk Barendregt and Tobias Nipkow, editors, *Types for Proofs and Programs*, LNCS 806. Springer-Verlag, 1994. Selected papers from the Int. Workshop TYPES '93, Nijmegen, May 1993.
22. Per Martin-Löf. A theory of types. manuscript, 1971.
23. Conor McBride. *Dependently Typed Functional Programs and their Proofs*. PhD thesis, University of Edinburgh, 1999. Available from `http://www.lfcs.informatics.ed.ac.uk/reports/00/ECS-LFCS-00-419/`.
24. Conor McBride. Faking It (Simulating Dependent Types in Haskell). *Journal of Functional Programming*, 12(4& 5):375–392, 2002. Special Issue on Haskell.

25. Conor McBride. First-Order Unification by Structural Recursion. *Journal of Functional Programming*, 13(6), 2003.
26. Conor McBride. Epigram, 2004. `http://www.dur.ac.uk/CARG/epigram`.
27. Conor McBride and James McKinna. The view from the left. *Journal of Functional Programming*, 14(1), 2004.
28. Fred McBride. *Computer Aided Manipulation of Symbols*. PhD thesis, Queen's University of Belfast, 1970.
29. Robin Milner, Mads Tofte, Robert Harper, and David MacQueen. *The Definition of Standard ML, revised edition*. MIT Press, 1997.
30. Chris Okasaki. *Purely Functional Data Structures*. Cambridge University Press, 1998.
31. Chris Okasaki. From Fast Exponentiation to Square Matrices: An Adventure in Types. In *ACM International Conference on Functional Programming '99*, 1999.
32. Simon Peyton Jones and John Hughes, editors. *Haskell'98: A Non-Strict Functional Language*, 1999. Available from `http://www.haskell.org/definition`.
33. Simon Peyton Jones, Geoffrey Washburn, and Stephanie Weirich. Wobbly types: type inference for generalised algebraic data types. Unpublished, 2004.
34. Dag Prawitz. *Natural Deduction—A proof theoretical study*. Almquist and Wiksell, Stockholm, 1965.
35. Bengt Nordström, Kent Petersson, and Jan Smith. *Programming in Martin-Löf's type theory: an introduction*. Oxford University Press, 1990.
36. Alan Robinson. A Machine-oriented Logic Based on the Resolution Principle. *Journal of the ACM*, 12:23–41, 1965.
37. David Turner. Elementary Strong Functional Programming. In *Functional Programming Languages in Education, First International Symposium*, volume 1022 of *LNCS*. Springer-Verlag, 1995.
38. Philip Wadler. Views: A way for pattern matching to cohabit with data abstraction. In *Proceedings of POPL '87*. ACM, 1987.
39. Hongwei Xi. *Dependent Types in Practical Programming*. PhD thesis, Department of Mathematical Sciences, Carnegie Mellon University, 1998.
40. Hongwei Xi and Frank Pfenning. Eliminating array bound checking through dependent types. In *Proceedings of the Conference on Programming Language Design and Implementation (PLDI'98)*. ACM Press, 1998.

# Combining Datatypes and Effects

Alberto Pardo

Instituto de Computación, Universidad de la República,
Julio Herrera y Reissig 565, 11300 Montevideo, Uruguay
pardo@fing.edu.uy

**Abstract.** Recursion schemes over datatypes constitute a powerful tool
to structure functional programs. Standard schemes, like map and fold,
have traditionally been studied in the context of purely-functional programs. In this paper we propose the generalization of well-known recursion schemes with the aim to obtain structuring mechanisms for programs
with effects, assuming that effects are modelled by monads. We analyze
the definition as well as the algebraic laws associated with the new recursion schemes. The way monads encapsulate effects plays an important
role in the definition of the monadic recursion schemes, as it permits to
focus on the structure of the recursive programs with effects disregarding the specific details of the effects involved. We illustrate the use of
the recursion schemes and their laws with some traversal algorithms on
graphs.

## 1 Introduction

In functional programming, it is common to find programs written using a compositional design, where a program is constructed as a collection of simple and
easy to write functions which communicate through function composition. Programs so defined are modular and have many benefits, such as clarity and main-
tainability, but unfortunately they are inefficient. Each function composition
$f \circ g$ implies passing information from one function to the other through an intermediate data structure which is produced by $g$ and consumed by $f$. This has
associated a computational cost, since the nodes of the intermediate data structure need to be allocated, filled, inspected and finally discarded from memory.

Intermediate data structures can be removed by the application of a program
transformation technique known as *deforestation* [30]. Diverse approaches to deforestation can be found in the literature [30,11,10,27,23]. In this paper we follow
an approach based on recursive program schemes over data types [18,6,4,8]. By
program schemes we mean higher-order functions that capture common patterns
of computation over data types and help in structuring programs. Typical examples are functions like *map* and *fold* [3], but there are many others. Recursion
schemes have associated algebraic laws, which are useful for formal reasoning
about programs as well as for program transformation purposes. In connection
with deforestation, there is a particularly relevant subset of these laws, the so-
called *fusion laws*, which involve the elimination of intermediate data structures.

V. Varmo and T. Uustalu (Eds.): AFP 2004, LNCS 3622, pp. 171–209, 2005.

The purpose of this paper is to study recursion schemes for programs with effects, assuming that effects are modelled by *monads* [2]. Most of the standard recursion schemes can only deal with purely-functional programs (i.e. effect-free programs). This means that they fail when we try to use them to represent programs with effects. Basically, the problem is with the shape of recursion that such programs possess, which is different from that of purely-functional ones. This raises the necessity of generalizing the existing recursion schemes to cope with the patterns of computations of programs with effects.

The compositional style of programming still holds in the context of programs with effects. This means that we will be interested in eliminating intermediate data structures generated by the composition of monadic programs, but now produced as the result of monadic computations. Our strategy will be therefore the derivation of fusion laws associated with the program schemes for programs with effects in order to restore deforestation in the presence of effects.

The paper is built on previous work on recursion schemes for programs with effects [20,25,24]. In contrast to [25,24], where a more abstract style of presentation based on category theory was followed, in this paper concepts and definitions are described in a functional programming style, using a Haskell-like notation.

The paper is organized as follows. In Section 2 we review some standard recursion schemes and their associated fusion laws. Section 3 presents background material on monads. Section 4 is devoted to the analysis of recursion schemes for programs with effects. We also present examples which illustrate the use of the program schemes and their laws. In Section 5, we conclude the paper with a brief description of a program fusion tool which integrates many of the ideas discussed in the paper.

## 2    Recursive Program Schemes

The program schemes described in the paper encapsulate common patterns of computation of recursive functions and have a strong connection with datatypes. Before presenting well-known recursion schemes for purely-functional programs, we will show a general construction used to capture datatype declarations. Based on that construction, we will be able to give a generic definition of the recursion schemes, parameterised by the structure of some of the datatypes involved.

Throughout we shall assume we are working in the context of a lazy functional language with a *cpo* semantics, in which types are interpreted as pointed cpos (complete partial orders with a least element $\perp$) and functions are interpreted as continuous functions between pointed cpos. As usual, a function $f$ is said to be *strict* if it preserves the least element, i.e. $f \perp = \perp$.

### 2.1    Data Types

The general construction relies on the concept of a *functor*. A functor consists of two components, both denoted by $F$: a type constructor $F$, and a function $F :: (a \rightarrow b) \rightarrow (F\ a \rightarrow F\ b)$, which preserves identities and compositions:

$$F \; id = id \qquad\qquad F \; (f \circ g) = F \, f \circ F \, g$$

A standard example of a functor is that formed by the *List* type constructor and the well-known *map* function, which applies a function to the elements of a list, building a new list with the results.

$$
\begin{aligned}
map & :: (a \to b) \to (List \; a \to List \; b) \\
map \; f \; Nil & = Nil \\
map \; f \; (Cons \; a \; as) & = Cons \; (f \; a) \; (map \; f \; as)
\end{aligned}
$$

We will use functors to capture the structure (or signature) of datatypes. In this paper we will only consider a restricted class of datatypes, called *regular datatypes*. These are datatypes whose declarations contain no function spaces and have recursive occurrences with the same arguments from left-hand sides. The functors corresponding to regular datatypes' signatures will be characterised by an inductive definition, composed by the following basic functors.

**Identity Functor.** The identity functor is defined as the identity type constructor and the identity function (on functions):

**type** $I \; a = a$

$$
\begin{aligned}
I \quad & :: (a \to b) \to (I \; a \to I \; b) \\
I \; f & = f
\end{aligned}
$$

**Constant Functor.** For any type $t$, we can construct a constant functor defined as the constant type constructor and the constant function that maps any function to the identity on $t$:

**type** $\underline{t} \; a = t$

$$
\begin{aligned}
\underline{t} \quad & :: (a \to b) \to (\underline{t} \; a \to \underline{t} \; b) \\
\underline{t} \; f & = id
\end{aligned}
$$

**Product Functor.** The product functor is an example of a *bifunctor* (a functor on two arguments). The product type constructor gives the type of pairs as result. The mapping function takes two functions which are applied to each component of the input pair.

**data** $a \times b \quad = (a, b)$

$$
\begin{aligned}
(\times) \quad & :: (a \to c) \to (b \to d) \to (a \times b \to c \times d) \\
(f \times g) \; (a, b) & = (f \; a, g \; b)
\end{aligned}
$$

The elements of a product can be inspected using the projection functions.

$$
\begin{aligned}
\pi_1 \quad & :: a \times b \to a \\
\pi_1 \; (a, b) & = a
\end{aligned}
$$

$$
\begin{aligned}
\pi_2 \quad & :: a \times b \to b \\
\pi_2 \; (a, b) & = b
\end{aligned}
$$

The split operation allows us to construct a product from a given object.

$$(\triangle) \qquad :: (c \to a) \to (c \to b) \to (c \to a \times b)$$
$$(f \triangle g)\, x = (f\, x, g\, x)$$

Among others, the following laws hold:

$$(f \triangle g) \circ h = (f \circ h) \triangle (g \circ h)$$
$$(f \times g) \circ (h \triangle k) = (f \circ h) \triangle (g \circ k)$$

**Sum Functor.** The sum functor builds the disjoint sum of two types, which are unions of tagged elements.

**data** $a + b \qquad = Left\ a \mid Right\ b$

$$(+) \qquad\qquad :: (a \to c) \to (b \to d) \to (a + b \to c + d)$$
$$(f + g)\,(Left\ a) = Left\,(f\ a)$$
$$(f + g)\,(Right\ b) = Right\,(g\ b)$$

Associated with sums we can define a case analysis operator:

$$(\triangledown) \qquad\qquad :: (a \to c) \to (b \to c) \to (a + b \to c)$$
$$(f \triangledown g)\,(Left\ a) = f\ a$$
$$(f \triangledown g)\,(Right\ b) = g\ b$$

which satisfies the following properties:

$$f\ \text{strict} \;\Rightarrow\; f \circ (g \triangledown h) = f \circ g \triangledown f \circ h$$
$$(f \triangledown g) \circ (h + k) = f \circ h \triangledown g \circ k$$

**Functor Composition.** The composition of two functors $F$ and $G$ is denoted by $F\ G$. In particular, we can define the composition of the bifunctors $\times$ and $+$ with functors $F$ and $G$, written $F \times G$ and $F + G$, as follows:

**type** $(F \times G)\ a = F\ a \times G\ a$
$\phantom{\textbf{type}}(F \times G)\ f \quad = F\ f \times G\ f$

**type** $(F + G)\ a \ = F\ a + G\ a$
$\phantom{\textbf{type}}(F + G)\ f \quad = F\ f + G\ f$

**Regular Functors.** Regular functors are functors built from identities, constants, products, sums, compositions and type functors.

$$F ::= I \mid \underline{t} \mid F \times F \mid F + F \mid F\ F \mid D$$

$D$ stands for type functors, which are functors corresponding to polymorphic recursive datatypes (the *List* functor is an example). Their definition is given in Section 2.3.

**The General Construction.** The idea is to describe the top level structure of a datatype by means of a functor. Consider a regular datatype declaration,

$$\textbf{data } \tau = C_1\ \tau_{1,1} \cdots \tau_{1,k_1} \mid \cdots \mid C_n\ \tau_{n,1} \cdots \tau_{n,k_n}$$

The assumption that $\tau$ is regular implies that each $\tau_{i,j}$ is restricted to the following forms: some constant type $t$ (like $Int$, $Char$, or even a type variable); a type constructor $D$ (e.g. $List$) applied to a type $\tau'_{i,j}$; or $\tau$ itself.

The derivation of a functor from a datatype declaration then proceeds as follows:

- pack the arguments of the constructors in tuples; for constant constructors (i.e. those with no arguments) we place the empty tuple ();
- regard alternatives as sums, replacing | by +; and
- substitute the occurrences of $\tau$ by a type variable $a$ in every $\tau_{i,j}$.

As a result, we obtain the following type constructor:

$$F\ a = \sigma_{1,1} \times \cdots \times \sigma_{1,k_1} + \cdots + \sigma_{n,1} \times \cdots \times \sigma_{n,k_n}$$

where $\sigma_{i,j} = \tau_{i,j}[\tau := a]$[1]. The body of the mapping function $F :: (a \to b) \to (F\ a \to F\ b)$ is similar to that of $F\ a$, with the difference that now we substitute the occurrences of the type variable $a$ by a function $f :: a \to b$, and write identities in the other positions:

$$Ff = \overline{\sigma}_{1,1} \times \cdots \times \overline{\sigma}_{1,k_1} + \cdots + \overline{\sigma}_{n,1} \times \cdots \times \overline{\sigma}_{n,k_n}$$

with

$$\overline{\sigma}_{i,j} = \begin{cases} f & \text{if } \sigma_{i,j} = a \\ id & \text{if } \sigma_{i,j} = t, \text{ for some type } t \\ D\,\overline{\sigma}'_{i,j} & \text{if } \sigma_{i,j} = D\,\sigma'_{i,j} \end{cases}$$

*Example 1.*

- For the datatype of natural numbers,

    **data** $Nat = Zero \mid Succ\ Nat$

    we can derive a functor $N$ given by

    **type** $N\ a = () + a$

    $N \qquad :: (a \to b) \to (N\ a \to N\ b)$
    $N\ f \quad = id + f$

    As a functorial expression, $N = \underline{()} + I$.

- For a datatype of arithmetic expressions:

    **data** $Exp = Num\ Int \mid Add\ Exp\ Exp$

    we can derive a functor $E$ given by

    **type** $E\ a = Int + Exp \times Exp$

    $E \qquad :: (a \to b) \to (E\ a \to E\ b)$
    $E\ f \quad = id + f \times f$

    As a functorial expression, $E = \underline{Int} + I \times I$.

---

[1] By $s[t := a]$ we denote the replacement of every occurrence of $t$ by $a$ in $s$.

– For the datatype of lists,

$$List\ a = Nil \mid Cons\ a\ (List\ a)$$

we can derive a functor $L_a$ given by

**type** $L_a\ b = () + a \times b$

$$
\begin{aligned}
L_a & \quad :: (b \to c) \to (L_a\ b \to L_a\ c) \\
L_a\ f & \quad = id + id \times f
\end{aligned}
$$

As a functorial expression, $L_a = () + \underline{a} \times I$. Notice that in this case the functor is parameterised. This happens with the signature of every polymorphic datatype, since it is necessary to reflect in the functor the presence of the type parameter. A parameterised functor $F_a$ is actually the partial application of a bifunctor $F$: **type** $F_a\ b = F\ a\ b$ and $F_a\ f = F\ id\ f$.    □

Every (recursive) regular datatype is then understood as a solution of an equation $Fx \cong x$, being $F$ the functor that captures its signature. A solution to this equation corresponds to a fixed point of the functor $F$, given by a type $t$ and an isomorphism between $F\ t$ and $t$. The underlying semantics in terms of cpos ensures the existence of a unique (up to isomorphism) fixed point to every regular functor $F$ whose type is denoted by $\mu F$. The isomorphism is provided by the strict functions,

$$F\mu F \xrightleftharpoons[out_F]{in_F} \mu F$$

each the inverse of the other, such that $in_F$ ($out_F$) packs the constructors (destructors) of the datatype. The type $\mu F$ contains partial, finite as well as infinite values. Further details can be found in [1,8].

*Example 2.*

– In the case of the datatype of natural numbers, the corresponding isomorphism is given by the type $\mu N = Nat$ and the functions $in_N$ and $out_N$:

$$
\begin{aligned}
in_N & \quad :: N\ Nat \to Nat \\
in_N & \quad = const\ Zero \bigtriangledown Succ
\end{aligned}
$$

$$
\begin{aligned}
out_N & \quad :: Nat \to N\ Nat \\
out_N\ Zero & \quad = Left\ () \\
out_N\ (Succ\ n) & \quad = Right\ n
\end{aligned}
$$

$$
\begin{aligned}
const & \quad :: a \to b \to a \\
const\ a\ b & \quad = a
\end{aligned}
$$

– In the case of the datatype of lists, the corresponding isomorphism is given by the type $\mu L_a = List\ a$ and the functions $in_{L_a}$ and $out_{L_a}$:

$$
\begin{aligned}
in_{L_a} & \quad :: L_a\ (List\ a) \to List\ a \\
in_{L_a} & \quad = const\ Nil \bigtriangledown uncurry\ Cons
\end{aligned}
$$

$$out_{L_a} \qquad\qquad :: List\ a \to L_a\ (List\ a)$$
$$out_{L_a}\ Nil \qquad\quad = Left\ ()$$
$$out_{L_a}\ (Cons\ a\ as) = Right\ (a, as)$$

$$uncurry \qquad\qquad :: (a \to b \to c) \to (a \times b \to c)$$
$$uncurry\ f\ (a, b) \quad = f\ a\ b \qquad\qquad\qquad\qquad\qquad\qquad\qquad \Box$$

## 2.2 Fold

Fold is a pattern of recursion that captures funcion definitions by structural recursion. The best known example of fold is the definition for lists,

$$fold_L \qquad\qquad :: (b, a \to b \to b) \to List\ a \to b$$
$$fold_L\ (h_1, h_2) = f_L$$
**where**
$$f_L\ Nil \qquad\quad = h_1$$
$$f_L\ (Cons\ a\ as) = h_2\ a\ (f_L\ as)$$

which corresponds to the *foldr* operator [3], but the same construction can be generalized to any regular datatype.

The general definition of *fold* can be represented by the following diagram:

$$
\begin{array}{ccc}
\mu F & \xrightarrow{\ fold\ h\ } & a \\[4pt]
{\scriptstyle in_F}\big\uparrow & & \big\uparrow{\scriptstyle h} \\[4pt]
F\mu F & \xrightarrow[F\ (fold\ h)]{} & F\ a
\end{array}
$$

Since $out_F$ is the inverse of the isomorphism $in_F$, we can write:

$$fold \quad :: (F\ a \to a) \to \mu F \to a$$
$$fold\ h = h \circ F\ (fold\ h) \circ out_F$$

A function $h :: F\ a \to a$ is called an *F-algebra*. The functor $F$ plays the role of signature of the algebra, as it encodes the information about the operations of the algebra. The type $a$ is called the carrier of the algebra. An *F-homomorphism* between two algebras $h :: F\ a \to a$ and $k :: F\ b \to b$ is a function $f :: a \to b$ between the carriers that commutes with the operations. This is specified by the condition $f \circ h = k \circ F\ f$. Notice that fold is a homomorphism from $in_F$ to $h$.

*Remark 1.* When writing the instances of the program schemes, we will adopt the following notational convention for algebras: We will write $(h'_1, \ldots, h'_n)$ instead of $h_1 \triangledown \cdots \triangledown h_n :: F\ a \to a$, such that, $h'_i = v$ when $h_i = const\ v :: () \to a$, or $h'_i :: \tau_1 \to \cdots \to \tau_k \to a$ is the curried version of $h_i :: \tau_1 \times \cdots \times \tau_k \to a$. For example, given an algebra $const\ v \triangledown f :: L_a\ b \to b$ we will write $(e, curry\ f) :: (b, a \to b \to b)$. $\qquad \Box$

*Example 3.* The following are instances of fold for different datatypes.

*Natural numbers*

$$fold_N \qquad :: (a, a \to a) \to Nat \to a$$
$$fold_N\ (h_1, h_2) = f_N$$
$$\textbf{where}$$
$$\qquad f_N\ Zero \quad = h_1$$
$$\qquad f_N\ (Succ\ n)\ = h_2\ (f_N\ n)$$

For instance, addition can be defined as:

$$add \quad :: Nat \to Nat \to Nat$$
$$add\ m = fold_N\ (m, Succ)$$

*Leaf-labelled binary trees*

$$\textbf{data}\ Btree\ a = Leaf\ a \mid Join\ (Btree\ a)\ (Btree\ a)$$

$$\textbf{type}\ B_a\ b \quad = a + b \times b$$

$$B_a \qquad\qquad :: (b \to c) \to (B_a\ b \to B_a\ c)$$
$$B_a\ f \qquad\quad = id + f \times f$$

$$fold_B \qquad\qquad :: (a \to b, b \to b \to b) \to Btree\ a \to b$$
$$fold_B\ (h_1, h_2) = f_B$$
$$\textbf{where}$$
$$\qquad f_B\ (Leaf\ a) \quad = h_1\ a$$
$$\qquad f_B\ (Join\ t\ t') = h_2\ (f_B\ t)\ (f_B\ t')$$

For instance,

$$mirror \qquad\qquad :: Btree\ a \to Btree\ a$$
$$mirror\ (Leaf\ a) \quad = Leaf\ a$$
$$mirror\ (Join\ t\ t') = Join\ (mirror\ t')\ (mirror\ t)$$

can be defined as:

$$mirror = fold_B\ (Leaf, \lambda t\ t' \to Join\ t'\ t) \qquad\qquad \square$$

Fold enjoys some algebraic laws that are useful for program transformation. A law that plays an important role is *fold fusion*. It states that the composition of a fold with a homomorphism is again a fold.

$$f\ strict\ \wedge\ f \circ h = k \circ F\ f\ \Rightarrow\ f \circ fold\ h = fold\ k$$

The next law is known as *acid rain* or *fold-fold fusion*. The goal of acid rain is to combine functions that produce and consume elements of an intermediate data structure. The intermediate datatype is required to be generated by a fold whose algebra is given in terms of a polymorphic function.

$$\tau :: \forall\ a\ .\ (F\ a \to a) \to (G\ a \to a)$$
$$\Rightarrow$$
$$fold\ h \circ fold\ (\tau\ in_F) = fold\ (\tau\ h)$$

*Remark 2.* We will adopt a samilar notational convention as for algebras for writing functions $\tau$ as part of the instances of programs schemes. Concretely, in the instances we will regard a function $\tau$ as a function between tuples. That is, if $h_1 \triangledown \cdots \triangledown h_m = \tau(k_1 \triangledown \cdots \triangledown k_n)$, then we will understand this transformation between algebras as $(h'_1, \ldots, h'_m) = \tau(k'_1, \ldots, k'_n)$, where each $h'_i$ and $k'_j$ is obtained from $h_i$ and $k_j$, respectively, by the convention for algebras. The following example uses this convention.                    □

*Example 4.* We use acid-rain to show that

$$size_B \circ mirror = size_B$$

where

$$size_B :: Btree\ a \rightarrow Int$$
$$size_B = fold_B\ (const\ 1, (+))$$

counts the number of leaves of a binary tree. The proof proceeds as follows:

$$
\begin{aligned}
&size_B \circ mirror\\
=\quad&\{\ \text{definition of } size_B \text{ and } mirror\ \}\\
&fold_B\ (const\ 1, (+)) \circ fold_B\ (Leaf, \lambda t\ t' \rightarrow Join\ t'\ t)\\
=\quad&\{\ \text{define } \tau\ (h_1, h_2) = (h_1, \lambda x\ x' \rightarrow h_2\ x'\ x)\ \}\\
&fold_B\ (const\ 1, (+)) \circ fold_B\ (\tau\ in_{B_a})\\
=\quad&\{\ \text{acid rain}\ \}\\
&fold_B\ (\tau\ (const\ 1, (+)))\\
=\quad&\{\ \text{definition of } \tau\ \}\\
&fold_B\ (const\ 1, \lambda x\ x' \rightarrow x' + x)\\
=\quad&\{\ \text{commutativity of } +, \text{section } (+)\ \}\\
&fold_B\ (const\ 1, (+))\\
=\quad&\{\ \text{definition of } size_B\ \}\\
&size_B
\end{aligned}
$$

□

## 2.3   Type Functors

Every polymorphic regular datatype gives rise to a polymorphic type constructor $D\ a = \mu F_a$, which can be made into a functor (called a type functor) by defining its mapping function:

$$D\quad :: (a \rightarrow b) \rightarrow (D\ a \rightarrow D\ b)$$
$$D\ f = fold\ (in_{F_b} \circ F\ f\ id)$$

*Example 5.*

*Lists* The list type functor corresponds to the standard *map* function [3]:

$$List\quad :: (a \rightarrow b) \rightarrow (List\ a \rightarrow List\ b)$$
$$List\ f = fold_L\ (Nil, \lambda a\ bs \rightarrow Cons\ (f\ a)\ bs)$$

that is,

$$List\ f\ Nil \qquad\quad = Nil$$
$$List\ f\ (Cons\ a\ as) = Cons\ (f\ a)\ (List\ f\ as)$$

*Leaf-labelled binary trees*

$$Btree \quad :: (a \to b) \to (Btree\ a \to Btree\ b)$$
$$Btree\ f = fold_B\ (Leaf \circ f, Join)$$

that is,

$$Btree\ f\ (Leaf\ a) \quad = Leaf\ (f\ a)$$
$$Btree\ f\ (Join\ t\ t') = Join\ (Btree\ f\ t)\ (Btree\ f\ t') \qquad \qquad \square$$

*Example 6.* Rose trees are multiway branching structures:

**data** *Rose a = Fork a (List (Rose a))*

The signature of rose trees is captured by a functor $R_a$ given by

**type** $R_a\ b = a\ \times\ List\ b$

$$R_a \qquad :: (b \to c) \to (R_a\ b \to R_a\ c)$$
$$R_a\ f \qquad = id\ \times\ List\ f$$

As a functorial expression, $R_a = \underline{a}\ \times\ List$. The fold operator is defined by,

$$fold_R \quad :: (R_a\ b \to b) \to Rose\ a \to b$$
$$fold_R\ h = f_R$$
$$\textbf{where}$$
$$f_R\ (Fork\ a\ rs) = h\ a\ (List\ f_R\ rs)$$

$$\square$$

A standard property of type functors is *map-fold fusion*. This law states that a map followed by a fold is a fold.

$$fold\ h \circ D\ f = fold\ (h \circ F\ f\ id)$$

## 2.4   Unfold

Let us now analyze the dual case. The corresponding pattern of recursion, called *unfold* [9,12], captures function definitions by structural corecursion. By corecursion we understand functions whose structure is dictated by that of the values produced as result. Unfold has a pattern of recursion given by the following scheme:

Proceeding as with fold, since $in_F$ is the inverse of $out_F$, we can write:

$$unfold \quad :: (a \to F\ a) \to a \to \mu F$$
$$unfold\ g = in_F \circ F\ (unfold\ g) \circ g$$

*Example 7.* The following are instances of unfold for different datatypes.

*Natural numbers*

$$unfold_N \quad :: (a \to N\ a) \to a \to Nat$$
$$unfold_N\ g\ a = \textbf{case}\ (g\ a)\ \textbf{of}$$
$$\qquad Left\ () \quad \to Zero$$
$$\qquad Right\ a' \to Succ\ (unfold_N\ g\ a')$$

*Lists*

$$unfold_L \quad :: (b \to L_a\ b) \to b \to List\ a$$
$$unfold_L\ g\ b = \textbf{case}\ (g\ b)\ \textbf{of}$$
$$\qquad Left\ () \quad\quad \to Nil$$
$$\qquad Right\ (a, b') \to Cons\ a\ (unfold_L\ g\ b')$$

*Leaf-labelled binary trees*

$$unfold_B \quad :: (b \to B_a\ b) \to b \to Btree\ a$$
$$unfold_B\ g\ b = \textbf{case}\ (g\ b)\ \textbf{of}$$
$$\qquad Left\ a \quad\quad \to Leaf\ a$$
$$\qquad Right\ (b1, b2) \to Join\ (unfold_B\ g\ b1)\ (unfold_B\ g\ b2)$$

*Rose trees*

$$unfold_R \quad :: (b \to R_a\ b) \to b \to Rose\ a$$
$$unfold_R\ g\ b = \textbf{let}\ (a, bs) = g\ b$$
$$\qquad\quad \textbf{in}\ Fork\ a\ (List\ (unfold_R\ g)\ bs)$$

□

A function $g :: a \to F\ a$ is called an *F-coalgebra*. A *F-homomorphism* between two coalgebras $g :: a \to F\ a$ and $g' :: b \to F\ b$ is a function $f :: a \to b$ such that $g' \circ f = F\ f \circ g$.

There is a corresponding *fusion* law for unfold, which states that the composition of a homomorphism with an unfold is again an unfold.

$$g' \circ f = F\ f \circ g \quad \Rightarrow \quad unfold\ g' \circ f = unfold\ g$$

There is also an acid rain law, called *unfold-unfold fusion*.

$$\sigma :: \forall a\ .\ (a \to F\ a) \to (a \to G\ a)$$
$$\Rightarrow$$
$$unfold\ (\sigma\ out_F) \circ unfold\ g = unfold\ (\sigma\ g)$$

## 2.5  Hylomorphism

Now we look at functions given by the composition of a fold with an unfold. They capture the idea of general recursive functions whose structure is dictated by that of a virtual data structure.

Given an algebra $h :: F\ b \to b$ and a coalgebra $g :: a \to F\ a$, a *hylomorphism* [18,19,27,23] is a function $hylo\ h\ g :: a \to b$ defined by

$$hylo\ h\ g\ =\ a\ \xrightarrow{\ unfold\ g\ }\ \mu F\ \xrightarrow{\ fold\ h\ }\ b \tag{1}$$

An alternative definition of hylomorphism shows that it is not necessary to construct the intermediate data structure:

$$hylo :: (F\ b \to b) \to (a \to F\ a) \to a \to b$$
$$hylo\ h\ g = h \circ F\ (hylo\ h\ g) \circ g$$

that is,

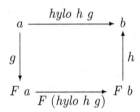

From this definition it is easy to see that fold and unfold are special cases of hylomorphism.

$$fold\ h = hylo\ h\ out_F \qquad\qquad unfold\ g = hylo\ in_F\ g$$

*Example 8.* We show the definition of hylomorphism for different datatypes.

*Lists*

$$hylo_L \qquad\qquad :: (c, a \to c \to c) \to (b \to L_a\ b) \to b \to c$$
$$hylo_L\ (h_1, h_2)\ g\ b = hylo$$
$$\textbf{where}$$
$$\quad hylo\ b = \textbf{case}\ (g\ b)\ \textbf{of}$$
$$\qquad\qquad Left\ () \qquad \to h_1$$
$$\qquad\qquad Right\ (a, b') \to h_2\ a\ (hylo\ b')$$

For example, the function that computes the factorial of a number

$$fact \qquad\qquad :: Int \to Int$$
$$fact\ n \mid n < 1 \quad\ = 1$$
$$\qquad \mid otherwise = n * fact\ (n - 1)$$

can be written as:

$$fact = hylo_L\ (1, (*))\ g$$
$$\quad \textbf{where}$$
$$\qquad g\ n \mid n < 1 \quad\ = Left\ ()$$
$$\qquad\quad \mid otherwise = Right\ (n, n - 1)$$

The reason of presenting *fact* as a hylomorphism associated with lists is because there is a virtual list that can be seen reflected in the form of the call-tree. Such a list can be made explicit by using (1):

$$fact = prod \circ upto$$

$$prod :: List\ Int \to Int$$
$$prod = fold_L\ (1, (*))$$

$$upto \qquad\qquad :: Int \rightarrow List\ Int$$
$$upto\ n \mid n < 1 \quad = Nil$$
$$\mid otherwise = Cons\ n\ (upto\ (n - 1))$$

*Internally-labelled binary trees*

**data** *Tree a*     $= Empty \mid Node\ (Tree\ a)\ a\ (Tree\ a)$

**type** $T_a\ b$     $= () + b \times a \times b$

$$T_a \qquad\qquad :: (b \rightarrow c) \rightarrow (T_a\ b \rightarrow T_a\ c)$$
$$T_a\ f \qquad\qquad = id + f \times id \times f$$

$$hylo_T \qquad\qquad :: (c, c \rightarrow a \rightarrow c \rightarrow c) \rightarrow (b \rightarrow T_a\ b) \rightarrow b \rightarrow c$$
$$hylo_T\ (h_1, h_2)\ g = hylo$$
$$\textbf{where}$$
$$hylo\ b = \textbf{case}\ (g\ b)\ \textbf{of}$$
$$\qquad Left\ () \qquad\qquad \rightarrow h_1$$
$$\qquad Right\ (b1, a, b2) \rightarrow h_2\ (hylo\ b1)\ a\ (hylo\ b2)$$

For example, the usual definition of quicksort

$$qsort \qquad\qquad :: Ord\ a \Rightarrow List\ a \rightarrow List\ a$$
$$qsort\ Nil \qquad\quad = Nil$$
$$qsort\ (Cons\ a\ as) = qsort\ [x \mid x \leftarrow as; x \leqslant a]$$
$$\qquad\qquad\qquad\quad +\!\!+\ wrap\ a\ +\!\!+$$
$$\qquad\qquad\qquad\quad qsort\ [x \mid x \leftarrow as; x > a]$$

$$wrap \qquad\qquad :: a \rightarrow List\ a$$
$$wrap\ a \qquad\qquad = Cons\ a\ Nil$$

can be written as a hylomorphism as follows:

$$qsort = hylo_T\ (Nil, h)\ g$$
$$\qquad \textbf{where}$$
$$\qquad h\ ys\ a\ zs \qquad = ys\ +\!\!+\ wrap\ a\ +\!\!+\ zs$$
$$\qquad g\ Nil \qquad\qquad = Left\ ()$$
$$\qquad g\ (Cons\ a\ as) = Right\ ([x \mid x \leftarrow as; x \leqslant a], a, [x \mid x \leftarrow as; x > a])$$

$$\square$$

The following fusion laws are a direct consequence of (1).

**Hylo Fusion.**

$$f\ strict \wedge f \circ h = k \circ F\ f \;\Rightarrow\; f \circ hylo\ h\ g = hylo\ k\ g$$
$$g' \circ f = F\ f \circ g \;\Rightarrow\; hylo\ h\ g' \circ f = hylo\ h\ g$$

**Hylo-Fold Fusion.**

$$\tau :: \forall a\ .\ (F\ a \rightarrow a) \rightarrow (G\ a \rightarrow a)$$
$$\Rightarrow$$
$$fold\ h \circ hylo\ (\tau\ in_F)\ g = hylo\ (\tau\ h)\ g$$

**Unfold-Hylo Fusion.**

$$\sigma :: \forall\, a \,.\, (a \to F\ a) \to (a \to G\ a)$$

$$\Rightarrow$$

$$hylo\ h\ (\sigma\ out_F) \circ unfold\ g = hylo\ h\ (\sigma\ g)$$

## 3    Monads

It is well-known that computational effects, such as exceptions, side-effects, or input/output, can be uniformly modelled in terms of algebraic structures called monads [21,2]. In functional programming, monads are a powerful mechanism to structure functional programs that produce effects [31].

A *monad* is usually presented as a *Kleisli triple* $(m, return, \ggg)$ composed by a type constructor $m$, a polymorphic function *return* and a polymorphic operator $(\ggg)$ often pronounced *bind*. The natural way to define a monad in Haskell is by means of a class.

    **class** *Monad m* **where**
       $return :: a \to m\ a$
       $(\ggg)\ :: m\ a \to (a \to m\ b) \to m\ b$

Computations delivering values of type $a$ are regarded as objects of type $m\ a$, and can be understood as terms with remaining computation steps. The bind operator describes how computations are combined. An expression of the form $m \ggg \lambda x \to m'$ is read as follows: evaluate computation $m$, bind the variable $x$ to the resulting value of this computation, and then continue with the evaluation of computation $m'$. How the effect is passed around is a matter for each monad. In some cases, we may not be interested in binding the result of the first computation to be used in the second. This can be performed by an operator pronounced *then*,

    $(\gg)\qquad :: Monad\ m \Rightarrow m\ a \to m\ b \to m\ b$
    $m \gg m' = m \ggg \lambda\_ \to m'$

Formally, to be a monad, the components of the triple must satisfy the following equations:

$$m \ggg return = m \tag{2}$$

$$return\ a \ggg \lambda x \to m = m\ [x := a] \tag{3}$$

$$(m \ggg \lambda x \to m') \ggg \lambda y \to m'' = m \ggg \lambda x \to (m' \ggg \lambda y \to m'') \tag{4}$$

In (4) $x$ cannot appear free in $m''$. The expression $m\ [x := a]$ means the substitution of all free occurrences of $x$ by $a$ in $m$.

With the introduction of monads the focus of attention is now on functions of type $a \to m\ b$, often referred to as *monadic functions*, which produce an effect when applied to an argument. Given a monadic function $f :: a \to m\ b$, we define $f^\star :: m\ a \to m\ b$ as $f^\star\ m = m \ggg f$. Using the same idea it is possible to define the *Kleisli composition* of two monadic functions,

$$(\bullet) \qquad :: Monad\ m \Rightarrow (b \rightarrow m\ c) \rightarrow (a \rightarrow m\ b) \rightarrow (a \rightarrow m\ c)$$
$$(f \bullet g)\ a = g\ a \ggg f$$

Now we can assign a meaning to the laws of Kleisli triples. The first two laws amount to say that *return* is a left and right identity with respect to Kleisli composition, whereas the last one expresses that composition is associative. Note that $f \bullet g = f^{*} \circ g$.

Associated with every monad we can define also a map function, which applies a function to the result yielded by a computation, and a lifting operator, which turns an arbitrary function into a monadic function.

$$mmap \qquad :: Monad\ m \Rightarrow (a \rightarrow b) \rightarrow (m\ a \rightarrow m\ b)$$
$$mmap\ f\ m = m \ggg \lambda a \rightarrow return\ (f\ a)$$

$$(\widehat{\phantom{f}}) \qquad :: (a \rightarrow b) \rightarrow (a \rightarrow m\ b)$$
$$\widehat{f} \qquad = return \circ f$$

Using the Kleisli triple's laws it can be easily verified that both *mmap* and $(\widehat{\phantom{f}})$ happen to be functorial on functions:

$$mmap\ id\ =\ id \qquad\qquad \widehat{id}\ =\ return$$
$$mmap\ (f \circ g)\ =\ mmap\ f \circ mmap\ g \qquad\qquad \widehat{f \circ g}\ =\ \widehat{f} \bullet \widehat{g}$$

*Example 9.* The *exception monad* models the occurrence of exceptions in a program.

**data** *Exc a*  $= Ok\ a \mid Fail\ Exception$
**type** *Exception* $= String$

**instance** *Monad Exc* **where**
   $return\ a \qquad = Ok\ a$
   $(Ok\ a) \ggg f = f\ a$
   $(Fail\ e) \ggg f = Fail\ e$

This monad captures computations which either succeed returning a value, or fail raising a specific exception signaled by a value of type *Exception*. The *return* operation takes a value and returns a computation that always succeeds, whereas bind may be thought of as a kind of *strict* function application that propagates an exception if one occurs.

When there is a unique exception value, the exception monad is often referred to as the *maybe monad*.

**data** *Maybe a* $= Just\ a \mid Nothing$

**instance** *Monad Maybe* **where**
   $return\ a \qquad = Just\ a$
   $(Just\ a) \ggg f = f\ a$
   $Nothing \ggg f = Nothing$

□

*Example 10.* State-based computations are modelled by the *state monad.* These are computations that take an initial state and return a value and a possibly modified state.

**newtype** *State s a = State (s → (a, s))*

**instance** *Monad (State s)* **where**
    *return x*      *= State (λs → (x, s))*
    *State c ≫ f = State (λs →* **let** *(a, s')*  *= c s*
                              *State c' = f a*
                  **in** *c' s')*

The bind operator combines two computations in sequence so that the state and value resulting from the first computation are supplied to the second one.

The state monad has been used as an effective tool for encapsulating actual imperative features, such as, mutable variables, destructive data structures, and input/output, while retaining fundamental properties of the language (see [26,14,13]). The idea is to hide the *real* state in an abstract data type (based on the monad) which is equipped with primitive operations that internally access the real state [31,5,13].       □

*Example 11.* The *list monad* enables us to describe computations that produce a list of results, which can be used to model a form of nondeterminism.

**instance** *Monad List* **where**
    *return*           *= wrap*
    *Nil*        *≫ f = Nil*
    *(Cons a as) ≫ f = f a ++ (as ≫ f)*

This monad can be seen as a generalization of the maybe monad: a computation of type *List a* may succeed with several outcomes, or fail by returning no result at all.       □

With the aim at improving readability of monadic programs, Haskell provides a special syntax called the *do notation.* It is defined by the following translation rules:

$$\textbf{do } \{x \leftarrow m; m'\} = m \gg\!\!= \lambda x \rightarrow \textbf{do } \{m'\}$$
$$\textbf{do } \{m; m'\} = m \gg \textbf{do } \{m'\}$$
$$\textbf{do } \{m\} = m$$

## 4 Recursion with Monadic Effects

Recursion and monads turn out to be two important structuring devices in functional programming. In this section we combine them with the aim to obtain structuring mechanisms for recursive programs with effects. A natural result of this combination will be the generalization of the existing recursion schemes to work with programs with effects. The way monads encapsulate effects turns out to be essential for this integration, since it permits to focus on the relevant structure of recursive programs disregarding the specific details of the effects they produce.

The fusion laws associated with the monadic program schemes are particularly interesting because they encapsulate new cases of deforestation. However, as we will see later, some of the fusion laws require very strong conditions for their application, reducing dramatically their possibilities to be considered in practice. To overcome this problem we will introduce alternative fusion laws, which, though not so powerful, turn out to be useful in practice.

Two alternative approaches can be adopted to the definition of monadic program schemes. One of them, to be presented first, is a strictly structural approach based on a *lifting* construction. This means to translate to the monadic universe the constructions that characterize the recursion schemes, as well as the concepts that take part in them. The other approach, to be presented in Subsection 4.8, is more pragmatical and turns out to be more useful in practice.

## 4.1 Lifting

Let us start explaining the notion of lifting. Our goal is to define program schemes that capture the recursion structure of functions with effects. Consider the pattern of recursion captured by hylomorphism:

$$
\begin{array}{ccc}
a & \xrightarrow{\ hylo\ } & b \\
g \downarrow & & \uparrow h \\
F\ a & \xrightarrow[F\ hylo]{} & F\ b
\end{array}
$$

By lifting we mean that we view each arrow of this diagram as an effect-producing function (a somehow *imperative* view). By thinking functionally, we make the effects explicit, giving rise to the following recursion scheme:

$$
\begin{array}{ccc}
a & \xrightarrow{\ mhylo\ } & m\ b \\
g \downarrow & & \uparrow h^\star \\
m\ (F\ a) & \xrightarrow[(\widehat{F}\ mhylo)^\star]{} & m\ (F\ b)
\end{array}
\tag{5}
$$

where $h :: F\ b \to m\ b$, $g :: a \to m\ (F\ a)$ and $\widehat{F} :: (a \to m\ b) \to (F\ a \to m\ (F\ b))$, for an arbitrary monad $m$. These ingredients are monadic versions of the notions of algebra, coalgebra and functor, respectively. Before introducing the monadic versions of fold, unfold and hylomorphism, we analyze first the $\widehat{F}$ construction, since it plays an essential role in the strictly structural approach to the definition of the monadic recursive program schemes.

## 4.2   Monadic Extension of a Functor

The *monadic extension* of a functor $F$ [7,28,24] is a function

$$\widehat{F} :: (a \to m\ b) \to (F\ a \to m\ (F\ b))$$

whose action embodies that of $F$. Monadic extensions are used to express the structure of the recursive calls in monadic functions. Every monadic extension $\widehat{F}$ is in one-to-one correspondence with a *distributive law*

$$dist_F :: F\ (m\ a) \to m\ (F\ a)$$

a polymorphic function that performs the distribution of a functor over a monad. In fact, for each distributive law $dist_F$, the action of $\widehat{F}$ on a function $f :: a \to m\ b$ can be defined by

$$\widehat{F}\ f\ =\ F\ a\ \xrightarrow{\ F\ f\ }\ F\ (m\ b)\ \xrightarrow{\ dist_F\ }\ m\ (F\ b) \tag{6}$$

Hence, $\widehat{F}\ f$ first applies $f$ to each argument position of type $a$ within a compound value of type $F\ a$, and then joins the monadic effects produced in each function application into a computation that delivers a compound value of type $F\ b$. Conversely, given a monadic extension $\widehat{F}$, the corresponding distributive law is given by $dist_F = \widehat{F}\ id$.

A definition of the distributive law $dist_F :: F\ (m\ a) \to m\ (F\ a)$ for each regular functor $F$ can be given by induction on the structure of $F$:

$$
\begin{aligned}
dist_I &= id & dist_{F \times G} &= dist_\times \circ (dist_F \times dist_G) \\
dist_{\underline{t}} &= return & dist_{F+G} &= dist_+ \circ (dist_F + dist_G) \\
dist_{FG} &= dist_F \circ F\ dist_G & dist_D &= fold\ (mmap\ in_{Fa} \circ dist_F)
\end{aligned}
$$

where

$$
\begin{aligned}
dist_+ &:: m\ a + m\ b \to m\ (a + b) \\
dist_+ &= \lambda s \to \textbf{case } s \textbf{ of} \\
&\qquad\qquad Left\ ma\ \to \textbf{do}\ a \leftarrow ma \\
&\qquad\qquad\qquad\qquad\quad return\ (Left\ a) \\
&\qquad\qquad Right\ mb \to \textbf{do}\ b \leftarrow mb \\
&\qquad\qquad\qquad\qquad\quad return\ (Right\ b)
\end{aligned}
$$

In the case of $dist_D$, with $D\ a = \mu F_a$, $dist_F :: F\ (m\ a)\ (m\ b) \to m\ (F\ a\ b)$ represents a distributive law for the bifunctor $F$. Distributive laws for regular bifunctors can be defined analogously by induction.

The inductive definition of $dist_F$ given above is parametric in the distributive law for the product functor

$$dist_\times :: (m\ a, m\ b) \to m\ (a, b)$$

Here we have two equally valid alternatives to choose. One is to define $dist_\times$ as a left-to-right product distribution,

$$dist_\times\ (m, m') = \textbf{do}\ \{a \leftarrow m; b \leftarrow m'; return\ (a, b)\}$$

combining a pair of computations by first evaluating the first one and then the second. The other alternative is to evaluate the computations from right-to-left,

$$dist_\times \ (m, m') = \mathbf{do} \ \{ b \leftarrow m'; a \leftarrow m; return \ (a, b) \}$$

A monad is said to be *commutative* if both alternatives produce the same result on the same input. Monads like identity or state reader [31] are commutative. Examples of noncommutative monads are state and list.

*Example 12.* Assuming that $dist_\times$ proceeds from left-to-right, the following are examples of distributive laws:

$$dist_N \ :: \ Monad \ m \Rightarrow N \ (m \ a) \rightarrow m \ (N \ a)$$
$$dist_N \ = \lambda x \rightarrow \mathbf{case} \ x \ \mathbf{of}$$
$$\qquad\qquad Left \ () \quad \rightarrow return \ (Left \ ())$$
$$\qquad\qquad Right \ ma \rightarrow \mathbf{do} \ a \leftarrow ma$$
$$\qquad\qquad\qquad\qquad\qquad return \ (Right \ a)$$

$$dist_{L_a} \ :: \ Monad \ m \Rightarrow L \ a \ (m \ b) \rightarrow m \ (L \ a \ b)$$
$$dist_{L_a} \ = \lambda x \rightarrow \mathbf{case} \ x \ \mathbf{of}$$
$$\qquad\qquad Left \ () \qquad \rightarrow return \ (Left \ ())$$
$$\qquad\qquad Right \ (a, mb) \rightarrow \mathbf{do} \ b \leftarrow mb$$
$$\qquad\qquad\qquad\qquad\qquad return \ (Right \ (a, b))$$

$$dist_{B_a} \ :: \ Monad \ m \Rightarrow B \ a \ (m \ b) \rightarrow m \ (B \ a \ b)$$
$$dist_{B_a} \ = \lambda x \rightarrow \mathbf{case} \ x \ \mathbf{of}$$
$$\qquad\qquad Left \ a \qquad\qquad \rightarrow return \ (Left \ a)$$
$$\qquad\qquad Right \ (mb, mb') \rightarrow \mathbf{do} \ b \ \leftarrow mb$$
$$\qquad\qquad\qquad\qquad\qquad\qquad b' \leftarrow mb'$$
$$\qquad\qquad\qquad\qquad\qquad\qquad return \ (Right \ (b, b'))$$

$$dist_{R_a} \ :: \ Monad \ m \Rightarrow R \ a \ (m \ b) \rightarrow m \ (R \ a \ b)$$
$$dist_{R_a} \ = \lambda(a, mbs) \rightarrow \mathbf{do} \ bs \leftarrow sequence \ mbs$$
$$\qquad\qquad\qquad\qquad\qquad return \ (a, bs)$$

where *sequence* is a distributive law corresponding to the list type functor:

$$sequence \qquad\qquad\qquad :: \ Monad \ m \Rightarrow List \ (m \ a) \rightarrow m \ (List \ a)$$
$$sequence \ Nil \qquad\qquad = return \ Nil$$
$$sequence \ (Cons \ m \ ms) = \mathbf{do} \ a \ \leftarrow m$$
$$\qquad\qquad\qquad\qquad\qquad as \leftarrow sequence \ ms$$
$$\qquad\qquad\qquad\qquad\qquad return \ (Cons \ a \ as)$$

$\square$

An inductive definition of $\widehat{F}$ can be derived from the definition of $dist_F$:

$$\widehat{I} f \ \ = f \qquad\qquad\qquad (\widehat{F + G}) f = dist_+ \circ (\widehat{F} f + \widehat{G} f)$$
$$\widehat{\underline{t}} f \ \ = return \qquad\qquad (\widehat{F \times G}) f = dist_\times \circ (\widehat{F} f \ \times \ \widehat{G} f)$$
$$\widehat{FG} f = \widehat{F} \ \widehat{G} f \qquad\qquad \widehat{D} f \qquad = fold \ (mmap \ in_{Fa} \circ \widehat{F} \ (f, id))$$

In the case of $\widehat{D}$, $\widehat{F}$ is the monadic extension of the bifunctor $F$, where $\mu F_a = Da$.

*Example 13.* Assuming that $dist_\times$ proceeds from left to right, the following are examples of monadic extensions:

$$\widehat{N} \quad :: Monad\ m \Rightarrow (a \to m\ b) \to (N\ a \to m\ (N\ b))$$

$\widehat{N} f = \lambda x \to$ **case** $x$ **of**

$\qquad\qquad Left\ () \to return\ (Left\ ())$

$\qquad\qquad Right\ a \to$ **do** $b \leftarrow f\ a$

$\qquad\qquad\qquad\qquad return\ (Right\ b)$

$$\widehat{L_a} \quad :: Monad\ m \Rightarrow (b \to m\ c) \to (L\ a\ b \to m\ (L\ a\ c))$$

$\widehat{L_a} f = \lambda x \to$ **case** $x$ **of**

$\qquad\qquad Left\ () \to return\ (Left\ ())$

$\qquad\qquad Right\ (a, b) \to$ **do** $c \leftarrow f\ b$

$\qquad\qquad\qquad\qquad return\ (Right\ (a, c))$

$$\widehat{B_a} \quad :: Monad\ m \Rightarrow (b \to m\ c) \to (B\ a\ b \to m\ (B\ a\ c))$$

$\widehat{B_a} f = \lambda x \to$ **case** $x$ **of**

$\qquad\qquad Left\ a \to return\ (Left\ a)$

$\qquad\qquad Right\ (b, b') \to$ **do** $c \leftarrow f\ b$

$\qquad\qquad\qquad\qquad c' \leftarrow f\ b'$

$\qquad\qquad\qquad\qquad return\ (Right\ (c, c'))$

$$\widehat{R_a} \quad :: Monad\ m \Rightarrow (b \to m\ c) \to (R\ a\ b \to m\ (R\ a\ c))$$

$\widehat{R_a} f = \lambda(a, bs) \to$ **do** $cs \leftarrow mapM\ f\ bs$

$\qquad\qquad\qquad return\ (a, cs)$

where $mapM$ is a monadic extension $\widehat{List}$ of the list type functor:

$mapM \qquad\qquad\qquad :: Monad\ m \Rightarrow (a \to m\ b) \to (List\ a \to m\ (List\ b))$

$mapM\ f\ Nil \qquad\qquad = return\ Nil$

$mapM\ f\ (Cons\ a\ as) =$ **do** $b \leftarrow f\ a$

$\qquad\qquad\qquad\qquad bs \leftarrow mapM\ f\ as$

$\qquad\qquad\qquad\qquad return\ (Cons\ b\ bs)$

$\qquad\qquad\qquad\qquad\qquad\qquad\qquad\qquad\qquad\qquad\qquad\qquad\qquad\qquad\quad \square$

A monadic extension is said to be a *lifting* whenever it behaves like a functor with respect to monadic functions. That is, when it preserves identities (returns) and Kleisli composition.

$$\widehat{F}\ return = return \qquad\qquad \widehat{F}\ (f \bullet g) = \widehat{F}\ f \bullet \widehat{F}\ g$$

As established by Mulry [22], a monadic extension is a lifting iff its associated distributive law satisfies the following conditions:

$$dist_F \circ F\ return = return \qquad\qquad\qquad (7)$$

$$dist_F \circ F\ join = dist_F \bullet dist_F \qquad\qquad\qquad (8)$$

where

$$join \quad :: Monad\ m \Rightarrow m\ (m\ a) \rightarrow m\ a$$
$$join\ m = \mathbf{do}\ \{m' \leftarrow m; m'\}$$

Equation (7) ensures the preservation of identities, while (8) makes $\widehat{F}$ distribute over Kleisli composition.

An interesting case to analyze is that of the product functor.[2] It is easy to verify that (7) is valid for every monad:

$$dist_\times \circ (return \times return) = return$$

For example, assuming that $dist_\times$ proceeds from left to right, we have that:

$$\begin{aligned}
& (dist_\times \circ (return \times return))\ (a, b) \\
=\ & \quad \{\ \text{definition } dist_\times\ \} \\
& \mathbf{do}\ \{x \leftarrow return\ a; y \leftarrow return\ b; return\ (x, y)\} \\
=\ & \quad \{\ (3)\ \} \\
& \mathbf{do}\ \{y \leftarrow return\ b; return\ (a, y)\} \\
=\ & \quad \{\ (3)\ \} \\
& return\ (a, b)
\end{aligned}$$

The same holds if $dist_\times$ is right to left. However, equation (8),

$$
\begin{array}{ccc}
(m^2\ a, m^2\ b) & \xrightarrow{\ join\ \times\ join\ } & (m\ a, m\ b) \\
\Big\downarrow{\scriptstyle dist_\times} & & \Big\downarrow{\scriptstyle dist_\times} \\
m\ (m\ a, m\ b) & \xrightarrow[\ dist_\times^\star\ ]{} & m\ (a, b)
\end{array}
$$

does not always hold, since it requires the monad to be commutative. To see the problem, let us calculate the expressions corresponding to each side of the equation. Again, assume that $dist_\times$ is left to right. We start with the left-hand side:

$$\begin{aligned}
& (dist_\times \circ (join \times join))\ (m2, m2') \\
=\ & \quad \{\ \text{definition of } dist_\times\ \} \\
& \mathbf{do}\ \{a \leftarrow join\ m2; b \leftarrow join\ m2'; return\ (a, b)\} \\
=\ & \quad \{\ \text{definition of } join\ \} \\
& \mathbf{do}\ \{a \leftarrow \mathbf{do}\ \{m \leftarrow m2; m\}; b \leftarrow \mathbf{do}\ \{m' \leftarrow m2'; m'\}; return\ (a, b)\} \\
=\ & \quad \{\ (4)\ \} \\
& \mathbf{do}\ \{m \leftarrow m2; a \leftarrow m; m' \leftarrow m2'; b \leftarrow m'; return\ (a, b)\}
\end{aligned}$$

Now, the right-hand side:

$$\begin{aligned}
& (dist_\times \bullet dist_\times)\ (m2, m2') \\
=\ & \quad \{\ \text{definition of } dist_\times \text{ and Kleisli composition}\ \} \\
& \mathbf{do}\ \{(n, n') \leftarrow \mathbf{do}\ \{m \leftarrow m2; m' \leftarrow m2'; return\ (m, m')\}; \\
& \qquad a \leftarrow n; b \leftarrow n'; return\ (a, b)\} \\
=\ & \quad \{\ (3) \text{ and } (4)\ \} \\
& \mathbf{do}\ \{m \leftarrow m2; m' \leftarrow m2'; a \leftarrow m; b \leftarrow m'; return\ (a, b)\}
\end{aligned}$$

---

[2] A detailed analysis for all regular functors can be found in [25,24].

Both expressions involve exactly the same computations, but they are executed in different order. If we were working with the state monad, for example, the order in which computations are performed is completely relevant both for the side-effects produced and for the values delivered by the computations.

The failure of (8) for functors containing products makes it necessary to add the hypothesis of preservation of Kleisli composition in those fusion laws in which that condition is required. There are some functors involving products for which (8) holds. These are functors containing product expressions of the form $F = \underline{t} \times I$ (or symmetric). For example, for that $F$, the distributive law $dist_F :: (t, m\ a) \to m\ (t, a)$, given by,

$$
\begin{aligned}
&dist_F\ (t, m) \\
=\ &\quad \{\ \text{inductive definition}\ \} \\
&(dist_\times \circ (return \times id))\ (t, m) \\
=\ &\quad \{\ dist_\times\ \text{left-to-right}\ \} \\
&\mathbf{do}\ \{\, x \leftarrow return\ t;\ a \leftarrow m;\ return\ (x, a)\,\} \\
=\ &\quad \{\ (3)\ \} \\
&\mathbf{do}\ \{\, a \leftarrow m;\ return\ (t, a)\,\}
\end{aligned}
$$

satisfies (8) for every monad, as can be verified:

$$
\begin{aligned}
&(dist_F \circ (id \times join))\ (t, m2) \\
=\ &\quad \{\ \text{definition of}\ dist_F\ \} \\
&\mathbf{do}\ \{\, a \leftarrow join\ m2;\ return\ (t, a)\,\} \\
=\ &\quad \{\ \text{definition of}\ join\ \} \\
&\mathbf{do}\ \{\, a \leftarrow \mathbf{do}\ \{\, m \leftarrow m2;\ m\,\};\ return\ (t, a)\,\} \\
=\ &\quad \{\ (4)\ \} \\
&\mathbf{do}\ \{\, m \leftarrow m2;\ a \leftarrow m;\ return\ (t, a)\,\} \\
=\ &\quad \{\ (3)\ \} \\
&\mathbf{do}\ \{(x, n) \leftarrow \mathbf{do}\ \{\, m \leftarrow m2;\ return\ (t, m)\,\};\ a \leftarrow n;\ return\ (x, a)\,\} \\
=\ &\quad \{\ \text{definition of}\ dist_F\ \text{and Kleisli composition}\ \} \\
&(dist_F\ \bullet\ dist_F)\ (t, m2)
\end{aligned}
$$

## 4.3   Monadic Fold

*Monadic fold* [7] is a pattern of recursion that captures structural recursive functions with monadic effects. A definition of monadic fold is obtained by instantiating (5) with $g = \widehat{out_F}$:

$$
\begin{array}{ccc}
\mu F & \xrightarrow{\ \ mfold\ h\ \ } & m\ a \\
{\scriptstyle \widehat{out_F}}\Big\downarrow & & \Big\uparrow{\scriptstyle h^\star} \\
m\ (F\ \mu F) & \xrightarrow[\ (\widehat{F}\ (mfold\ h))^\star\ ]{} & m\ (F\ a)
\end{array}
$$

By (3) this can be simplified to:

$$
\begin{array}{ccc}
\mu F & \xrightarrow{\quad mfold\ h \quad} & m\ a \\
out_F \downarrow & & \uparrow h^\star \\
F\ \mu F & \xrightarrow[\widehat{F}\ (mfold\ h))]{} & m\ (F\ a)
\end{array}
$$

Therefore,

$$mfold \quad :: Monad\ m \Rightarrow (F\ a \to m\ a) \to \mu F \to m\ a$$
$$mfold\ h = h \bullet \widehat{F}\ (mfold\ h) \circ out_F$$

*Example 14.* The following are instances of monadic fold for different datatypes. We assume a left-to-right product distribution $dist_\times$.

*Lists*

$$mfold_L \qquad\qquad :: Monad\ m \Rightarrow (m\ b, a \to b \to m\ b) \to List\ a \to m\ b$$
$$mfold_L\ (h_1, h_2) = mf_L$$
$$\mathbf{where}$$
$$\qquad mf_L\ Nil \qquad\quad = h_1$$
$$\qquad mf_L\ (Cons\ a\ as) = \mathbf{do}\ y \leftarrow mf_L\ as$$
$$\qquad\qquad\qquad\qquad\qquad h_2\ a\ y$$

For instance, the function that sums the numbers produced by a list of computations (performed from right to left),

$$msum_L \qquad\qquad :: Monad\ m \Rightarrow List\ (m\ Int) \to m\ Int$$
$$msum_L\ Nil \qquad\quad = return\ 0$$
$$msum_L\ (Cons\ m\ ms) = \mathbf{do}\ \{\, y \leftarrow msum_L\ ms; x \leftarrow m; return\ (x + y)\,\}$$

can be defined as:

$$msum_L = mfold_L\ (return\ 0, \lambda m\ y \to \mathbf{do}\ \{\, x \leftarrow m; return\ (x + y)\,\})$$

*Leaf-labelled binary trees*

$$mfold_B \qquad\qquad :: Monad\ m \Rightarrow (a \to m\ b, b \to b \to m\ b) \to Btree\ a \to m\ b$$
$$mfold_B\ (h_1, h_2) = mf_B$$
$$\mathbf{where}$$
$$\qquad mf_B\ (Leaf\ a) \quad = h_1\ a$$
$$\qquad mf_B\ (Join\ t\ t') = \mathbf{do}\ y \leftarrow mf_B\ t$$
$$\qquad\qquad\qquad\qquad\qquad y' \leftarrow mf_B\ t'$$
$$\qquad\qquad\qquad\qquad\qquad h_2\ y\ y'$$

For instance, the function that sums the numbers produced by a tree of computations (performed from left to right),

$$msum_B \qquad\qquad :: Monad\ m \Rightarrow Btree\ (m\ Int) \rightarrow m\ Int$$
$$msum_B\ (Leaf\ m) = m$$
$$msum_B\ (Join\ t\ t') = \mathbf{do}\ \{y \leftarrow msum_B\ t; y' \leftarrow msum_B\ t'; return\ (y + y')\}$$

can be defined as:

$$msum_B = mfold_B\ (id, \lambda y\ y' \rightarrow return\ (y + y'))$$

*Rose trees*

$$mfold_R \quad :: Monad\ m \Rightarrow (a \rightarrow List\ b \rightarrow m\ b) \rightarrow Rose\ a \rightarrow m\ b$$
$$mfold_R\ h = mf_R$$

   **where**

$$mf_R\ (Fork\ a\ rs) = \mathbf{do}\ ys \leftarrow mapM\ mf_R\ rs$$
$$h\ a\ ys$$

In this case, the function that sums the numbers produced by a tree of computations,

$$msum_R \qquad\qquad :: Monad\ m \Rightarrow Rose\ (m\ Int) \rightarrow m\ Int$$
$$msum_R\ (Fork\ m\ rs) = \mathbf{do}\ ys \leftarrow mapM\ msum_R\ rs$$
$$x \leftarrow m$$
$$return\ (x + sum_L\ ys)$$

$$sum_L :: List\ Int \rightarrow Int$$
$$sum_L = fold_L\ (0, (+))$$

can be defined as:

$$msum_R = mfold_R\ (\lambda m\ ys \rightarrow \mathbf{do}\ \{x \leftarrow m; return\ (x + sum_L\ ys)\})$$

$\square$

Functions of type $F\ a \rightarrow m\ a$ are called *monadic F-algebras*; the type $a$ is called the carrier of the algebra. Like purely-functional algebras, monadic algebras may be thought of as structures. The difference is that they return a computation instead of simply a value. As could be seen in Example 14, we adopt a similar notational convention as for algebras to write monadic algebras in instances of the schemes.

A structure-preserving mapping between two monadic algebras is a function between their carriers that preserves their structures, and is *compatible* with their monadic effects. We identify two forms of structure-preserving mappings.

A *F-homomorphism* between two monadic algebras $h :: F\ a \rightarrow m\ a$ and $k :: F\ b \rightarrow m\ b$ is a monadic function $f :: a \rightarrow m\ b$ such that $f \bullet h = k \bullet \widehat{F} f$. The use of $\widehat{F}$ in the definition of homomorphism is essential, since it is necessary to join the effects produced by the occurrences of $f$ within the expression $F f$. Homomorphisms are closed under composition provided $\widehat{F}$ preserves Kleisli compositions.

A weaker notion of mapping between two monadic algebras $h :: F\ a \rightarrow m\ a$ and $k :: F\ b \rightarrow m\ b$ is what we call a *pure homomorphism*: a function $f :: a \rightarrow b$ such that $mmap\ f \circ h = k \circ F\ f$. A pure homomorphism may be thought of as a means of changing the 'representation' of a monadic algebra while maintaining the effects that it produces.

The following are fusion laws for monadic fold. In all of them it is necessary to assume that function $mmap :: (a \to b) \to (m\ a \to m\ b)$ is strictness-preserving, in the sense that it maps strict functions to strict functions.

**MFold Fusion.** If $\widehat{F}$ preserves Kleisli compositions,

$$f\ strict\ \wedge\ f \bullet h = k \bullet \widehat{F}\ f\ \Rightarrow\ f \bullet mfold\ h = mfold\ k$$

**MFold Pure Fusion.**

$$f\ strict\ \wedge\ mmap\ f \circ h = k \circ F\ f\ \Rightarrow\ mmap\ f \circ mfold\ h = mfold\ k$$

**MFold-Fold Fusion.**

$$\Rightarrow \quad \begin{aligned} &\tau :: \forall\ a\ .\ (F\ a \to a) \to (G\ a \to m\ a) \\ &mmap\ (fold\ h) \circ mfold\ (\tau\ in_F) = mfold\ (\tau\ h) \end{aligned}$$

We will adopt a similar notational convention as for the case of algebras to write this kind of functions $\tau$ in instances of the program schemes.

*Example 15.* In Example 14, we showed that $msum_L$ can be defined as a monadic fold. Assuming that $mmap$ is strictness-preserving, we use fusion to show that:

$$msum_L = mmap\ sum_L \circ lsequence$$

being *lsequence* the function that performs a list of computations from right to left:

$$\begin{aligned} lsequence &:: Monad\ m \Rightarrow List\ (m\ a) \to m\ (List\ a) \\ lsequence\ Nil &= return\ Nil \\ lsequence\ (Cons\ m\ ms) &= \mathbf{do}\ as \leftarrow lsequence\ ms \\ &\qquad\qquad a \leftarrow m \\ &\qquad\qquad return\ (Cons\ a\ as) \end{aligned}$$

We can express *lsequence* as a monadic fold,

$$\begin{aligned} lsequence = mfold_L\ (&return\ Nil, \\ &\lambda m\ as \to \mathbf{do}\ \{\,a \leftarrow m;\ return\ (Cons\ a\ as)\,\}) \end{aligned}$$

such that it is possible to write its monadic algebra as $\tau\ (Nil, Cons)$, where

$$\begin{aligned} \tau &\quad :: (b, a \to b \to b) \to (b, m\ a \to b \to m\ b) \\ \tau\ (h_1, h_2) &= (return\ h_1, \\ &\quad\ \lambda m\ b \to \mathbf{do}\ \{\,a \leftarrow m;\ return\ (h_2\ a\ b)\,\}) \end{aligned}$$

Finally, we calculate

$$\begin{aligned} &mmap\ sum_L \circ lsequence \\ =\quad &\{\ \text{definition of } sum_L \text{ and } lsequence\ \} \\ &mmap\ (fold_L\ (0, (+))) \circ mfold_L\ (\tau\ (Nil, Cons)) \\ =\quad &\{\ \text{mfold-fold fusion}\ \} \\ &mfold_L\ (\tau\ (0, (+))) \\ =\quad &\{\ \text{definition of } \tau \text{ and } msum_L\ \} \\ &msum_L \end{aligned}$$

$\square$

## 4.4   Monadic Unfold

Now we turn to the analysis of corecursive functions with monadic effects. Like monadic fold, the definition of monadic unfold can be obtained from (5), now taking $h = \widehat{in_F}$.

$$
\begin{array}{ccc}
a & \xrightarrow{\quad munfold\ g \quad} & m\ \mu F \\
g \downarrow & & \downarrow \widehat{in_F}^{\star} \\
m\ (F\ a) & \xrightarrow{\quad (\widehat{F}\ (munfold\ g))^{\star} \quad} & m\ (F\ \mu F)
\end{array}
$$

that is,

$$munfold \quad :: Monad\ m \Rightarrow (a \to m\ (F\ a)) \to (a \to m\ \mu F)$$
$$munfold\ g\ a = (return \circ in_F) \bullet \widehat{F}\ (unfold\ g) \bullet g$$

*Example 16.* We show the definition of monadic unfold for different datatypes. Again, we assume a left to right product distribution $dist_\times$.

*Lists*

$$munfold_L \quad :: Monad\ m \Rightarrow (b \to m\ (L\ a\ b)) \to (b \to m\ (List\ a))$$
$$munfold_L\ g\ b = \mathbf{do}\ x \leftarrow g\ b$$
$$\qquad \mathbf{case}\ x\ \mathbf{of}$$
$$\qquad\qquad Left\ () \qquad \to return\ Nil$$
$$\qquad\qquad Right\ (a, b') \to \mathbf{do}\ as \leftarrow munfold_L\ g\ b'$$
$$\qquad\qquad\qquad\qquad\qquad return\ (Cons\ a\ as)$$

*Leaf-labelled binary trees*

$$munfold_B \quad :: Monad\ m \Rightarrow (b \to m\ (B\ a\ b)) \to (b \to m\ (Btree\ a))$$
$$munfold_B\ g\ b = \mathbf{do}\ x \leftarrow g\ b$$
$$\qquad \mathbf{case}\ x\ \mathbf{of}$$
$$\qquad\qquad Left\ a \qquad\quad \to return\ (Leaf\ a)$$
$$\qquad\qquad Right\ (b1, b2) \to \mathbf{do}\ t1 \leftarrow munfold_B\ g\ b1$$
$$\qquad\qquad\qquad\qquad\qquad t2 \leftarrow munfold_B\ g\ b2$$
$$\qquad\qquad\qquad\qquad\qquad return\ (Join\ t1\ t2)$$

*Rose trees*

$$munfold_R \quad :: Monad\ m \Rightarrow (b \to m\ (R\ a\ b)) \to (b \to m\ (Rose\ a))$$
$$munfold_R\ g\ b = \mathbf{do}\ (a, bs) \leftarrow g\ b$$
$$\qquad\qquad rs \quad\ \leftarrow mapM\ (munfold_R\ g)\ bs$$
$$\qquad\qquad return\ (Fork\ a\ rs) \qquad\qquad\qquad\qquad\qquad\qquad \square$$

A function $g :: a \to m\ (F\ a)$ is called a *monadic F-coalgebra*. Structure-preserving mappings between monadic coalgebras play an important role in the fusion laws for monadic unfold. A *F-homomorphism* between two monadic coalgebras $g :: a \rightarrow m\ (F\ a)$ and $g' :: b \rightarrow m\ (F\ b)$ is a function $f :: a \rightarrow m\ b$ such that $g' \bullet f = \widehat{F}\ f \bullet g$. Homomorphisms between monadic coalgebras are closed under composition provided $\widehat{F}$ preserves Kleisli compositions.

Like with monadic algebras, we can define a weaker notion of structure-preserving mapping. A *pure homomorphism* between two coalgebras $g :: a \rightarrow m\ (F\ a)$ and $g' :: b \rightarrow m\ (F\ b)$ is a function $f :: a \rightarrow b$ between their carriers such that $g' \circ f = mmap\ (F\ f) \circ g$. Again, a pure homomorphism may be regarded as a representation changer.

The following are fusion laws for monadic unfold.

**MUnfold Fusion.** If $\widehat{F}$ preserves Kleisli compositions,

$$g' \bullet f = \widehat{F}\ f \bullet g \quad \Rightarrow \quad munfold\ g' \bullet f = munfold\ g$$

**MUnfold Pure Fusion.**

$$g' \circ f = mmap\ (F\ f) \circ g \quad \Rightarrow \quad munfold\ g' \circ f = munfold\ g$$

**Unfold-MUnfold Fusion.**

$$\Rightarrow \quad \begin{array}{l} \sigma :: \forall\ a\ .\ (a \rightarrow F\ a) \rightarrow (a \rightarrow m\ (G\ a)) \\[4pt] munfold\ (\sigma\ out_F) \circ unfold\ g = munfold\ (\sigma\ g) \end{array}$$

### 4.5   Graph Traversals

A *graph traversal* is a function that takes a list of roots (entry points to a graph) and returns a list containing the vertices met along the way. In this subsection we show that classical graph traversals, such as DFS or BFS, can be formulated as a monadic unfold.

We assume a representation of graphs that provides a function *adj* which returns the *adjacency list* for each vertex.

**type** $Graph\ v = ...$

$adj :: Eq\ v \Rightarrow Graph\ v \rightarrow v \rightarrow List\ v$

In a graph traversal vertices are visited at most once. Hence, it is necessary to maintain a set where to keep track of vertices already visited in order to avoid repeats. Let us assume an abstract data type of finite sets over $a$, with operations

$emptyS :: Set\ a$
$insS\quad :: Eq\ a \Rightarrow a \rightarrow Set\ a \rightarrow Set\ a$
$memS\ :: Eq\ a \Rightarrow a \rightarrow Set\ a \rightarrow Bool$

where *emptyS* denotes the empty set, *insS* is set insertion and *memS* is a membership predicate.

We handle the set of visited nodes in a state monad. A standard technique to do so is to encapsulate the set operations in an abstract data type based on the monad [31]:

**type** $M\ a\ b$ $\quad\quad = State\ (Set\ a)\ b$

$runMS$ $\quad\quad\quad\quad :: M\ a\ b \to b$
$runMS\ (State\ f) = \pi_1\ (f\ emptyS)$

$insMS$ $\quad\quad\quad\quad :: Eq\ a \Rightarrow a \to M\ a\ ()$
$insMS\ a$ $\quad\quad\quad = State\ (\lambda s \to ((), insS\ a\ s))$

$memMS$ $\quad\quad\quad\quad :: Eq\ a \Rightarrow a \to M\ a\ Bool$
$memMS\ a$ $\quad\quad\quad = State\ (\lambda s \to (memS\ a\ s, s))$

Such a technique makes it possible to consider, if desired, an imperative representation of sets, like e.g. a *characteristic vector* of boolean values, which allows $O(1)$ time insertions and lookups when implemented by a mutable array. In that case the monadic abstract data type has to be implemented in terms of the ST monad [14].

Now, we define graph traversal:

**type** $Policy\ v = Graph\ v \to v \to List\ v \to List\ v$

$graphtrav$ $\quad\quad :: Eq\ v \Rightarrow Policy\ v \to Graph\ v \to List\ v \to List\ v$
$graphtrav\ pol\ g = runMS \circ gtrav\ pol\ g$

$gtrav$ $\quad\quad\quad :: Eq\ v \Rightarrow Policy\ v \to Graph\ v \to List\ v \to M\ v\ (List\ v)$
$gtrav\ pol\ g\ vs$ $\quad = $ **do** $xs \leftarrow mdropS\ vs$
$\quad\quad\quad\quad\quad\quad\quad$ **case** $xs$ **of**
$\quad\quad\quad\quad\quad\quad\quad\quad\quad Nil \quad\quad\quad \to return\ Nil$
$\quad\quad\quad\quad\quad\quad\quad\quad\quad Cons\ v\ vs \to$ **do** $insMS\ v$
$\quad\quad\quad\quad\quad\quad\quad\quad\quad\quad\quad\quad\quad\quad zs \leftarrow gtrav\ pol\ g\ (pol\ g\ v\ vs)$
$\quad\quad\quad\quad\quad\quad\quad\quad\quad\quad\quad\quad\quad\quad return\ (Cons\ v\ zs)$

$mdropS$ $\quad\quad\quad\quad :: Eq\ v \Rightarrow List\ v \to M\ v\ (List\ v)$
$mdropS\ Nil$ $\quad\quad\quad = return\ Nil$
$mdropS\ (Cons\ v\ vs) = $ **do** $b \leftarrow memMS\ a$
$\quad\quad\quad\quad\quad\quad\quad\quad\quad\quad$ **if** $b$ **then** $mdropS\ vs$
$\quad\quad\quad\quad\quad\quad\quad\quad\quad\quad$ **else** $return\ (Cons\ v\ vs)$

Given an initial list of roots, *graphtrav* first creates an empty set, then executes *gtrav*, obtaining a list of vertices and a set, and finally discards the set and returns the resulting list. In each iteration, the function *gtrav* starts with an exploration of the current list of roots in order to find a vertex that has not been visited yet. To this end, it removes from the front of that list every vertex $u$ that is marked as visited until, either an unvisited vertex is met, or the end of the list is reached. This task is performed by the function *mdropS*.

After the application of *mdropS*, we visit the vertex at the head of the input list, if still there is any, and mark it (by inserting it in the set). A new 'state' of the list of roots is also computed. This is performed by an auxiliary function, called *pol*, which encapsulates the administration policy used for the list of pending roots. That way, we obtain a formulation of graph traversal parameterized by a strategy.

Function $gtrav$ can be expressed as a monadic unfold:

$gtrav\ pol\ g = munfold_L\ k$
   **where**
      $k$    $:: List\ v \rightarrow M\ v\ (L\ v\ (List\ v))$
      $k\ vs = $ **do** $xs \leftarrow mdropS\ vs$
            **case** $xs$ **of**
               $Nil$         $\rightarrow return\ (Left\ ())$
               $Cons\ v\ ys \rightarrow$ **do** $insMS\ v$
                           $return\ (Right\ (v, pol\ g\ v\ ys))$

Particular traversal strategies are obtained by providing specific policies:

*Depth-First Traversal.* This is achieved by managing the list of pending roots as a stack.

$dfsTrav$        $:: Eq\ v \Rightarrow Graph\ v \rightarrow List\ v \rightarrow List\ v$
$dfsTrav\ g$     $= graphtrav\ dfsPol\ g$

$dfsPol\ g\ v\ vs = adj\ g\ v \mathbin{+\!\!+} vs$

*Breath-First Traversal.* This is achieved by managing the list of pending roots as a queue.

$bfsTrav$        $:: Eq\ v \Rightarrow Graph\ v \rightarrow List\ v \rightarrow List\ v$
$bfsTrav\ g$     $= graphtrav\ bfsPol\ g$

$bfsPol\ g\ v\ vs = vs \mathbin{+\!\!+} adj\ g\ v$

## 4.6   Monadic Hylomorphism

Monadic hylomorphism is a pattern of recursion that represents general recursive monadic functions.

$mhylo$      $:: Monad\ m \Rightarrow (F\ b \rightarrow m\ b) \rightarrow (a \rightarrow m\ (F\ a)) \rightarrow (a \rightarrow b)$
$mhylo\ h\ g = h \bullet \widehat{F}\ (mhylo\ h\ g) \bullet g$

*Example 17.* The following are instances of monadic hylomorphism for specific datatypes. Again, we assume a left to right product distribution $dist_\times$.

*Lists*

$mhylo_L :: Monad\ m \Rightarrow$
          $(m\ c, a \rightarrow c \rightarrow m\ c) \rightarrow (b \rightarrow m\ (L\ a\ b)) \rightarrow (b \rightarrow m\ c)$
$mhylo_L\ (h_1, h_2)\ g = mh_L$
   **where**
      $mh_L\ b = $ **do** $x \leftarrow g\ b$

$$
\begin{array}{ll}
\textbf{case } x \textbf{ of} \\
\quad Left\ () & \rightarrow h_1 \\
\quad Right\ (a, b') & \rightarrow \textbf{do } c \leftarrow mh_L\ b' \\
& \quad\quad h_2\ a\ c
\end{array}
$$

*Leaf-labelled binary trees*

$$mhylo_B :: Monad\ m \Rightarrow$$
$$\quad\quad (a \rightarrow m\ c, c \rightarrow c \rightarrow m\ c) \rightarrow (b \rightarrow m\ (B\ a\ b)) \rightarrow (b \rightarrow c)$$
$$mhylo_B\ (h_1, h_2)\ g = mh_B$$
$$\quad \textbf{where}$$
$$\quad\quad mh_B\ b = \textbf{do } x \leftarrow g\ b$$

$$
\begin{array}{ll}
\quad\quad\quad\quad \textbf{case } x \textbf{ of} \\
\quad\quad\quad\quad\quad Left\ a & \rightarrow h_1\ a \\
\quad\quad\quad\quad\quad Right\ (b1, b2) & \rightarrow \textbf{do } c1 \leftarrow mh_B\ b1 \\
& \quad\quad\quad\quad c2 \leftarrow mh_B\ b2 \\
& \quad\quad\quad\quad h_2\ c1\ c2
\end{array}
$$

*Rose trees*

$$mhylo_R :: Monad\ m \Rightarrow$$
$$\quad\quad (a \rightarrow [c] \rightarrow m\ c) \rightarrow (b \rightarrow m\ (R\ a\ b)) \rightarrow (b \rightarrow m\ c)$$
$$mhyloh\ h\ g\ b = \textbf{do } (a, bs) \leftarrow g\ b$$
$$\quad\quad\quad\quad cs \quad\quad \leftarrow mapM\ (mhylo_R\ h\ g)\ bs$$
$$\quad\quad\quad\quad h\ a\ cs \hfill \square$$

The fusion laws for monadic hylomorphism are a consequence of those for monadic fold and monadic unfold.

**MHylo Fusion.** If $\widehat{F}$ preserves Kleisli compositions,

$$f \text{ strict } \wedge\ f \bullet h = k \bullet \widehat{F}\ f \ \Rightarrow\ f \bullet mhylo\ h\ g = mhylo\ k\ g$$
$$g' \bullet f = \widehat{F}\ f \bullet g \ \Rightarrow\ mhylo\ h\ g' \bullet f = mhylo\ h\ g$$

In the first law *mmap* needs to be strictness-preserving.

**MHylo Pure Fusion.**

$$f \text{ strict } \wedge\ mmap\ f \circ h = k \circ F\ f \ \Rightarrow\ mmap\ f \circ mhylo\ h\ g = mhylo\ k\ g$$
$$g' \circ f = mmap\ (F\ f) \circ g \ \Rightarrow\ mhylo\ h\ g' \circ f = mhylo\ h\ g$$

In the first law *mmap* needs to be strictness-preserving.

**MHylo-Fold Fusion.** If *mmap* is strictness-preserving,

$$\tau :: \forall\ a\ .\ (F\ a \rightarrow a) \rightarrow (G\ a \rightarrow m\ a)$$
$$\Rightarrow$$
$$\quad\quad mmap\ (fold\ h) \circ mhylo\ (\tau\ in_F)\ g = mhylo\ (\tau\ h)\ g$$

**Unfold-MHylo Fusion.**

$$\Rightarrow \quad \frac{\sigma :: \forall\ a\ .\ (a \to F\ a) \to (a \to m\ (G\ a))}{mhylo\ h\ (\sigma\ out_F) \circ unfold\ g = mhylo\ h\ (\sigma\ g)}$$

## 4.7   Depth-First Search Algorithms

The references [16,17,15] show the advantages of explicitly maintaining the *depth-first spanning forest* of a graph when implementing DFS algorithms in a lazy functional language. The construction of the depth-first forest is performed in two stages. In the first phase a forest of (possibly infinite) trees is generated. Each tree is rooted with a vertex from a given list of entry points to the graph and contains all vertices in the graph reachable from that root. The second phase runs a prune process, which traverses the forest in depth-first order, discarding all subtrees whose roots have occurred previously. This *generate-then-prune* strategy turns out to be the natural solution in the context of a lazy functional language. Indeed, because of lazy evaluation, deeper levels of the trees are generated only if and when demanded by the prune process.

In this subsection, we show that the depth-first forest construction can be structured using monadic recursion schemes.

**Generation.** Like in Subsection 4.5, we assume a graph representation that supports a function $adj :: Eq\ v \Rightarrow Graph\ v \to v \to List\ v$ which returns the adjacency list of each node of a graph.

The generation of a (rose) tree containing all vertices in the graph reachable from a vertex $v$ is defined by,

$$gen \qquad :: Eq\ v \Rightarrow Graph\ v \to v \to Rose\ v$$
$$gen\ g\ v = Fork\ v\ (List\ (gen\ g)\ (adj\ g\ v))$$

This function is naturally an unfold

$$gen\ g = unfold_R\ (id\ \triangle\ adj\ g)$$

The generation of a forest from a given list of vertices is then obtained by mapping each vertex of the list with function *gen*.

$$fgen \quad :: Eq\ v \Rightarrow Graph\ v \to List\ v \to List\ (Rose\ a)$$
$$fgen\ g = List\ (gen\ g)$$

**Pruning.** Pruning traverses the forest in depth-first order, discarding all subtrees whose roots have occurred previously. Analogous to graph traversals, pruning needs to maintain a set (of *marks*) to keep track of the already visited nodes. This suggest the use of the same monadic abstract data type.

In the pruning process we will use a datatype of rose trees extended with an empty tree constructor.

**data** $ERose\ a = ENull\ |\ EFork\ a\ (List\ (ERose\ a))$

**type** $ER_a\ b\ \ = ()\ +\ a\ \times\ List\ b$

$$ER_a \qquad \quad :: (b \rightarrow c) \rightarrow (ER_a\ b \rightarrow ER_a\ c)$$
$$ER_a\ f \qquad = id + id\ \times\ List\ f$$

When we find a root that has occurred previously, we prune the whole subtree. The function that prunes an individual rose tree is defined by

$prune_R ::$           $Eq\ v \Rightarrow Rose\ v \rightarrow M\ v\ (ERose\ v)$
$prune_R\ (Fork\ v\ rs) = \mathbf{do}\ b \leftarrow memMS\ v$
                    $\mathbf{if}\ b$
                    $\mathbf{then}\ return\ ENull$
                    $\mathbf{else\ do}\ insMS\ v$
                             $rs' \leftarrow mapM\ prune_R\ rs$
                             $return\ (EFork\ v\ rs')$

This function can be written as a monadic unfold:

$prune_R = munfold_{ER}\ g$
    $\mathbf{where}$
       $g\ (Fork\ v\ rs) = prStep\ (v, rs)$
       $prStep\ (v, rs) = \mathbf{do}\ b \leftarrow memMS\ v$
                     $\mathbf{if}\ b$
                     $\mathbf{then}\ return\ (Left\ ())$
                     $\mathbf{else\ do}\ insMS\ v$
                           $return\ (Right\ (v, rs))$

such that its coalgebra can be written as $g = prStep \circ out_{R_v}$.

Pruning a forest just consists of pruning the trees in sequence:

$fpruneR :: Eq\ v \Rightarrow List\ (Rose\ a) \rightarrow M\ a\ (List\ (ERose\ v))$
$fpruneR = mapM\ prune_R$

A drawback of this solution is that the resulting forest contains many unnecessary empty trees, which could be dropped if we convert the resulting extended rose trees into rose trees again. The conversion is performed by simply traversing the forest of extended rose tress, *cleaning* all occurrences of the empty tree:

$fclean :: List\ (ERose\ a) \rightarrow List\ (Rose\ a)$
$fclean = collect \circ List\ clean$

$clean \qquad\qquad\quad :: ERose\ a \rightarrow Maybe\ (Rose\ a)$
$clean\ ENull \qquad\ = Nothing$
$clean\ (EFork\ a\ rs) = Just\ (Fork\ a\ (fclean\ rs))$

$collect \qquad\qquad\quad :: List\ (Maybe\ a) \rightarrow List\ a$
$collect\ Nil = Nil$
$collect\ (Cons\ m\ ms) = \mathbf{case}\ m\ \mathbf{of}$
                            $Nothing \rightarrow collect\ ms$
                            $Just\ a \quad \rightarrow Cons\ a\ (collect\ ms)$

Clearly, both *clean* and *collect* are folds, $clean = fold_{ER}\ cl$ and $collect = fold_L\ coll$, for suitable algebras $cl$ and $coll = (coll1, coll2)$, respectively.

Finally, we define the function that prunes a forest of rose trees, returning the rose trees that remain:

$$prune :: Eq\ v \Rightarrow List\ (Rose\ a) \to M\ a\ (List\ (Rose\ a))$$
$$prune = mmap\ fclean \circ fpruneR$$

**Computing the Depth-First Forest.** Now we define a function *dfs* that computes the depth-first spanning forest of a graph reachable from a given list of vertices.

$$dfs\quad :: Eq\ v \Rightarrow Graph\ v \to List\ v \to List\ (Rose\ v)$$
$$dfs\ g = runMS \circ prune \circ fgen\ g$$

We use function *runMS* to hide the monadic state from the outside world. That way, *dfs* is externally regarded as a purely functional. The internal components of *dfs* can be fused as the following calculation shows.

$$prune \circ fgen\ g$$
$$= \quad \{\ \text{function definitions}\ \}$$
$$mmap\ (collect \circ List\ clean) \circ mapM\ (prune_R) \circ List\ (gen\ g)$$
$$= \quad \{\ mapM = \widehat{List}\ \text{and property:}\ \widehat{F}\ f \circ F\ g = \widehat{F}\ (f \circ g)\ \}$$
$$mmap\ (collect \circ List\ clean) \circ mapM\ (prune_R \circ gen\ g)$$
$$= \quad \{\ \text{functor}\ mmap\ \}$$
$$mmap\ collect \circ mmap\ (List\ clean) \circ mapM\ (prune_R \circ gen\ g)$$

$$= \quad \{\ \text{property:}\ mmap\ (F\ f) \circ \widehat{F}\ g = \widehat{F}\ (mmap\ f \circ g)\ \}$$
$$mmap\ collect \circ mapM\ (mmap\ clean \circ prune_R \circ gen\ g)$$
$$= \quad \{\ \text{define:}\ gpc\ g = mmap\ clean \circ prune_R \circ gen\ g\ \}$$
$$mmap\ collect \circ mapM\ (gpc\ g)$$
$$= \quad \{\ \text{property:}\ mmap\ (fold\ h) \circ \widehat{D}\ f = fold\ (mmap\ h \circ \widehat{F}\ f\ id)\ \}$$
$$fold_L\ (mmap\ coll \circ \widehat{L}\ (gpc\ g)\ id)$$

We call *gp* (for generate then prune) the resulting fold. Inlining, we get the following recursive definition:

$$gp \qquad\qquad :: Eq\ v \Rightarrow Graph\ v \to List\ v \to M\ v\ (List\ (Rose\ v))$$
$$gp\ g\ Nil \qquad = return\ Nil$$
$$gp\ g\ (Cons\ v\ vs) = \mathbf{do}\ x \leftarrow gpc\ g\ v$$
$$\qquad\qquad\qquad rs \leftarrow gp\ g\ vs$$
$$\qquad\qquad\qquad return\ (\mathbf{case}\ x\ \mathbf{of}$$
$$\qquad\qquad\qquad\qquad Left\ ()\ \to rs$$
$$\qquad\qquad\qquad\qquad Right\ r \to Cons\ r\ rs)$$

Now, let us analyze function *gpc*, which expresses how individual trees are generated, pruned and cleaned in a shot.

$$gpc \quad :: Eq \; v \Rightarrow Graph \; g \rightarrow v \rightarrow M \; v \; (Maybe \; (Rose \; a))$$
$$gpc \; g = mmap \; clean \circ prune_R \circ gen \; g$$

This definition can also be simplified:

$$mmap \; clean \circ prune_R \circ gen \; g$$
$$= \quad \{ \text{ function definitions } \}$$
$$mmap \; (fold_{ER} \; cl) \circ munfold_{ER} \; (prStep \circ out_{R_v}) \circ unfold_R \; (id \; \vartriangle \; adj \; g)$$
$$= \quad \{ \text{ define: } \sigma \; j = prStep \circ j \; \}$$
$$mmap \; (fold_{ER} \; cl) \circ munfold_{ER} \; (\sigma \; out_{R_v}) \circ unfold_R \; (id \; \vartriangle \; adj \; g)$$
$$= \quad \{ \text{ unfold-munfold fusion } \}$$
$$mmap \; (fold_{ER} \; cl) \circ munfold_{ER} \; (\sigma \; (id \; \vartriangle \; adj \; g))$$
$$= \quad \{ \text{ factorization prop.: } mmap \; (fold \; h) \circ munfold \; g = mhylo \; \widehat{h} \; g \; \}$$
$$mhylo_{ER} \; \widehat{cl} \; (prStep \circ (id \; \vartriangle \; adj \; g))$$

Inlining, we obtain:

$$gpc \; g \; v = \textbf{do} \; b \leftarrow memMS \; v$$
$$\textbf{if} \; b$$
$$\textbf{then} \; return \; Nothing$$
$$\textbf{else do} \; insMS \; v$$
$$ms \leftarrow mapM \; (gpc \; g) \; (adj \; g \; v)$$
$$return \; (Just \; (Fork \; v \; (collect \; ms)))$$

**Depth-First Traversal.** To illustrate the use of the depth-first forest, we compute the depth-first traversal of a graph by traversing the forest in preorder. Other DFS algorithms under the same approach can be found in [16,17,15,24].

The preorder of a forest can be defined by

$$fpreorder \; :: List \; (Rose \; v) \rightarrow List \; v$$
$$fpreoredr = concat \circ List \; preorder$$

$$preorder \; :: Rose \; v \rightarrow List \; v$$
$$preorder \; = fold_R \; (Cons \circ (id \; \times \; concat))$$

We compute the depth-first traversal of a graph by listing the depth-first forest in preorder:

$$dfsTrav \quad :: Eq \; v \Rightarrow Graph \; g \rightarrow List \; v \rightarrow List \; v$$
$$dfsTrav \; g = fpreorder \circ dfs \; g$$

We show now how the generation of the intermediate depth-first forest can be eliminated using fusion.

$$fpreorder \circ dfs \; g$$
$$= \quad \{ \text{ function definitions } \}$$
$$concat \circ List \; preorder \circ runMS \circ mmap \; collect \circ mapM \; (gpc \; g)$$
$$= \quad \{ \text{ parametricity property: } f \circ runMS = runMS \circ mmap \; f \; \}$$
$$runMS \circ mmap \; (concat \circ List \; preorder) \circ mmap \; collect \circ mapM \; (gpc \; g)$$

$=$    { functor $mmap$ }

$runMS \circ mmap\ (concat \circ List\ preorder \circ collect) \circ mapM\ (gpc\ g)$

$=$    { map-fold fusion, define $pjoin = uncurry\ (\mathbin{+\!\!+}) \circ (preorder \times id)$ }

$runMS \circ mmap\ (fold_L\ (Nil, pjoin) \circ collect) \circ mapM\ (gpc\ g)$

$=$    { define: $\tau$ (see below) }

$runMS \circ mmap\ (fold_L\ (Nil, pjoin) \circ fold_L\ (\tau\ (Nil, Cons))) \circ mapM\ (gpc\ g)$

$=$    { fold-fold fusion }

$runMS \circ mmap\ (fold_L\ (\tau\ (Nil, pjoin))) \circ mapM\ (gpc\ g)$

$-$    { property: $mmap\ (fold\ h) \circ \widehat{D}\ f = fold\ (M\ h \circ \overset{..}{F}\ f\ id)$ }

$runMS \circ fold_L\ (mmap\ (\tau\ (Nil, pjoin)) \circ \widehat{L}\ (gpc\ g)\ id)$

Function $\tau$ is given by:

$\tau$         $:: (b, a \to b \to b) \to (b, Maybe\ a \to b \to b)$

$\tau\ (h_1, h_2) = (h_1,$

$\qquad\quad \lambda m\ b \to$ **case** $m$ **of**

$\qquad\qquad\quad Nothing \to b$

$\qquad\qquad\quad Just\ a\ \ \to h_2\ a\ b)$

The property $f \circ runMS = runMS \circ mmap\ f$ is an example of a *parametricity property* or *free theorem* [29], which are properties that can be directly derived from the type of polymorphic functions.

Calling $mtrav$ the $fold_L$ obtained in the derivation and inlining, we obtain this program:

$mtrav$                    $:: Eq\ v \Rightarrow Graph\ g \to List\ v \to M\ v\ (List\ v)$

$mtrav\ g\ Nil$            $= return\ Nil$

$mtrav\ g\ (Cons\ v\ vs) =$ **do** $x\ \leftarrow\ gpc\ g\ v$

$\qquad\qquad\qquad\qquad\ as \leftarrow\ mtrav\ g\ vs$

$\qquad\qquad\qquad\qquad\ return\ ($**case** $x$ **of**

$\qquad\qquad\qquad\qquad\qquad\qquad Nothing \to as$

$\qquad\qquad\qquad\qquad\qquad\qquad Just\ r\ \ \to preorder\ r \mathbin{+\!\!+} as)$

## 4.8   A More Practical Approach

The monadic program schemes shown so far were all derived from the lifting construction presented in Subsection 4.1.

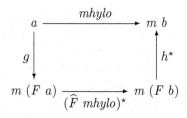

However, despite its theoretical elegance, this construction suffers from an important drawback that hinders the practical use of the program schemes derived from it. The origin of the problem is the compulsory use of the distributive law $dist_F$ associated with $\widehat{F}$ as unique way of joining the effects produced by the recursive calls. It is not hard to see that this structural requirement introduces a restriction in the kind of functions that can be formulated in terms of the monadic program schemes. To see a simple example, consider the following function that prints the values contained in a leaf-labelled binary tree, with a '+' symbol in between.

$$
\begin{array}{lll}
printTree & :: Show\ a \Rightarrow Btree\ a \rightarrow IO\ () \\
printTree\ (Leaf\ a) & = putStr\ (show\ a) \\
printTree\ (Join\ t\ t') & = \mathbf{do}\ \{\,printTree\ t;\ putStr\ \texttt{"+"};\ printTree\ t'\,\}
\end{array}
$$

For instance, when applied to the tree $Join\ (Join\ (Leaf\ 1)\ (Leaf\ 2))\ (Leaf\ 3)$, $printTree$ returns an I/O action that, when performed, prints the string $\texttt{"1+2+3"}$ on the standard output. Since it is a monadic function defined by structural recursion on the input tree, one could expect that it can be written as a monadic fold. However, this is impossible. To see why, recall that the definition of monadic fold for binary trees follows a pattern of recursion of this form:

$$
\begin{array}{ll}
mf_B\ (Leaf\ a) & = h_1\ a \\
mf_B\ (Join\ t\ t') & = \mathbf{do}\ \{\,y \leftarrow mf_B\ t;\ y' \leftarrow mf_B\ t';\ h_2\ y\ y'\,\}
\end{array}
$$

when a left to right product distribution $dist_\times$ is assumed. According to this pattern, in every recursive step the computations returned by the recursive calls must be performed in sequence, one immediately after the other. This means that there is no way of interleaving additional computations between the recursive calls, precisely the contrary of what $printTree$ does. This limitation is a consequence of having fixed the use of a monadic extension $\widehat{F}$ as unique alternative to structure the recursive calls in monadic program schemes. In other words, the fault is in the lifting construction itself.

This problem can be overcome by introducing a more flexible construction for the definition of monadic hylomorphism:

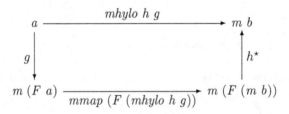

There are two differences between this definition and the one shown previously. First, this definition avoids the use of a monadic extension $\widehat{F}$, and second, the type of $h$ has changed with respect to the type it had previously. Now, its type is $F\ (m\ b) \rightarrow m\ b$. Therefore, strictly speaking, $h$ is not more a monadic $F$-algebra, but an $F$-algebra with monadic carrier. As a consequence of these modifications, in the new scheme the computations returned by the recursive calls are not performed apart in a separate unit any more. Instead, they are provided to the algebra $h$, which will specify the order in that these computations are performed, as well as their possible interleaving with other computations.

It is easy to see that this new version of monadic hylomorphism subsumes the previous one. In fact, a previous version of monadic hylomorphism (with monadic algebra $h :: F\ b \to m\ b$) can be represented in terms of the new one by taking $h \bullet dist_F$ as algebra, that is, $mhylo_{old}\ h\ g = mhylo\ (h \bullet dist_F)\ g$. This means that the definitions, examples and laws based on the lifting construction can all be regarded as special cases of the new construction.

Of course, we can derive new definitions of monadic fold and unfold from the new construction. For monadic unfold, the algebra of the monadic hylomorphism should only join the effects of the computations returned by the recursive calls, and build the values of the data structure using the constructors. Therefore,

$$munfold \quad :: Monad\ m \Rightarrow (a \to m\ (F\ a)) \to a \to m\ \mu F$$
$$munfold\ g = mhylo\ (\widehat{in_F} \bullet dist_F)\ g$$

Interestingly, this definition turns out to be equivalent to the one presented in Subsection 4.4. A definition of monadic fold is obained by taking $g = \widehat{out_F}$. By applying simplifications concerning the monad operations, we obtain:

$$mfold \quad :: Monad\ m \Rightarrow (F\ (m\ a) \to m\ a) \to \mu F \to m\ a$$
$$mfold\ h = h \circ F\ (mfold\ h) \circ out_F$$

Observe that this is nothing but the definition of fold (see Subsection 2.2) with the additional restriction that the algebra must be of monadic carrier. For instance, for leaf-labelled binary trees, $h :: (a \to m\ b, m\ b \to m\ b \to mb)$. Now, we can write $printTree$ as a monadic fold:

$$printTree = mfold_B\ (putStr \circ show, \lambda m\ m' \to \mathbf{do}\ \{\, m; putStr\ \texttt{"+"}; m'\,\})$$

Finally, we present a pair of fusion laws for the new version of monadic hylomorphism.

**MHylo-Fold Fusion.** If $mmap$ is strictness-preserving,

$$\tau :: \forall\ a\ .\ (F\ a \to a) \to (G\ (m\ a) \to m\ a)$$
$$\Rightarrow$$
$$mmap\ (fold\ h) \circ mhylo\ (\tau\ in_F)\ g = mhylo\ (\tau\ h)\ g$$

**Unfold-MHylo Fusion.**

$$\sigma :: \forall\ a\ .\ (a \to F\ a) \to (a \to m\ (G\ a))$$
$$\Rightarrow$$
$$mhylo\ h\ (\sigma\ out_F) \circ unfold\ g = mhylo\ h\ (\sigma\ g)$$

## 5   A Program Fusion Tool

The research presented in this paper motivated the development of an interactive program fusion tool that performs the automatic elimination of intermediate data structures from both purely-functional programas and programs with effects. The system accepts as input standard functional programs written in a subset of Haskell and translates them into an internal representation in terms of (monadic) hylomorphism. The tool is based on ideas and algorithms used in the design of the HYLO system [23]. In addition to the manipulation of programs with effects, our system extends HYLO with the treatment of some other shapes of recursion for purely-functional programs.

The following web page contains documentation and versions of the tool:

http://www.fing.edu.uy/inco/proyectos/fusion

# References

1. S. Abramsky and A. Jung. Domain theory. In S. Abramsky, D. M. Gabbay, and T. S. E. Maibaum, editors, *Handbook of Logic in Computer Science*, volume 3, pages 1–168. Clarendon Press, 1994.
2. N. Benton, J. Hughes, and E. Moggi. Monads and Effects. In *APPSEM 2000 Summer School,* LNCS 2395. Springer-Verlag, 2002.
3. R. Bird. *Introduction to Functional Programming using Haskell,* 2nd edition. Prentice-Hall, UK, 1998.
4. R.S. Bird and O. de Moor. *Algebra of Programming.* Prentice Hall, UK, 1997.
5. Chih-Ping Chen and P. Hudak. Rolling Your Own Mutable ADT—A Connection Between Linear Types and Monads. In *24th Symposium on Principles of Programming Languages*, pages 54–66. ACM, January 1997.
6. M.M. Fokkinga. *Law and Order in Algorithmics.* PhD thesis, Universiteit Twente, The Netherlands, 1992.
7. M.M. Fokkinga. Monadic maps and folds for arbitrary datatypes. Memoranda Informatica 94-28, University of Twente, June 1994.
8. J. Gibbons. Calculating Functional Programs. In *Algebraic and Coalgebraic Methods in the Mathematics of Program Construction,* LNCS 2297, pages 148–203. Springer-Verlag, January 2002.
9. J. Gibbons and G. Jones. The Under-Appreciated Unfold. In *3rd. International Conference on Functional Programming.* ACM, September 1998.
10. A. Gill. *Cheap Deforestation for Non-strict Functional Languages.* PhD thesis, Department of Computing Science, University of Glasgow, UK, 1996.
11. A. Gill, J. Launchbury, and S. Peyton Jones. A Shortcut to Deforestation. In *Conference on Functional Programming and Computer Architecture*, 1993.
12. G. Hutton. Fold and Unfold for Program Semantics. In *3rd. International Conference on Functional Programming.* ACM, September 1998.
13. S. Peyton Jones. Tackling the awkward squad: monadic input/output, concurrency, exceptions, and foreign language calls in Haskell. In *Engineering theories of software construction, Marktoberdorf Summer School 2000.* NATO ASI Series, IOS press, 2001.
14. S. Peyton Jones and J. Launchbury. Lazy functional state threads. In *Symposium on Programming Language Design and Implementation (PLDI'94)*, pages 24–35. ACM, 1994.
15. D. King. *Functional Programming and Graph Algorithms.* PhD thesis, Department of Computing Science, University of Glasgow, UK, March 1996.

16. D. King and J. Launchbury. Structuring depth-first search algorithms in Haskell. In *22nd Symposium on Principles of Programming Languages*, pages 344–354. ACM, 1995.

17. J. Launchbury. Graph Algorithms with a Functional Flavour. In *Advanced Functional Programming*, LNCS 925. Springer-Verlag, 1995.

18. E. Meijer, M. Fokkinga, and R. Paterson. Functional Programming with Bananas, Lenses, Envelopes and Barbed Wire. In *Functional Programming Languages and Computer Architecture'91*, LNCS 523. Springer-Verlag, August 1991.

19. E. Meijer and G. Hutton. Bananas in space: Extending fold and unfold to exponential types. In *Functional Programming Languages and Computer Architecture'95*, pages 324–333, 1995.

20. E. Meijer and J. Jeuring. Merging Monads and Folds for Functional Programming. In *Advanced Functional Programming*, LNCS 925, pages 228–266. Springer-Verlag, 1995.

21. E. Moggi. Notions of Computation and Monads. *Information and Computation*, 93:55–92, 1991.

22. P.S. Mulry. Lifting Theorems for Kleisli Categories. In *9th International Conference on Mathematical Foundations of Programming Semantics*, LNCS 802, pages 304–319. Springer-Verlag, 1993.

23. Y. Onoue, Z. Hu, H. Iwasaki, and M. Takeichi. A Calculational Fusion System HYLO. In *IFIP TC 2 Working Conference on Algorithmic Languages and Calculi, Le Bischenberg, France*, pages 76–106. Chapman & Hall, February 1997.

24. A. Pardo. *A Calculational Approach to Recursive Programs with Effects*. PhD thesis, Technische Universität Darmstadt, October 2001.

25. A. Pardo. Fusion of Recursive Programs with Computational Effects. *Theoretical Computer Science*, 260:165–207, 2001.

26. S. Peyton-Jones and P. Wadler. Imperative Functional Programming. In *20th Annual Symposium on Principles of Programming Languages*, Charlotte, North Carolina, 1993. ACM.

27. A. Takano and E. Meijer. Shortcut to Deforestation in Calculational Form. In *Functional Programming Languages and Computer Architecture'95*, 1995.

28. D. Tuijnman. *A Categorical Approach to Functional Programming*. PhD thesis, Fakultät für Informatik, Universität Ulm, Germany, January 1996.

29. P. Wadler. Theorems for free! In *4th International Conference on Functional Programming and Computer Architecture*, London, 1989.

30. P. Wadler. Deforestation: transforming programs to eliminate trees. *Theoretical Computer Science*, 73:231–248, 1990.

31. P. Wadler. Monads for functional programming. In *Advanced Functional Programming*, LNCS 925. Springer-Verlag, 1995.

# GEC: A Toolkit for Generic Rapid Prototyping of Type Safe Interactive Applications

Peter Achten, Marko van Eekelen,
Rinus Plasmeijer, and Arjen van Weelden

Nijmeegs Instituut voor Informatica en Informatiekunde,
Radboud Universiteit Nijmegen, Toernooiveld 1,
6525 ED Nijmegen, The Netherlands
{P.Achten, rinus, arjenw}@cs.ru.nl, marko@niii.ru.nl

**Abstract.** Programming GUIs with conventional GUI APIs is notoriously tedious. In these notes we present the GEC toolkit in which the programmer can create user interfaces without any knowledge of low-level I/O handling. Instead, he works with Graphical Editor Components (GEC). A GEC is an interactive component that is automatically derived from an arbitrary monomorphic data type, including higher order types. It contains a value of that data type, visualizes it, and allows the user to manipulate it in a type-safe way. The toolkit has a library of data types that represent standard GUI elements such as buttons, text fields, and so on. As a consequence, the programmer works with data types that model the interactive system that he is interested in. Programs are constructed as a collection of communicating GECs. This communication can be arranged in an ad-hoc way, or in a disciplined way, using a combinator library based on arrows. GECs are suitable for rapid prototyping of real world applications, for teaching and for debugging. These notes focus on the *use* of the GEC toolkit for functional programmers, only briefly explaining its inner workings and underlying principles.

## 1  Introduction

In the last decade, Graphical User Interfaces (GUIs) have become *the* standard for user interaction. Programming these interfaces can be done without much effort when the interface is rather static, and for many of these situations excellent tools are available. However, when there is more dynamic interaction between interface and application logic, such applications require tedious manual programming in any programming language. Programmers need to be skilled in the use of a large programming toolkit.

The goal of the *Graphical Editor* project is to obtain a concise programming toolkit that is *abstract*, *compositional*, and *type-directed*. Abstraction is required to reduce the size of the toolkit, compositionality reduces the effort of putting together (or altering) GUI code, and type-directed automatic creation of GUIs allows the programmer to focus on the data model. In contrast to visual programming environments, programming toolkits can provide ultimate flexibility,

V. Vene and T. Uustalu (Eds.): AFP 2004, LNCS 3622, pp. 210–244, 2005.

type safety, and dynamic behavior within a single framework. We use a *pure functional* programming language (Clean [22]) because functional programming languages have proven to be very suitable for creating abstraction layers on top of each other. Additionally, they have strong support for type definitions and type safety.

Our programming toolkit utilizes the *Graphical Editor Component* (*GEC*) [6] as universal building block for constructing GUIs. A *GEC*$_t$ is a graphical editor for values of any *monomorphic first-order* type t. This type-directed creation of *GEC*s has been obtained by *generic programming* techniques [9,16,15]. With generic programming one defines a family of functions that depend on the structure of types. The *GEC* toolkit project is to our knowledge the first project in which generic programming techniques are used for the creation of GUI applications. It is not the purpose of these notes to explain the inner workings of the *GEC* building blocks. The reader is referred to [6] for that. Instead we focus on the *use* of these building blocks and on *how* the toolkit is built using the basic blocks.

The basic first order *GEC* building blocks from [6] have been extended in two ways, such that we *can* construct higher-order value editors [8]. The first extension uses run-time *dynamic typing* [1,21], which allows us to include them in the *GEC* toolkit, but this does not allow type-directed GUI creation. It does, however, enable the toolkit to use polymorphic higher-order functions and data types. The second extension uses compile-time static typing, in order to gain monomorphic higher-order type-directed GUI creation of *abstract* types. It uses the *abstraction mechanism* of the *GEC* toolkit [7].

Apart from putting all the earlier published work together in a single context, focusing on the use of the toolkit and explaining the extensions using the basic building blocks, these notes also introduce a library for composing *GEC*s which is based on the arrows [17] concept. Furthermore, these notes contain exercises at the end of each section to encourage the reader to get familiar with the treated *GEC* concepts.

These notes are structured as follows. Section 2 contains an overview of the basic first-order *GEC* toolkit. In Sect. 3 it is explained how *GEC*s can be composed to form larger applications both using *GEC*s directly as well as using a new arrows library. The *GEC*-abstraction for model-view programming is treated in Sect. 4. Extensions for working with higher order types, dynamically and statically are covered in Sect. 5. Related work is discussed in Sect. 6 and conclusions are summarized in Sect. 7.

A note on the implementation and the examples in this paper. The project has been realized in Clean. Familiarity with Haskell is assumed, relevant differences between Haskell and Clean are explained in footnotes. The GUI code is mapped to Object I/O [4], which is Clean's library for GUIs. Given sufficient support for dynamic types, the results of this project can be transferred to Generic Haskell [19], using the Haskell [20] port of Object I/O [3]. The complete code of all examples (including the complete *GEC* implementation in Clean) can be downloaded from http://www.cs.ru.nl/~clean/gec.

Finally, we need to point out that Clean uses an explicit multiple environment passing style [2] for I/O programming. As *GEC*s are integrated with Clean Object I/O, the I/O functions that are presented in these notes are state transition functions on the program state (PSt ps). The program state represents the external world of an interactive program, tailored for GUI operations. In these notes the identifier env is a value of this type. The uniqueness type system [10] of Clean ensures single threaded use of the environment. To improve the readability, uniqueness type attributes that actually appear in the type signatures are not shown. Furthermore, the code has been slightly simplified, leaving out a few details that are irrelevant for these notes.

## 2   The Basic *GEC* Programming Toolkit

With the *GEC* programming toolkit [6], one constructs GUI applications in a *compositional* way using a high level of *abstraction*. The basic building block is the Graphical Editor Component (*GEC*).

**Graphical Editor Components.** A $GEC_t$ is an editor for values of type t. It is generated with a generic function. The power of a generic scheme is that we obtain an editor for free for any data type. This makes the approach particularly suitable for *rapid prototyping*.

The standard appearance of a *GEC* is illustrated by the following example that uses many functions and types that will be explained below:

```
module Editor
import StdEnv, StdIO, StdGEC

Start :: *World → *World[1]
Start world = startIO MDI[2] Void[3] myEditor world

myEditor = generateEditor ("List",[1])

generateEditor :: (String, t) (PSt ps) → PSt ps[4] |[5] gGEC{|*|}[6] t
generateEditor (windowName,initialValue) env = newenv
where
    (gecInterface, newenv)
        = gGEC{|*|} (windowName, initialValue, const id) env
```

---

[1] This function is equivalent with Haskell main::IO ().
[2] MDI selects Object I/O's Multiple Document Interface.
[3] Void is equivalent with Haskell ().
[4] Clean separates the types of function arguments by whitespace, instead of →.
[5] In a function type, | introduces all overloading class restrictions.
[6] Use the generic instance of kind * of gGEC.

**Fig. 1.** Generated editor for the standard list type, initially with value [1]

The complete GUI application is shown in Fig. 1.

The generic function gGEC creates *GEC*s. The way it is defined is explained in [6]. Here, we will focus on its use. It takes a *definition* (GECDef t env) of a $GEC_t$ and *creates* the $GEC_t$ object in the environment. It returns an *interface* (GECInterface t env) to that $GEC_t$ object. The environment env is in this case (PSt ps), since gGEC uses Object I/O.

**generic**[7] gGEC t :: GECFunction t (PSt ps)

:: GECFunction t env
   :==[8] (GECDef t env) env → (GECInterface t env, env)

The (GECDef t env) consists of three elements. The first is a string that identifies the top-level Object I/O element (window or dialog) in which the editor must be created. The second is the initial value of type t of the editor. The third is a callback function of type t → env → env. This callback function tells the editor which parts of the program need to be informed of user actions. The editor uses this function to respond to changes to the value of the editor by the application user.

:: GECDef t env :== (String,t,CallBackFunction t env)
:: CallBackFunction t env :== t env → env

The (GECInterface t env) is a record that contains all *methods* of the newly created $GEC_t$.

:: GECInterface t env =   { gecGetValue :: GecGet t env
                          , gecSetValue :: GecSet t env
                          }[9]
:: GecGet      t env :== env → (t, env)
:: GecSet      t env :== Update t env → env
:: Update          =   YesUpdate | NoUpdate

The gecGetValue method returns the current value, and gecSetValue sets the current value of the associated $GEC_t$ object. The gecSetValue method has an argument of type Update indicating whether or not the call-back function has to be called propagating the change of the value through the system.

In Fig. 2 the basic use of the function gGEC is illustrated by showing the corresponding GUI for several alternative definitions of myEditor (as in the example

---

[7] **generic** $f\ t\ ::\ T(t)$ introduces a generic function $f$ with type scheme $T(t)$.
[8] :== introduces a type synonym.
[9] A record type with fields $f_i$ of types $t_i$ is denoted as $\{f_i :: t_i\}$.

**Alternative definition of** `myEditor`:          **Corresponding GUI:**

```
myEditor2
= generateEditor ("Integer",0)
```

```
myEditor3
= generateEditor ("String","Hello World!")
```

```
myEditor4
= generateEditor ("Tuple of Integer and String",(0,"Hello World!"))
```

```
myEditor5
  = generateEditor
        ("Tree",Node Leaf 1 Leaf)

:: Tree a
      = Node (Tree a) a (Tree a) | Leaf
derive gGEC Tree
```

**Fig. 2.** Automatically derived editors for standard types

above). This generates an editor for the argument data type. All you have to specify is the name of the window and an initial value. On the right the editor is shown.

For standard types a version of **gGEC** is derived automatically. For user-defined types it is required that a version of **gGEC** is explicitly derived for the given type. For the type `Tree` this is explicitly done in the example. In the rest of these notes these **derives** are not shown.

Programs can consist of several editors. Editors can communicate with each other by tying together the various `gecSetValue` and `gecGetValue` methods. In Sect. 3.2 it is shown how an arrow combinator library [5] can be used for the necessary plumbing. In this section we use the function `selfGEC` (explained in Sect. 3.1) to create 'self-correcting' editors:

```
selfGEC ::
    String (t → t) t (PSt ps) → (PSt ps) | gGEC{|*|} t & bimap{|*|}10 ps
```

Given function f of type $t \rightarrow t$ on the data model of type t and an initial value v of type t, selfGEC gui f v creates the associated $GEC_t$ using gGEC (hence the context restriction). selfGEC creates a feedback loop that sends every edited output value back as input to the same editor, after applying f.

An example of the use of selfGEC is given by the following program that creates an editor for a *self-balancing* binary tree:

---

[10] The generic **gGEC** function requires an instantiation of the predefined generic function **bimap**.

```
myEditor    = selfGEC "Tree" balanceTree (Node Leaf 1 Leaf)

balanceTree = fromListToBalTree o¹¹ fromTreeToList

fromTreeToList Leaf = [ ]
fromTreeToList (Node l x r)
                = fromTreeToList l ++¹² [x:fromTreeToList r]¹³

fromListToBalTree  = balance o sort¹⁴
where balance [ ]        = Leaf
      balance [x]        = Node Leaf x Leaf
      balance xs         = Node (balance bs) b (balance as)
      where (as, [b:bs]) = splitAt (length xs / 2) xs
```

In this example, we create a $GEC_{(Tree\ Int)}$ which displays the indicated initial value Node Leaf 1 Leaf (left screen shot in Fig. 3). The user can manipulate this value in any desired order, producing new values of type Tree Int (e.g., turning the upper Leaf into a Node with the pull-down menu, the result of which is shown in the right screen shot in Fig. 3). Each time a new value is created or edited, the feedback function balanceTree is applied. balanceTree takes an argument of type Tree a and returns the tree after balancing it. The shape and lay-out of the tree being displayed adjusts itself automatically. Default values are generated by the editor when needed.

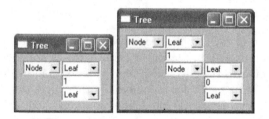

**Fig. 3.** A self-correcting editor for balanced trees

Note that the only things that need to be specified by the programmer are the initial value of the desired type, and the feedback function.

**Customizing Types.** Clean allows generic functions to be overruled by custom definitions for arbitrary types. gGEC is no exception to this rule. The left screenshot in Fig. 4 shows the default interface of the definition below for the ubiquitous *counter* example, and the code that creates it:

Although the definition of the counter is a sensible one, its visual interface clearly is not. In [6] we show how to change the representation of all values

---

[11] o is the function composition operator.

[12] ++ is the list concatenation operator.

[13] In Clean, list denotations are always delimited by [ and ].

[14] sort :: [a] → [a] | Ord a.

```
myEditor = selfGEC "Counter" updCntr (0,Neutral)
```

```
updCntr :: Counter → Counter
updCntr (n,Up)   = (n+1,Neutral)
updCntr (n,Down) = (n-1,Neutral)
updCntr any      = any
```

```
:: Counter :== (Int,UpDown)
:: UpDown  = UpPressed | DownPressed | Neutral
```

**Fig. 4.** The default (left) and customized (right) editor of the counter example

of type `Counter` to the screenshot shown at the right in Fig. 4. Because it has been explained in detail in [6], we will not repeat the code, but point out the important points:

- In this particular example, only the definitions of ( , ) (hide the constructor and place its arguments next to each other) and `UpDown` (display ⬍ instead of |Neutral ▼|) need to be changed.
- Normally `gGEC` creates the required logical (value passing) and visual infrastructure (GUI components). The programmer, when customizing `gGEC`, only needs to define the visual infrastructure. The programmer must be knowledgeable about Object I/O programming.
- The overruled instance works not only at the top-level. Every nested occurrence of the `Counter` type is now represented as shown right in Fig. 4.

For the creation of GUI applications, we need to model both specific GUI elements (such as buttons) and layout control (such as horizontal, vertical layout). In a way similar to the one shown above for the spin button, this has also been done by specializing `gGEC` for a number of other types that either represent GUI elements or layout. Below the predefined specialized editors are shown for a number of types. The specialized editor for `Display` creates a non-editable GUI; for `Button` a button is created; for `<|>` and `<->` two editors are created below each other, respectively next to each other; and finally `Hide` creates no GUI at all which is useful for remembering state.

For large data structures it may be infeasible to display the complete data structure. Customization can be used to define a $GEC_t$ that creates a view on a finite subset of such a large data structure with buttons to browse through the rest of the data structure. This same technique can also be used to create $GEC$s for lazy infinite data structures. For these infinite data structures customization is a must since clearly they can never be fully displayed.

*Exercise 1.* **A single address** $GEC$. Write a $GEC$ for editing a single record containing standard data base data such as name, address and location.

*Exercise 2.* **A List GEC (advanced).** Write a specialized $GEC$ that edits a lazy list with buttons to go to editing the next element.

**Type of the value given to** `myEditor`:                **Corresponding GUI:**

`:: Display a = Display a`

`:: Button = Button String`
`          | Pressed`

`:: <|> a b = a <|> b`

`:: <-> a b = a <-> b`

`:: Hide a = Hide a`

**Fig. 5.** Effect of some predefined customized editors on "Hello World!"

*Exercise 3.* **An address data base GEC.** Combine the applications above to write a GEC that edits a list of addresses.

## 3   Composition of GECs

In this section we present a number of examples to show how *GEC*s can be combined using the callback mechanism and method invocation (Sect. 3.1). In Sect. 3.2 we show how these examples can be expressed using arrow combinators.

### 3.1   Manual Composition of GECs

**Functionally Dependent GECs.** The first composition example establishes a functional dependency of type $a \to b$ between a source editor $GEC_a$ and destination editor $GEC_{Display\ b}$:

```
applyGECs :: (String,String) (a → b) a (PSt ps) → PSt ps
          |  gGEC{|*|} a & gGEC{|*|} b & bimap{|*|} ps
applyGECs (sa,sb) f va env
    #15 (gec_b, env) = gGEC{|*|} (sb, Display (f va), const id)   env
    #   (gec_a, env) = gGEC{|*|} (sa, va, set gec_b f) env
    =   env
```

---

[15] The #-notation of Clean has a special scope rule such that the same variable name can be used for subsequent non-recursive #-definitions. For mutually recursive definitions (as in `apply2GECs`) a standard **where**-definition has to be used with a different name for each variable.

```
set :: (GECInterface b (PSt ps)) (a → b) a (PSt ps) → (PSt ps)
set gec f va env = gec.¹⁶gecSetValue NoUpdate (Display (f va)) env
```

The callback function of $GEC_a$ uses the gecSetValue interface method of $GEC_b$ to update the current b value whenever the user modifies the a value. As a simple example, one can construct an interactive editor for lists (see Fig. 6) that are mapped to balanced trees by:

```
myEditor
    = applyGECs ("List","Balanced Tree") fromListToBalTree [1,5,2]
```

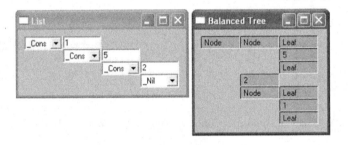

**Fig. 6.** Turning lists into balanced binary trees

Of course, the same can be done for binary functions with slightly more effort:

```
apply2GECs :: (String,String,String) (a → b → c) a b (PSt ps)
              → (PSt ps)
              | gGEC{|*|} a & gGEC{|*|} b & gGEC{|*|} c & bimap{|*|} ps
apply2GECs (sa,sb,sc) f va vb env = env3
where
    (gec_c,env1) = gGEC{|*|} (sc,Display (f va vb),const id)     env
    (gec_b,env2) = gGEC{|*|} (sb,vb,combine gec_a gec_c (flip f)) env1
    (gec_a,env3) = gGEC{|*|} (sa,va,combine gec_b gec_c f)       env2

combine :: (GECInterface y (PSt ps)) (GECInterface z (PSt ps))
                         (x → y → z) x (PSt ps) → PSt ps
combine gy gc f x env
    # (y,env) = gy.gecGetValue                                  env
    # env     = gc.gecSetValue NoUpdate (Display (f x y)) env
    = env
```

Notice that, due to the explicit environment passing style, it is trivial in Clean to connect $GEC_b$ with $GEC_a$ and vice versa. In Haskell's monadic I/O one needs to tie the knot with fixIO.

As an example, one can construct two interactive list editors, that are merged and put into a balanced tree (Fig. 7 shows the result):

---

¹⁶ $r.f$ denotes the selection of field $f$ of record $r$.

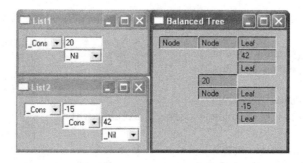

**Fig. 7.** Merging two lists into a balanced binary tree

```
myEditor
   = apply2GECs ("List1","List2","Balanced Tree") makeBalTree [1] [1]
where
   makeBalTree l1 l2 = fromListToBalTree (l1 ++ l2)
```

**Self-correcting GECs.** In this example we give the implementation of the *self-correcting* editor function gGEC that was already used in Sect. 2. Self-correcting editors update *themselves* in response to user edit operations. The function definition is concise:

```
selfGEC :: String (a → a) a (PSt ps) → (PSt ps)
        |  gGEC{|*|} a & bimap{|*|} ps
selfGEC s f v env = env1
where
   (gec,env1) = gGEC{|*|} (s,f v,λx → gec.gecSetValue NoUpdate (f x)) env
```

As an example, one can now construct a *self-sorting* list as follows:

```
myEditor = selfGEC "Self Sorting List" sort [5,1,2]
```

It is impossible for a user of this editor to create a stable non-sorted list value.

**Mutually Dependent GECs.** In a similar way one can define mutually dependent *GEC*s. Take the following definition of mutualGEC.

```
mutualGEC :: (String,String) a (a → b) (b → a) (PSt ps) → (PSt ps)
        |  gGEC{|*|} a & gGEC{|*|} b & bimap{|*|} ps
mutualGEC (gui1,gui2) va a2b b2a env = env2
where (gec_b,env1) = gGEC{|*|} (gui1, a2b va, set gec_a b2a) env
      (gec_a,env2) = gGEC{|*|} (gui2,     va, set gec_b a2b) env1
```

This function displays two *GEC*s. It is given an initial value va of type a, a function a2b :: a → b, and a function b2a :: b → a. The gec_a initially displays va, while gec_b initially displays a2b va. Each time one of the *GEC*s is changed, the other is updated automatically. The order in which changes are made is irrelevant. For example, the application mutualGEC ("Euros","Pounds")

```
exchangerate = 1.4
```

```
:: Pounds = {pounds :: Real}
:: Euros  = {euros  :: Real}
```

```
toPounds :: Euros → Pounds
toPounds {euros} = {pounds = euros / exchangerate}
```

```
toEuros :: Pounds → Euros
toEuros {pounds} = {euros = pounds ⋆ exchangerate}
```

**Fig. 8.** Mutually dependent $GEC_{\text{Pounds}}$ and $GEC_{\text{Euros}}$

{euros = 3.5} toPounds toEuros results in an editor that calculates the exchange between pounds and euros (see Fig. 8) and vice versa.

The example of Fig. 8 may look a bit like a tiny spreadsheet, but it is essentially different since standard spreadsheets do not allow mutual dependencies between cells. Notice also the separation of concerns: the way *GEC*s are coupled is defined completely separate from the actual functionality.

### 3.2   Combinators for GEC Composition

The examples in Sect. 3.1 show that *GEC*s can be composed by writing appropriate callback functions that use the GECInterface methods gecGetValue (get the value of a *GEC*) and gecSetValue (set its value). This explicit plumbing can become cumbersome when larger and more complex situations must be specified. What is needed, is a disciplined, and more abstract way of combining components. *Monads* [26] and *arrows* [17] are the main candidates for such a discipline. Monads abstract from computations that produce a value, whereas arrows abstract from computations that, *given certain input*, produce values. Because *GEC*s also have input and produce values, arrows are the best match. In this section we show how arrows can be used successfully for the composition of *GEC*s, resulting in structures that resemble *circuits of GECs*.

It is the task of our arrow model to introduce a standardized way of combining *GEC*s. As explained in Sect. 2, one uses a $GEC_t$ through its interface of type GECInterface t env. Method gecSetValue :: GecSet t env sets a new value of type t in the associated $GEC_t$, and gecGetValue :: GecGet t env reads its current value of type t.

If we generalize these types, then we can regard a *GEC-to-be-combined* as a component that has input a and output b (where a = b = t in case of a 'pure' $GEC_t$). This generalization of a *GEC-to-be-combined* has type GecCircuit a b because of its resemblance with electronic circuits. Consequently, this GecCircuit a b has a slightly more general interface, namely a method to *set* values of type GecSet a env, and a method to *get* values of type GecGet b env. This generalized flow of control of a circuit is visualized in Fig. 9.

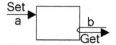

**Fig. 9.** A *GEC* Circuit (external view)

**Fig. 10.** A *GEC* Circuit (internal view)

When circuits are combined this will yield a double connection (one forward *set* and one backward *get* for each circuit). It is essential to realize that usage of the *set* method is restricted to the circuit that produces that input, and, likewise, usage of the *get* method is restricted to the circuit that needs that output.

Moreover, a *GEC-to-be-combined* of type `GecCircuit a b` needs to know where to send its output to, and where to obtain its input from. More precisely, it is only completely defined if it is provided with a corresponding *set* method (of type `GecSet b env`) and a *get* method (of type `GecGet a env`). These methods correspond exactly with the 'missing' methods in Fig. 9. Put in other words, a `GecCircuit a b` behaves as a *function*. Indeed, the way we obtain the restricted communication is by passing *continuation functions*. Through these continuations values are passed and set throughout the circuit. Each `GecCircuit a b` is a function that takes two continuations as arguments (one for the input and one for the output) and produces two continuations. The way a circuit takes its continuation arguments, creates a circuit and produces new continuations, can be visualized with the internal view of a circuit (see Fig. 10).

A `GecCircuit` is not only a continuation pair transformation function but it also transforms an Object I/O environment since it has to be able to incorporate the environment functions for the creation of graphical editor components. These environment functions are of type `(PSt ps) → (PSt ps)`.

The global idea sketched above motivates the following full definition of the `GecCircuit a b` type:

```
:: GecCircuit a b
   = GecCircuit (∀ ps:
        (GecSet b (PSt ps),GecGet a (PSt ps),PSt ps)
      → (GecSet a (PSt ps),GecGet b (PSt ps),PSt ps))
```

The circuits do not depend on the program state `ps`. This is expressed elegantly using a rank-2 polymorphic function type.

A `GecCircuit a b` generalizes *GEC*s by accepting input values of type `a` and produces output values of type `b`. Clearly, for every *GEC*$_a$ there exists a `GecCircuit a a`. This relation is expressed concisely with the function `edit`:

```
edit :: String → GecCircuit a a | gGEC{|*|} a
```

We will provide an instantiation of the standard arrow class for our *GEC* arrows of type GecCircuit. This standard arrow class definition is given below. It describes the basic combinators >>> (serial composition), arr (function lifting), and first (saving values across computations). The other definitions below can all be derived in the standard way from these basic arrow combinators. They are repeated here because we use them in our examples.

```
class Arrow arr where
    arr   ::  (a → b)  →  arr a b
    (>>>) ::  (arr a b) → (arr b c) → arr a c
    first ::  (arr a b) →  arr (a,c) (b,c)
```

```
// Combinators for free:
second :: (arr a b) → arr (c, a) (c, b)
second gec   = arr swap >>> first gec >>> arr swap
where  swap t = (snd t,fst t)
```

```
returnA :: arr a a
returnA = arr id
```

```
(<<<) infixr 1 :: (arr b c) (arr a b) → arr a c
(<<<) l r = r >>> l
```

```
(***) infixr 3 :: (arr a b) (arr c d) → arr (a,c) (b,d)
(***) l r = first l >>> second r
```

```
(&&&) infixr 3 :: (arr a b) (arr a c) → arr a (b,c)
(&&&) l r = arr (λx → (x,x)) >>> (l *** r)
```

We use the arrow combinator definitions in the examples below. For each example of Sect. 3.1, we give the definition using arrow combinators, and some of the circuit structures as figures.

However, we first need to show how such a circuit comes to life in Object I/O. This is done with the function startCircuit which basically turns a circuit into an Object I/O state transition function. As such it can be used in the myEditor function of Sect. 2.

```
startCircuit :: (GecCircuit a b) a (PSt ps) → PSt ps
startCircuit (GecCircuit k) a env
    = let (_,_,env1) = k (setb,geta,env) in env1
where geta      env  = (a,env)
       setb _ _ env  = env
```

Upon creation, the circuit function is applied to a geta function producing the initial argument and a dummy set function that just passes the environment.

**Functionally Dependent GECs.** The first arrow example (of which the external view is given in Fig. 11) implements applyGECs of Sect. 3.1.

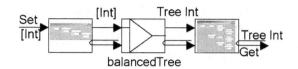

**Fig. 11.** applyGECs using arrows balancing a tree, external view

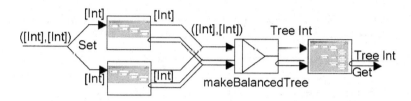

**Fig. 12.** apply2GECs using arrows creating a balanced tree from two lists, external view

```
myEditor
    = startCircuit (applyGECs ("List","Balanced Tree")
                    (Display o fromListToBalTree)) [1,5,2]

applyGECs :: (String,String) (a → b) → GecCircuit a b
                                    | gGEC{|*|} a & gGEC{|*|} b
applyGECs (sa, sb) f = edit sa >>> arr f >>> edit sb
```

Two visual editors are shown. The first allows the user to edit the (initial) list, and the second shows (and allows the user to edit) the resulting balanced tree. In the hand coded examples, the initial value of a *GEC* was specified at the time of its creation. Using the arrow combinators to construct a GecCircuit, we specify the initial values for all *GEC*s when we start the circuit.

The next example shows the arrow combinator version of apply2GECs (see Fig. 12 for its external view):

```
myEditor = startCircuit (apply2GECs ("List1","List2","Balanced Tree")
                makeBalTree) ([1],[2])
```
**where**
```
    makeBalTree (l1,l2) = Display (fromListToBalTree (l1 ++ l2))

apply2GECs :: (String,String,String) ((a,b) → c) → GecCircuit (a,b) c
                            | gGEC{|*|} a & gGEC{|*|} b & gGEC{|*|} c
apply2GECs (sa, sb, sc) f = edit sa *** edit sb >>> arr f >>> edit sc
```

The initial values for the input lists are paired, to allow the delayed initialization using startCircuit. The example clearly shows that combining *GEC*s using arrow combinators is much more readable than the (often) recursive handwritten functions. The linear flow of information between *GEC*s, using the >>> combinator, corresponds directly with the code. Although splitting points in flow of information, using the *** combinator, is less clear, it is still easier on the eyes than the examples of Sect. 3.1.

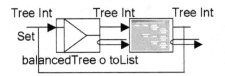

**Fig. 13.** `selfGEC` using arrows, self balancing a tree, external view

**Self-correcting GECs.** The example below shows the arrow combinator version of the `selfGEC` example (see its external view in Fig. 13).

```
myEditor = startCircuit selfGEC Leaf
```

```
selfGEC :: String (a → a) → GecCircuit a a | gGEC{|*|} a
selfGEC s f = feedback (arr f >>> edit s)
```

The way the `feedback` combinator constructs a feedback circuit is by taking the value of the circuit and feeding it back again into the circuit. This is done in such a way that it will not be propagated further when it arrives at a *GEC* editor.

When a feedback circuit contains no editor at all, the meaning of the circuit is undefined since in that case the calculation of the result would depend on itself in a circular way. A feedback circuit in which each path of the circuit contains an editor, is called *well-formed*. It is easy to check syntactically whether feedback circuits are well-formed. Consider the following examples of non well-formed and well-formed feedback circuits.

```
nonWellFormed1 = feedback (arr id >>> arr ((+) 1))
nonWellFormed2 = feedback (arr id &&& edit "Int" >>>
                          arr (λ(x, y) → x + y)    )
wellFormed = feedback (edit "Int" >>> arr ((+) 1))
```

It should be clear that the `selfGEC` function is well-formed. This completes the arrow combinator versions of the examples of Sect. 3.1. The counter example (Sect. 2) is also conveniently, and concisely, expressed below using `arr` and `>>>`.

```
myEditor = startCircuit (selfGEC "Counter" updCntr) (0,Neutral)
```

*Exercise 4.* **An intelligent form.** Write using the combinators a GEC for an intelligent form which calculates some of its values from others (VAT e.g.).

*Exercise 5.* **An editor for editors (advanced exercise).** Write an editor with which it is possible to create editors. An optional basic design scheme of such a *GEC* for *GEC*s is shown below.

```
myEditor = startCircuit (designEditor    >>>
                        arr convert      >>>
                        applicationEditor) initvalue
```

```
designEditor :: GecCircuit DesignEditor DesignEditor
```

```
designEditor = feedback (
                    toDesignEditor                      >>>
                    edit "design"                       >>>
                    arr (updateDesign o fromDesignEditor))


applicationEditor :: GecCircuit ApplicationEditor ApplicationEditor
applicationEditor = feedback (
                        arr (toApplicEditor o updateApplication) >>>
                        edit "application"                       >>>
                        arr fromApplicEditor                     )
```

It uses two quite complex *GEC*s that allow the user to edit the type and visual appearance of another *GEC*: an editor for designing a *GEC*, as well as an editor that displays, and allows the designer to interact with the designed *GEC*. Note that the information flow between these editors is nicely expressed using the arrow combinator >>> and that both feedback loops are well-formed.

## 4 Compositional Model-View Programming

When constructing a GUI application, the need arises to incrementally build and modify the GUI under construction. From what is explained in the previous sections, this means that one needs to modify the data structures, and hence also the dependent code, when changing the application. In this section we explain how to obtain a good separation between the *logic* of a GUI application (the *model*) and the way it is presented to the user (the *view*). This way of separating concerns is an instance of the *model-view* paradigm [18]. We show that it can be incorporated smoothly within our toolkit by inventing a new way to realize abstraction and composition based on the specialization mechanism that is used by the generic framework of the GEC toolkit.

The technique is illustrated by means of the following running example of a record with three fields, one of which contains the sum of the other two fields.

The code fragment below shows the *data model*. The data model is a record of type MyDataModel. The intention is that whenever the user edits one of the fields d_value1 or d_value2, then these new values are summed and displayed in field d_sum. This behavior is defined by updDataModel. We want to emphasize that the types and code shown in Fig. 14 are 'carved in stone': they do not change in the rest of this section.

As a trivial starting point we take the view model equal to the data model resulting in the following code and corresponding window (see Fig. 15).

The aim of this section is to show how the *view* on this data model can be varied without any modifications to this data model. Some of the kind of variations we would like to make easily are shown in Fig. 16 from left to right: a non-editable field for the result, additionally one of the fields implemented as a

---

[17] The record update $\{r \& f_1 = v_1, \ldots f_n = v_n\}$ denotes a new record equal to $r$, but with fields $f_i$ having values $v_i$.

```
:: MyDataModel
   = { d_value1 :: Int, d_value2 :: Int, d_sum :: Int }

initDataModel :: (Int,Int) → MyDataModel
initDataModel (v1,v2)
   = { d_value1 = v1, d_value2 = v2, d_sum = v1 + v2 }

updDataModel :: MyDataModel → MyDataModel
updDataModel d = { d &¹⁷ d_sum = d.d_value1 + d.d_value2 }

myEditor = selfGEC "View on Data"
                (toMyViewModel o updDataModel o fromMyViewModel)
                (toMyViewModel (initDataModel (0,0)))
```

**Fig. 14.** The code that is carved in stone for the running sum-example of this section

```
:: MyViewModel
   = { v_value1 :: Int, v_value2 :: Int, v_sum :: Int }

toMyViewModel :: MyDataModel → MyViewModel
toMyViewModel d = { v_value1 = d.d_value1
                  , v_value2 = d.d_value2
                  , v_sum    = d.d_sum }

fromMyViewModel :: MyViewModel → MyDataModel
fromMyViewModel v = { d_value1 = v.v_value1
                    , d_value2 = v.v_value2
                    , d_sum    = v.v_sum }
```

**Fig. 15.** The running sum-example, with trivial view

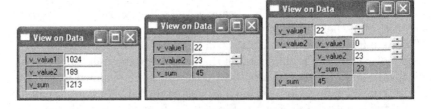

**Fig. 16.** 3 Model-View Variations of the sum-example of Fig. 15

counter to see variations and all editable fields as counter fields with one of the fields itself calculated as a sum of other fields.

In the following sections we show step by step how this can be accomplished. First, in Sect. 4.1 we show how to construct self-contained editors that take care of their own update and conversion behavior. In Sect. 4.2 we turn these self-contained editors into *abstract reusable* editors, thus encapsulating all information about their implementation and behaviour. We show how this is possible although *abstract* types seem to be at odds with generic programming. Finally, we show in Sect. 4.3 that these self-contained editors are truly reusable elements themselves. In that section we will also show (in Fig. 17) how to produce the variations (given in Fig. 16) of the running example (shown in Fig. 15).

## 4.1  Defining Self-contained Editors

If we want to reuse an existing editor, it is not enough to reuse its type. We also want to reuse its functionality: each editor should take care of its own update. For this purpose we need a type in which we can store the functionality of an editor. If want to create a view v on a domain model d, we need to be able to replace a standard editor for type d by a self-contained editor for some isomorphic view type v. Furthermore, since we generally also have to perform conversions between these types, we like to store them as well, such that each editor can take care of its own conversions. Finally, it is generally useful to take into account the old value of of v when converting from d since editors may have an internal state. Therefore we define a new type, ViewGEC d v (and a corresponding creation function mkViewGEC), in which we can store the update and conversion functions:

```
:: ViewGEC d v = { d_val    :: d
                 , d_to_v   :: d → (Maybe v) → v
                 , update_v :: v → v
                 , v_to_d   :: v → d }
```

```
mkViewGEC :: d (d → (Maybe b) → v) (v → v) (v → d) → ViewGEC d v
mkViewGEC d fdvv fvv fvd
            = { d_val    = d
              , d_to_v   = fdvv
              , update_v = fvv
              , v_to_d   = fvd }
```

For convenience, we define the creation function mkSimpleViewGEC that has a slightly simpler interface. In Exercise 6 you can practice with the more general interface for managing state.

```
mkSimpleViewGEC :: d (d → v) (v → v) (v → d) → ViewGEC d v
mkSimpleViewGEC d fdv fvv fvd = mkViewGEC d fdvv fvv fvd
where fdvv d Nothing  = fdv d
      fdvv _ (Just v) = v
```

Next, we define a specialized version of our generic editor gGEC for this type. The top-level definition is given below. Notice that in gGEC{|ViewGEC|} two additional parameters appear: gGECd and gGECv. This is caused by the fact that generic functions in Clean are kind-indexed functions. As ViewGEC d v is of kind $\star \to \star \to \star$, the generic function has two additional parameters, one for type d and one for type v.

```
gGEC{|ViewGEC|} gGECd gGECv (vName, viewGEC, viewGECCallback) env
    = ({ gecSetValue = viewSetValue vInterface
       , gecGetValue = viewGetValue vInterface }, new_env)
where (vInterface,new_env)
            = gGECv ( vName
                    , viewGEC.d_to_v viewGEC.d_val Nothing
                    , viewCallback vInterface
                    ) env
```

The ViewGEC editor does the following. The value of type d is stored in the ViewGEC record, but a d-editor (gGECd) for it is not created. Taking the old value of v into account, the d-value is converted to a v-value using the conversion function d_to_v :: d → (Maybe v) → v. For this v-value we do generate a generic v-editor (gGECv) to store and edit the v-value.

What remains to be defined are the callback function for the view editor (viewCallback) and the GECInterface (ViewGEC d v) methods (viewSetValue and viewGetValue). We discuss the most complicated one, the callback function, first. Whenever the application user creates a new v-value with this editor, the call-back function of the v-editor is called (viewCallback) and the update_v :: v → v function is applied. This is similar to applying (selfGEC update_v) to the corresponding new value of type v. The resulting new v-value is shown in the v-editor again, and it is converted back to a d-value as well, using the function v_to_d :: v → d. This new d-value is then stored in the ViewGEC record in the d_val field, and the call-back function for the ViewGEC editor is called (viewGECCallback).

```
viewCallback vInterface new_v env
    = viewGECCallback {viewGEC & d_val = new_d} new_env
where new_upd_v = viewGEC.update_v new_v
      new_env   = vInterface.gecSetValue new_upd_v env
      new_d     = viewGEC.v_to_d new_upd_v
```

The two interface methods to write (viewSetValue) and read (viewGetValue) are fairly straightforward. Writing a value of type ViewGEC d v amounts to writing a value of type v using the current old value of type v and the new value of type d that is stored in the ViewGEC record. Reading a value of type ViewGEC d v amounts to reading the current v value and wrap it up in the record after converting it to a d value.

```
viewSetValue vInterface new_viewGEC env
    = vInterface.gecSetValue new_v new_env
where new_v = new_viewGEC.d_to_v new_viewGEC.d_val (Just old_v)
      (old_v,new_env) = vInterface.gecGetValue env

viewGetValue vInterface env
    = ({viewGEC & d_val = viewGEC.v_to_d current_v},new_env)
where (current_v,new_env) = vInterface.gecGetValue env
```

The concrete behavior of the generated ViewGEC editor now not only depends on the type, but also on the concrete information stored in a value of type ViewGEC. A self-contained reusable editor, such as counterGEC below, is now quickly constructed. The corresponding editor takes care of the conversions and the update. The displayGEC does a trivial update (identity) and also takes care of the required conversions.

```
counterGEC :: Int → ViewGEC Int Counter
counterGEC i = mkViewGEC i toCounter updCntr fromCounter

displayGEC :: a → ViewGEC a (Display a)
displayGEC x = mkViewGEC x toDisplay id fromDisplay
```

Making use of these new self-contained editors we can attach a *view model* to the *data model* that was presented in the start of this section by giving appropriate definitions of the conversion functions toMyViewModel and fromMyViewModel. All other definitions remain the same.

```
:: MyViewModel  = { v_value1 :: ViewGEC Int Counter
                  , v_value2 :: ViewGEC Int Counter
                  , v_sum    :: ViewGEC Int (Display Int) }

toMyViewModel :: MyDataModel → MyViewModel
toMyViewModel d = { v_value1 = counterGEC d.d_value1
                  , v_value2 = counterGEC d.d_value2
                  , v_sum    = displayGEC d.d_sum }

fromMyViewModel :: MyViewModel → MyDataModel
fromMyViewModel v = { d_value1 = v.v_value1.d_val
                    , d_value2 = v.v_value2.d_val
                    , d_sum    = v.v_sum.d_val }
```

In the definition of toMyViewModel we can now choose any suitable self-contained editor. Each editor handles the needed conversions and updates itself automatically. To obtain the value we are interested in, we just have to address the d_val field.

The example shows that we have indeed obtained proper compositional behavior but the programming method is not truly compositional. If we would replace a self-contained editor by another in toMyViewModel, all other code remains the same. However, we *do* have to change the type of MyViewModel. In this type it is completely visible what kind of editor has been used. In the following section it is shown how to create a complete compositional abstraction using a special abstract data type for our self-contained editors.

## 4.2  Abstract Self-contained Editors

The concrete value of type ViewGEC d v is used by the generic mechanism to generate the desired self-contained editors. The ViewGEC d v type depends on the type of the editor v that is being used. Put in other words, the type still reveals information about the implementation of editor v. This is undesirable for two reasons: one can not exchange views without changing types, and the type of composite views reflects their composite structure. For these reasons, a type is required that *abstracts* from the concrete editor type v.

However, if we manage to hide these types, how can the generic mechanism generate the editor for it? The generic mechanism can only generate an editor for a given concrete type, not for an abstract type of which the content is unknown. The solution is as follows. When the abstraction is being made, we *do* know the contents and its type. Hence, we can store the *generic editor function* (of type GECFunction, see Sect. 2) in the abstract data structure itself where the abstraction is being made. The stored editor function can be applied later when we really need to construct the editor. Therefore, it is possible to define an abstract data structure (AGEC d) in which the ViewGEC d v is stored with its corresponding generic gGEC function for v. Technically this requires a type system that supports existentially quantified types as well as rank-2 polymorphism.

```
:: AGEC d
   = ∃v: AGEC (ViewGEC d v) (∀ps: GECFunction (ViewGEC d v) (PSt ps))

mkAGEC :: (ViewGEC d v) → AGEC d | gGEC{|*|} v
mkAGEC viewGEC = AGEC viewGEC (gGEC{|* → * → *|} undef gGEC{|*|})

gGEC{|AGEC|} = ···  // similar to gGEC{|ViewGEC|}, but apply function in AGEC
```

The function mkAGEC creates the desired AGEC given a viewGEC. Looking at the type of AGEC, the generic system can deduce that the editor to store has to be a generic editor for type ViewGEC d v. To generate this editor, the generic system by default requires an editor for type d and type v as well. *We* know that in this particular case we do not use the d-editor at all. We can tell this to the generic system by making use of the fact that generic functions in Clean are kind indexed. The system allows us, if we wish, to explicitly specify the editors for type d (undef) and type v (gGEC{|*|}) to be used by the editor for ViewGEC (gGEC{|* → * → *|}). In this case we know that we do not need an editor for type d (hence the undef), and use the standard generic editor for type v. The overloading context restriction in the type of mkAGEC ( | gGEC{|*|} v) states that for making an AGEC d out of a ViewGEC d v only an editor for type v is required.

We also have to define a specialized version of gGEC for the AGEC type. The corresponding generated editor applies the stored editor to the stored ViewGEC.

The types and kind indexed generic programming features we have used here may look complicated, but for the programmer an abstract editor is easy to make. To use a self-contained editor of type v as editor for type d, a ViewGEC d v has to be defined. Note that the editor for type v is automatically derived for the programmer by the generic system! The function mkAGEC stores them both into an AGEC. The functions counterAGEC and displayAGEC show how easy AGEC's can be made. One might be surprised that the overloading context for displayAGEC still requires a d-editor ( | gGEC{|*|} d). This is caused by the fact that in this particular case type d is used in the definition of type `Display`.

```
counterAGEC :: Int → AGEC Int
counterAGEC i = mkAGEC (counterGEC i)

displayAGEC :: d → AGEC d | gGEC{|*|} d
displayAGEC x = mkAGEC (displayGEC x)
```

We have chosen to export `AGEC d` as a Clean abstract data type. This implies that code that uses such an abstract value can not apply record selection to access the d value. For this purpose we provide the following obvious projection functions to retrieve the d-value from an `AGEC d` (^^) and to store a new d-value in an existing `AGEC d` (the infix operator ^=).

```
(^^) :: (AGEC d) → d                    // Read current value
(^^) (AGEC viewGEC gGEC) = viewGEC.d_val

(^=) infixl :: (AGEC d) d → (AGEC d)    // Set new value
(^=) (AGEC viewGEC gGEC) nval = AGEC {viewGEC & d_val=nval} gGEC
```

Using abstract editors we can refine the *view model* data type and conversion functions:

```
:: MyViewModel   = { v_value1 :: AGEC Int
                   , v_value2 :: AGEC Int
                   , v_sum    :: AGEC Int }

toMyViewModel    :: MyDataModel → MyViewModel
toMyViewModel    d = { v_value1 = counterAGEC d.d_value1
                     , v_value2 = counterAGEC d.d_value2
                     , v_sum    = displayAGEC d.d_sum }

fromMyViewModel :: MyViewModel → MyDataModel
fromMyViewModel v = { d_value1 = ^^ v.v_value1
                    , d_value2 = ^^ v.v_value2
                    , d_sum    = ^^ v.v_sum }
```

The advantage of the use of the `AGEC`-type is that, if we want to pick another editor, we only have to tell which one to pick in the definition of `toMyViewModel`. The types used in `MyViewModel` all remain the same (`AGEC Int`), no matter which editor is chosen. Also the definition of `fromMyViewModel` remains unaffected.

## 4.3   Abstract Editors Are Compositional

In order to show the compositional nature of abstract editors, we first turn the running example into an abstract editor: `sumAGEC :: AGEC Int`. It can be used *itself* as an `Int`-editor. We follow the scheme introduced above:

```
sumAGEC :: Int → AGEC Int                          // see counterAGEC (4.2)
sumAGEC i = mkAGEC (sumGEC i)
where sumGEC :: Int → ViewGEC Int MyViewModel // see counterGEC (4.1)
      sumGEC i = mkSimpleViewGEC i toV updV fromV
        where toV   = toMyViewModel o toMyData
              fromV = fromMyData   o fromMyViewModel
              updV  = toMyViewModel o updDataModel o fromMyViewData

              toMyData  i = {d_value1 = 0, d_value2 = i, d_sum = i}
              fromMyData d = d.sum
```

Now sumAGEC, counterAGEC, and displayAGEC are interchangeable components. If we want to experiment with variants of the running example, we pick the instance of our choice in the toMyViewModel function (in this way achieving the wanted examples of the beginning of this section: see Fig. 17).

**Alternative definition of toMyViewModel:**        **Corresponding GUI:**

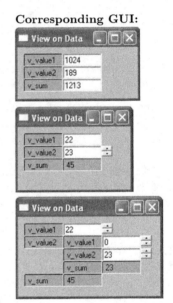

```
toMyViewModel1 d
  = { v_value1 = idAGEC       d.d_value1
    , v_value2 = idAGEC       d.d_value2
    , v_sum    = displayAGEC d.d_sum }


toMyViewModel2 d
  = { v_value1 = idAGEC       d.d_value1
    , v_value2 = counterAGEC d.d_value2
    , v_sum    = displayAGEC d.d_sum }




toMyViewModel3 d
  = { v_value1 = counterAGEC d.d_value1
    , v_value2 = sumAGEC      d.d_value2
    , v_sum    = displayAGEC d.d_sum }
```

**Fig. 17.** *Plug-and-play* your favorite abstract editors. The only code that changes is the function toMyViewModel. The values have been edited by the user.

We have set up a library of abstract components. One of these library functions idAGEC (which takes a value of any type and promotes it to an abstract editor component for that type) is used in the example above. With this library it is possible to rapidly create GUIs in a declarative style. This is useful e.g. for prototyping, education, tracing and debugging purposes.

Below, we summarize only those functions of the collection that are used in the examples in these notes:

```
vertlistAGEC :: [a] → AGEC [a] | gGEC{|*|} a
                                            // all elements displayed in a column
counterAGEC  :: a → AGEC a | gGEC{|*|}, IncDec a
                                            // a special number editor
hidAGEC      :: a → AGEC a                   // identity, no editor
displayAGEC  :: a → AGEC a | gGEC{|*|} a // identity, non-editable editor
```

*Exercise 6.* **Abstract Lists (advanced).** Modify the solution of Exercise 2 in such a way that it is an abstract editor for lists. Make use of the general mkViewGEC function that manipulates the state of the view.

*Exercise 7.* **Abstract Intelligent Form.** Experiment with your solution for Exercise 4. Replace parts of it by *AGEC*s and experiment with different editors at the basic level.

## 5   Higher-Order GECs

In the previous sections all functionality had to be encoded in the program. A user could only edit data values, no functions.

In this section we explain how basic *GEC*s have been extended with the ability to deal with functions and expressions allowing the user to edit functional values.

Consider as a motivating example the running example of the previous section. It had the function sum encoded in the program. In order to change it to product e.g. the user would have to ask a programmer to change the program. Of course, a user would prefer to have the ability to change (and add) functionality.

A user would like to be able to type in expressions using e.g. twice and map and let the *GEC* react accordingly. In Fig. 18 we show how such an editor could look like. On the left there is a *GEC* in which a user has typed in a partial application of the map function, on the right the twice function has been used.

Looking carefully one can imagine that it is not an easy task to achieve such functionality. Depending on what functional value is typed in, the number of other fields will vary.

Suppose the expression field is the twice function λf x → f (f x) as in the right example of Fig. 18. If the first argument is the increment function ((+) 1),

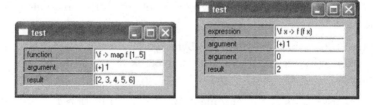

**Fig. 18.** Two *GEC*s editing functional values

there is one further argument, an `Int`, and of course a field for the result. However, if the first argument would also be the twice function then an extra argument would be required!

The number of argument fields depend on the type of the functional value that is typed in by the user (or of the actual arguments that are given to it by the user). These examples of Fig. 18 are created in the sections below.

Because functions are opaque, the solution requires a means of interpreting functional expressions as functional values. Instead of writing our own parser/interpreter/type inference system we use the *Esther* shell [24]. Esther enables the user to enter expressions (using a subset of Clean) that are dynamically typed, and transformed to values and functions using compiled code. It is also possible to reuse earlier created functions, which are stored on disk. Its implementation relies on the *dynamic type system* [1,21,25] of Clean.

The shell uses a text-based interface, and hence it makes sense to create a special *string*-editor (Sect. 5.1), which converts any string into the corresponding dynamically typed value. This special editor has the same power as the Esther command interpreter and can deliver any dynamic value, including higher-order polymorphic functions. In addition we show that the actual *content* of a dynamic value can be influenced by the very same generic mechanism, using type dependent functions (Sect. 5.2). With this mechanism, dynamics can be used in a type-directed way, but only for monomorphic types in dynamics.

## 5.1   Dynamically Typed Higher-Order GECs

We first introduce the foundations of the Esther shell, and proceed by showing how to construct an editor for functions.

**Dynamics in Clean.** A *dynamic* is a value of static type `Dynamic`, which contains an expression as well as a representation of its static type, e.g., **dynamic** 42 :: `Int`, **dynamic** `map fst` :: $\forall$a b: $[(a, b)] \rightarrow [a]$. Basically, dynamic types turn every (first and higher-order) type into a first-order type, while providing runtime access to the original type and value.

Function alternatives and case patterns can match on values of type `Dynamic`. Such a pattern match consists of a value pattern and a type pattern, e.g., $[4, 2]$ :: $[Int]$. The compiler translates a pattern match on a type into run-time type unification. If the unification is successful, type variables in a type pattern are bound to the offered type. Applying dynamics at run-time will be used to create an editor that changes according to the type of entered expressions (Sect. 5.1, Example 2).

```
dynamicApply :: Dynamic Dynamic → Dynamic
dynamicApply (f :: a → b) (x :: a) = dynamic f x      :: b
dynamicApply       df         dx    = dynamic "Error" :: String
```

`dynamicApply` tests if the argument type of the function `f`, inside its first argument, can be unified with the type of the value `x`, inside the second argument. `dynamicApply` can safely apply `f` to `x`, if the type pattern match succeeds. It yields a value of the type that is bound to the type variable b by unification, wrapped in a dynamic. If the match fails, it yields a string in a dynamic.

Type variables in type patterns can also relate to type variables in the static type of a function. A ^ behind a variable in a pattern associates it with the same type variable in the static type of the function.

```
matchDynamic :: Dynamic → t | TC t
matchDynamic (x :: t^) = x
```

The static type variable t, in the example above, is determined by the static context in which it is used, and imposes a restriction on the actual type that is accepted at run-time by matchDynamic. The function becomes overloaded in the predefined TC (type code) class. This makes it a type dependent function [21].

The dynamic run-time system of Clean supports writing dynamics to disk and reading them back again, possibly in another program or during another execution of the same program. This provides a means of type safe communication, the ability to use compiled plug-ins in a type safe way, and a rudimentary basis for mobile code. The dynamic is read in lazily after a successful run-time unification. The amount of data and code that the dynamic linker links is, therefore, determined by the evaluation of the value inside the dynamic.

```
writeDynamic :: String Dynamic env → (Bool,env) | FileSystem env
readDynamic  :: String env → (Bool,Dynamic,env) | FileSystem env
```

Programs, stored as dynamics, have Clean types and can be regarded as a typed file system. We have shown that dynamicApply can be used to type check any function application at run-time using the static types stored in dynamics. Combining both in an interactive 'read expression – apply dynamics – evaluate and show result' loop, already gives a simple shell that supports the type checked run-time application of programs to documents. The composeDynamic function below, taken from the Esther shell, applies dynamics and infers the type of an expression.

```
composeDynamic    :: String env → (Dynamic,env) | FileSystem env
showValueDynamic  :: Dynamic → String
```

composeDynamic *expr env* parses *expr*. Unbound identifiers in *expr* are resolved by reading them from the file system. In addition, overloading is resolved. Using the parse tree of *expr* and the resolved identifiers, the dynamicApply function is used to construct the (functional) value $v$ *and* its type $\tau$. These are packed in a **dynamic** $v :: \tau$ and returned by composeDynamic. In other words, if $env \vdash expr :: \tau$ and $[\![expr]\!]_{env} = v$ **then** composeDynamic *expr env* $= (v :: \tau, env)$. The showValueDynamic function yields a string representation of the value inside a dynamic.

**Creating a GEC for the Type Dynamic.** With the composeDynamic function, an editor for dynamics can be constructed. This function needs an appropriate environment to access the dynamic values and functions (plug-ins) that are stored on disk. The standard (PSt ps) environment used by the generic gGEC function (Sect. 2) is such an environment. This means that we can use composeDynamic in a specialized editor to offer the same functionality as the command line interpreter. Instead of Esther's console we use a String editor as interface to the application user. In addition we need to convert the provided string into the corresponding dynamic. We therefore define a composite data type DynString and a specialized gGEC-editor for this type (a $GEC_{\text{DynString}}$) that performs the required conversions.

```
:: DynString = DynStr Dynamic String
```

The choice of the composite data type is motivated mainly by simplicity and convenience: the string can be used by the application user for typing in the expression. It also stores the original user input, which cannot be extracted from the dynamic when it contains a function.

Now we specialize gGEC for this type DynString. The complete definition of gGEC{|DynString|} is given below.

```
gGEC{|DynString|} (gui,DynStr _ expr,dynStringUpd) env
  # (stringGEC,env) = gGEC{|*|} (gui,expr,stringUpd dynStringUpd) env
  = ({ gecSetValue = dynSetValue stringGEC.gecSetValue
     , gecGetValue = dynGetValue stringGEC.gecGetValue },env)
where dynSetValue stringSetValue (DynStr _ expr) env
         = stringSetValue expr env
      dynGetValue stringGetValue env
         # (nexpr,env) = stringGetValue env
         # (ndyn, env) = composeDynamic nexpr env
         = (DynStr ndyn nexpr,env)
      stringUpd dynStringUpd nexpr env
         # (ndyn,env) = composeDynamic nexpr env
         = dynStringUpd (DynStr ndyn nexpr) env
```

The created $GEC_{\text{DynString}}$ displays a box for entering a string by calling the standard generic gGEC{|*|} function for the value expr of type String, yielding a stringGEC. The DynString-editor is completely defined in terms of this String-editor. It only has to take care of the conversions between a String and a DynString. This means that its gecSetValue method dynSetValue sets the string component of a new DynString in the underlying String-editor. Its gecGetValue method dynGetValue retrieves the string from the String-editor, converts it to the corresponding Dynamic by applying composeDynamic, and combines these two values in a DynString-value. When a new string is created by the application user, this will call the callback function stringUpd. It invokes the callback function dynStringUpd (provided as an argument upon creation of the DynString-editor), after converting the String to a DynString.

It is convenient to define a constructor function mkDynStr that converts any input $expr$, that has value $v$ of type $\tau$, into a value of type DynString guaranteeing that if $v :: \tau$ and $[\![expr]\!] = v$, then (DynStr $(v::\tau)$ $expr$) :: DynString.

```
mkDynStr :: a → DynString | TC a
mkDynStr x = let dx = dynamic x in DynStr dx (showValueDynamic dx)
```

**Function Test Example.** We construct an interactive editor that can be used to test functions. It can be a newly defined function, say $\lambda x \to x\^2$, or any existing function stored on disk as a `Dynamic`. Hence the tested function can vary from a small function, say `factorial`, to a large complete application.

```
:: MyRecord = { function :: DynString
              , argument :: DynString
              , result   :: DynString }
myEditor
= selfGEC "test" guiApply (initval id 0)
where
  initval f v
    = { function = mkDynStr f
      , argument = mkDynStr v
      , result   = mkDynStr (f v) }
  guiApply
      r=:18{ function = DynStr (f::a → b) _
           , argument = DynStr (v::a)    _ }
    = {r & result = mkDynStr (f v)}
  guiApply r = r
```

MyRecord has three `DynString` fields: `function`, `argument`, and `result`. The user can use this editor to enter a function definition and its argument. The `selfGEC` function ensures that each time a new string is created with the editor "test", the function `guiApply` is applied that provides a new value of type `MyRecord` to the editor. The function `guiApply` tests, in a similar way as the function `dynamicApply` (see Sect. 5.1), whether the type of the supplied function and argument match. If so, a new result is calculated. If not, nothing happens.

This editor can only be used to test functions with one argument. What happens if we edit the function and the argument in such a way that the result is not a plain value but a function itself? Take, e.g., as function the twice function $\lambda f\ x \to f\ (f\ x)$, and as argument the increment function $((+)\ 1)$. Then the result is also a function $\lambda x \to ((+)\ 1)\ ((+)\ 1\ x)$. The editor displays `<function>` as result. There is no way to pass an argument to the resulting function.

With an editor like the one above, the user can enter expressions that are automatically converted into the corresponding `Dynamic` value. As in the shell, unbound names are expected to be dynamics on disk. Illegal expressions result in a `Dynamic` containing an error message.

To have a properly higher-order dynamic application example one needs an editor in which the user can type in functions of arbitrary arity, and subsequently enter arguments for this function. The result is then treated such that, if it is a function, editors are added dynamically for the appropriate number of arguments. This is explained in the following example.

---

[18] $x =: e$ binds $x$ to $e$.

**Expression Test Example.** We construct a test program that accepts arbitrary expressions and adds the proper number of argument editors, which again can be arbitrary expressions. The number of arguments cannot be statically determined and has to be recalculated each time a new value is provided. Instead of an editor for a record we therefore create an editor for a list of tuples. Each tuple consists of a string used to prompt to the user, and a DynString-value. The tuple elements are displayed below each other using the predefined list editor vertlistAGEC (Sect. 4.3) and access operator `^^` (Sect. 4.2). The selfGEC function is used to ensure that each change made with the editor is tested with the guiApply function and the result is shown in the editor.

```
myEditor
= selfGEC "test" (guiApply o (^^))
      (vertlistAGEC [show "expression " 0])
where
 guiApply [df=:(_,DynStr f _):args]
   = vertlistAGEC [df:check f args]
 where
   check (f::a → b)
         [arg=:(_,DynStr (x::a) _):args]
       = [arg : check (dynamic f x) args]
   check (f::a → b) _
       = [show "argument " "??"]
   check (x::a) _
       = [show "result " x]
```

show s v = (Display s,mkDynStr v)

The key part of this example is formed by the function check which calls itself recursively on the result of the dynamic application. As long as function and argument match, and the resulting type is still a function, it requires another argument which is checked for type consistency. If the resulting type is a plain value, it is evaluated and shown using the predefined function display, which creates a non-editable editor that just displays its value. As soon as a type mismatch is detected, a question mark is displayed to prompt the user to try again. With this editor, any higher-order polymorphic function can be entered and tested.

## 5.2   Statically Typed Higher-Order *GEC*s

The editors presented in the previous section are flexible because they deliver a Dynamic (packed into the type DynString). They have the disadvantage that the programmer has to program a check, such as the check function in the previous example, on the type consistency of the resulting Dynamics.

In many applications it is statically known what the type of a supplied function must be. In this section we show how the run-time type check can be replaced by a compile-time check, using the abstraction mechanism for *GEC*s. This gives the programmer a second solution for higher-order types that is statically typed, which allows, therefore, type-directed generic GUI creation.

**Adding Static Type Constraints to Dynamic GECs.** The abstraction mechanism provided by *AGEC*s is used to build type-directed editors for higher-order types, which check the type of the entered expressions dynamically. These statically typed higher-order editors are created using the function dynamicAGEC. The full definition of this function is specified and explained below.

```
dynamicAGEC :: d → AGEC d | TC d
dynamicAGEC x
   = mkAGEC (mkSimpleViewGEC x toView (updView x) (fromView x))
where
       toView :: d → (DynString,AGEC DynString)
       toView newx = let dx = mkDynStr newx in (dx,hidAGEC dx)

       fromView :: d (DynString,AGEC DynString) → d | TC d
       fromView _ (_,oldx) = case ^^oldx of DynStr (x::d^) _ → x

       updView :: d (DynString,AGEC DynString)
                   → (DynString,AGEC DynString) | TC d
       updView _ (newx=:(DynStr (x::d^) _),_) = (newx,hidAGEC newx)
       updView _ (_,oldx)                     = (^^oldx,oldx)
```

The abstract Dynamic editor, which is the result of the function dynamicAGEC initially takes a value of some statically determined type d. It converts this value into a value of type DynString, such that it can be edited by the application user as explained in Sect. 5.1. The application user can enter an expression of arbitrary type, but now it is ensured that only expressions of type d are approved.

The function updView, which is called in the abstract editor after any edit action, checks, using a type pattern match, whether the newly created dynamic can be unified with the type d of the initial value (using the ^-notation in the pattern match as explained in Sect. 5.1). If the type of the entered expression is different, it is rejected and the previous value is restored and shown. To do this, the abstract editor has to remember in its internal state also the previously accepted correctly typed value. Clearly we do not want to show this part of the internal state to the application user. This is achieved using the abstract editor hidAGEC (Sect. 4.3), which creates an invisible editor, i.e., a store, for any type.

**Function Test Example, Revisited.** Consider the following variation of the function test example on page 237:

```
:: MyRecord a b = { function :: AGEC (a → b)
                  , argument :: AGEC a
                  , result   :: AGEC b }
```

```
myEditor = selfGEC "test" guiApply (initval ((+) 1.0) 0.0)
where
    initval f v
        = { function = dynamicAGEC f
          , argument = dynamicAGEC v
          , result   = displayAGEC (f v) }

    guiApply myrec=:{ function = af, argument
        = {myrec & result = displayAGEC ((^^af) (^^av))}
```

The editor above can be used to test functions of a certain statically determined type. Due to the particular choice of the initial values ((+) 1.0 :: Real → Real and 0.0 :: Real), the editor can only be used to test functions of type Real → Real applied to arguments of type Real. Notice that it is now statically guaranteed that the provided dynamics are correctly typed. At runtime the dynamicAGEC-editors take care of the required checks and they reject ill-typed expressions. The programmer therefore does not have to perform any checks anymore. The abstract dynamicAGEC-editor delivers a value of the proper type just like any other abstract editor.

The code in the above example is not only simple and elegant, but it is also very flexible. The dynamicAGEC abstract editor can be replaced by any other abstract editor, provided that the statically derived type constraints (concerning f and v) are met. This is illustrated by the next example.

**Function Test Example, Once Again Revisited.** If one prefers a counter as input editor for the argument value, one only has to replace dynamicAGEC by counterAGEC in the definition of initval:

```
initval f v
    = { function = dynamicAGEC f
      , argument = counterAGEC v
      , result   = displayAGEC (f v) }
```

The dynamicAGEC is typically used when *expression* editors are preferred over *value* editors of a type, and when application users need to be able to enter functions of a statically fixed monomorphic type.

One can create an editor for any higher-order type t, even if it contains polymorphic functions. It is required that all higher-order parts of t are abstracted, by wrapping them with an *AGEC* type. Basically, this means that each part of t of the form a → b must be changed into AGEC (a → b). For the resulting type t' an edit dialog *can* be automatically created, e.g., by applying selfGEC. However, the initial value that is passed to selfGEC must be monomorphic, as usual for any instantiation of a generic function. Therefore, editors for polymorphic types cannot be created automatically using this statically typed generic technique. As explained in Sect. 5.1 polymorphic types can be handled with dynamic type checking.

Summarizing, we have shown two ways to create editors that can deal with higher order types. Firstly, one can create dynamically typed higher-order editors, which have the advantages that we can deal with polymorphic higher order types and overloading. This has the disadvantage that the programmer has to check type safety in the editor. Secondly, we have treated a method in which the compiler can ensure type correctness of higher-order types in statically typed editors, but then the resulting editors can only edit monomorphic types.

*Exercise 8.* **Dynamically Adaptable Intelligent Form.** Change your solutions from exercises 4 and 7 such that the intelligence can be dynamically changed by typing in the function that is applied.

# 6   Related Work

We distinguish three areas of related work:

**Grammars Instead of Types:** Taking a different perspective on the type-directed nature of our approach, one can argue that it is also possible to obtained editors by starting from a grammar specification instead of a type. Such toolkits require a grammar as input and yield an editor GUI as result. Projects in this flavor are for instance the recent Proxima project [23], which relies on XML and its DTD (Document Type Definition language), and the Asf+Sdf Meta-Environment [11] which uses an Asf syntax specification and Sdf semantics specification. The major difference with such an approach is that these systems need both a grammar and some kind of interpreter. In our system higher-order elements are immediately available as a functional value that can be applied and passed to other components.

**GUI Programming Toolkits:** From the abstract nature of the *GEC* toolkit it is clear that we need to look at GUI toolkits that also offer a high level of abstraction. Most GUI toolkits are concerned with the low level management of widgets in an imperative style. One well-known example of an abstract, compositional GUI toolkit based on a combinator library is Fudgets [12]. These combinators are required for plumbing when building complex GUI structures from simpler ones. In our system far less plumbing is needed. Most work is done automatically by the generic function gGEC. The only plumbing needed in our system is for combining the *GEC*-editors themselves. Any application will only have a very limited number of *GEC*-editors. Furthermore, the Fudget system does not provide support for editing function values or expressions.

A *GEC*$_t$ is a t-stateful object, hence it makes sense to look at object oriented approaches. The power of abstraction and composition in our functional framework is similar to *mixins* [13] in object oriented languages. One can imagine an OO GUI library based on compositional and abstract mixins in order to obtain a similar toolkit. Still, such a system lacks higher-order data structures.

**Visual Programming Languages:** Due to the extension of the *GEC* programming toolkit with higher-order types, *visual programming languages* have come within reach as *application domain*. One interesting example is the Vital system [14] in which Haskell-like scripts can be edited. Both systems allow direct manipulation of expressions and custom types, allow customization of views, and have guarded data types (the `selfGEC` function). In contrast with the Vital system, which is a dedicated system and has been implemented in Java, our system is a general purpose toolkit. We could use our toolkit to construct a visual environment in the spirit of Vital.

## 7   Conclusions

We have presented the *GEC* toolkit for rapid prototyping of type safe interactive applications. The toolkit

1. *produces type-safe interactive applications* composed from *G*raphical *E*ditor *C*omponents;
2. is highly *automatic* due to generic generative programming techniques;
3. can be used for first order and *higher order* types;
4. can be *customized* to create any kind of user interface;
5. allows *abstraction* using model-view programming to hide details and allow type-safe view changes;
6. is *compositional* on various levels:
   **Types** standard composition of types lead to composition of corresponding graphical editor components;
   **Expressions** the user can enter expressions in which values and functions can be defined/used compositionally; these functions can even be compiled functions (possibly taken from complete applications) that are read from disk, linked in dynamically and applied in a compositional way;
   **GECs** *GEC*s can be composed in an ad-hoc way by standard functional programming or in a structured way using arrow combinators;
   **AGECs** AGECs can be composed in a statically type safe way.
7. enables the programmer to *focus on a data type* representing the interaction with the user instead of on the many nasty details of a graphical toolkit;
8. can be *downloaded* from `http://www.cs.ru.nl/~clean/gec`.

## Acknowledgements

The authors would like to thank the referees for their detailed comments.

## References

1. M. Abadi, L. Cardelli, B. Pierce, G. Plotkin, and D. Rèmy. Dynamic typing in polymorphic languages. In *Proc. of the ACM SIGPLAN Workshop on ML and its Applications*, San Francisco, June 1992.

2. P. Achten. *Interactive Functional Programs - models, methods, and implementations*. PhD thesis, University of Nijmegen, The Netherlands, 1996.
3. P. Achten and S. Peyton Jones. Porting the Clean Object I/O library to Haskell. In M. Mohnen and P. Koopman, editors, *Proc. of the 12th International Workshop on the Implementation of Functional Languages, IFL'00, Selected Papers*, volume 2011 of *LNCS*, pages 194–213. Aachen, Germany, Springer, Sept. 2001.
4. P. Achten and R. Plasmeijer. Interactive Functional Objects in Clean. In C. Clack, K. Hammond, and T. Davie, editors, *Proc. of the 9th International Workshop on the Implementation of Functional Languages, IFL 1997, Selected Papers*, volume 1467 of *LNCS*, pages 304–321. St.Andrews, UK, Springer, Sept. 1998.
5. Achten, Peter and van Eekelen, Marko and Plasmeijer, Rinus and van Weelden, Arjen. Arrows for Generic Graphical Editor Components. Technical report NIII-R0416, Nijmegen Institute for Computing and Information Sciences, University of Nijmegen, The Netherlands, 2004. available at http://www.niii.kun.nl/research/reports/full/NIII-R0416.pdf.
6. Achten, Peter, van Eekelen, Marko and Plasmeijer, Rinus. Generic Graphical User Interfaces. In Greg Michaelson and Phil Trinder, editors, *Selected Papers of the 15th Int. Workshop on the Implementation of Functional Languages, IFL03*, volume 3145 of *LNCS*. Edinburgh, UK, Springer, 2003.
7. Achten, Peter, van Eekelen, Marko and Plasmeijer, Rinus. Compositional Model-Views with Generic Graphical User Interfaces. In *Practical Aspects of Declarative Programming, PADL04*, volume 3057 of *LNCS*, pages 39–55. Springer, 2004.
8. Achten, Peter, van Eekelen, Marko, Plasmeijer, Rinus and van Weelden, Arjen. Automatic Generation of Editors for Higher-Order Data Structures. In Wei-Ngan Chin, editor, *Second ASIAN Symposium on Programming Languages and Systems (APLAS 2004)*, volume 3302 of *LNCS*, pages 262–279. Springer, 2004.
9. A. Alimarine and R. Plasmeijer. A Generic Programming Extension for Clean. In T. Arts and M. Mohnen, editors, *The 13th International workshop on the Implementation of Functional Languages, IFL'01, Selected Papers*, volume 2312 of *LNCS*, pages 168–186. Älvsjö, Sweden, Springer, Sept. 2002.
10. E. Barendsen and S. Smetsers. *Graph Rewriting Aspects of Functional Programming*, chapter 2, pages 63–102. World scientific, 1999.
11. M. v. d. Brand, A. van Deursen, J. Heering, H. de Jong, M. de Jonge, T. Kuipers, P. Klint, L. Moonen, P. Olivier, J. Scheerder, J. Vinju, E. Visser, and J. Visser. The Asf+Sdf Meta-Environment: a Component-Based Language Development Environment. In R. Wilhelm, editor, *Compiler Construction 2001 (CC'01)*, pages 365–370. Springer-Verlag, 2001.
12. M. Carlsson and T. Hallgren. FUDGETS - a graphical user interface in a lazy functional language. In *Proc. of the ACM Conference on Functional Programming and Computer Architecture, FPCA '93*, Kopenhagen, Denmark, 1993.
13. M. Flatt, S. Krishnamurthi, and M. Felleisen. Classes and mixins. In *The 25TH ACM SIGPLAN-SIGACT Symposium on Principles of Programming Languages (POPL98)*, pages 171–183, San Diego, California, 1998. ACM, New York, NY.
14. K. Hanna. Interactive Visual Functional Programming. In S. P. Jones, editor, *Proc. Intnl Conf. on Functional Programming*, pages 100–112. ACM, October 2002.
15. R. Hinze. A new approach to generic functional programming. In *The 27th Annual ACM SIGPLAN-SIGACT Symposium on Principles of Programming Languages*, pages 119–132. Boston, Massachusetts, January 2000.
16. R. Hinze and S. Peyton Jones. Derivable Type Classes. In G. Hutton, editor, *2000 ACM SIGPLAN Haskell Workshop*, volume 41(1) of *ENTCS*. Montreal, Canada, Elsevier Science, 2001.

17. J. Hughes. Generalising Monads to Arrows. *Science of Computer Programming*, 37:67–111, May 2000.
18. G. Krasner and S. Pope. A cookbook for using the Model-View-Controller user interface paradigm in Smalltalk-80. *Journal of Object-Oriented Programming*, 1(3):26–49, August 1988.
19. A. Löh, D. Clarke, and J. Jeuring. Dependency-style generic haskell. In *ICFP '03: Proc. of the eighth ACM SIGPLAN international conference on Functional programming*, pages 141–152. ACM Press, 2003.
20. S. Peyton Jones and Hughes J. et al. *Report on the programming language Haskell 98*. University of Yale, 1999. http://www.haskell.org/definition/.
21. M. Pil. Dynamic types and type dependent functions. In K. Hammond, T. Davie, and C. Clack, editors, *Implementation of Functional Languages (IFL '98)*, LNCS, pages 169–185. Springer Verlag, 1999.
22. R. Plasmeijer and M. van Eekelen. *Concurrent CLEAN Language Report (version 2.0)*, December 2001. http://www.cs.kun.nl/~clean/contents/contents.html.
23. M. Schrage. *Proxima, a presentation-oriented editor for structured documents*. PhD thesis, University of Utrecht, 2004.
24. A. van Weelden and R. Plasmeijer. A functional shell that dynamically combines compiled code. In P. Trinder and G. Michaelson, editors, *Selected Papers Proc. of the 15th International Workshop on Implementation of Functional Languages, IFL'03*. Heriot Watt University, Edinburgh, Sept. 2003.
25. M. Vervoort and R. Plasmeijer. Lazy dynamic input/output in the lazy functional language Clean. In R. Peña and T. Arts, editors, *The 14th International Workshop on the Implementation of Functional Languages, IFL'02, Selected Papers*, volume 2670 of *LNCS*, pages 101–117. Springer, Sept. 2003.
26. P. Wadler. Comprehending Monads. In *Proc. of the 1990 ACM Conference on Lisp and Functional Programming*, pages 61–77, Nice, France, 1990.

# A Functional Shell That Operates
# on Typed and Compiled Applications

Rinus Plasmeijer and Arjen van Weelden

Nijmeegs Instituut voor Informatica en Informatiekunde,
Radboud Universiteit Nijmegen, Toernooiveld 1,
6525 ED Nijmegen, The Netherlands
{rinus, arjonw}@cs.kun.nl

**Abstract.** Esther is the interactive shell of Famke, a prototype implementation of a strongly typed operating system written in the functional programming language Clean. As usual, the shell can be used for manipulating files, applications, data and processes at the command line. A special feature of Esther is that the shell language provides the basic functionality of a strongly typed lazy functional language, at the command line. The shell type checks each command line and only executes well-typed expressions. Files are typed as well, and applications are simply files with a function type.

The type checking/inferencing performed by the shell is actually performed by the hybrid static/dynamic type system of Clean. The shell behaves like an interpreter, but it actually executes a command line by combining existing compiled code of functions/programs on disk. Clean's dynamic linker is used to store (and retrieve) any expression (both data and code) with its type on disk. This linker is also used to communicate values of any type, e.g., data, closures, and functions (i.e., compiled code), between running applications in a type safe way.

The shell combines the advantages of interpreters (direct response) and compilers (statically typed, fast code). Applications (compiled functions) can be used, in a type safe way, in the shell, and functions defined in the shell can be used by any compiled application.

## 1   Introduction

Functional programming languages like Haskell [1] and Clean [2,3] offer a very flexible and powerful static type system. Compact, reusable, and readable programs can be written in these languages while the static type system is able to detect many programming errors at compile time. However, this works only within a single application.

Independently developed applications often need to communicate with each other. One would like the communication of objects to take place in a type safe manner as well. And not only simple objects, but objects of any type, including functions. In practice, this is not easy to realize: the compile time type information is generally not available to the compiled executable at run-time. In

V. Varmo and T. Uustalu (Eds.): AFP 2004, LNCS 3622, pp. 245–272, 2005.

real life therefore, applications often only communicate simple data types like streams of characters, ASCII text, or use some ad-hoc defined (binary) format.

Programming languages, especially pure and lazy functional languages like Clean and Haskell, provide good support for abstraction (e.g., subroutines, overloading, polymorphic functions), composition (e.g., application, higher-order functions, module system), and verification (e.g., strong type checking and inference). In contrast, command line languages used by operating system shells usually have little support for abstraction, composition, and especially verification. They do not provide higher-order subroutines, complex data structures, type inference, or type checking *before* evaluation. Given their limited set of types and their specific area of application (in which they have been, and still are, very successfull), this is not experienced as a serious problem.

Nonetheless, we think that command line languages can benefit from some of the programming language facilities, as this will increase their flexibility, reusability, and security. We have previously done research on reducing run-time errors (e.g., memory access violations, type errors) in operating systems by implementing a micro kernel in Clean that provides type safe communication of any value of any type between functional processes, called Famke (*Function*Al *M*icro *K*ernel *E*xperiment) [4]. This has shown that (moderate) use of dynamic typing [5], in combination with Clean's dynamic run-time system and dynamic linker [6,7], enables processes to communicate any data (and even code) of any type in a type safe way.

During the development of a shell/command line interface for our prototype functional operating system it became clear that a normal shell cannot really make use (at run-time) of the type information derived by the compiler (at compile-time). To reduce the possibility of run-time errors during execution of scripts or command lines, we need a shell that supports abstraction and verification (i.e., type checking) in the same way as the Clean compiler does. In order to do this, we need a better integration of compile-time (i.e., static typing) and run-time (i.e., interactivity) concepts.

Both the shell and micro kernel are built on top of Clean's hybrid static/dynamic type system and its dynamic I/O run-time support. It allows programmers to save any Clean expression, i.e., a graph that can contain data, references to functions, and closures, to disk. Clean expressions can be written to disk as a *dynamic*, which contains a representation of their (polymorphic) static type, while preserving sharing. Clean programs can load dynamics from disk and use run-time type pattern matching to reintegrate it into the statically typed program. In this way, new functionality (e.g., plug-ins) can be added to a running program in a type safe way. This paper stresses type safety and assumes that we can trust the compiler.

The shell is called Esther (*E*xtensible *S*hell with *T*ype c*H*ecking Expe*R*iment), and is capable of:

- reading an expression from the console, using Clean's syntax for a basic, but complete, functional language. It offers application, lambda abstraction, recursive let, pattern matching, function definitions, and even overloading;

- using compiled Clean programs as typed functions at the command line;
- defining new functions, which can be used by other compiled Clean programs (without using the shell or an interpreter);
- extracting type information (and indirectly, code) from dynamics on disk;
- type checking the expression and resolving overloading, *before* evaluation;
- constructing a new dynamic containing the correct type and code of the expression.

## 1.1   Esther Example: An Application That Uses a Shell Function

Figure 1 shows a sequence of screenshots of a calculator program written in Clean. Initially, the calculator has no function buttons. Instead, it has buttons to add and remove function buttons. These will be loaded dynamically after adding dynamics that contain tuples of String and Real Real $\rightarrow$ Real.

The lower half of Fig. 1 shows a command line in the Esther shell that writes such a tuple as a dynamic named "2a-b2.u.dyn" to disk.

Its button name is 2*a-b^2 and the function is $\lambda$a b $\rightarrow$ 2.0 * a $-$ b * b. Pressing the Add button on the calculator opens a file selection dialog, shown at the bottom of Fig. 1. After selecting the dynamic named "2a-2b.u.dyn", it becomes available in the calculator as the button 2*a-b^2, and it is applied to 8 and 3 yielding 7.

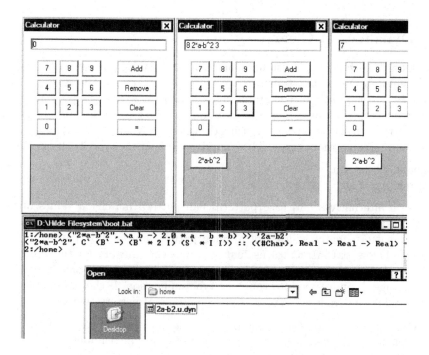

**Fig. 1.** A combined screenshot of the calculator and Esther in action

The calculator itself is a separately compiled Clean executable that runs without using Esther. Alternatively, one can write the calculator, which has type [(String, Real Real → Real)] *World → *World, to disk as a dynamic. The calculator can then be started from Esther, either in the current shell or as a separate process.

## 1.2  Overview

First, we introduce the static/dynamic hybrid type system and dynamic I/O of Clean in Sect. 2. The type checking and combining of compile code features of Esther are directly derived from Clean's dynamic implementation. In Sect. 3 we give an overview of the expressive power of the shell command language using tiny examples of commands that can be given. In Sect. 4 we show how to construct a dynamic for each kind of subexpression such that it has the correct semantics and type, and how to compose them in a type checked way. Related work is discussed in Sect. 5 and we conclude and mention future research in Sect. 6. We assume the reader to be familiar with Haskell, and will indicate syntactic difference with Clean in footnotes. The implementation has been done in Clean because it has more support for (de)serializing dynamics than Haskell. Unfortunately, Clean's dynamic linker, which is required for Esther, has only been implemented for Microsoft Windows. The implementation, which is reasonably stable but always under development, can be downloaded from: http://www.cs.ru.nl/~arjenw.

## 2   Dynamics in Clean

Clean offers a hybrid type system: in addition to its static type system it also has a (polymorphic) dynamic type system [5,6,7]. A dynamic in Clean is a value of static type *Dynamic*, which contains an expression as well as a representation of the (static) type of that expression. Dynamics can be formed (i.e., lifted from the static to the dynamic type system) using the keyword **dynamic** in combination with the value and an optional type. The compiler will infer the type if it is omitted[1].

**dynamic** 42 :: Int[2]
**dynamic** map fst :: A[3].a b: [(a, b)] → [a]

Function alternatives and case patterns can pattern match on values of type Dynamic, i.e., bring them from the dynamic back into the static type system. Such a pattern match consist of a value pattern and a type pattern. In the example below, matchInt returns Just the value contained inside the dynamic if it has type Int; and Nothing if it has any other type. The compiler translates a pattern match on a type into run-time type unification. If the unification fails, the next alternative is tried, as in a common (value) pattern match.

---

[1] Types containing universally quantified variables are currently not inferred by the compiler. We will sometimes omit these types for ease of presentation.

[2] Numerical denotations are not overloaded in Clean.

[3] Clean's syntax for Haskell's **forall**.

```
::⁴Maybe a = Nothing | Just a

matchInt :: Dynamic → Maybe Int
matchInt (x :: Int) = Just x
matchInt  other     = Nothing
```

A type pattern can contain type variables which, provided that run-time unification is successful, are bound to the offered type. In the example below, dynamicApply tests if the argument type of the function f inside its first argument can be unified with the type of the value x inside the second argument. If this is the case then dynamicApply can safely apply f to x. The type variables a and b will be instantiated by the run-time unification. At compile time it is generally unknown what type a and b will be, but if the type pattern match succeeds, the compiler can safely apply f to x. This yields a value with the type that is bound to b by unification, which is wrapped in a dynamic.

```
dynamicApply :: Dynamic Dynamic → Dynamic⁵
dynamicApply (f :: a → b) (x :: a) = dynamic f x :: b⁶
dynamicApply      df           dx  = dynamic "Error: cannot apply"
```

Type variables in dynamic patterns can also relate to a type variable in the static type of a function. Such functions are called type dependent functions [5]. A caret (^) behind a variable in a pattern associates it with the type variable with the same name in the static type of the function. The static type variable then becomes overloaded in the predefined TC (or type code) class. The TC class is used to 'carry' the type representation. The compiler generates instances for this class, which contain the necessary methods to convert values to dynamics and vice versa. In the example below, the static type variable t will be determined by the (static) context in which it is used, and will impose a restriction on the actual type that is accepted at run-time by matchDynamic. It yields Just the value inside the dynamic (if the dynamic contains a value of the required context dependent type) or Nothing (if it does not).

```
matchDynamic :: Dynamic → Maybe t | TC t⁷
matchDynamic (x :: t^) = Just x
matchDynamic  other    = Nothing
```

## 2.1  Reading and Writing of Dynamics

The dynamic run-time system of Clean supports writing dynamics to disk and reading them back again, possibly in another application or during another execution of the same application. This is not a trivial feature, since Clean is not an interpreted language: it uses compiled code. Since a dynamic may contain

---

⁴ Defines a new data type in Clean, Haskell uses the data keyword.
⁵ Clean separates argument types by whitespace, instead of →.
⁶ The type b is also inferred by the compiler.
⁷ Clean uses | to announce context restrictions. In Haskell this would be written as (TC t) ⇒ Dynamic → Maybe t.

unevaluated functions, reading a dynamic implies that the corresponding code produced by the compiler has to be added to the code of the running application. To make this possible one needs a dynamic linker. Furthermore, one needs to to be able to retrieve the type definitions and function definitions that are associated with a stored dynamic. With the ability to read and write dynamics, type safe plug-ins can be realized in Clean relatively easily.

**Writing a Dynamically Typed Expression to File.** A dynamic of any value can be written to a file on disk using the writeDynamic function.

```
writeDynamic :: String Dynamic *⁸World → (Bool, *World)
```

In the producer example below a dynamic is created which consists of the application of the function sieve to an infinite list of integers. This dynamic is then written to file using the writeDynamic function. Evaluation of a dynamic is done lazily. The producer does not demand the result of the application of sieve to the infinite list. As a consequence, the application in its unevaluated form is written to file. The file therefore contains a calculation that will yield a potential infinite integer list of prime numbers.

```
producer :: *World → *World
producer world = writeDynamic "primes" (dynamic sieve [2..]) world
where
    sieve :: [Int] → [Int]
    sieve [prime:rest] = [prime:sieve filter]
    where
        filter = [h \\ h <- rest | h mod prime <> 0]
```

When the dynamic is stored to disk, not only the dynamic expression and its type has to be stored somewhere. To allow the dynamic to be used as a plug-in by any other application additional information has to be stored as well. One also has to store:

- the code corresponding to the function definitions that are referred to in closures inside the dynamic;
- the definitions of all the types involved needed to check type consistency when matching on the type of the dynamic in another Clean program.

The required code and type information will be generated by the compiler and is stored in a special data base when an application is compiled and linked. For the detail of the bookkeeping of the code data base, we refer to [7]. The code and type information is created and stored once at compile-time, while the dynamic value and dynamic type can be created and stored several times at run-time.

---

[8] This is a uniqueness attribute, indicating that the world environment is passed around in a single threaded way. Unique values allow safe destructive updates and are used for I/O in Clean. The value of type World corresponds to the hidden state of the IO monad in Haskell.

The run-time system has to be able to find both kinds of information when a dynamic is read in.

**Reading a Dynamically Typed Expression from File.** A dynamic can be read from disk using the `readDynamic` function.

```
readDynamic :: String *World → (Bool, Dynamic, *World)
```

This `readDynamic` function is used in the `consumer` example below to read the earlier stored dynamic. The dynamic pattern match checks whether the dynamic expression is an integer list. In case of success the first 100 elements are taken. In case that the read in dynamic is not of the indicated type, the consumer aborts. Actually, it is not possible to do something with a read-in dynamic (besides passing it around to other functions or saving it to disk again), unless the dynamic matches some type or type scheme specified in the pattern match of the receiving application.

```
consumer :: *World → [Int]
consumer world
#⁹ (ok, dyn, world) = readDynamic "primes" world
= take 100 (extract dyn)
where
    extract :: Dynamic → [Int]
    extract (list :: [Int]) = list
    extract other           = abort "dynamic type check failed"
```

To turn a dynamically typed expression into a statically typed expression, the following steps are performed by the run-time system of Clean:

- The type of the dynamic and the type specified in the pattern are unified with each other. If the unification fails, the dynamic pattern match also fails.
- If the unification is successful, it is checked that the type definitions of equally named types coming from different applications are equal as well. If one of the involved type definitions differs, the dynamic pattern match fails. Equally named types are equivalent if and only if their type definitions are syntactically the same (modulo alpha-conversion and the order of algebraic data constructors).
- If all patterns match, the corresponding function alternative is chosen and evaluated.
- It is possible that for the evaluation of the, now statically typed, expression parts of its representation on disk are required. In that case, the expression is reconstructed out of the information stored in the dynamic on disk, the corresponding code needed for the evaluation of the expression is added to the running application, after which the expression can be evaluated.

Running `prog1` and `prog2` in the example below will write a function and a value to dynamics on disk. Running `prog3` will create a new dynamic on disk that

---

⁹ Clean uses environment passing, instead of monads, for side effects. It supports let-before (#) to increase readability.

contains the result of 'applying' (using the `dynamicApply` function) the dynamic with the name "function" to the dynamic with the name "value". The closure 40 + 2 will not be evaluated until the * operator needs it. In this case, because the 'dynamic application' of `df` to `dx` is lazy, the closure will not be evaluated until the value of the dynamic on disk named "result" is needed. Running `prog4` tries to match the dynamic `dr`, from the file named "result", with the type `Int`. After this succeeds, it displays the value by evaluating the expression, which is semantically equal to `let x = 40 + 2 in x * x`, yielding 1764.

```
prog1 world = writeDynamic "function" (dynamic (*)) world

prog2 world = writeDynamic "value" (dynamic 40 + 2) world

prog3 world = let (ok1, df, world1) = readDynamic "function" world
                  (ok2, dx, world2) = readDynamic "value" world1
              in  writeDynamic "result" (dynamicApply df dx) world2

prog4 world = let (ok, dr, world1) = readDynamic "result" world
              in  (case dr of (x :: Int) → x, world1)
```

A dynamic will be read in lazily after a successful run-time unification (triggered by a pattern match on the dynamic). The dynamic linker will take care of the actual linking of the code to the running application and the checking of the type definitions referenced by the dynamic being read. The dynamic linker is able to find the code and type definitions in the data base in which they are stored by the compiler. The amount of data and code that the dynamic linker will link depends on how far the dynamic expression is evaluated.

Dynamics written by one application program can safely be read by any other application. Only when the linker confirms that both programs agree on the used types, it can be plugged in so that the application can do something with it. The reading program is extended with the new types found in the dynamic. Known types and constructors in the dynamic are mapped to the corresponding types in the program. In this way two Clean applications can communicate values of any type they like, including function types, in a type safe manner.

## 3    Overview of the Shell

Like any other shell, our Esther shell enables users to start pre-compiled programs, provides simple ways to combine multiple programs, e.g., pipelining and concurrent execution, and supports execution-flow controls, e.g., if-then-else constructs. It provides a way to interact with the underlying operating system and the file system, using a textual command line/console interface.

A special feature of the Esther shell is that it offers a complete typed functional programming language with which programs can be constructed. The shell type checks a command line before performing any actions. Traditional shells provide very limited error checking before executing the given command line. This is mainly because the applications mentioned at the command line are practically untyped because they work on, and produce, streams of characters. The intended meaning of these streams of characters varies from one program to the other. The choice to make our shell language typed also has consequences for the underlying operating system and file system: they should be able to deal with types as well.

In this section we give a brief overview of the functionality of the Esther shell and the underlying operating system and file system it relies on.

### 3.1  Famke: A Type Safe Micro Kernel

A shell has to be able to start applications and to provide a way to connect applications (e.g., by creating a pipe-line) such that they can communicate. Since our shell is typed, process communication should be type safe as well. The Windows Operating System that we use does not provide such a facility. We therefore have created a micro kernel on top of Windows. Our micro-kernel, Famke, provides Clean programs with ways to start new (possibly distributed running) processes, and the ability to communicate any value in a type safe way. It should be no surprise that Famke uses dynamics for this purpose. Dynamics can be send between applications as strings (see [7]), which makes it possible to use conventional interprocess communication system such as TCP/IP for the actual communication.

### 3.2  A Typed File System

A shell works on applications and data stored on disk. Our shell is typed; it can only work if all files it operates on are typed as well. We therefore assume that all files have a proper type.

For applications written in Clean this can be easily realized. Any data, function, or even any large complete Clean application (which is a function as well) can be written as dynamic to disk, thus forming a rudimentary typed file system.

Applications written in other languages are usually untyped. We can in principle incorporate such an application into in our typed file system, by writing a properly typed Clean wrapper application around it, which is then stored again as dynamic on disk. We could also wrap them automatically, or via a function, and give them the type `String String → String` (commandline, stdin → stdout). Obviously, this type does not really help type checking and is, therefore, not implemented in this prototype that promotes type checking.

We assume that all documents and compiled applications are stored in a dynamic of appropriate type. Applications in our file system are just dynamics that contain a function type. This typed file system makes it possible for the shell to ensure (given an ideal world where all programs are stored as dynamics) that it is type safe to apply a printing application (`print :: WordDocument →` `PostScript`) to a document (`myDocument :: WordDocument`). The Clean dynamic type system will ensure that the types will indeed fit. This is, of course, not a very realistic example. It is for illustration purposes only.

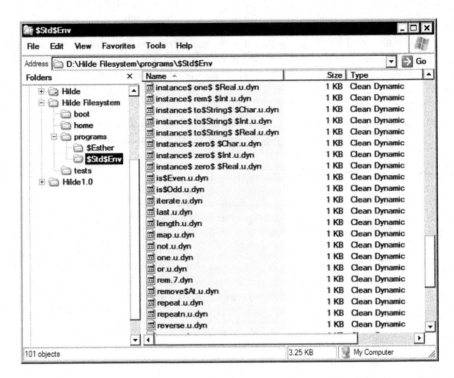

**Fig. 2.** A screenshot of the typed file system; implemented as dynamic on disk

Normal directory manipulation operations still apply, but one no longer reads bytes from a file. Instead, one reads whole files (only conceptually, the dynamic linker reads it lazily), and one can pattern match on the dynamic to check the type. This removes the need for explicit (de)serialization, as data structures are stored directly as graphs in dynamics. Serialization, parsing, and printing are often significant parts of existing software (up to thirty percent), which may be reduces by providing these operations in the programming language and/or operating system.

The shell contains no built-in commands. The commands it knows are determined by the files (dynamics) stored on disk. To find a command, the shell searches its directories in a specific order as defined in its search paths, looking for a file with that name.

The shell is therefore pretty useless unless a collection of useful dynamics has been stored. When the system is initialized, a standard file system is created (see Fig. 2) in a Windows folder. It contains:

- almost all functions from the Clean standard environment[10], such as +, −, map, and foldr (stored as dynamic on disk);
- common commands to manipulated the file system (mkdir, rmdir, and the like);

---

[10] Similar to Haskell's Prelude.

- commands to create processes directly based on the functionality offered by Famke (`famkeNewProcess`, and the like).

All folders are common Window folders, all files contain dynamics created by Clean applications using the `writeDynamic`-function. The implementation of dynamics on disk is organized in such a way ([7]) that a user can safely rename, copy or delete files, either using the Esther shell or directly using Windows.

### 3.3    Esther: A Type Checking Shell

The last example of Sect. 2 shows how one can store and retrieve values, expressions, and functions of any type to and from the file system. It also shows that the `dynamicApply` function can be used to type check an application at run-time using the static types stored in dynamics. Combining both in an interactive 'read expression – apply dynamics – evaluate and show result' loop gives a very simple shell that already supports the type checked run-time application of programs to documents. For maximum flexibility, the shell contains almost no built-in functions. Any Clean function can be saved to disk using dynamics, and can thus be used by Esther.

Esther performs the following steps in a loop:

- it reads a string from the console and parses it like a Clean expression. It supports Clean's basic and predefined types, application, infix operators, lambda abstraction, functions, overloading, let(rec), and case expressions;
- identifiers that are not bound by a lambda abstraction, a let(rec), or a case pattern are assumed to be names of dynamics on disk, and they are read from disk;
- type checks the expression using dynamic run-time unification and type pattern matching, which also infers types;
- if the command expression does not contain type errors, Esther displays the result of the expression and the inferred type. Esther will automatically be extended with any code necessary to display the result (which requires evaluation) by the dynamic linker.

For instance, if the user types in the following expression:

```
> map ((+) 1) [1..10]
```

the shell reacts as follows:

```
[2,3,4,5,6,7,8,9,10,11] :: [Int]
```

Roughly the following happens. The shell parses the expression. The expression consists of typical Clean-like syntactical constructs (such as (, ), and [ .. ]), constants (such as 1 and 10), and identifiers (such as `map` and +).

The names `map` and + are unbound (do not appear in the left hand side of a let, case, lambda expression, or function definition) in this example, and the shell therefore assumes that they are names of dynamics on disk. They are

read from disk (with help of `readDynamic`), practically extending its functionality with these functions, and inspects the types of the dynamics. It uses the
types of map (let us assume that the file `map` contains the type that we expect:
$(a \rightarrow b)$ $[a] \rightarrow [b]$), + (for simplicity, let us assume: Int Int $\rightarrow$ Int) and the
list comprehension (which has type: $[Int]$) to type-check the command line. If
this succeeds, which it should given the types above, the shell applies the partial
application of + with the integer one to the list of integers from one to ten,
using the map function. The application of one dynamic to another is done using
the `dynamicApply` function from Sect. 2, extended with better error reporting.
How this is done exactly, is explained in more detail in Sect. 4. With the help
of the `dynamicApply` function, the shell constructs a new function that performs
the computation map $((+)\ 1)\ [1..10]$. This function uses the compiled code of
map, +, and $[\ ..\ ]$, which is implemented as a generator function called `_from_to`
in Clean.

Our shell can therefore be regarded as a hybrid interpreter/compiler, where
the command line is interpreted/compiled to a function that is almost as efficient
as the same function written directly in Clean and compiled to native code. If
functions, such as map and +, are used in other commands later on, the dynamic
linker will notice that they are already have been used and linked in, and it will
reuse their code. As a consequence, the shell will react even quicker, because no
dynamic linking is required anymore in such a case. For more details on Clean's
dynamic linker we refer to Vervoort and Plasmeijer [7].

### 3.4    The Esther Command Language

Here follow some command line examples with an explanation of how they are
handled by the shell. Figure 3 show two example sessions with Esther. The right
Esther window in Fig. 3 shows the same directory as the Windows Explorer

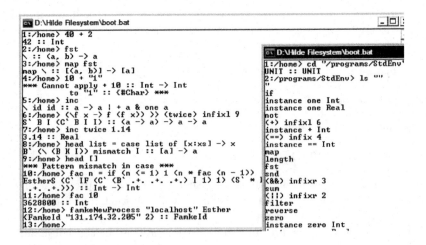

**Fig. 3.** A combined screenshot of the two concurrent sessions with Esther

window in Fig. 2. We explain Esther's syntax by example below. Like a common UNIX shell, the Esther shell prompts the user with something like 1:/home> for typing in a new command. For readability we use only > in the examples below.

**Expressions.** Here are some more examples of expressions that speak for themselves. Application:

```
> map
map :: (a -> b) [a] -> [b]
```

Expressions that contain type errors:

```
> 40 + "5"
*** cannot apply + 40 :: Int -> Int
            to  "5" :: {#Char} ***
```

**Saving Expressions to Disk.** Expressions can be stored as dynamics on disk using >>:

```
> 2 >> two
2 :: Int
> two
2 :: Int

> (+) 1 >> inc
+ 1 :: Int -> Int
> inc 41
42 :: Int
```

The >> operator is introduced mostly for convenience. Most expressions of the form expr >> name can be written as:

writeDynamic "name" (**dynamic** expr) world

Unfortunately, it does not work to specify the >> operator as

(>>) expr name = writeDynamic "name" (**dynamic** expr)

because this can require a rank-2 type that neither Esther, nor the Clean's compiler, can infer. Furthermore, >> uses writeDynamic as is therefore a function with side-effects, and it has type $*World \to (Bool, *World)$. Functions of this type must be treated specially by Esther, which must pass them the world environment[11]. By defining the >> operator at the syntax level, we circumvent these problems.

**Overloading.** Esther resolves overloading in almost the same way as Clean. It is currently not possible to define new classes at the command line, but they can be introduced using a simple Clean program that stores the class as an overloaded

---

[11] Execute them in the IO monad.

function. It is also not possible to save overloaded command-line expressions using the >> described above. Arithmetic operations are overloaded in Esther, just as they are in Clean:

```
> +
+ :: a a -> a | + a

> one
one :: a | one a

> (+) one
(+) one :: a -> a | + a & one a
```

**Function Definitions.** One can define new functions at the command line:

```
> dec x = x - 1
dec :: Int -> Int
```

This defines a new function with the name dec. This function is written to disk in a file with the same name (dec) such that from now on it can be used in other expressions.

```
> fac n = if (n < 2) 1 (n * fac (dec n))
S (C‘ IF (C‘ < I 2) 1) (S‘ * I (B (S .+. .+.) (C‘ .+. .+. .+.)))
:: Int -> Int
```

The factorial function is constructed by Esther using combinators (see Sect. 4), which explains why Esther responds in this way. The internals of the function shown by Esther proved useful while debugging Esther itself, but this may change in the future.

Functions can not only be reused within the shell itself, but also used by any other Clean program. Such a function is a dynamic and can be used (read in, dynamically linked, copied, renamed, communicated across a network) as usual.

Notice that dynamics are read in before executing the command line, so it is not possible to change the meaning of a part of the command line by overwriting a dynamic.

**Lambda Expressions.** It is possible to define lambda expressions, just as in Clean.

```
> (\f x -> f (f x)) ((+) 1) 0
2 :: Int
```

```
> (\x x -> x) "first-x" "second-x"
"second-x" :: String
```

Esther parses the example above as: $\lambda x \rightarrow (\lambda x \rightarrow x)$. This is not standard, and may change in the future.

**Let Expressions.** To introduce sharing and to construct both cyclic and infinite data structures, one can use let expressions.

```
> let x = 4 * 11 in x + x
88 :: Int

> let ones = [1:ones] in take 10 ones
[1,1,1,1,1,1,1,1,1,1] :: [Int]
```

**Case Expressions.** It is possible to do a simple pattern match using case expressions. Nested patterns are not yet supported, but one can always nest case expressions by hand. An exception `Pattern mismatch in case` is raised if a case fails.

```
> hd list = case list of [x:xs] -> x
B' (\ (B K I)) mismatch I :: [a] -> a

> hd [1..]
1 :: Int

> hd []
*** Pattern mismatch in case ***

> sum l = case l of [x:xs] -> x + sum xs; [] -> 0
B' (\ (C' (B' .+.) I (B .+. .+.))) (\ 0 mismatch) I
:: [Int] -> Int
```

The interpreter understands Clean denotations for basic types like `Int`, `Real`, `Char`, `String`, `Bool`, tuples, and lists. But how can one perform a pattern match on a user defined constructor defined in some application? It is not (yet) possible to define new types in the shell itself. But one can define the types in any Clean module, and construct an application writing the constructors as dynamic to disk.

**module** NewType

```
:: Tree a = Node (Tree a) (Tree a) | Leaf a

Start world
    # (ok, world) = writeDynamic "Node"
              (dynamic Node :: A.a: (Tree a) (Tree a) → Tree a) world
    # (ok, world) = writeDynamic "Leaf"
                  (dynamic Leaf :: A.a: a → Tree a) world
    # (ok, world) = writeDynamic "myTree"
                  (dynamic Node (Leaf 1) (Leaf 2)) world
    = world
```

These constructors can then be used by the shell to pattern match on a value of that type.

```
> leftmost tree = case tree of Leaf x -> x; Node l r -> leftmost l
leftmost :: (Tree a) -> a

> leftmost (Node (Node myTree myTree) myTree)
1 :: Int
```

**Typical Shell Commands.** Esther's search path also contains a directory with common shell commands, such a file system operations:

```
> mkdir "foo"
UNIT :: UNIT
```

Esther displays UNIT because mkdir has type World → World, i.e., has a side effect, but no result. Functions that operate on the Clean's World state are applied to the world by Esther.

More operations on the file system:

```
> cd "foo"
UNIT :: UNIT

> 42 >> bar
42 :: Int

> ls ""
"
bar
" :: {#Char}
```

**Processes.** Examples of process handling commands:

```
> famkeNewProcess "localhost" Esther
{FamkeId "131.174.32.197" 2} :: FamkeId
```

This starts a new, concurrent, incarnation of Esther at the same computer. IP addresses can be used to start processes on other computers. famkeNewProcess yields a new process id (of type FamkeId). It is necessary to have the Famke kernel running on the other computer, e.g., by starting a shell there, to be able to start a process on another machine. Starting Esther on another machine does not give remote access, the console of the new incarnation of Esther is displayed on the other machine.

## 4   Implementation of Esther Using Clean's Dynamics

In this section, we explain how one can use the type unification of Clean's dynamic run-time system to type check a shell command, and we show how the corresponding Clean expression is translated effectively using combinations of already existing compiled code.

Obviously, we could have implemented type checking ourselves using one of the common algorithms involving building and solving a list of type equations. Another option would be to use the Clean compiler to do the type checking and compilation of the command line expressions. Instead, we decided to use Clean's dynamic run-time unification, because we want to show the power of Clean's dynamics, and because this has several advantages:

- Clean's dynamics allow us to do type safe and lazy I/O of expressions;
- we do not need to convert between the (hidden) type representation used by dynamics and the type representation used by our type checking algorithm;
- it shows whether Clean's current dynamics interface is powerful enough to implement basic type inference and type checking;
- we get future improvements of Clean's dynamics interface for free, e.g., uniqueness attributes or overloading.

The parsing of a shell command line is trivial and we will assume here that the string has already been successfully parsed.

In order to support a basic, but complete, functional language in our shell we need to support function definitions, lambda, let(rec), and case expressions.

We will introduce the syntax tree constructors piecewise and show for each kind of expression how to construct a dynamic that contains the corresponding Clean expression and the type for that expression. Names occurring free in the command line are read from disk as dynamics before type checking. The expression can contain references other dynamics, and therefore references the compiled code of functions, which will be automatically linked by Clean's run-time system.

## 4.1  Application

Suppose we have a syntax tree for constant values and function applications that looks like:

```
:: Expr = (@) infixl 9¹² Expr Expr   //¹³ Application
        | Value Dynamic              // Constant or dynamic value from disk
```

We introduce a function compose, which constructs the dynamic containing a value with the correct type that, when evaluated, will yield the result of the given expression.

```
compose :: Expr → Dynamic
compose (Value d) = d
compose (f @ x)   = case (compose f, compose x) of
    (f :: a → b, x :: a) → dynamic f x :: b
    (df, dx)             → raise¹⁴ ("Cannot apply " +++ typeOf df
                                        +++ " to " +++ typeOf dx)
```

---

[12] This defines an infix constructor with priority 9 that is left associative.

[13] This a Clean comment to end-of-line, like Haskell's --.

[14] For easier error reporting, we implemented imprecise user-defined exceptions à la Haskell [8]. We used dynamics to make the set of exceptions extensible.

```
typeOf :: Dynamic → String
typeOf dyn = toString (typecodeOfDynamic dyn) // pretty print type
```

Composing a constant value, contained in a dynamic, is trivial. Composing an application of one expression to another is a lot like the **dynamicApply** function of Sect. 2. Most importantly, we added error reporting using the **typeOf** function for pretty printing the type of a value inside a dynamic.

In an application both dynamic arguments contain references to compiled code. If we write the resulting **dynamic** (f x) to disk, it contains references to the compiled code of f and CleanInlinex. Furthermore, we added a reference to the code of Clean's application. The resulting dynamic is self contained in the sense that the shell is not required to execute the code inside the dynamic. When the resulting dynamic is used in another Clean program, the referenced code is linked into the running program. Hence, we effectively combined existing code to form the new code of the resulting expression. This shows that the resulting code is not interpreted, but actually compiled via Clean's dynamics, even if not all conversions to dynamics (describe below) are as efficient one expects from a real compiler.

## 4.2   Lambda Expressions

Next, we extend the syntax tree with lambda expressions and variables.

```
:: Expr = ···                        // Previous def.
        | (~>) infixr 0 Expr Expr    // Lambda abstraction: λ .. → ..
        | Var String                 // Variable
        | S | K | I                  // Combinators
```

At first sight, it looks as if we could simply replace a $\leadsto$ constructor in the syntax tree with a dynamic containing a lambda expression in Clean:

```
compose (Var x ~> e) = dynamic (λy → composeLambda x y e :: ?)
```

The problem with this approach is that we have to specify the type of the lambda expression before the evaluation of **composeLambda**. Furthermore, **composeLambda** will not be evaluated until the lambda expression is applied to an argument. This problem is unavoidable because we cannot get 'around' the lambda. Fortunately, bracket abstraction [9] solves both problems.

Applications and constant values are **composed** to dynamics in the usual way. We translate each lambda expression to a sequence of combinators (S, K, and I) and applications, with the help of the function **ski**.

```
compose ···        // Previous def.
compose (x ~> e) = compose (ski x e)
compose I        = dynamic λx → x
compose K        = dynamic λx y → x
compose S        = dynamic λf g x → f x (g x)
```

```
ski :: Expr Expr → Expr   // common bracket abstraction
ski   x       (y ~> e)          = ski x (ski y e)
ski (Var x) (Var y) |¹⁵ x == y = I
ski   x       (f @ y)           = S @ ski x f @ ski x y
ski   x       e                 = K @ e
```

Composing lambda expressions uses `ski` to eliminate the ~> and `Var` syntax constructors, leaving only applications, dynamic values, and combinators. Composing a combinator simply wraps its corresponding definition and type as a lambda expression into a dynamic.

Special combinators and combinator optimization rules are often used to improve the speed of the generated combinator code by reducing the number of combinators [10]. One has to be careful not to optimize the generated combinator expressions in such a way that the resulting type becomes too general. In an untyped world this is allowed because they preserve the intended semantics when generating untyped (abstract) code. However, our generated code is contained within a dynamic and is therefore typed. This makes it essential that we preserve the principal type of the expression during bracket abstraction. Adding common eta-reduction, for example, results in a too general type for Var "f" ~> Var "x" ~> f x): $a \rightarrow a$, instead of: $(a \rightarrow b) \rightarrow a \rightarrow b$. Such optimizations might prevent us from getting the principal type for an expression. Simple bracket abstraction using S, K, and I, as performed by `ski`, does preserve the principal type [11].

Code combined by Esther in this way is not as fast as code generated by the Clean compiler. Combinators introduced by bracket abstraction are the main reason for this slowdown. Additionally, all applications are lazy and not specialized for basic types. However, these disadvantages only hold for the small (lambda) functions written at the command line, which are mostly used for plumbing. If faster execution is required, one can always copy-paste the command line into a Clean module that writes a dynamic to disk and running the compiler.

In order to reduce the number of combinators in the generated expression, our current implementation uses Diller's algorithm C [12] without eta-conversion in order to preserve the principal type, while reducing the number of generated combinators from exponential to quadratic. Our current implementation seems to be fast enough, so we did not explore further optimizations by other bracket abstraction algorithms.

## 4.3   Irrefutable Patterns

Here we introduce irrefutable patterns, e.g., (nested) tuples, in lambda expressions. This is a preparation for the upcoming let(rec) expressions.

```
:: Expr = ...                    // Previous def.
        | Tuple Int              // Tuple constructor
```

---

¹⁵ If this guard fails, we end up in the last function alternative.

```
compose ···           // Previous def.
compose (Tuple n) = tupleConstr n

tupleConstr :: Int → Dynamic
tupleConstr 2 = dynamic λx y → (x, y)
tupleConstr 3 = dynamic λx y z → (x, y, z)
tupleConstr ···  // and so on...16

ski :: Expr Expr → Expr
ski (f @ x)   e = ski f (x ↝ e)
ski (Tuple n) e = Value (matchTuple n) @ e
ski ···           // previous def.

matchTuple :: Int → Dynamic
matchTuple 2 = dynamic λf t → f (fst t) (snd t)
matchTuple 3 = dynamic λf t → f (fst3 t) (snd3 t) (thd3 t)
matchTuple ···  // and so on...
```

We extend the syntax tree with `Tuple` $n$ constructors (where $n$ is the number of elements in the tuple). This makes expressions like

```
Tuple 2 @ Var "x" @ Var "y" ↝ Tuple 2 @ Var "y" @ Var "z"
```

valid expressions. This example corresponds with the Clean lambda expression $\lambda(x, y, z) \to (x, z)$.

When the `ski` function reaches an application in the left-hand side of the lambda abstraction, it processes both sub-patterns recursively. When the `ski` function reaches a `Tuple` constructor it replaces it with a call to the `matchTuple` function. Note that the right-hand side of the lambda expression has already been transformed into lambda abstractions, which expect each component of the tuple as a separate argument. We then use the `matchTuple` function to extract each component of the tuple separately. It uses lazy tuple selections (using `fst` and `snd`, because Clean tuple patterns are always eager) to prevent non-termination of recursive let(rec)s in the next section.

## 4.4  Let(rec) Expressions

Now we are ready to add irrefutable let(rec) expressions. Refutable let(rec) expressions must be written as cases, which will be introduced in next section.

```
:: Expr = ···                        // Previous def.
        | Letrec [Def] Expr          // let(rec) .. in ..
        | Y                          // Combinator

:: Def = (:=:) infix 0 Expr Expr    // .. = ..
```

---

16 ...until 32. Clean does not support functions or data types with arity above 32.

```
compose ···                 // Previous def.
compose (Letrec ds e) = compose (letRecToLambda ds e)
compose Y                 = dynamic let y = f y in y :: A.a: (a → a) → a

letRecToLambda :: [Def] Expr → Expr
letRecToLambda ds e = let (p :=: d) = combine ds
                      in  ski p e @ (Y @ ski p d)

combine :: [Def] → Def
combine [p :=: e]      = p :=: c
combine [p1 :=: e1:ds] = let (p2 :=: e2) = combine ds
                         in  Tuple 2 @ p1 @ p2 :=: Tuple 2 @ e1 @ e2
```

When compose encounters a let(rec) expression it uses letRecToLambda to convert it into a lambda expression. The letRecToLambda function combines all (possibly mutually recursive) definitions by pairing definitions into a single (possibly recursive) irrefutable tuple pattern. This leaves us with just a single definition that letRecToLambda converts to a lambda expression in the usual way [13].

### 4.5   Case Expressions

Composing a case expression is done by transforming each alternative into a lambda Expression that takes the expression to match as an argument. This yields a function that, once composed, results in a dynamics that contains a functions that expects a value to match to. If the expression matches the pattern, the right-hand side of the alternative is taken. When it does not match, the lambda expression corresponding to the next alternative is applied to the expression, forming a cascade of if-then-else constructs. This results in a single lambda expression that implements the case construct, and we apply it to the expression that we wanted to match against.

```
:: Expr = ···                    // Previous def.
        | Case Expr [Alt]        // case .. of ..

:: Alt = (:>) infix 0 Expr Expr    // .. → ..

compose ···          // Previous def.
compose (Case e as) = compose (altsToLambda as @ e)
```

We translate the alternatives into lambda expressions below using altsToLambda below. If the pattern consists of an application we do bracket abstraction for each argument, just as we did for lambda expressions, in order to deal with each subpattern recursively. Matching against an irrefutable pattern, such as variables of tuples, always succeeds and we reuse the code of ski that does the matching for lambda expressions. Matching basic values is done using ifEqual that uses Clean's built-in equalities for each basic type. We always add a default alternative, using the mismatch function, that informs the user that none of the patterns matched the expression.

```
altsToLambda :: [Alt] → Expr
altsToLambda []                     = Value mismatch
altsToLambda [f @ x :> e:as]        = altsToLambda [f :> ski x e:as]
altsToLambda [Var x :> e:_]         = Var x ⤳ e
altsToLambda [Tuple n :> e:_]       = Tuple n ⤳ e
altsToLambda [Value dyn :> th:as]
    = let el = altsToLambda as
      in   case dyn of
                (i :: Int)  → Value (ifEqual i) @ th @ el
                (c :: Char) → Value (ifEqual c) @ th @ el
                ··· // for all basic types


ifEqual :: a → Dynamic | TC a & Eq a
ifEqual x = dynamic λth el y → if (x == y) th (el y)
                   :: A.b: b (aˆ → b) aˆ → b


mismatch = dynamic raise "Pattern mismatch" :: A.a: a
```

Matching against a constructor contained in a dynamic takes more work. For example, if we put Clean's list constructor [:] in a dynamic we find that it has type a → [a] → [a], which is a function type. In Clean, one cannot match closures or functions against constructors. Therefore, using the function makeNode below, we construct a node that contains the right constructor by adding dummy arguments until it has no function type anymore. The function ifMatch uses some low-level code to match two nodes to see if the constructor of the pattern matches the outermost constructor of the expression. If it matches, we need to extract the arguments from the node. This is done by the applyTo function, which decides how many arguments need to be extracted (and what their types are) by inspection of the type of the curried constructor. Again, we use some low-level auxiliary code to extract each argument while preserving laziness.

Some low-level code is necessary, because selecting an arbitrary argument of a node is not expressible in Clean. To keep the Clean language referential transparent, this cannot be expressed in general. Since we know that the resulting code and types are correct, we chose to write this in Clean's machine independent assembly code: ABC-code. Another option is to request destructors/maching function from the user. We chose to implement this hack using ABC-code because all information is available, from the Clean run-time system and the data and heap storage areas. We decided that the users convenience has priority over an elegant implementation in this case.

```
altsToLambda [Value dyn :> th:as] = let el = altsToLambda as
    in case dyn of
           ··· // previous definition for basic types
           constr → Value (ifMatch (makeNode constr))
                                    @ (Value (applyTo dyn) @ th) @ el
```

```
ifMatch :: Dynamic → Dynamic
ifMatch (x :: a)=dynamic λth el y → if (matchNode x y) (th y) (el y)
                            :: A.b: (a → b) (a → b) a → b
```

```
makeNode :: Dynamic → Dynamic
makeNode (f :: a → b) = makeNode (dynamic f undef :: b)
makeNode (x :: a)     = dynamic x :: a
```

```
applyTo :: Dynamic → Dynamic
applyTo ···                   // and so on, most specific type first...
applyTo (_ :: a b → c) = dynamic λf x → f (arg1of2 x) (arg2of2 x)
                            :: A.d: (a b → d) c → d
applyTo (_ :: a → b)   = dynamic λf x → f (arg1of1 x)
                            :: A.c: (a → c) b → c
applyTo (_ :: a)       = dynamic λf x → f :: A.b: b a → b
```

```
matchNode :: a a → Bool // low-level code; compares two nodes.
```

$argiof n$ :: a → b // low-level code; selects $i^{th}$ argument of an $n$-ary node

Pattern matching against user defined constructors requires that the constructors are available from, i.e., stored in, the file system. Esther currently does not support type definitions at the command line, and the Clean compiler must be used to introduce new types and constructors into the file system. For an example of this, we refer to the description of the use of case expressions in Sect. 3.4.

### 4.6 Overloading

Support for overloaded expressions within dynamics in Clean is not yet implemented (e.g., one cannot write **dynamic** (==) :: A.a: a a → Bool | Eq a). Even when a future dynamics implementation supports overloading, it cannot be used in a way that suits Esther. We want to solve overloading using instances/-dictionaries from the file system, which may change over time, and which is something we cannot expect from Clean's dynamic run-time system out of the box.

Below is the Clean version of the overloaded functions == and **one**. We will use these two functions as a running example.

```
class Eq  a where (==) infix 4 :: a a → Bool
class one a where one :: a
```

```
instance Eq  Int where (==) x y = // low-level code to compare integers
instance one Int where one      = 1
```

To mimic Clean's overloading, we introduce the type Overloaded to differentiate between 'overloaded' dynamics and 'normal' dynamics. The type Overloaded, shown below, has three type variables that represent: the dictionary type d, the 'original' type of the expression t, and the type of the name of the overloaded function o, which also contains the variable the expression is overloaded in. Values of the type Overloaded consists of a infix constructor ||| followed by the overloaded expression (of type d → t), and the context restrictions (of type o). A term Class c of type Context v is used for a single context restriction of the class c on the type variable v. Multiple context restrictions are combined in a tree of type Contexts.

```
:: Overloaded d t o = (|||) infix 1 (d → t) o
:: Contexts a b     = (&&&) infix 0 a b
:: Context v        = Class String
```

```
(==) = dynamic id ||| Class "Eq"
           :: A.a: Overloaded (a a → Bool) (a a → Bool) (Context a)
one  = dynamic id ||| Class "one" :: A.a: Overloaded a a (Context a)
```

```
instance_Eq_Int  = dynamic λx y → x == y :: Int Int → Bool
instance_one_Int = dynamic 1              :: Int
```

The dynamic (==), in the example above, is Esther's representation of Clean's overloaded function ==. The overloaded expression itself is the identity function because the result of the expression *is* the dictionary. The name of the class is Eq. The dynamic (==) is overloaded in a single variable a, the type of the dictionary is a → a → Bool as expected, the 'original' type is the same, and the type of the name is Context a. Likewise, the dynamic one is Esther's representation of Clean's overloaded function one.

By separating the different parts of the overloaded type (the expression, the dictionary, and the variable) we obtain direct access to the variable in which the expression is overloaded. This makes it easy to detect if the overloading has been resolved: the variable no longer unifies with A.a: a.a. By separating the dictionary type and the 'original' type of the expression, it becomes easier to check if the application of one overloaded dynamic to another is allowed. We can check if a value of type Overloaded _ (a → b) _ can be applied to a value of type Overloaded _ a _).

To apply one overloaded dynamic to another, we combine the overloading information using the Contexts type in the way shown below in the function applyOverloaded.

```
applyOverloaded :: Dynamic Dynamic → Dynamic
applyOverloaded (f ||| of :: Overloaded df (a → b) cf) (x :: a)
    = dynamic (λd_f → f d_f x) ||| of :: Overloaded df b cf
applyOverloaded (f :: a → b) (x ||| ox :: Overloaded dx a cx)
    = dynamic (λd_x → f (x d_x)) ||| ox :: Overloaded dx b cx
applyOverloaded (f ||| of :: Overloaded df (a → b) cf)
               (x ||| ox :: Overloaded dx a cx)
    = dynamic (λ(d_f, d_x) → f d_f (x d_x)) ||| of &&& ox
       :: Overloaded (df, dx) b (Contexts cf cx)
```

`applyOverloaded` applies an overloaded function to a value, a function to an overloaded value, or an overloaded function to an overloaded value. The `compose` function from the beginning of this section is extended in the same way to handle 'overloaded dynamics'.

We use the (private) data type `Contexts` instead of tuples because this allows us to differentiate between a pair of two context restrictions and a single variable that has been unified with a tuple.

Applying `applyOverloaded` to (`==`) and `one` yields an expression semantically equal to `isOne` below. The overloaded expression `isOne` needs a pair of dictionaries to build the expression (`--`) `one` and has two context restrictions on the same variable. The 'original' type is a → `Bool`, and it is overloaded in `Eq` and `one`. Esther will pretty print this as: `isOne :: a → Bool | Eq a & one a`.

```
isOne = dynamic (λ(d_Eq, d_one) → id d_Eq (id d_one))
              ||| Class "Eq" &&& Class "one"
          :: A.a: Overloaded ((a a → Bool, a) (a → Bool))
              (Contexts (Context a) (Context a))
```

Applying `isOne` to the integer 42 will bind the variable `a` to `Int`. Esther is now able to choose the right instance for both `Eq` and `one`. It searches the file system for the files named "instance Eq Int" and "instance one Int", and applies the code of `isOne` to the dictionaries after applying the overloaded expression to 42. The result will look like `isOne42` in the example below, where all overloading has been removed from the type.

```
isOne42 = dynamic (λ(d_Eq, d_one) → id d_Eq (id d_one) 42)
              (instance_Eq_Int, instance_one_Int)     :: Bool
```

Although overloading is resolved in the example above, the plumbing/dictionary passing code is still present. This will increase evaluation time, and it is not clear yet how this can be prevented.

## 5  Related Work

We have not yet seen an interpreter or shell that equals Esther's ability to use pre-compiled code, and to store expressions as compiled code, which can be used in other already compiled programs, in a type safe way.

Es [14] is a shell that supports higher-order functions and allows the user to construct new functions at the command line. A UNIX shell in Haskell [15] by Jim Mattson is an interactive program that also launches executables, and provides pipelining and redirections. Tcl [16] is a popular tool to combine programs, and to provide communications between them. None of these programs provides a way to read and write typed objects, other than strings, from and to disk. Therefore, they cannot provide our level of type safety.

A functional interpreter with a file system manipulation library can also provide functional expressiveness and either static or dynamic type checking of part of the command line. For example, the Scheme Shell (ScSh) [17] integrates common shell operations with the Scheme language to enable the user to use the full expressiveness of Scheme at the command line. Interpreters for statically typed functional languages, such as Hugs [18], even provide static type checking in advance. Although they do type check source code, they cannot type check the application of binary executables to documents/data structures because they work on untyped executables.

The BeanShell [19] is an embeddable Java source interpreter with object scripting language features, written in Java. It is capable of inferring types for variables and to combine shell scripts with existing Java programs. While Esther generates compiled code via dynamics, the BeanShell interpreter is invoked each time a script is called from a normal Java program.

Run-time code generation in order to specialize code at run-time to certain parameters is not related to Esther. Esther only combines existing code into new code, by adding code for function application and combinators in between, using Clean's dynamic I/O system.

There are concurrent versions of both Haskell and Clean. Concurrent Haskell [20] offers lightweight threads in a single UNIX process and provides M-Vars as the means of communication between threads. Concurrent Clean [21] is only available on multiprocessor Transputers and on a network of single-processor Apple Macintosh computers. Concurrent Clean provides support for native threads on Transputer systems. On a network of Apple computers, it runs the same Clean program on each processor, providing a virtual multiprocessor system. Concurrent Clean provided lazy graph copying as the primary communication mechanism. Neither concurrent system can easily provide type safety between different programs or between multiple incarnations of a single program.

Both Lin [22] and Cooper and Morrisett [23] have extended Standard ML with threads (implemented as continuations using call/CC) to form a small functional operating system. Both systems implement the basics needed for a stand-alone operating system. However, none of them support the type-safe communication of any value between different computers.

Erlang [24] is a functional language specifically designed for the development of concurrent processes. It is completely dynamically typed and primarily uses interpreted byte-code, while Famke is mostly statically typed and executes native code generated by the Clean compiler. A simple spelling error in a token used during communication between two processes is often not detected by Erlang's dynamic type system, sometimes causing deadlock.

Back et al. [25] built two prototypes of a Java operating system. Although they show that Java's extensibility, portable byte code and static/dynamic type system provides a way to build an operating system where multiple Java programs can safely run concurrently, Java does not support dynamic type unification, higher-order functions, and closures in the comfortable way that our functional approach does.

# 6   Conclusions

We have shown how to build a shell that provides a simple, but powerful strongly typed functional programming language. We were able to do this using only Clean's support for run-time type unification and dynamic linking, albeit syntax transformations and a few low-level functions were necessary. The shell named Esther supports type checking and type inference before evaluation. It offers application, lambda abstraction, recursive let, pattern matching, and function definitions: the basics of any functional language. Additionally, infix operators and support for overloading make the shell easy to use.

By combining code from compiled functions/programs, Esther allows the use of any pre-compiled program as a function in the shell. Because Esther stores functions/expressions constructed at the command line as a Clean dynamic, it supports writing compiled programs at the command line. Furthermore, these expressions written at the command line can be used in any pre-compiled Clean program. The evaluation of expressions using recombined compiled code is not as fast as using the Clean compiler. Speed can be improved by introducing fewer combinators during bracket abstraction, but it seams unfeasible to make Esther perform the same optimizations as the Clean compiler. In practice, we find Esther responsive enough, and more optimizations do not appear worth the effort at this stage. One can always construct a Clean module using the same syntax and use the compiler to generate a dynamic that contains more efficient code.

# References

1. S. Peyton Jones and J. Hughes et al. *Report on the programming language Haskell 98*. University of Yale, 1999. http://www.haskell.org/definition/
2. M. J. Plasmeijer and M. C. J. D. van Eekelen. *Functional Programming and Parallel Graph Rewriting*. Addison Wesley, 1993.
3. R. Plasmeijer and M. van Eekelen. *Concurrent Clean Language Report version 2.1*. University of Nijmegen, November 2002. http://cs.kun.nl/~clean.
4. A. van Weelden and R. Plasmeijer. Towards a Strongly Typed Functional Operating System. In R. Peña and T. Arts, editors, *14th International Workshop on the Implementation of Functional Languages, IFL'02*, pages 215–231. Springer, September 2002. LNCS 2670.
5. M. Abadi, L. Cardelli, B. Pierce, and G. Plotkin. Dynamic Typing in a Statically Typed Language. *ACM Transactions on Programming Languages and Systems*, 13(2):237–268, April 1991.
6. M. Pil. Dynamic Types and Type Dependent Functions. In T. Davie, K. Hammond and C. Clack, editors, *Proceedings of the 10th International Workshop on the Implementation of Functional Languages*, volume 1595 of *Lecture Notes in Computer Science*, pages 171–188. Springer-Verlag, 1998.
7. M. Vervoort and R. Plasmeijer. Lazy Dynamic Input/Output in the Lazy Functional Language Clean. In R. Peña and T. Arts, editors, *14th International Workshop on the Implementation of Functional Languages, IFL'02*, pages 101–117. Springer, September 2002. LNCS 2670.

8. S. L. Peyton Jones, A. Reid, F. Henderson, C. A. R. Hoare, and S. Marlow. A Semantics for Imprecise Exceptions. In *SIGPLAN Conference on Programming Language Design and Implementation*, pages 25–36, 1999.

9. M. Schönfinkel. Über die Bausteine der mathematischen Logik. In *Mathematische Annalen*, volume 92, pages 305–316. 1924.

10. H. B. Curry and R. Feys. *Combinatory Logic*, volume 1. North-Holland, Amsterdam, 1958.

11. J. Roger Hindley and J. P. Seldin. *Introduction to Combinators and lambda-Calculus*. Cambridge University Press, 1986. ISBN 0521268966.

12. A. Diller. *Compiling Functional Languages*. John Wiley and Feys Sons Ltd, 1988.

13. S. L. Peyton Jones. *The Implementation of Functional Programming Languages*. Prentice-Hall, 1987.

14. P. Haahr and B. Rakitzis. Es: A shell with higher-order functions. In *USENIX Winter*, pages 51–60, 1993.

15. J. Mattson. The Haskell Shell. http://www.informatik.uni−bonn.de/~ralf/software/examples/Hsh.html.

16. J. K. Ousterhout. Tcl: An Embeddable Command Language. In *Proceedings of the USENIX Winter 1990 Technical Conference*, pages 133–146, Berkeley, CA, 1990. USENIX Association.

17. O. Shivers. A Scheme Shell. Technical Report MIT/LCS/TR-635, 1994.

18. M. P. Jones, A. Reid, the Yale Haskell Group, the OGI School of Science, and Engineering at OHSU. *The Hugs 98 User Manual*, 1994–2002. http://cvs.haskell.org/Hugs/.

19. P. Niemeyer. Beanshell 2.0. http://www.beanshell.org.

20. S. Peyton Jones, A. Gordon, and S. Finne. Concurrent Haskell. In *Conference Record of POPL '96: The 23$^{rd}$ ACM SIGPLAN-SIGACT Symposium on Principles of Programming Languages*, pages 295–308, St. Petersburg Beach, Florida, 21–24 1996.

21. E.G.J.M.H. Nocker, J.E.W. Smetsers, M.C.J.D. van Eekelen, and M.J. Plasmeijer. Concurrent Clean. In E.H.L. Aarts, J. van Leeuwen, and M. Rem, editors, *PARLE '91: Parallel Architectures and Languages Europe, Volume II*, volume 506 of *Lecture Notes in Computer Science*, pages 202–219. Springer, 1991.

22. A.C. Lin. *Implementing Concurrency For An ML-based Operating System*. PhD thesis, Massachusetts Institute of Technology, February 1998.

23. E.C. Cooper and J.G. Morrisett. Adding Threads to Standard ML. Technical Report CMU-CS-90-186, Pittsburgh, PA, 1990.

24. J. Armstrong, R. Virding, C. Wikström, and M. Williams. *Concurrent Programming in Erlang*. Prentice-Hall, second edition, 1996.

25. G. Back, P. Wullmann, L. Stoller, W. C. Hsieh, and J. Lepreau. Java Operating Systems: Design and Implementation. Technical Report UUCS-98-015, 6, 1998.

# Declarative Debugging with Buddha

Bernard Pope

Department of Computer Science and Software Engineering,
University of Melbourne, Victoria 3010, Australia
bjpop@cs.mu.oz.au

**Abstract.** Haskell is a very safe language, particularly because of its type system. However there will always be programs that do the wrong thing. Programmer fallibility, partial or incorrect specifications and typographic errors are but a few of the reasons that make bugs a fact of life. This paper is about the use and implementation of a debugger, called Buddha, which helps Haskell programmers understand why their programs misbehave. Traditional debugging tools that examine the program execution step-by-step are not suitable for Haskell because of its unorthodox evaluation strategy. Instead, a different approach is taken which abstracts away the evaluation order of the program and focuses on its high-level logical meaning.

This style of debugging is called Declarative Debugging, and it has its roots in the Logic Programming community. At the heart of the debugger is a tree which records information about the evaluation of the program in a manner which is easy to relate to the structure of the source code. It resembles a call graph annotated with the arguments and results of function applications, shown in their most evaluated form. Logical relationships between entities in the source are reflected in the links between nodes in the tree. An error diagnosis algorithm is applied to the tree in a top-down fashion in the search for causes of bugs.

## 1  Introduction

Debugging Haskell is interesting as a topic for research because, quite frankly, it is hard, and conventional debugging technologies do not suit it well.

On the one hand, Haskell is a very safe language. Implicit memory management, pure functions, and static type checking all tend to reduce the kind of bugs that can be encountered. Trivial programming mistakes tend to be caught early on in the development process. To use an old adage, there are fewer ways that a Haskell programmer can "shoot themselves in the foot". On the other hand, no language can stop a programmer from making logical errors. Furthermore, logical errors can be the hardest to find, due to subtle differences between what the programmer intended, and what they actually wrote. Therefore, debugging tools that relate program execution with the source code are vital for finding logical errors that aren't obvious from reading the source code. Typically there is a wide gap between the structure of Haskell code and the way it is evaluated, and

V. Varmo and T. Uustalu (Eds.): AFP 2004, LNCS 3622, pp. 273–308, 2005.
© Springer-Verlag Berlin Heidelberg 2005

this makes the task of debugging hard, in particular it rules out the step-based debugging style widely employed in imperative languages.

Purely functional languages, along with logic languages, are said to be *declarative*. The uniting theme of these languages is that they emphasise *what* a program computes rather than *how* it should do it. Or to put it another way, declarative programs focus on logic rather than evaluation strategy. The declarative style can be adopted in most languages, however the functional and logic languages tend to encourage a declarative mode of thinking, and are usually used most productively in that way. Proponents of declarative programming argue that the style allows programmers to focus on problem solving, and that the resulting programs are concise, and easier to reason about than equivalent imperative implementations. The declarative style allows more freedom in the way that programs are executed because the logic and evaluation strategy are decoupled. This means that declarative languages can take advantage of novel execution mechanisms without adding to the complexity of the source code. The non-strict semantics of Haskell and backtracking search of Prolog are examples of this.

Despite the many advantages of declarative programming, there are situations when the programmer must reason about *how* a program is evaluated. That is, the evaluation strategy is occasionally very important. For example, when performing input and output (I/O) the relative order of side-effects is crucial to the correctness of the program. The inclusion of monads and the statement-based *do notation* in Haskell reflect this, and where necessary one may adopt an imperative style of programming. Also, efficiency considerations sometimes require that the programmer can influence the evaluation strategy — for example strict evaluation may lead to better memory consumption.

Debugging is another task that suffers when the evaluation strategy is unknown to the programmer. The usual approach to debugging is to step through the program evaluation one operation at a time. However, to make any sense, this method requires the programmer to have an accurate mental model of the evaluation strategy — which is the very thing that the declarative style eschews. Forming an accurate mental model of lazy evaluation is quite a challenge. Logical relationships, such as "X depends on Y", which are evident in the source code, may not be apparent in the reduction order.

The other main factor that complicates debugging in Haskell is the tendency for programs to make extensive use of higher-order functions. The difficulty stems from three things: the function type is abstract and more difficult to display than structured data, the relationship between the static and dynamic call graphs is more complicated, and the specification of correctness much more demanding.

A very basic facility of debugging tools is to print out values from a running program. Functions are first-class in Haskell but they have no inherent printable representation. One might suppose that showing the name of a function would suffice, however not all functions in Haskell have a name (*i.e.* lambda abstractions). Also, there is a tendency to construct new functions dynamically by partial application and composition. If the user of the debugger is to have any hope of understanding what their program is doing, functions must be made observable, and the way they are shown must be easily related to the user's mental model of the program.

Higher-order functions make holes in the static call graph that are only filled in when the program is executed. Curried functions can pick up their arguments in a piecemeal fashion, and there may be a lengthy delay between when the initial application is made and when the function has received enough arguments for a reduction to take place. Whilst the extra flexibility in the call graph is good for abstraction and modularity, the effect for debugging is similar to the problem identified with non-strict evaluation — it is harder to relate the dynamic behaviour of the program with its static description.

Lastly, fundamental questions like: *"Is this function application doing what it should?"* have less obvious answers in the higher-order context. Understanding the meaning of a function is often hard enough, but understanding the meaning of a function that takes another function as its argument, or returns one as its result, exacerbates the problem. A significant challenge in the design of debugging systems for Haskell is how to reduce the cognitive load on the user, especially when there is a large number of higher-order functions involved. This is an issue that has seen little attention in the design of debugging systems for mainstream imperative languages because higher-order code is much less prevalent there.

The debugger we describe in this paper, called Buddha, is based on the philosophy that declarative languages deserve declarative debuggers. Or in other words, an effective way to deal with the problem of non-strict evaluation and higher-order functions is to aim the debugging tool at the declarative level of reasoning. The result is a powerful debugging facility that goes far beyond the capabilities of step-wise debuggers, extending the benefits of the declarative style from program development to program maintenance.

## Overview

In this paper we explain how Buddha is used, how it is implemented and the overall philosophy of Declarative Debugging. You, the reader, are assumed to be comfortable with Haskell, or a similar language, though by no means do you have to be an expert.

A number of exercises are sprinkled throughout the text for you to ponder over as you read along. In many cases the questions are open ended, and there may be more than one "right" answer. Some questions might even be research topics on their own! Of course there is no obligation to answer them all, they are merely an aid to help you consolidate the material in between.

The rest of the paper goes as follows:

- Section 2: using Buddha on an example buggy program.
- Section 3: summary of the important parts of Buddha's implementation.
- Section 4: deciding on the correctness of function applications.
- Section 5: controlling Buddha's resource usage.
- Section 6: pointers to related work.
- Section 7: conclusion.

## 2  An Example Debugging Session

Let's consider a short debugging session. Figure 1 contains a program with a bug.[1] It is supposed to print the digits of 341 as a list, but instead it prints [1,10,10].

This is the intended algorithm:

1. Compute a list of "base ten prefixes" of the number, by integer-dividing it by increasing powers of ten, starting at $10^0$. For example, the prefixes of 341 are are '[341, 34, 1, 0, 0, ...]' This is the job of prefixes.
2. Take numbers from the front of the above list while they are not zero. The output should be [341, 34, 3]. This is the job of the leadingNonZeros function.
3. For each number in the above list, obtain the last digit. The output should be [1,4,3]. This is the job of the lastDigits function.
4. Reverse the above list to give the digits in the desired order.

Normally, functions defined in the standard libraries are trusted by Buddha, making them invisible in the debugging session. To flesh out this example we have re-defined a number of Prelude functions within the module, hence the hiding clause in the import statement on line 3.

Debugging with Buddha takes place in five steps:

1. Program transformation. To make a debugging executable, the source code of the original program (the *debuggee*) is transformed into a new Haskell program. The transformed code is compiled and linked with a declarative debugging library, resulting in a program called debug.
2. Program execution. The debug program is executed, which runs the debuggee to completion and then starts the debugger.
3. Declarative debugging. An interactive dialogue begins between the debugger and the user. The debugger chooses function applications that were evaluated during the execution of the debuggee and prints them on the screen. The user judges them for correctness.
4. Diagnosis. The debugging dialogue continues until either the user terminates the session or the debugger makes a diagnosis.
5. Retry. For a given set of input values there might be more than one cause of an erroneous program execution. To find all the causes the user must repeat the above steps until no more bugs are found.

Each step is outlined below. Boxed text simulates user interaction on an operating system terminal. Italicised text indicates user-typed input, the rest is output. The operating system prompt is indicated by ▷.

**Transformation.** Buddha is based on program transformation. That is, to make a debugging executable, the source code of the original program (the *debuggee*) is

---

[1] Adapted from an example in the HOOD user documentation: www.haskell.org/hood/documentation.htm.

```
1       module Main where

        import Prelude hiding (reverse, map, (.), takeWhile, iterate)

5       main = print (digits 341)

        digits :: Int -> [Int]
        digits = reverse . lastDigits . leadingNonZeros . prefixes

10      prefixes :: Int -> [Int]
        prefixes = iterate ('div' 10)

        leadingNonZeros :: [Int] -> [Int]
        leadingNonZeros = takeWhile (/= 0)
15
        lastDigits :: [Int] -> [Int]
        lastDigits = map (10 'mod')

        reverse :: [a] -> [a]
20      reverse xs
           = revAcc xs []
           where
           revAcc [] acc = acc
           revAcc (x:xs) acc = revAcc xs (x:acc)
25
        map :: (a -> b) -> [a] -> [b]
        map f [] = []
        map f (x:xs) = f x : map f xs

30      takeWhile :: (a -> Bool) -> [a] -> [a]
        takeWhile p [] = []
        takeWhile p (x:xs)
           | p x = x : takeWhile p xs
           | otherwise = []
35
        iterate :: (a -> a) -> a -> [a]
        iterate f x = x : iterate f (f x)

        (.) :: (b -> c) -> (a -> b) -> a -> c
40      (.) f g x = f (g x)
```

**Fig. 1.** A program with a bug. It is supposed to compute the digits of 341 as a list ([3,4,1]), but instead it produces [1,10,10]. Line numbers are indicated on the left hand side.

transformed into a new Haskell program. The transformed code is compiled and linked with a declarative debugging library, resulting in a program called **debug**. When **debug** is executed it behaves exactly like the debuggee — it accepts the same command line arguments and performs the same I/O. Where the debuggee would have terminated, debug initiates an interactive debugging session. The details of the transformation are dealt with in Sec. 3.5.

To use Buddha on a program you must first ask it to transform the program source (and compile it *etcetera*). A program called buddha is provided for this job.[2]

Suppose that the program resides in a file called Digits.hs. The first thing to do is transform it, which goes as follows:

```
▷ buddha Digits.hs
buddha 1.2: initialising
buddha 1.2: transforming: Digits.hs
buddha 1.2: compiling
Chasing modules from: Main.hs
Compiling Main_B              ( ./Main_B.hs, ./Main_B.o )
Compiling Main                ( Main.hs, Main.o )
Linking ...
buddha 1.2: done
```

For each module X in the program, buddha transforms the code in that module and stores the result in a file called X_B.hs. To avoid cluttering the working directory with the new files, buddha does all of its work in a sub-directory called Buddha, which is created during its initialisation phase. Compilation and linking are done by the Glasgow Haskell Compiler (GHC).

**Program Execution.** The debugging executable (debug) is stored in the Buddha directory, so you must move to that directory and run it:

```
▷ cd Buddha
▷ ./debug
[1,10,10]
```

The first thing done by debug is to imitate the behaviour of the debuggee — in this simple example, it just prints the list [1,10,10].

**Declarative Debugging.** Where the debuggee would have terminated, debug initiates an interactive debugging session:

```
Welcome to buddha, version 1.2
A declarative debugger for Haskell
Copyright (C) 2004, Bernie Pope
http://www.cs.mu.oz.au/~bjpop/buddha

Type h for help, q to quit
```

---

[2] Don't confuse Buddha with buddha (the font and capitalisation are significant). Buddha is the name for the whole debugging system, whilst buddha is the name of the executable program for performing program transformation. We probably should have called the latter buddha-trans, but that would require more typing!

Buddha introduces itself with the above banner message. Following this is something called a *derivation*, and then the prompt (which is underlined):

```
[1] Main 5 main
    result = <IO>

buddha:
```

A derivation records information about the evaluation of a function application or a constant. In the above case, the derivation reports that the constant main evaluated to an I/O action (which is abstract). Each derivation also indicates in which module the entity was defined, and on what line its definition begins. In this case main was defined in module Main on line 5. If the entity is a function application the derivation will also show representations of its arguments. The number inside square brackets is unique to the derivation, and thus gives it an identity — we'll see how this is useful in a moment.

The derivations are stored in a tree, one per node, called an Evaluation Dependence Tree (EDT).[3] It looks just like a call graph. The root always contains a derivation for main because all Haskell programs begin execution there. Debugging is a traversal of this tree, one derivation at a time.

The evaluation of a function application or constant will often depend on other applications and constants. If you look back at Fig. 1, you will see that the definition of main depends on a call to print and a call to digits. The execution of these calls at runtime forms the *children* of the derivation for main, and conversely, main is their *parent*.

An important concept is that of the *current derivation*. The current derivation is simply the one that is presently under consideration. In our example the current derivation is the one for main. If you ever forget what the current derivation is you can get a reminder by issuing the refresh command.

You can ask Buddha to show you the children of the current derivation by issuing the kids command:

```
buddha: kids
```

To save typing, many of Buddha's commands can be abbreviated to one letter, normally the first letter of the long version. For example, kids can be abbreviated to k. For the remainder of this example we will use the long versions of each command for clarity, but you will probably want to use the short version in practice.

Buddha responds to kids as follows:

```
Children of the current derivation:

[2] Main 8 digits
    arg 1  = 341
    result = [1, 10, 10]
```

---

[3] The term *EDT* was coined by Nilsson and Sparud [1].

Surprisingly Buddha says that the derivation for main has only one child, namely an application of digits. What happened to the derivation for print? Since print is defined in the Prelude it is trusted to be correct. To reduce the size of the EDT and hopefully save time spent debugging, Buddha does not record derivations for trusted functions.

Note that kids does not change the current derivation, it just allows you to look ahead one level in the EDT. At this point in the example the current derivation is still main.

*Exercise 1.* If print was not trusted what would its derivation look like in this case?

Buddha can help you visualise the shape of the EDT with the draw command:

```
buddha: draw edt
```

This generates a graphical representation of the top few levels of the EDT, using the *Dot* language [2], and saves it to a file called buddha.dot. You can use a tool such as *dotty*[4] to view the graph:

```
▷ dotty buddha.dot
```

Figure 2 illustrates the kind of graph produced by the draw command. It is worth noting that the resulting graph differs from the EDT in that nodes do not include function arguments or results (or even line numbers *etcetera*).

It is very difficult to say anything about the correctness of the derivation for main because its result, an I/O value, is abstract. Therefore, it is a good idea to consider function applications that do not give I/O results.[5]

The child of main is suspicious looking, and thus worthy of further scrutiny. Here's where the unique number of the derivation becomes useful. You can change the current derivation using the jump command. The derivation for digits is numbered 2, and you can jump to it as follows:

```
buddha: jump 2
```

Although not needed here, it is worth noting that jumps can be undone with the back command, which takes you back to the derivation that you jumped from, and allows you to resume debugging from where you left off.

After making the jump Buddha shows the new current derivation:

```
[2] Main 8 digits
    arg 1  = 341
    result = [1, 10, 10]
```

---

[4] www.research.att.com/sw/tools/graphviz

[5] The version of Buddha described in this paper does not support debugging of functions that perform I/O, however future versions should remove this limitation.

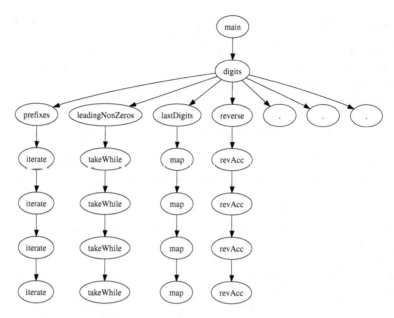

**Fig. 2.** A representation of the function call graph produced by the `draw` command, which shows the relationship between calls in the EDT. Note that the dot (.) is Haskell's name for function composition.

This derivation says that `digits` was applied to 341 and it returned the list [1, 10, 10]. This is definitely wrong — it should be [3, 4, 1]. When a derivation is found to be wrong you can declare this information by issuing a *judgement*. Function applications or constants that do not agree with your intended interpretation of the program should be judged as erroneous:

```
buddha: erroneous
```

Buddha's objective is to find a *buggy* derivation. A buggy derivation is one that is erroneous, and which either has no children, or all of its children are correct. Such a derivation indicates a function or constant which is improperly defined — it is the cause of at least one bug in the program.

A nice feature of the debugging algorithm is that, if the EDT is finite (and it always is for terminating programs), once you find an erroneous node you are guaranteed to find a buggy node.

*Exercise 2.* Provide an informal argument for the above proposition. What assumptions (if any) do you have to make, and will they be significant in practice?

We have established that the call to `digits` is erroneous, now Buddha must determine if it is buggy. This requires an inspection of its children. In Fig. 2 we see that the application of `digits` has seven children. Each child corresponds to an instance of a function which is mentioned in the body of the definition of digits. You might be surprised to see the EDT structured this way, because none of the function applications in the body of digits are saturated. In a language that allows partial application of functions, the evaluation contexts in which a function is first mentioned and when it is fully applied can be quite disconnected. For example, the definition of digits refers to prefixes. However, it is not until prefixes is applied (dynamically) in the body of compose that it becomes saturated. Therefore it might also be reasonable to make the call to prefixes a child of a call to compose. The parent-child relationship between nodes in the EDT is based on the idea of logical evaluation dependence. The idea is that the correctness of the parent depends, in part, on the correctness of the child. Higher-order programming tends to muddy the waters, and we can see that there is some degree of flexibility as to the positioning of calls to functions which are passed as arguments to other functions. Buddha's approach is to base the parent-child relationship on the dependency which is evident in the static definition of functions. Statically, the definition of digits depends on a reference to prefixes. Dynamically, a call to digits will give rise to a partial application of prefixes. All the *full* applications of this particular instance of prefixes will become children of the application of digits. The same logic is applied to all the other functions which are mentioned in the body of digits.

There are two possible scenarios that can lead Buddha to a diagnosis. In the first scenario all the children of digits are correct. The conclusion in that case is that digits is buggy. In the second scenario one or more of the children of digits is incorrect. In that case the erroneous children or one or more of their descendents are buggy. Buddha could collect a *set* of buggy nodes as its diagnosis, but for simplicity it stops as soon as one such node has been identified. The idea is that you find and fix one bug at a time.

In this example Buddha will move to the first child of digits. If that child is correct it will move to the next child, and so on. If all the children are found to be correct the diagnosis is complete. If one of the children is erroneous, Buddha will recursively consider the EDT under that child in the search for a bug.

*Exercise 3.* Will the order that the children are visited affect the diagnosis of the bug? Can you think of any heuristics that might reduce the number of derivations considered in a debugging session?

As it happens, the first child visited by Buddha is a call to compose, which becomes the new current derivation:

```
[3] Main 40 .
    arg 1  = { [341, 34, 3, 0, ..? -> [1, 10, 10] }
    arg 2  = { 341 -> [341, 34, 3, 0, ..? }
    arg 3  = 341
    result = [1, 10, 10]
```

The first two arguments of compose are much more complicated than the examples we have seen before. The complexity comes from two sources. First, this is an instance of *higher order* programming — compose is a function which takes functions as its first two arguments. Printing functions is more difficult than other values, and understanding derivations that contain them can be more taxing on the brain. Second, we have encountered a partially evaluated list — the list that ends with '..?'. This arises because Haskell is non-strict, and the value of the tail of the list was never needed. Again, partial values can make derivations harder to comprehend.

Buddha indicates functional values using the notation:

{ app$_1$, ..., app$_n$ }

where each app$_i$ represents a function application of the form:

```
input -> output
```

Typically this is only a partial representation of the function — it only reports the value of the function for the actual values it was applied to.[6] Nonetheless, this is enough information to proceed with debugging. Thus the first argument to compose is a function that maps '[341, 34, 3, 0, ..?' to '[1, 10, 10]'.

*Exercise 4.* Can you think of any other way to show the value of functions that appear as arguments or results in derivations? What benefits/costs do the alternatives have in comparison to the one used by Buddha?

A consequence of the non-strict semantics of Haskell is that some expressions may never reach a normal form throughout the execution of the program. In this derivation we have a list whose prefix was evaluated four elements deep and whose tail, after those four elements, was unevaluated — in functional programming jargon, a *thunk*. Note carefully that Buddha shows all values to the extent that they were evaluated at the end of the execution of the debuggee.

When Buddha encounters a thunk it prints a question mark, although if the thunk appears at the end of a list it uses square bracket notation for the start of the list and '..?' to indicate the thunk at the end.

The judgement of derivations involving partial values is considered in more detail in Sec. 4.2. In this particular case it is not too hard to judge this derivation to be correct, since it is clearly the intention that:

(.) {Y -> Z} {X -> Y} X = Z

However, we will take this opportunity to reveal another feature of Buddha. It is quite common during declarative debugging to be faced with a very difficult derivation. In many cases it is better to look for simpler derivations that might also lead to a bug diagnosis, rather than struggle with the most difficult ones first.

The **defer** command tells Buddha to postpone judgement of the current derivation and move on to another one if possible. Where does it get the next one from? Remember that there were seven children of the derivation for **digits**.

---

[6] This representation resembles the idea of *minimal function graphs*, which were introduced as part of a data-flow analysis of functional languages in [3].

We were in the process of checking those children for correctness. In fact we've only looked at one so far, and we found it to be too complicated. Buddha treats the children as a circular queue. Deferral simply moves the current derivation to the end of the queue and makes the next derivation the current one. If we keep deferring we'll eventually get back to the start again.

```
buddha: defer
```

This leads us to two more applications of compose. Again these could be judged correct, but for the point of demonstration we'll defer them both:

```
[4] Main 40 .
    arg 1  = { [341, 34, 3] -> [1, 10, 10] }
    arg 2  = { [341, 34, 3, 0, ..? -> [341, 34, 3] }
    arg 3  = [341, 34, 3, 0, ..?
    result = [1, 10, 10]
```

```
buddha: defer
```

```
[5] Main 40 .
    arg 1  = { [10, 10, 1] -> [1, 10, 10] }
    arg 2  = { [341, 34, 3] -> [10, 10, 1] }
    arg 3  = [341, 34, 3]
    result = [1, 10, 10]
```

```
buddha: defer
```

Finally something which is easy to judge:

```
[6] Main 20 reverse
    arg 1  = [10, 10, 1]
    result = [1, 10, 10]
```

Clearly this application of **reverse** is correct:

```
buddha: correct
```

*Exercise 5.* The type of **reverse** is:

$$\forall\ a\ .\ [a] \rightarrow [a]$$

How could this polymorphic type be used to simplify derivations of **reverse**? Hint: **reverse** doesn't care about the value of the items in the list, just their relative order.

A correct child cannot be held responsible for an error identified in its parent. Thus there is no need to consider the subtree under the child, so Buddha moves on to the next of its siblings:

```
[8] Main 17 lastDigits
     arg 1  = [341, 34, 3]
     result = [10, 10, 1]
```

At last we find a child of `digits` which is erroneous (we expect that the last digits of [341, 34, 3] to be [1, 4, 3]).

```
buddha: erroneous
```

*Exercise 6.* The definition of `lastDigits` in Fig. 1 is accompanied by a type annotation. The annotation says that `lastDigits` is a function of one argument, however the argument is not mentioned in its definition (`lastDigits` is defined as a constant). How is this possible? Something interesting happens in Buddha if you remove that annotation — the derivation for `lastDigits` changes to the following:

```
[8] Main 16 lastDigits
     result = { [341, 34, 3] -> [10, 10, 1] }
```

Can you explain what has happened here? Why does the type annotation make a difference? Will it influence the diagnosis of the bug?

The discovery of this error causes the focus to shift from the children of `digits` to the sub-tree which is rooted at the derivation for `lastDigits`. The new goal is to decide whether `lastDigits` or one of its descendents is buggy.

As it happens the derivation of `lastDigits` has only one child, which is a call to `map`:

```
[9] Main 27 map
     arg 1  = { 3 -> 1, 34 -> 10, 341 -> 10 }
     arg 2  = [341, 34, 3]
     result = [10, 10, 1]
```

*Exercise 7.* It would appear from the code in Fig. 1 that `lastDigits` calls two functions. However Buddha only gives it one child. What is the other child, and what happened to it?

Despite the fact that `map`'s first argument is a function it should be pretty clear that this application is correct:

```
buddha: correct
```

**Diagnosis.** This last judgement leads us to a buggy node, which Buddha indicates as follows:

```
Found a buggy node:
  [8] Main 17 lastDigits
      arg 1  = [341, 34, 3]
      result = [10, 10, 1]
```

Here is where the debugging session ends. However we haven't yet achieved what we set out to do: find the bug in the program. Buddha has helped us a lot, but we have to do a little bit of thinking on our own.

*Exercise 8.* Why did Buddha stop here? Trace through the steps in the diagnosis that lead it to this point. Are you convinced it has found a bug? What about those deferred derivations involving compose, is it okay to simply ignore them?

The diagnosis tells us that `lastDigits` returns the wrong result when applied to [341, 34, 3]. We also know that every application depended on by `lastDigits` to produce this value is correct.

*Exercise 9.* What is the bug in the program in Fig. 1? Provide a definition of `lastDigits` that amends the problem.

**Retry.** When we get to this point it is tempting to dust our hands, congratulate ourselves, thank Buddha and move on to something else. However our celebrations may be premature. Buddha only finds one buggy node at a time, but there may be more lurking in the same tree. A diligent bug finder will re-run the program on the same inputs that cause the previous bug, to see whether it has been resolved, or whether there is more debugging to be done. Of course it is prudent to test our programs on a large number and wide variety of inputs as well — the testing suite QuickCheck can be very helpful for this task [4].

## 2.1   Try It for Yourself

Now it's your turn to use Buddha to debug a program.

Figure 3 contains a small program for converting numbers written in base ten notation to other bases. It is an extension of the program in Figure 1. It reads two numbers from the user: the number to convert, and the desired base of the output. It prints out the number written in the new base. The intended algorithm goes as follows (all numbers are written in base ten to avoid confusion):

1. Prompt the user to enter a number and a base. Read each as a string, and convert them to integers using the library function **read** (which assumes its argument is in base ten).
2. Compute a list of "prefixes" of the number in the desired base. For example, if the number is 1976, and the base is 10, the prefixes are '[1976, 197, 19, 1]'. This is the job of **prefixes**.

3. For each number in the above list, obtain the last digit in the desired base. For example if the list is '[1976, 197, 19, 1]', the output should be '[6, 7, 9, 1]'. This is the job of lastDigit.

4. Convert each (numerical) digit into a character. Following the hexadecimal convention, numbers above 9 are mapped to a letter in the alphabet. For example, 10 becomes 'a', 11 becomes 'b' and so on. This is the job of toDigit.

5. Reverse the above list to give the digits in the desired order.

*Exercise 10.* Your job is to test the program to find example input values that cause it to return the wrong result. For each set of inputs that give rise to the

```
1    module Main where

     main = do putStrLn "Enter a number"
               num <- getLine
5              putStrLn "Enter base"
               base <- getLine
               putStrLn (convert (read base) (read num))

     convert :: Int -> Int -> String
10   convert base
         = reverse          .
           map toDigit       .
           map (lastDigit base) .
           prefixes base
15
     toDigit :: Int -> Char
     toDigit i
         = index i digitChars
         where
20       digitChars = ['0' .. 'z']

     prefixes :: Int -> Int -> [Int]
     prefixes base n
         | n <= 0 = []
25       | otherwise = n : prefixes (n 'div' base) base

     lastDigit :: Int -> Int -> Int
     lastDigit x = \y -> mod x y

30   index :: Int -> [a] -> a
     index n list
         | n == 0 = head list
         | otherwise = index (n - 1) (tail list)
```

**Fig. 3.** A program for converting numbers in base 10 notation to other bases. The program has a number of bugs.

wrong behaviour, use Buddha to diagnose the cause of the bug. Fix the program, and repeat the process until you are convinced that the program is bug free. To get started, try using the program to convert 1976 to base 10. The expected output is 1976, however program produces :0:.

# 3   Implementation

In this section we look at how Buddha is implemented. Space constraints necessitate a fair degree of generalisation, and you should treat it as a sketch, rather than a blueprint.

We begin with a definition of the EDT using Haskell types. Then we look at a useful abstraction called the Oracle, which plays the part of judge in the debugger. After the Oracle, we consider a simple bug diagnosis algorithm over the EDT. Then we discuss the process of turning arbitrary values into textual forms which are suitable for printing on the terminal. Of particular interest is the way that functions are handled. Lastly, we compare two transformation algorithms that introduce code into the debuggee for constructing the EDT.

## 3.1   The Evaluation Dependence Tree

The Evaluation Dependence Tree (EDT) provides a high-level semantics for the evaluation of a Haskell program, and is at the heart of Buddha. Nodes in the tree contain derivations which show the value of function applications and constants that were needed in the course of the program execution. Edges between the nodes indicate an evaluation dependence which can be related directly to the structure of the source code. Figure 4 illustrates the EDT for the program studied in the previous section. Figure 5 shows Haskell types for describing the EDT.

Each node in the EDT has a unique integer identity, a derivation, and zero or more children nodes. Each derivation names a function or a constant, zero or more argument values, a result value and a source location (constants have zero arguments and functions have at least one).

Perhaps the most interesting type in Fig. 5 is Value. It has one constructor, called V, which is polymorphic in the type of its argument, however that type is concealed. This means that the EDT can refer to a heterogeneous collection of types without breaking Haskell's typing rules. You might wonder how we retrieve something from its Value wrapper. The solution to this problem is discussed later in Sec. 3.4.

Explicit quantification of type variables are not part of the Haskell 98 standard, however the style used here is widely supported.

## 3.2   The Oracle

The debugging example in Sec. 2 shows how Buddha interacts with the user. A basic assumption of the Declarative Debugging algorithm is the existence of someone or something that knows how to judge derivations. It is natural to think

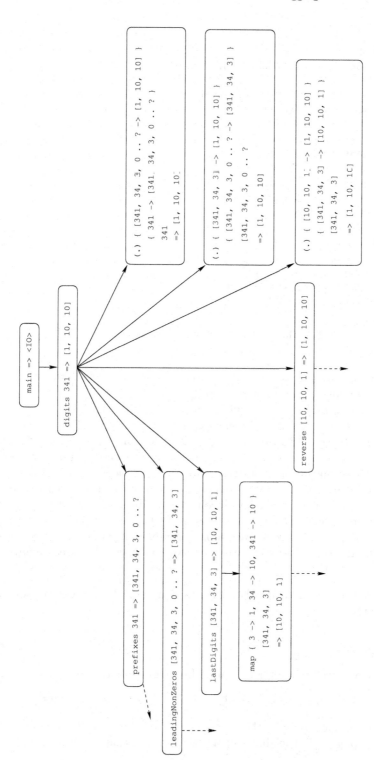

**Fig. 4.** An EDT for the program in Fig. 1. Dotted edges indicate subtrees which have been truncated for brevity.

```
type Identifier  = String
type LineNumber  = Int
type FileName    = String
type SrcLoc      = (FileName, LineNumber)

-- note the explicit quantifier in this type
data Value = forall a . V a

data Derivation
   = Derivation
       { name     :: Identifier
       , args     :: [Value]
       , result   :: Value
       , location :: SrcLoc }

data EDT
   = EDT
       { nodeID     :: Int
       , derivation :: Derivation
       , children   :: [EDT] }
```

**Fig. 5.** Haskell types for implementing the EDT

of the judge as a person sitting behind a computer terminal. However the role of judge can be automated to a certain degree.

Buddha delegates the task of judgement to an entity called the Oracle. Currently the Oracle is a hybrid of software and human input. The diagnosis algorithm passes derivations to the Oracle which returns a judgement. The goal of the software part is to reduce the number of derivations seen by the user. It keeps a database that records pairs of derivations and judgements, which is populated by prior responses from the user. If a derivation has been seen before, the corresponding judgement is retrieved from the database. Derivations never seen before are printed on the terminal and judged by the user, and the judgement is saved in the database. There is much room for improvement on the software side. An obvious extension is to allow the database to be saved between debugging sessions.

*Exercise 11.* Can you think of other features that might be useful in the software part of the Oracle?

### 3.3  Diagnosis

Figure 6 shows a very simple Declarative Debugging algorithm in Haskell.

*Exercise 12.* Extend the diagnosis algorithm to collect a set of buggy nodes.

The method for obtaining the EDT depends on the underlying implementation of the debugger. In the above diagnosis algorithm that detail is left abstract.

```
data Judgement = Correct | Erroneous
data Diagnosis = NoBugs  | Buggy Derivation

debug :: Diagnosis -> [EDT] -> IO Diagnosis
debug diagnosis [] = return diagnosis
debug diagnosis (node:siblings)
    = do let thisDerivation = derivation node
         judgement <- askOracle thisDerivation
         case judgement of
            Correct -> debug diagnosis siblings
            Erroneous
               -> debug (Buggy thisDerivation) (children node)

askOracle :: Derivation -> IO Judgement
askOracle derivation = ... -- abstract

-- the top level of the debugger
main :: IO ()
main
    = do root <- get the root of the EDT
         diagnosis <- debug NoBugs [root]
         case diagnosis of
            NoBugs -> output: no bugs found
            Buggy derivation -> output: this derivation is buggy
```

**Fig. 6.** Pseudo Haskell code for a Declarative Debugging diagnosis algorithm

Later, in Sec. 3.5, we'll see two different ways that have been used in Buddha to produce the tree.

## 3.4  Observation

Buddha must be able to turn values into text if it is going to print them on the terminal. An important condition is that it must be able to print *any* value. In short, we want a universal printer. Unfortunately there is no standard way of doing this in Haskell, and GHC does not supply one, so Buddha must provide its own.[7]

There are a number of requirements that make the task quite hard:

– It must be possible to observe partial values, and reveal their unevaluated parts without forcing them any further.
– Some values can have cyclic representations. The printer must not generate infinite strings for these.
– It must be able to print functions.

---

[7] Hugs does have a universal printer of sorts, but it has poor support for functions, and regardless, Hugs is too slow to support Buddha.

To implement the printer we need reflection, however Haskell is not particularly strong in this regard. For example, there is no facility to determine whether something is a thunk. We work around the restrictions at the Haskell level by interfacing with the runtime environment via the Foreign Function Interface (FFI). That is, we extend GHC's runtime environment with reflective facilities, by the use of C code that observes the representation of values on the GHC heap. The C code constructs a Haskell data structure, of type Graph, that mirrors the heap representation, including the presence of thunks and cycles.

Graph has the following definition:

```
data Graph
    = AppNode      Word String [Graph]
    | CharNode     Char
    | IntNode      Int
    | IntegerNode  Integer
    | FloatNode    Float
    | DoubleNode   Double
    | Cycle        Word
    | Thunk
    | Function
```

AppNode represents applications of data constructors. It has three arguments: its address on the heap, the name of the constructor and a list of the arguments to the application (for nullary constructors the list is empty). Specialised Graph constructors are provided for the primitive types (CharNode *etcetera*). Cycles in the heap representation are encoded with the Cycle constructor, its argument is the address of a constructor application — in other words it is a pointer back to some other part of the object. Unevaluated heap objects are mapped to Thunk, and all functions are mapped to Function (although this apparent limitation will be addressed shortly).

*Exercise 13.* In Sec. 2 we saw the partial list [341,34,3,0,..?. Recall that the tail of the list indicated by ..? is a thunk. Provide a Graph encoding of that list. You can assume that the numbers are of type Int. The memory addresses of constructor applications are not important — just make them up.

The interface to the reflection facility is as follows:

```
reifyValue :: Value -> IO Graph
reifyValue (V x) = reify x


reify :: a -> IO Graph
reify x = ...  -- call C code via the FFI
```

The function reifyValue retrieves an item encapsulated inside a Value, and passes it to reify, which maps it into a Graph. The typing rules of Haskell forbid us from exposing the type of the item. Thus it is crucial that reify is polymorphic in its first argument. This is easily satisfied by performing all the

**Graph** construction work in C. From the C perspective all values have the same type (a heap object), so there is no limitation on the type of value that can be passed down through **reify**.

*Exercise 14.* What have we sacrificed by observing values on the heap via the FFI?

The result of **reify** has an **IO** type. This is necessary because multiple applications of **reify** to the same value may give back different **Graphs**. For example, the presence or absence of thunks and cycles in a value depends on *when* it is observed. Buddha ensures that values are observed in their most evaluated form by delaying all calls to **reify** until the evaluation of the debuggee has run to completion — at that point it knows their heap representations will not change.

**Cycles.** Cyclic values are not uncommon in Haskell. The classic example is the infinite list of ones:

```
ones = 1 : ones
```

The non-strict semantics of Haskell allow programs to operate on this list without necessarily causing non-termination. It is worth pointing out that the language definition does not require this list to be implemented as a cyclic structure, however all of the popular compilers currently do. Here is a **Graph** representation of the list, assuming that it lies at address 12:

```
AppNode 12 ":" [IntNode 1, Cycle 12]
```

Buddha's default mode of showing cyclic values is rather naive. It prints this list as:

```
[1, <cycle>
```

This indicates the origin of the cycle, but not its destination. Buddha has another mode of printing which uses recursive equations to show cycles. You can turn this mode on with the **set** command:

```
buddha: set cycles True
```

In this mode the list is printed as:

```
let _x1 = [1, _x1 in _x1
```

You might wonder why Buddha doesn't use the second mode by default. Our experience is that for larger values with cycles it can actually make the output harder to comprehend! In any case, it is often preferable to view complex structures as a diagram, which can be done with the **draw** command. In Sec. 2 we saw how to use **draw** to produce a diagram of the EDT, using the Dot graph language. You can also use this command for printing values that appear as arguments or results in derivations.

Suppose the current derivation contains **ones**. The following command renders the result of **ones** and saves the output in the file **buddha.dot**:

> **buddha:** *draw result*

As before, you can view the diagram with the *dotty* program, the output of which looks like this:

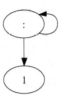

If you want to draw an argument at position 3, for instance, you can issue the command:

> **buddha:** *draw arg 3*

**Functions.** Functions are more troublesome beasts when it comes to printing because they are abstract types. Ordinary data structures have constructors which can be inspected in the heap and printed in a straightforward manner, but the internal, compiled representation of functions is very hard to reconcile with the source code.

The solution goes as follows. Each function that could possibly be printed is assigned a unique integer. An entry is added to a global table whenever such a function is applied, recording the number of the function, its argument and its result. Table entries have this type:

```
type FunApplication = (Int, Value, Value)
```

*Exercise 15.* Why is it possible to record only one argument? How do you think multi-argument functions are handled?

Functions and their unique number are "wrapped up" inside a new type called **F**:

```
data F a b = F Int (a->b)
```

This ensures that the function and the number are always together. Wrappers are introduced as part of the program transformation, however the unique numbers are created dynamically.

Wrapped functions are passed to **reify** in the usual way, resulting in a **Graph** value such as:

```
AppNode 28 "F" [IntNode 4, Function]
```

Obviously the printer does not treat this like an ordinary data structure. The presence of the F constructor indicates that the Graph represents a function. In the above example, the function is identified by the number 4. The printer scans the global table and collects all records that correspond to this function.

For example, suppose the global table contains these records:

```
[ (1, V True, V False)
, (2, V 12, V 3)
, (1, V False, V True)
, (4, V "ren", V 3)
, (3, V ('a', 'b'), V 'a')
, (4, V "stimpy", V 6)
, (2, V 16, V 4)
]
```

The entries pertaining to function number 4 are underlined. The arguments and results in the records are Values that must be converted to Graphs before they can be printed. In this example function number 4 would be printed in the following way:

```
{ "ren" -> 3, "stimpy" -> 6 }
```

The part of the transformation that deals with function wrapping is quite simple. It consists of three parts. First, wrappers must be introduced where functional values are created (lambda abstractions and partial applications). Second, when a wrapped function is applied it must be unwrapped and the application must be recorded in the global table. Third, function types must be changed to reflect the wrapping.

Let's consider a small example using code from Fig. 1. In lastDigits's body, map is applied to the expression (10 `mod`). That expression is a function which must be wrapped up. We introduce a family of wrappers, $fun_n$, where $n$ indicates the arity of the function to be wrapped. The first three of those wrappers have the following types:

```
fun₁ :: (a -> b) -> F a b
fun₂ :: (a -> b -> c) -> F a (F b c)
fun₃ :: (a -> b -> c -> d) -> F a (F b (F c d))
```

*Exercise 16.* Why do we have multiple wrapping functions? Would one suffice?

In our example, the expression (10 `mod`) has an arity of one, so the definition of lastDigits is transformed like so:

```
lastDigits :: Int -> Int
lastDigits = map (fun₁ (10 `mod`))
```

The definition of map must also be transformed:

```
map :: F a b -> [a] -> [b]
map f [] = []
map f (x:xs) = apply f x : map f xs
```

The first parameter, called f, will be bound to a wrapped function when map is applied. This requires two changes. First, the type is changed to indicate the wrapping: (a->b) becomes F a b. Second, where f is applied to x, it must be unwrapped, and the application must be recorded. The job of unwrapping and recording is done by apply, which has this definition:

```
apply :: F a b -> a -> b
apply (F unique f) x
   = let result = f x in updateTable unique x result

updateTable :: Int -> a -> b -> b
```

Updates to the global table are made by updateTable, by means of (gasp) impure side-effecting code!

A curious user can view the contents of the global table using the dump command as follows:

```
buddha: dump funs
```

Use this command with caution: the table can get quite big.

*Exercise 17.* The transformation of map shows that some function type annotations must be changed to accommodate wrapping. Where else in the program will types have to be changed?

*Exercise 18.* We have multiple wrapping functions, one for each level of function arity, yet we only have one apply. How is this possible?

## 3.5   Transformation

The purpose of the transformation is to introduce code into the debuggee for constructing the EDT. In the development of Buddha we have experimented with two different styles of transformation. The first style builds the tree in a purely functional way, whilst the second style builds the tree in a table by means of impure side-effects. The current version of Buddha employs the second style for a combination of efficiency concerns and programming convenience.

To help with the presentation we'll consider both styles of transformation applied to the following code for naive reverse:

```
rev :: [a] -> [a]
rev xs
   = case xs of
          []   -> []
          y:ys -> append (rev ys) [y]

append :: [a] -> [a] -> [a]
append xs ys
   = case xs of
          []   -> ys
          z:zs -> z : append zs ys
```

**The Purely Functional Style.** In the first style each function definition is transformed to return a pair containing its original value and an EDT node. Applications in the body of the function return nodes which make up its children.

Figure 7 shows the result of transforming `rev` using this style.

```
rev xs
   = case xs of
        []    -> let result   = []
                     children = []
                     node = edt name args result children
                 in (result, node)
        y:ys -> let (v1, t1) = rev ys
                    (v2, t2) = append v1 [y]
                    result   = v2
                    children = [t1, t2]
                    node = edt name args result children
                in (result, node)
     where
     name = "rev"
     args = [V xs]
```

**Fig. 7.** Purely functional style transformation of `rev`

Note the decomposition of the nested function application from the second branch of the case statement:

| before | after |
|---|---|
| append (rev ys) [y]  $\longrightarrow$ | (v1, t1) = rev ys |
| | (v2, t2) = append v1 [y] |

The variables v1 and v2 are bound to the original value of the intermediate applications, and t1 and t2 are bound to EDT nodes.

Figure 8 shows the transformation of **append**, which follows the same pattern as **rev**.

Upon first inspection the effect of the transformation might appear somewhat daunting. However, it is actually only doing two things: constructing a new EDT node for the application of the function and, in the process of doing that, collecting its children nodes from the applications that appear in the body. To simplify things we make use of a helper function called **edt** which constructs a new EDT node from the function's name, arguments, result and children (we've skipped the source location for simplicity). The apparent complexity is largely due to the fact that the computation of the original value and the EDT node are interwoven.

This style of transformation is quite typical in the literature on Declarative Debugging. Variants have been proposed by [5], [6], and [7], amongst others.

The main attraction of this style is that it is purely functional. However, support for higher-order functions is somewhat challenging. The naive version of the transformation assumes that all function applications result in a value *and*

```
append xs ys
  = case xs of
       []   -> let result   = ys
                   children = []
                   node = edt name args result children
               in (result, node)
       z:zs -> let (v1, t1) = append zs ys
                   result   = z : v1
                   children = [t1]
                   node = edt name args result children
               in (result, node)
  where
  name = "append"
  args = [V xs, V ys]
```

**Fig. 8.** Purely functional style transformation of append

an EDT node, although this is only true for saturated applications. An initial solution to this problem was proposed in [7] and improved upon in [8].

*Exercise 19.* What are the types of the transformed versions of rev and append?

*Exercise 20.* Apply this style of transformation to the definition of map from Fig. 1? How will you deal with the application of the higher-order argument f in the body of the second equation?

**The Table-Based Approach.** The second style is based on the concept of reduction numbering. It introduces code which, at runtime, causes each reduced function application to be uniquely numbered. For each application, the function name, its arguments and its result are stored in a global table, which is indexed by the number of the application. The global table is thus a collection of all the derivations in the EDT. Table entries also record the parent number of the derivation. Parent numbers are passed down through the call graph to their children by extending each function with a new integer argument. When execution of the debuggee is complete a single pass is made over the table to construct the EDT.

Figure 9 shows the transformation of rev in this style.

```
rev :: Int -> [a] -> [a]
rev parent xs
  = addNode parent "rev" [V xs]
        (\n -> case xs of
                   []   -> []
                   y:ys -> append n (rev n ys) [y])
```

**Fig. 9.** Table-based transformation of rev

Notice the new type of rev, in particular its first argument is now an integer which corresponds to the unique number of its parent. The task of assigning new unique numbers for each application of rev is performed by the helper function addNode, whose type is as follows:

```
addNode :: Int -> String -> [Value] -> (Int -> a) -> a
```

Each call to addNode does four things:

1. generate a new unique number for the current application;
2. pass that number into the body of the transformed function;
3. record an entry for the application in the global table;
4. return the value of the application as the result.

Writes to the global table are achieved via impure side effects.

The number for each application of rev is passed to the calls in its body through the variable n, which is introduced by lambda abstraction around the original function body. The idea is that the new function body — the lambda abstraction — is applied to each new number for rev inside addNode. Hence the type of addNode's fourth argument is (Int -> a), where n takes the value of the Int and a matches with the type of the original function's result.

Figure 10 shows the transformation of append, which follows the same pattern as rev.

```
append :: Int -> [a] -> [a] -> [a]
append parent xs ys
    = addNode parent "append" [V xs, V ys]
        (\n -> case xs of
                []    -> ys
                z:zs -> z : append n zs ys)
```

**Fig. 10.** Table-based transformation of append

*Exercise 21.* Consider the transformation of some constant, such as:

```
goodDay = (12, January, 1976)
```

The discussion of the transformation above suggests that we would give goodDay an integer argument to represent its parent number. Can you foresee any problem(s) with this in regards to how often goodDay is evaluated? How might you fix it? Hint: Ideally each constant should have at most one entry in the global table. However, you will still want to record each time another entity refers to a constant.

You might have noticed some similarity between the use of a global table in this section to record derivations and the use of a global table to record applications of higher-order functions in Sec. 3.4. Indeed they share some underlying machinery for performing impure updates of the tables. Just like the function table, you can also see the contents of the derivation table, using the dump command:

```
buddha: dump calls
```

Again, for long running programs the table can get quite large, so be careful with this command, it can produce a *lot* of output.

The main advantage of the impure table transformation over the purely functional is that it tends to decouple the generation of the EDT and and evaluation of the debuggee. This means that we can stop the debuggee at any point and still have access to the tree produced up to that point. Declarative diagnosis can often be applied to a partial tree. In the purely functional style this is possible but more complicated. The separation makes the handling of errors easier. It doesn't matter if the debuggee crashes with an exception, the table is still easily accessible to the debugging code. In the purely functional style the evaluation of the debuggee and the production of the EDT are interwoven, which makes it harder to access the EDT if the debuggee crashes.

The main problem with the second transformation style is that it relies on impure side effects to generate new unique numbers and make updates to the global table. It is possible that with some clever programming the side effects could be avoided, but we speculate that this will be at a significant cost to performance. Without more investigation it is difficult to be definitive on that point. The problem with the use of impure side effects is that they do not sit well with the semantics of Haskell. As the old saying goes:

*If you lie to the compiler, it will get its revenge.*

This is certainly true with GHC, which is a highly optimising compiler. Covert uses of impure facilities tend to interact very badly with the optimisations that it performs, and one must program very carefully around them. We could turn the optimisations off, however that would come at the cost of efficiency in the debugging executable, which is something we want to avoid.

## 4    Judgement

The Oracle is assumed to have an internal set of beliefs about the intended meaning of each function and constant in the program. We call this the *Intended Interpretation* of the program. Derivations in the EDT reveal the actual behaviour of the program. Judgement is the process of comparing the actual behaviour of functions and constants with their intended behaviour. Differences between the two are used to guide the search for buggy nodes.

### 4.1    Partial Functions

In the simple debugging algorithm described in Sec. 3.3 judgement is a binary decision: a derivation is either correct or erroneous. Our experience is that the binary system does not always suit the intuition of the user and we extend it with two more values: *unknown* and *inadmissible*.

Some derivations are just too complicated to be judged. Perhaps they contain very large values, or lots of higher-order code, or lots of thunks. The best choice is to defer judgement of these derivations. However, deferral might only postpone the inevitable need for a judgement. If deferral does not lead to another path to a bug the Oracle can judge a difficult derivation as unknown. If a buggy node is found which has one or more unknown children, Buddha will report those children in its final diagnosis, and remind the user that their correctness was unknown. The idea is that the true bug may be either due to the buggy node or one or more of its unknown children, or perhaps one of their descendents.

For some tasks it is either convenient or necessary to write partial functions: functions which are only defined on a subset of their domain. Most functional programmers have at some point in their life experienced program crash because they tried to take the head of an empty list. An important question is how to judge derivations where the function is actually applied to arguments for which there is no intended result?

Consider the `merge` function which takes two sorted lists as arguments and returns a sorted list as output containing all the values from the input lists. Due to a bug in some other part of the program it might happen that `merge` is given an unsorted list as one of its arguments. In this case Buddha might ask the Oracle to judge the following derivation:

```
[32] Main 12 merge
    arg 1  = [3,1,2]
    arg 2  = [5,6]
    result = [3,1,2,5,6]
```

Let's assume for the moment that our definition of `merge` is correct for all sorted arguments. Is this derivation correct or erroneous? If we judge it to be erroneous then Buddha will eventually diagnose `merge` as buggy, assuming that `merge` only calls itself. This is a bad diagnosis because the bug is not due to `merge`, rather it is due to which ever function provided the invalid argument. To find the right buggy node we could judge the derivation to be correct. However, it feels counter-intuitive to say that a derivation is correct when it should never have happened in the first place. In such circumstances it is more natural to say that the derivation is inadmissible. It has exactly the same effect as judging the derivation to be correct, yet it is a more accurate expression of the user's beliefs.

## 4.2   Partial Values

Non-strict evaluation means that not all computations will necessarily reach normal forms in the execution of a program. Consider the following definition of boolean conjunction:

```
(&&) :: Bool -> Bool -> Bool
(&&) False _ = False
(&&) True  x = x
```

In the application '(&&) False exp', the value of exp is not needed, so it will remain as a thunk. It would not be prudent for the debugger to force the evaluation of exp to find its value, first because the computation might be expensive, and second, in the worst case is might trigger divergence (exp might be non-terminating or it might raise an exception).

Thunks that remain at the end of the program execution cannot be the cause of any observed bugs, so it ought to be possible to debug without knowing their value. Therefore, thunks are treated by Buddha as unknown entities, and it prints a question mark whenever it encounters one. In the above example, this would lead to the following derivation:

```
[19] Main 74 &&
     arg 1  = False
     arg 2  = ?
     result = False
```

How do you judge derivations that have question marks in them? One approach is to assume that the Oracle has an intended meaning for functions with all possible combinations of partial arguments and results. This is convenient for us as designers of the debugger, but it is not very helpful for the user.

Generally it is easier for the user to model their intended interpretation on complete values. It tends to simplify the task of saying what a function should do if you ignore the effects of computation (*i.e.* strictness and non-termination) and think in terms of abstract mathematical functions. In this sense you can say the intended interpretation of && is merely the relation:

```
(True, True, True),   (True, False, False)
(False, True, False), (False, False, False)
```

A derivation with partial arguments is correct if and only if all possible instantiations of those partial arguments agree with the intended interpretation. The above derivation for && is correct because, according to the relation above, it doesn't matter whether we replace the question mark with True or False, the result is always False.

Of course && is a very simple example, and many interesting functions are defined over large or even infinite domains, where it is not feasible to enumerate all mappings of the function. In such cases the user might have to do some reasoning before they can make a judgement.

*Exercise 22.* Judge these derivations (the module names, line numbers and derivation numbers are irrelevant).

```
[6] Main 55 length
    arg 1  = ?
    result = 0

[99] Main 55 length
     arg 1  = [?]
     result = 1
```

It is also possible to encounter partial values in the result of a derivation. Consider the swap function:

```
swap :: (a,b) -> (b,a)
swap (x,y) = (y,x)
```

It might be the case that the program only needs the first component of the output tuple, while the second component remains a thunk, such as:

```
[19] Boo 7 swap
    arg 1  = (?, 12)
    result = (12, ?)
```

When the output contains a partial value the derivation is correct if and only if for all possible instances of the arguments there *exists* a instance of the result which agrees with the intended interpretation.

*Exercise 23.* Judge these derivations:

```
[6] Main 22 reverse
    arg 1  = [1,2,3]
    result = ?

[99] Main 22 reverse
    arg 1  = [1,2,?]
    result = [1,?,?]
```

## 5   Resource Usage

For all but the briefest runs of a program it is totally infeasible to consider every function application. In long running programs you will be swamped with derivations, and most likely all of your available heap space will be consumed. One way to reduce the number of derivations (and memory usage at the same time) is to limit the range of functions considered by the debugger. Hopefully you will have some feeling for where the bug is in your program, and also which parts are unlikely to be involved. Unit testing can be quite helpful in this regard. Instead of just testing the program as a whole, one may test smaller pieces of code separately. A failed unit test gives a much narrower scope for the bug, and allows any code not touched by the test to be trusted. One may even debug specialised versions of the program that only execute the top call in a failed test case, thus avoiding the extra cost of executing large amounts of trusted code. This idea is discussed in the context of tracing in [9]. Unit tests are supported in Haskell by QuickCheck [4], and also HUnit[8].

The EDT maintains references to the arguments and results of each function application. This means that such values cannot be garbage collected as they might have been in the evaluation of the original program. By not creating nodes

---

[8] http://hunit.sourceforge.net

for every function application we allow some values to be garbage collected. Fewer nodes generally means less memory is needed and less questions will be asked.

How do you reduce the number of nodes in this tree? You can prune it statically by telling Buddha which functions you trust and which ones you suspect. For each module in the program you can provide an options file that tells Buddha what to do for each function in the module. If the module's name is X, the options file is called called X.opt, and it must be stored in the Buddha directory. The syntax of the options file is very simple. It has a number of lines and each line specifies what kind of transformation you want for a given function.

Here's what you might write for some program:

```
_ ; Trust
prefixes ; Suspect
convert ; Suspect
```

Each line contains the name of the function, a semi-colon and then an option as to what kind of EDT node you want. The underscore matches with anything (just like in Haskell patterns), so the default is specified on the first line to be Trust. Any function which is not mentioned specifically gets the default option. If there is no such default option in the whole file, then the *default* default is Suspect. In the case when no option file is present for a module, every function in the module is transformed with the Suspect option.

What do the options mean?

- Suspect: Create a full node for each application of this function. Such a node will record the name of the function, its arguments and result, its source location and will have links to all of its children. However, the children will be transformed with their own options which will not necessarily be Suspect. This option tends to make Buddha use a lot of memory, especially for recursive functions, so please use it sparingly.
- Trust: Don't create a node for applications of this function, but collect any children that this function has.

Another way to reduce the size of the EDT is to make use of re-evaluation. The idea is that only the top few levels of the EDT are produced by the initial execution of the debuggee. Debugging commences with only a partial tree. Eventually the traversal of the EDT might come to a derivation whose children were not created in the initial run. The debugger can regenerate the children nodes by forcing the re-evaluation of the function application at the parent. In the first execution of the debuggee, the children are pruned from the EDT. The purpose of re-evaluating the call at the parent is to cause the previously pruned children nodes to be re-generated. This allows the EDT to be constructed in a piecemeal fashion, at the cost of some extra computation time during the debugging session — a classic space/time tradeoff. Re-evaluation was implemented in a previous version of Buddha, for the purely functional style of transformation, see [10]. However, it has yet to be incorporated into the latest transformation style.

# 6   Further Reading

Phil Wadler once wrote:

> *Constructing debuggers and profilers for lazy languages is recognised as difficult. Fortunately, there have been great strides in profiler research, and most implementations of Haskell are now accompanied by usable time and space profiling tools. But the slow rate of progress on debuggers for lazy functional languages makes us researchers look, well lazy.* [11]

While it is true that debugging technology for lazy functional languages hasn't set the world on fire, there has nonetheless been a fair amount of improvement since Wadler made that remark.

Perhaps the most significant tool for debugging Haskell is Hat [12]. Like Buddha, Hat is based on program transformation. However Hat-transformed programs produce a very detailed program trace, called a Redex Trail, which explains the reduction history of each expression in the program. The trace is written to a file rather than main memory. This means that the memory usage of a transformed program stays proportional to the usage of the original program, although at the expense of very large trace files. The best feature of the trace is that it can be viewed in many different ways. Hat provides a handful of browsing tools, that are useful for diagnosing different kinds of bugs. A very helpful tutorial on the use of Hat in combination with with QuickCheck was presented at the Advanced Functional Programming School in 2002 [9]. Much of the technology in Hat is based on earlier work by Sparud [6], who also proposed a program transformation for Declarative Debugging, quite similar to Buddha.

A popular debugging tool for Haskell is Hood [13]. Hood provides a library function called observe, which can be used to log the evaluation of expressions in the program. In essence it provides a sophisticated form of the so-called printf style of diagnostic debugging. A particularly nice aspect of Hood is that it can observe functional values and partial data structures, without changing the declarative semantics of the underlying program. A negative aspect of Hood is that the user must modify the source code of their program to insert the observations. Such modifications can be a problem for program maintenance.

Another declarative debugger, called Freya, was implemented by Nilsson, for a large subset of Haskell [14]. The main difference from Buddha is that Freya makes use of a modified runtime environment to construct the EDT, rather than by program transformation. An advantage of the Freya approach is that the debugger has intimate knowledge and influence over the mechanics of program evaluation. The most obvious benefit is a sophisticated re-evaluation scheme which allows the EDT to be created in a piecemeal fashion [15]. The downside of the Freya approach is that it requires a whole new compiler and runtime environment, which is difficult to maintain and port.

Buddha is based predominantly on the pioneering work of Naish and Barbour [16,17,18,5,19]. Their ideas have also influenced the development of a declarative debugger for logic/functional languages such as Toy and Curry [7].

Optimistic evaluation of Haskell can reduce the gap between the structure of the code and the evaluation order by reducing most function arguments eagerly [20]. This is the basis for a step-based debugger called HsDebug [21], built on top of an experimental version of the Glasgow Haskell Compiler. However, to preserve non-strict semantics the evaluator must sometimes suspend one computation path and jump to another. This irregular flow of control is likely to be hard to follow in the step-based debugging style.

Of course no paper on Declarative Debugging would be complete without a reference to the seminal work of Shapiro, who's highly influential thesis introduced Algorithmic Debugging to the Prolog language [22], from which the ideas of Declarative Debugging have emerged.

# 7    Conclusion

Buddha is by no means a finished product. At the time of writing the latest version is 1.2, which supports all of the Haskell 98 standard. In terms of program coverage there are a number of small improvements that need to be made, including support for the FFI, hierarchical modules, and programs spread over more than one directory. It seems that a fair proportion of people who have expressed an interest in using Buddha cannot do so because their code makes use of non-standard features, like multi-parameter type classes and functional dependencies. The next few development cycles of Buddha will look at supporting the most commonly used language extensions.

The biggest limitation of Buddha is the size of the EDT. If we are going to debug long running programs we need to manage the growth of the EDT more effectively. On the one hand, main memory sizes are ever growing, and are becoming increasingly cheaper. At first this looks good for Buddha because we can fit more EDT nodes into memory. On the other hand, the rapid advances in hardware have also given us faster CPUs, which can fill the memory more quickly. Even if we can fit enormous EDTs into main memory we will have to come up with smarter debugging algorithms, lest we become swamped in an insurmountable number of derivations.

Another important area of research is Buddha's interface with the user. For example, at the moment, it is nigh impossible to judge a derivation that contains very large values. There are of course many avenues to explore in this regard. An interesting idea is to allow Buddha to be specialised to particular problem domains. For example, if you are writing digital circuit simulators, you might like custom printing routines that show the values in derivations in a fashion that is closer to your mental picture of an electronic component.

Buddha also has a place in education. Haskell is used extensively in Computer Science courses all over the world. Novice programmers often grapple with difficult concepts like recursion and higher-order functions, especially when they are explained statically in text or on the white board. Buddha can be quite helpful here, especially as an exploratory device. A few minutes spent browsing the EDT can be very enlightening, even if you are not debugging the program.

Lastly, while Declarative Debugging is a useful technique for locating logical errors in programs, it is not the final word on debugging. For starters, we need good testing tools, such as QuickCheck, to help us identify faulty behaviour in programs. Even better would be to automate the process of finding *small* input values that cause the program to go wrong. That way the debugging sessions are more likely to be within a manageable size. For bugs that relate to the operational behaviour of the program, like I/O, or resource usage, we will need to look elsewhere for help.

The Buddha web page provides the latest stable release of the source code, and online versions of the user documentation: `www.cs.mu.oz.au/~bjpop/buddha`.

## Acknowledgements

I would like to thank all the people who have helped with the preparation of this paper and who helped organise the 5th International Summer School on Advanced Functional Programming. In particular: the programme committee, Varmo Vene, Tarmo Uustalu, and Johan Jeuring, for countless hours of administration and preparation; the University of Tartu for providing such a great location; the volunteers who made the school run very smoothly; the various sponsors who supported the School; the reviewers of this paper for their most helpful constructive comments; and Lee Naish for all the years of collaboration on this project.

## References

1. Nilsson, H., Spaurd, J.: The evaluation dependence tree as a basis for lazy functional debugging. Automated Software Engineering **4** (1997) 121–150
2. Gansner, E., Koutsofios, E., North, S.:      Drawing  graphs  with  dot. `www.research.att.com/sw/tools/graphviz/dotguide.pdf` (2002)
3. Jones, N., Mycroft, A.: Dataflow analysis of applicative programs using minimal function graphs. In: Proceedings of the 13th ACM SIGACT-SIGPLAN symposium on Principles of Programming Languages, Florida, ACM Press (1986) 296–306
4. Claessen, K., Hughes, J.: Quickcheck: a lightweight tool for random testing of Haskell programs. In: International Conference on Functional Programming, ACM Press (2000) 268–279
5. Naish, L., Barbour, T.: Towards a portable lazy functional declarative debugger. Australian Computer Science Communications **18** (1996) 401–408
6. Sparud, J.: Tracing and Debugging Lazy Functional Computations. PhD thesis, Chalmers University of Technology, Sweden (1999)
7. Caballero, R., Rodri'guez-Artalejo, M.: A declarative debugging system for lazy functional logic programs. In Hanus, M., ed.: Electronic Notes in Theoretical Computer Science. Volume 64., Elsevier Science Publishers (2002)
8. Pope, B., Naish, L.: A program transformation for debugging Haskell-98. Australian Computer Science Communications **25** (2003) 227–236 ISBN:0-909925-94-1.
9. Claessen, K., Runciman, C., Chitil, O., Hughes, J., Wallace, M.: Testing and Tracing Lazy Functional Programs using QuickCheck and Hat. In: 4th Summer School in Advanced Functional Programming. Number 2638 in LNCS, Oxford (2003) 59–99

10. Pope, B., Naish, L.: Practical aspects of declarative debugging in Haskell-98. In: Fifth ACM SIGPLAN Conference on Principles and Practice of Declarative Programming. (2003) 230–240 ISBN:1-58113-705-2.
11. Wadler, P.: Why no one uses functional languages. SIGPLAN Notices **33** (1998) 23–27
12. Wallace, M., Chitil, O., Brehm, T., Runciman, C.: Multiple-view tracing for Haskell: a new hat. In: Preliminary Proceedings of the 2001 ACM SIGPLAN Haskell Workshop. (2001) 151–170
13. Gill, A.: Debugging Haskell by observing intermediate data structures. Technical report, University of Nottingham (2000) In Proceedings of the 4th Haskell Workshop, 2000.
14. Nilsson, H.: Declarative Debugging for Lazy Functional Languages. PhD thesis, Department of Computer and Information Science Linköpings Universitet, S-581 83, Linköping, Sweden (1998)
15. Nilsson, H.: How to look busy while being as lazy as ever: The implementation of a lazy functional debugger. Journal of Functional Programming **11** (2001) 629–671
16. Naish, L.: A declarative debugging scheme. Journal of Functional and Logic Programming **1997** (1997)
17. Naish, L., Barbour, T.: A declarative debugger for a logical-functional language. In Forsyth, G., Ali, M., eds.: Eighth International Conference on Industrial and Engineering Applications of Artificial Intelligence and Expert Systems — Invited and Additional Papers. Volume 2., Melbourne, DSTO General Document 51 (1995) 91–99
18. Naish, L.: Declarative debugging of lazy functional programs. Australian Computer Science Communications **15** (1993) 287–294
19. Naish, L.: A three-valued declarative debugging scheme. Australian Computer Science Communications **22** (2000) 166–173
20. Ennals, R., Peyton Jones, S.: Optimistic evaluation: an adaptive evaluation strategy for non-strict programs. In: Proceedings of the Eighth ACM SIGPLAN Conference on Functional Programming. (2003) 287–298
21. Ennals, R., Peyton Jones, S.: HsDebug: Debugging lazy programs by not being lazy. In Jeuring, J., ed.: ACM SIGPLAN 2003 Haskell Workshop, ACM Press (2003) 84–87
22. Shapiro, E.: Algorithmic Program Debugging. The MIT Press (1982)

# Server-Side Web Programming in WASH

Peter Thiemann

Institut für Informatik, Universität Freiburg,
Georges-Köhler-Allee 079, D-79110 Freiburg, Germany
thiemann@informatik.uni-freiburg.de

**Abstract.** WASH makes server-side Web programming as easy as programming a stand-alone application with an XHTML-based GUI. Starting from an interaction graph model of the application where nodes model web pages and edges correspond to form submissions, each node is implemented by a WASH function and the edges correspond to function invocation. Nodes can be decomposed further into "pagelets", which are XHTML fragments bundled with associated logic.

We give an introduction to the concepts of WASH programming with this methodology and advocate the design of interactive web functionality in terms of such pagelets. The two components of a pagelet may be specified monolithically or in separation. Pagelets may also be composed up to an entire WASH page. The development of a web-based logging application serves as a running example.

## 1  Introduction

The basic idea of a web-based application is to make a software system accessible to the general public by

- creating its user interface in terms of XHTML pages and
- placing the underlying functionality on a web server.

This approach has the appeal that deployment and maintenance of the application can be done centrally on the web server, the application works in a distributed setting without requiring the design of application-specific protocols, and no specific software needs to be installed on the clients. That is, input and output is based entirely on XHTML where input is specified either by navigation via hyperlinks or by using XHTML forms. A form provides an editable association list for entering strings and a means to specify where the association list is to be sent.

However, web applications suffer from some peculiarities that complicate their development. There are three principal causes for these peculiarities: the stateless nature of HTTP, the unusual navigation facilities offered by a web browser, and the reliance on untyped, string-based protocols.

The Hypertext Transfer Protocol [3] is build around the simple idea of a remote method invocation: a client sends a request message that determines an object on the server, a method that should be invoked on the object, and

V. Varmo and T. Uustalu (Eds.): AFP 2004, LNCS 3622, pp. 309–330, 2005.

parameters for this method. The server performs the requested operation and returns the results wrapped in a response message. After this exchange, the connection between client and server is closed (logically, at least) and the next message from the same client is treated like any other message because the HTTP-server does not keep any information about processed requests. Hence, there is no intrinsic notion of a session between a particular client and the server where the responses depend on the session history of the client. On the user level, however, most applications require a notion of session where a user proceeds step by step, is aware of the session's history, and can issue commands depending on the current state of the session. Clearly, there is a semantic gap between the interface provided by HTTP and the interface desired by the application program.

Web browsers offer advanced navigation that goes beyond the facilities typically offered in user interfaces [6]. In particular, browsers maintain a history list of previously visited web locations and offer forward and backward buttons to navigate freely within this list. Browsers also maintain bookmarks which are pointers to previously visited locations. Bookmarked locations may be revisited any time by selecting them from the appropriate menu. Some browsers allow to clone an existing window or open a link in a new window and continue independently with both windows. Finally, it is possible to save the contents of a window to a file and point the browser to that file later on. While these facilities are helpful and useful for browsing a static hypertext, they make it hard to define an appropriate concept of a session when each window is really a dynamically generated snapshot of the state of some application.

Typical web applications rely on XHTML forms as their input facility. Because an XHTML form yields an association list and a URL where the data should be sent, the main data exchanges in such applications are string based: input fields in forms are named with strings, the input values are strings, and the pointers in web pages are also strings, albeit in the format of a URL. In this context, it is very hard to guarantee any kind of consistency. To begin with, the field names present in a form must be a superset of the field names expected by the program processing the form input. Otherwise, the program expects values for inputs that are not present in the form It is even harder to give any typing guarantees for the entered values themselves because the form processor does not have this information.[1] Finally, there is no way to guarantee that the URLs mentioned in the hyperlinks and in a form's action attribute correspond to the intended functionality, in particular, when they point to scripts.

Implementors of web applications address these problems by defining their own support for sessions or by relying on third party libraries for sessions. Quite often, such libraries provide session objects of some sort which have to be maintained by the programmer. Unfortunately, many implementations of session objects only provide a mapping from a specific client to the application specific data of the client. They often fall short of keeping track of the current locus of

---

[1] The XForms [12] standard will improve on this situation, once implementations are widely available. Unfortunately, its development seems to be stalled.

control of the application.[2] Hence, the developers map the control information to file names and distribute the code of their application over as many programs as there are interaction states in the program, in the worst case. Clearly, this approach leads to complex dependencies between the different parts of the application. In addition, it is hard to detect if users have exercised the above-mentioned navigation facilities, which leads to further problems and unexpected responses from the application [5].

These considerations lead us to two questions. First, which abstractions may be employed to shield the programmer from the problems with sessions, navigation, and consistent use of strings? Second, given an answer to the first question, what then is a good approach for designing a web application?

The WASH system [11], a domain-specific language based on Haskell98 [7], has satisfactory answers to the first question. Its session abstraction handles data and control information transparently to the programmer: Data is available if and only if it is in scope and execution continues after a form submission with a selected callback function. Second, the implementation of sessions is compatible with arbitrary navigation. Users can go backwards and forwards, they may clone windows, and save pages without the application programmer providing extra code for it[3]. Finally, WASH provides strongly typed interfaces based on abstract datatypes for accessing the data entered into the application and for connecting a form with its functionality in terms of callbacks. It thus replaces external string consistency with lexical binding wherever possible. The implementation of WASH can address the consistency problems once and for all because lexical binding is fully controlled and checked by the compiler.

Our answer to the second question builds on compositionality. WASH inherits compositionality essentially for free from the underlying Haskell language. In the WASH context, compositionality means that web applications may be assembled from independent *pagelets*, *i.e.*, pieces of web pages which may be specified, implemented, and tested in isolation. That is, a pagelet integrates form and function and enables a kind of component-based programming. As pagelets are represented by Haskell values, Haskell functions can produce them and consume them, thus providing arbitrary means of parameterization for them. Pagelets are thus exceptionally amenable to reuse.

The present paper starts of with an introduction to the basic concepts of the WASH system in Section 2. The remainder, Section 3, considers a disciplined method for developing web applications using the example of web logging. It starts with a decomposition of the application into pagelets using a graphical notation. Then it considers two example pagelets and shows the final wiring. Each pagelet is naturally divided into a logic part and a presentation part. The final Section 4 gives a brief introduction to the implementation.

---

[2] Web programming systems that preserve the locus of control in the form of a server-side continuation include DrScheme [4] and the Cocoon framework [1].

[3] The astute reader may wonder if this claim is compatible with server-side state, like for example a database accessible through the server. We will comment on that point in Sec.4.

The spirit of the paper is that of an informal introduction and as such it is not self-contained. Firstly, it assumes that readers have a working knowledge of Haskell language [7] and of monadic programming[10]. Secondly, while it introduces the fundamental concepts underlying WASH programming, it does not attempt to cover the entire material. Please refer to the user manual and the online documentation [11] for full coverage. Thirdly, it does not spread much light on WASH's implementation because its discussion would exceed the scope of the paper. More details about the implementation may be found in the definitive article about WASH [9]. This article also contains a comprehensive discussion of related work, that is, other domain specific languages for web programming and functional approaches in particular.

## 2   WASH Basics

WASH provides roughly two layers of operations. The first layer provides the session level operations: displaying a web page, performing server-side I/O operations, and constructing callbacks for inclusion in forms. The second layer deals with the construction of XHTML output, in particular the generation of interactive widgets.

Both layers are implemented in a monad-based combinator library, each with its own monad. The CGI monad implements the session abstraction by keeping a log of all I/O operations. Hence, it is layered on top of the IO monad and mediates access to it. To avoid inconsistencies between the current view of the real world and its logged view for the running session, it is imperative that the main function of a WASH program does not perform any IO action before switching into the CGI monad using the function run :: CGI () -> IO ().

The document layer results from applying the monad transformer WithHTML x to the CGI monad. Its standard incarnation WithHTML x CGI is required to create interactive widgets. The additional functionality with respect to the base monad CGI is an abstract interface for the generation of XHTML documents. The extra parameter x in the type of a document constructor is not used in this exposition. It enables the compiler to guarantee the validity of the generated XHTML output just by providing suitable types to the constructors [9].

### 2.1   CGI Actions

The main operations inside of the CGI monad are io and ask:

```
io  :: (Read a, Show a) => IO a -> CGI a
ask :: WithHTML x CGI a -> CGI ()
```

The function io performs an IO operation and injects its value in the CGI monad. The type returned by the operation must be an instance of the type classes Read and Show because WASH relies on the methods of these classes for reading and writing the session log (cf. Sec.4).

The function ask takes the description of an XHTML document and displays the document on the web browser. The use of WithHTML x CGI in its type indicates that input widgets may be used to construct the document.

A WASH program is essentially a sequence of io and ask operations which are glued together using the monadic bind and return operations. The combinator ask takes as a parameter the description of a document in the WithHTML x CGI monad. This document description embeds submission buttons with attached callbacks of type CGI (). These callbacks take two kinds of parameters, form input values and standard function parameters.

## 2.2  Composing XHTML Documents

If m is a monad, then WithHTML x m is a monad that extends m and additionally creates a fragment of an XHTML document. In WASH, m is typically CGI or IO. The internal representation of a document fragment is a *sequence of document nodes*. There are several types of document nodes, inspired by the node types of the XML document object model (DOM) [8]. The type can be one of

- **Document** (single child: the root element)
- **Element** (children: elements, attributes, text, or comments)
- **Attribute** (no children)
- **Text** (no children)
- **Comment** (no children)

For maximum flexibility, all document operations work in terms of sequences of document nodes. First, there are the usual operations for manipulating sequences. The empty sequence is created with empty :: Monad m => WithHTML x m (). Its implementation is the return operator of the document monad. Sequences may be concatenated in several ways that differ mainly in the propagation of the computed value.

1. The monadic sequence operator (>>) :: Monad m => m a -> m b -> m b concatenates two sequences and returns the value computed while constructing the second sequence.
2. Dually,   (##) :: Monad m => m a -> m b -> m a   concatenates   the sequences and returns the value computed with the first sequence.
3. The do notation as well as the standard monadic bind operator (>>=) may also be used for concatenating sequences and for arbitrary manipulation of the computed values.

Each type of node has a (family of) constructor operations. The root node for a document (of type document) is constructed implicitly by the ask operator and its constructor is not directly accessible to the programmer. For each valid element name in XHTML, there is a constructor function of the same name that creates a corresponding document node. Its argument is a sequence of child nodes for the element and it returns a singleton sequence containing just the newly constructed element node. The element constructors automatically extract attribute nodes from the child sequence. Thus, while there are special constructors for attribute nodes, there are no special operations to attach an attribute to an element. This design differs from DOM where attributes are handled differently than other child nodes.

The attribute constructor

```
attr :: Monad m => String -> String -> WithHTML x m ()
```

takes an attribute name and its value (as strings) and creates a singleton sequence with just the new attribute node. Text nodes and comments also have their special constructor functions:

```
comment :: Monad m => String -> WithHTML x m ()
text    :: Monad m => String -> WithHTML x m ()
```

The argument to text and comment can be an arbitrary string. The WASH implementation takes care of all character escapes that may be required.

## 2.3  Native Syntax for XHTML

In practice, most of the operators introduced in the previous Section 2.2 can be avoided by directly putting the desired XHTML fragment into the code. The WASH preprocessor translates all XHTML fragments in the source program to constructor operations in the WithHTML x m monad. Inside an XHTML fragment, it is possible to escape to Haskell by enclosing the Haskell code in <% and %>. The Haskell code may be a term e or a single generator v <- e. As with the do notation, the generator binds the variable v to the result of computation e and the binding is available in the rest of the XHTML fragment. The type of such a term e must be WithHTML x CGI a and the term may again contain XHTML fragments. There is a specialized version of the code escape bracketed by <%= and %>. It expects an expression of type String and embed its string value as a text node in the XHTML fragment. That is, <%= e %> is equivalent to <% text (e) %>. Further syntax is available for creating attribute nodes, for embedding attribute values, and for including arbitrary XML files.

## 2.4  Example: showDate

Here is a complete program that displays the current date and time.

```
1    import CGI
2    import Time
3
4    main :: IO ()
5    main =
```

```
6      run showDate
7
8    showDate :: CGI ()
9    showDate =
10     do theDate <- io $ do clk <- getClockTime
11                           cal <- toCalendarTime clk
12                           return (calendarTimeToString cal)
13        ask <html>
14            <head><title>The current time</title></head>
15            <body>
16              <h1>The current time</h1>
17              <%= theDate %>
18            </body>
19          </html>
```

The functionality for calculating the time (lines 10-12) is implemented using the module Time (imported in line 2) from the standard library. It gets the current time from the system and converts it to a string using the local timezone and format information.

The import CGI in line 1 is required in every WASH program. Similarly, in line 5-6, the main function immediately invokes the main CGI action showDate through the run function. Because the computation of the date happens in the IO monad, the io operator must be employed (line 10) to lift its result to the CGI monad. Finally, the ask operator (line 13) is applied to an XHTML fragment that contains a string embedding in line 17.

Typically, web pages are not written in isolation but rather as part of a web site or application that comprises many pages with a similar design. Hence, a programmer would abstract over the elements that form a standard template for many documents. The construction of such a template does not involve any new concepts in WASH. It is sufficient to define the template as a function of appropriate type.

```
standardTemplate :: String -> WithHTML x CGI a -> CGI ()
standardTemplate title contents =
  ask <html>
        <head><title><%= title %></title></head>
        <body>
          <h1><%= title %></h1>
          <% contents %>
        </body>
      </html>
```

This template provides the standard skeleton of an XHTML document and abstracts over two aspects of it, a string for the title and a sequence of document nodes for the contents. In the context of an application, the template will include further material: stylesheet references, script references, meta information, and perhaps even parts of a standardized layout.

However, already with this simple template, the showData function becomes considerably more concise.

```
showDate :: CGI ()
showDate =
  do theDate <- io $ ...
     standardTemplate
       "The current time"
       (text theDate)
```

As this implementation uses `theDate` outside of an XHTML fragment, the `text` constructor is required to convert the string into a document node of type text.

## 2.5    Input Widgets

In GUI terminology, a widget is an area on the screen with some functionality attached to it. In an XHTML-based GUI, each widget corresponds to an element node in the document tree that describes the visual appearance of the GUI. To enable the transmission of the inputs to the widget from browser to server, all widgets have to be part of a form. In contrast to a GUI, XHTML only provides for string-based input widgets that work in an offline manner: each input action (filling out a text field, checking a box, making a selection, ...) only changes the state of the form in the browser. Only when an input action results in the submission of the form, the browser collects the current values of the widgets in a sequence of name-value pairs with the name indicating the widget and sends this sequence to the web server. A server-side application has to parse the stream of name-value pairs generated by the web browser's form submission, extract the needed parameters from it, and perform all desired activities on the input.

Like most web programming environments, WASH librates the programmer from dealing explicitly with the stream of name-value pairs. However, WASH takes the liberation one step further. The WASH programmer does *not* have to

– name the input widgets explicitly,
– extract the input values by widget name from some structure,
– parse strings into the actually expected values and take care of reporting parsing errors properly.

Instead, WASH provides typed abstractions for all XHTML input widgets. Each of them returns the input values directly in their internal representation. That is, integers are returned as values of type `Int`, checkboxes return values of type `Bool`, etc. In addition, programmers can define their own input value type by providing little more than a parser for it.

Instead of naming widgets by string, the WASH constructor of an input widget returns a handle for accessing the input (besides creating the XHTML required for displaying the widget). The type of the handle depends on the widget, but each handle-type constructor is an instance of the type class `InputHandle`.

```
class InputHandle h where ...
```

```
submit :: InputHandle h
          => h INVALID -> (h VALID -> CGI ()) -> HTMLField x y ()
```

The submit function is the primary means of creating a submission button in a form, attaching a server-side callback to the button, and to pass input values to the callback function.

Indeed, HTMLField x y a abbreviates WithHTML x CGI () -> WithHTML y CGI a, so that an XHTML field is a function that takes a sequence of (attribute) nodes as an argument and returns a (singleton) sequence consisting the newly constructed input field with the provided attribute nodes attached to it.

As the type of the submit function further indicates, an input handle may either be VALID or INVALID. An input handle can only be VALID after its associated widget received input that parses according to the requirements of the input handle. Hence, each constructor returns an INVALID handle because it has not yet received its input.

For instance, InputField a x is one of the handle types:

```
data InputField a x = ...
instance InputHandle (InputField a) where ...
```

The constructor for a textual input field, inputField, uses this type of handle:

```
inputField :: (Reason a, Read a)
           => WithHTML x CGI ()
           -> WithHTML y CGI (InputField a INVALID)
```

The type parameter a indicates the type of value that is acceptable to the input field. The constraint Read a indicates that a parser for this type must be available. The type a must also be an instance of class Reason, the members of which supply an explanation of the input format.

Once a handle has become valid, its value is available through the value function. The function value is also defined using a type class because it should be applicable to different handle types.

```
class HasValue i where
  value :: i a VALID -> a
instance HasValue InputField where ...
```

Suppose now that the values

```
ih :: InputField a INVALID
worker :: InputField a VALID -> CGI ()
```

are available. Then submit ih worker empty creates a submission button on the screen. When the button is clicked, submit attempts to transform the (invalid) handle into a valid one by parsing the values entered for the field ih. If this attempt is successful, submit passes the validated handle to the worker function, which will perform the next processing step and generate the corresponding document. If the handle cannot be validated, submit redisplays the previous document with the erroneous input marked.

Up to now, the type parameter a of the input handle is not necessarily bound. However, to read a value from the handle, the type must be fixed, for example, by a type declaration.

```
worker :: InputField Int VALID -> CGI ()
worker intF =
  let intValue = value intF in
  ...
```

The variable `intValue` has indeed type `Int` and it contains the input value.

One final problem remains to be solved. The `submit` function takes only one input handle as a parameter. What if there are multiple handles to pass to the worker function? It turns out that specially typed tuple constructors are required for this purpose, `F2`, `F3`, and so on. They form tuples of input handles that can be validated together. Of course, a value cannot be extracted directly from a tuple of handles, so the worker function first has to take the tuples apart. The example code in the next section contains a use of `F2`.

On some occasions, a program dynamically generates an arbitrary number of handles in a single web page. In most of these cases, each `submit` function still takes a finite number of handles. Here are some examples.

- A selection widget may present a statically unknown number of choices to the browser, but it only generates a single handle for accessing the input. See Sec. 3.3 for an example.
- Forms for accessing mailing list managers, contact data bases, and the like mostly just have a button to select a specific item from a displayed list. Specific actions with non-trivial input can only be taken on subsequent pages.

However, the following scenario requires a dynamic number of handles. Consider a form that provides a grade entry list for all students signed up for a particular course. For each student the form contains a subform with input fields for the grade and perhaps other information, too. There is only one type of handle involved because the information is uniform across all students. Hence, WASH provides the FL data constructor that turns a list of same-typed handles into a single handle. Validating an FL handle boils down to validating each handle in the list. Of course, the handle constructors FL, F2, F3, and so on may be nested arbitrarily.

The inconvenience of having specially typed constructors for tuples and lists of handles as well as the distinction between valid and invalid handles is due to the design decision that WASH should rely entirely on Haskell98. It is possible to employ advanced typing features (multi-parameter type classes) of Haskell to work around these inconveniences at the price of portability[4]. However, the inconvenience is much reduced by using the preprocessor which can generate most of the code for this wrapping and also for the extraction of the values from their handles.

## 2.6   Example: Adder

Figure 1 contains a complete example for a web page performing additions. It relies on a function `standardQuery`, which is defined similarly to `standardTemplate` but wraps a form around the entire body of the document.

---

[4] The distribution contains a suitable alternative implementation of `submit` for demonstration.

```
1    adder :: CGI ()
2    adder =
3      standardQuery "Adder/1"
4       <#>
5         <p>First  number to add <% sum1F <- inputField empty %></p>
6         <p>Second number to add <% sum2F <- inputField empty %></p>
7         <% submit (F2 sum1F sum2F) addThem <[value="Perform addition"]>%>
8       </#>
9
10   addThem (F2 sum1F sum2F) =
11     let sum1, sum2 :: Int
12         sum1 = value sum1F
13         sum2 = value sum2F
14         sum  = sum1 + sum2
15     in
16     standardQuery "Adder/2"
17       <#>
18         <p><%= show sum1 %> + <%= show sum2 %> = <%= show sum %></p>
19         <% submit0 adder <[value="Continue"]> %>
20       </#>
```

**Fig. 1.** A web page for additions

The entire application consists of two different screens, Adder/1 (line 3-8) and Adder/2 (line 15-19). The notation <#> and </#> just serves as a bracket to combine a number of element nodes to a sequence. In our application, the XHTML notation is preferable to using the raw document combinators. To see this, consider lines 5 (or 6) and 7. In line 5, the notation sum1F <- ... binds the variable sum1F to a handle to the first input field. By our convention, this binding is valid up to the end of the current XHTML fragment, that is, up to the closing </#>. Hence, the call to submit can refer directly to sum1F.

The call to submit takes as first argument a pair of handles constructed with the special F2 operator for pairing handles. Pairs formed with this constructor may be validated together and the callback function (line 10) can simply pattern-match against F2 to extract the (now validated) handles again. Finally, the function value extracts an Int value from each handle (lines 12,13) where the result type Int is enforced with the type declaration for sum1 and sum2 in line 11.

The callback function is set up so that application logic and presentation are kept strictly separate. It contains a submission button to restart the application. This button is constructed using submit0, a specialized version of submit that does not pass parameters to its callback action. The two submit buttons both make use of the bracketing notation <[ and ]> for attribute creation to set the value attribute of the underlying input element.

## 2.7 Fully Integrated XHTML Syntax

The WASH preprocessor packaged with version 2.2 enables further simplication. Many escapes from the XHTML notation to Haskell only contain the definition

```
1    adder :: CGI ()
2    adder =
3      standardQuery "Adder/1"
4        <#>
5          <p>First  number to add <input type="text" name="sum1"/></p>
6          <p>Second number to add <input type="text" name="sum2"/></p>
7          <input type="submit" WASH:call="addThem (sum1, sum2)"
8                          value="Perform addition" />
9        </#>
10
11   addThem (val1, val2) =
12     let sum :: Int
13         sum  = val1 + val2
14     in
15     standardQuery "Adder/2"
16       <#>
17         <p><%= show sum1 %> + <%= show sum2 %> = <%= show sum %></p>
18         <input type="submit" WASH:call="adder" value="Continue" />
19       </#>
```

**Fig. 2.** Web page for additions in XHTML notation

of a widget, *e.g.*, they construct an input field or a submission button. These escapes can be avoided by having the preprocessor translate the standard XHTML elements into the correct constructors. The **name** attribute of the input elements serves directly as a binding instance of a Haskell identifier for the corresponding handle. As an example, Fig. 2 contains two textual **input** elements that bind the identifiers **sum1** and **sum2** as well as a submit button.

The submit button makes use of an attribute in a special XML name space indicated by the prefix WASH. XML attributes in this name space provide extra information that does not fits into the standard XHTML attributes. In this case, the WASH:call attribute contains a call template for the callback function. The attribute value "addThem (sum1, sum2)" indicates that clicking the button invokes the callback function **addThem** on the *values* of the handles **sum1** and **sum2**. That is, the preprocessor eliminates the need for the F2, F3, ... tuple constructors and for the **value** function in many standard cases. Some cases, like having a dynamic number of input handles still require special treatment.

The translation of the **input** element of type **submit** eliminates the named tuple constructors in the user program as follows. Suppose that WASH:call="g $(p_1, p_2, \ldots, p_n)$".

- The parameter list is transformed to the nested named tuple

$$(F2 \ p_1 \ (F2 \ p_2 \ ( \ \ldots \ (F2 \ p_n \ F0)\ldots))).$$

This nested pair becomes the first parameter to the **submit** function.
- The callback function g is wrapped in a lambda abstraction

$$(\lambda \ (F2 \ p_1 \ (F2 \ p_2 \ ( \ \ldots \ (F2 \ p_n \ F0)\ldots)))$$
$$\rightarrow g \ (value \ p_1, \ value \ p_2, \ \ldots, \ value \ p_n)),$$

which becomes the second argument to submit. With this wrapper, the callback g becomes completely unaware of handles and of named tuples. It simply becomes a function that takes a tuple of input values and yields a CGI action.

If no parameters are present, then the preprocessor emits a call to submit0 and does not wrap the callback function in any way.

## 2.8  Customizing Widgets

WASH allows the creation of customized textual widgets in at least two different ways. The first way is to create a new data type with a specialized parser for that type. The other way is to combine and transform existing textual widgets.

**New Data Type with Custom Parser.** Any data type can serve as a data type for input fields if it is an instance of Read and an instance of Reason. To make a type $T$ an instance of Reason it is sufficient to say

```
instance Reason T
```

If you want to be really nice, you override the default definition of the method reason :: $T$ -> String to provide an explanation of $T$'s input syntax. reason must not touch its $T$ argument.

As an example, Figure 3 contains the implementation of a Password data type, which enforces the rule that a Password is a string of length $\geq 8$ with characters taken from at least three of the four sets: lower case characters, upper case characters, digits, and special characters.

```
newtype Password = Password { unPassword :: String }

instance Reason Password where
  reason _ = "Password string of length >= 8 with characters ..."

instance Read Password where
  readsPrec i str =
    let lower = any isLower str
        upper = any isUpper str
        digit = any isDigit str
        specl = any isSpecl str
        isSpecl c = isPrint c && not (isAlphaNum c)
        nclasses = sum (Prelude.map fromEnum [lower, upper, digit, specl])
    in
    if   length str >= 8 && nclasses >= 3
    then [(Password str, "")]
    else []
```

**Fig. 3.** Definition of a password field type

```
adder :: CGI () adder =
  standardQuery "Adder/1"
    <#>
      <p>Pair of numbers to add <% sumF <- inputField empty %></p>
      <% pairF <- return (concatFieldsWith pairUp sumF []) %>
      <% submit pairF addPair <[value="Perform addition"]> %>
    </#>
  where pairUp str = '(' : str ++ ")"

addPair pairF =
  let sum1, sum2 :: Int
      (sum1, sum2) = value pairF
  in
  standardQuery "Adder/2"
    <#>
      <p><%= show sum1 %> + <%= show sum2 %>=<%= show (sum1+sum2) %></p>
      <% submit0 adder <[value="Continue"]> %>
    </#>
```

**Fig. 4.** Addition with input field for pairs of integers

**Transforming and Combining Widgets.** As an example, where an input transformation would be appropriate, consider the task of creating an input field for pairs of integers or lists of integers. Of course, an input field for type (Int, Int) or [Int] will do the job. However, people that are not initiated to Haskell's Read syntax might enter 15,42 instead of (15,42) for a pair of integers or 1,2,3 instead of [1,2,3] for a list of integers. Hence, it would be nice to be able to have a widget that automatically adds the extra parentheses around the pair or the list unless they are already present.

The function concatFieldsWith builds a new input field out of existing ones. It takes a function argument, a base input field, and a list of further input fields. It applies the function to the strings entered in all fields and creates a new input field with the resulting, transformed string as input.

As an example, let's rewrite the addition web page created in the previous subsection to accept unparenthesized pairs of numbers as input. Figure 4 contains the result. Of course, it would be possible to perform the same task with a specialized field type but concatenating and transforming fields is much less effort.

Other uses of field transformations include error correction, format translation (*e.g.*, date and time formats), and more. It is also possible to combine two or more input fields and parse them according to a common syntax. For example, a date entry widget might use three fields for day, month, and year, whereas an existing date parser and verifier might expect the entire date specification in one string.

## 3    An Example Application

The section considers the disciplined construction of a WASH application with the example of a web logger. The contributions of the disciplined approach introduced here are twofold.

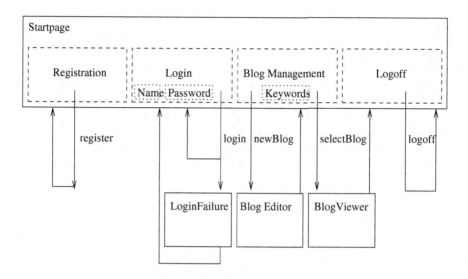

**Fig. 5.** Sketch of blogger architecture

- A graphical notation for structuring a web application in terms of pagelets.
- Programming guidelines for strictly separating the program's "business logic" from the presentation logic.

Interestingly, no new facilities are required to enforce the separation of concern between logic and presentation. Haskell's functional abstraction suffices entirely for this task. Haskell's type system automatically enforces consistency between the presentation skin and the logic even if their specifications are completely separate.

### 3.1 The Web Logger

A blogging[5] application supports the creation of categorized online diaries. The difference between a blog and a real diary is that the diary is a private record which is safely locked away in a drawer whereas the blog is publicly accessible, everyone can read it (without knowing the authors), and everyone can attach comments to entries in the blog if the blogging application supports this feature. The design of such an application is large enough to offer interesting insights and small enough to be presented concisely.

The diagram in Figure 5 describes the design of a very basic blogger. The diagram is a hierarchical hypergraph with several different kinds of nested nodes drawn as rectangles. Each solid rectangle in the diagram corresponds to one or more web pages displayed on the browser. The dashed rectangles correspond to pagelets, *i.e.*, XHTML fragments with attached functionality. They can only

---

[5] Contracted from *web logging*.

appear within web pages. The dotted rectangles correspond to widgets on the screen. They can only appear within pagelets. Arrows can start from web pages or pagelets and must end in web pages. Each arrow that starts from a pagelet models an operation. The widgets in the pagelet provide the input to its operation. An arrow may fan out to multiple ends if the operation has multiple exits. For instance, the `login` arrow splits into a successful end and a failure end.

Solid rectangles may be refined by subsidiary diagrams. Their outgoing arrows must be reconnected to web pages or pagelets in the refined diagram. Incoming arrows must be reconnected to subsidiary web pages.

Due to space and time constraints, we concentrate on the implementation of a few pagelets and on the final wiring of the pagelets.

## 3.2   A Login Pagelet

Login functionality is widely used in web applications. The idea is usually that more functionality is available to registered users, either as a reward for giving away some personal information and/or to be able to track down users that have violated the service provider's contents policy.

The corresponding pagelet should consist of two input fields, one for entering the user name and another for entering the password. The underlying functionality checks the name and password against some database. The pagelet should allow for some parameterization so that it becomes reusable. In particular, the definition of the functionality and the visual appearance should be separated from each other.

Here is a tentative signature for the `login` function.

```
type Skin = ...
type Name = String
type Password  = String
type PasswordChecker = Name -> Password -> IO Bool
type SuccessCont = Name -> CGI ()
type FailureCont = CGI ()
login :: Skin
         -> PasswordChecker
         -> SuccessCont
         -> FailureCont
         -> WithHTML x CGI ()
```

The first argument of type `Skin` describes the visual appearance of the pagelet. The `PasswordChecker` is a side-effecting function that is supposed to perform the password check. It is made into a parameter because its implementation is likely to differ between systems. The remaining two arguments, `SuccessCont` and `FailureCont`, are the actions taken if the password check succeeds or fails.

The skin argument is supposed to contain the entire visual formatting and including the choice of input widgets. It should not contain application or presentation logic. In the present case, it is a function taking the callback for the sole submit button in the pagelet.

```
loginSkin act =
  <table>
    <tr><td>Name       </td>
        <td><input type="text" name="l" /></td>
    </tr>
    <tr><td>Password </td>
        <td><input type="password" name="p" /></td>
    </tr>
    <tr><td></td>
        <td><input type="submit" WASH:call="act( l, p)"
                   value="Login" /></td>
    </tr>
  </table>
```

Clearly, the only implementation decisions taken in this code fragment regard the visual appearance of the login area: there is a textual input field, a password input field, and a submit button. The input fields are named l and p and both are passed to the callback that has to be provided to the submit function.

The logic of the login pagelet is completely separate in the function login.

```
login skin pwCheck scont fcont =
  skin $ \ (l, p) ->
    let logname = unNonEmpty l
        pw      = unPassword p
    in
    do registered <- io (pwCheck logname pw)
       if registered
          then scont logname
          else fcont
```

The application of the skin function to the callback function constructs the XHTML elements corresponding to the login pagelet. The callback function implements the logic: it retrieves the values from the input fields at their expected types, performs the password check, and invokes one of the continuation actions.

There is one unfortunate property of the chosen decomposition in XHTML skin and functionality. The skin already has to provide for the wiring between the input widgets and the submission buttons. In the extreme case, the skin writer (who might be using a tool with a graphical front end) does not know about the required wiring and may not be familiar with Haskell typing at all. In such a case, the skin "code" has to assume the worst: all input handles are passed to all submission buttons. In the worst case, the submit function itself can be made into a parameter and an appropriate projection function can be applied to the handle parameter before it is passed to submit.

The loginSkin and login functions are independent of each other and can be defined in different modules. The definition of the application's skin can thus be concentrated into a single separate module just by collecting all skin definitions.

## 3.3   A Selection Pagelet

Another commonly recurring functionality is to either select from a list of existing alternatives or to create a new alternative. This functionality may be subsumed by the following type.

```
type Skin = ...
type GetAlternatives = CGI [String]
type NewCont = String -> CGI ()
type OldCont = String -> CGI ()
selector :: Skin -> GetAlternatives -> NewCont -> OldCont
         -> WithHTML x CGI ()
```

Again, the pagelet may be split into the skin and the logic. The skin is only concerned with the visual appearance. However, it has more parameters than before because it contains a complicated widget, selectSingle, which creates a selection box essentially from a list of alternatives. As mentioned before, selectSingle yields exactly one input handle regardless of the number of items it selects from.

```
selectorSkin shower def selections act =
 <table>
   <tr><td>Enter new topic </td>
       <td><input type="text" name="nt" /></td></tr>
   <tr><td>Select existing topic </td>
       <td><% et <- selectSingle shower def selections empty %></td></tr>
   <tr><td></td>
       <td><input type="submit" WASH:call="act( nt, et)"
                  value="proceed" /></td></tr>
 </table>
```

The logic part has only one novelty. The program needs to lift the CGI computation getAlternatives to the WithHTML x CGI monad because the skin is defined in it. Otherwise the code is straightforward.

```
selector skin getAlternatives newCont oldCont =
  do alts <- lift getAlternatives
     let selections = Nothing : map Just alts
     skin (fromMaybe "<new entry>")
          (Just Nothing)
          selections
      $ \ (nt, et) ->
          case et of
            Just name ->
              oldCont name
            Nothing ->
              newCont (unText nt)
```

The use of unText forces the input field to accept (and return to the program) an arbitrary string of characters.

## 3.4    Final Wiring Up

Each pagelet is defined in a separate function and potentially in a separate module. Another module, Skins, contains the definitions of all skins. The main program in the module Blogger applies each pagelet to its skin and wires the resulting pagelets according the design.

```
-- build pagelets from logic and skin
startPage= StartPage.startPage Skins.startSkin
login    = Login.login Skins.loginSkin
logoff   = Logoff.logoff Skins.logoffSkin
register = Register.register Skins.registerSkin
selector = Select.selector Skins.selectorSkin

-- application code
blogger :: CGI ()
blogger =
  mainPage initialBloggerState ""

mainPage :: BloggerState -> String -> CGI ()
mainPage bs message =
  ask $ startPage message (userManager bs) (blogManager bs)

userManager :: BloggerState -> WithHTML x CGI ()
userManager bs =
  case loggedName bs of
    Nothing ->
      Skins.userManager1
        (login myPasswordCheck
               (\ user -> mainPage bs{ loggedName = Just user }
                                 "Login successful")
               (mainPage bs{ loggedName = Nothing }
                         "Login failed"))
        (register myPasswordSaver
               (\ user -> mainPage bs{ loggedName = Just user }
                                 "Registration successful"))
    Just user ->
      Skins.userManager2
        (logoff user (mainPage initialBloggerState
                               (user ++ " logged off")))

blogManager :: BloggerState -> WithHTML x CGI ()
blogManager bs@B{ status = Visiting } =
  selector myBlogTitles (BlogAccess.newBlog bs mainPage)
                        (BlogAccess.oldBlog bs mainPage)
```

The function mainPage generates a web page by passing to startPage a string and two sequences of document nodes, which are generated by the pagelets userManager and blogManager. All involve the blog state bs of type BloggerState as a central data structure. In our simple setting, the state contains the login name of the current user and some status information.

```
type UserName = String
type BlogName = String
data BloggerState =
  B { loggedName :: Maybe UserName, status :: BlogAction}
  deriving (Read, Show)

data BlogAction =
  Visiting | Editing BlogName | Reading BlogName
  deriving (Read, Show)
```

The code for the blogManager function is incomplete in the listing. It only deals with the case where a user without a login wants to access some blogs. The implementation of this access, is in the BlogAccess module which provides one (or more) web pages that either create a new blog or access an existing blog.

The main emphasis of the code is on clearly separating different concerns. The one part that deals exclusively with the graphical appearance is isolated in the Skins module. The module Blogger concentrates on the application logic whereas application specific functions, like myBlogTitles, myPasswordSaver, and myPasswordCheck, are kept completely separate. Our example implementation of these functions is in terms of the file system, but it is easy to replace them by database accesses through a suitable API.

## 4    A Taste of Implementation

This short section explains the main ideas underlying the implementation of WASH. It is provided because the implementation has a subtle impact on the way that WASH deals with server-side state and on the efficiency of a Web application programmed with WASH. While the efficiency consideration can be safely dismissed for small applications, the handling of server-side state is crucial for the semantics.

The main problem in WASH's implementation is the representation of a session, that is, a programmed sequence of forms that is driven by the user's interactive inputs. The concept of a session is fundamentally at odds with the stateless nature of HTTP as already explained in the introduction. The most portable way of running a program through HTTP is the Common Gateway Interface (CGI) [2]. Such a program is a CGI program. An HTTP request for a CGI program starts the selected program on the server and passes the parameters from the request to the program. The program acts on the parameters, produces some output—usually another form—that is returned to the browser, and terminates.

To continue the session, the terminated CGI program somehow has to remember the state of the interaction thus far. One common approach is to store this state on the server and include an pointer to the state into the returned form, so that the next CGI program can continue from that state. Unfortunately, this approach is neither scalable nor compatible with the browser's navigation features (the back-button, in particular; see [9] for more discussion). Hence, the implementation of WASH has made another choice.

When a WASH program executes, each input to the program is logged in a session log. The session log has entries for the results of IO actions and for inputs from form submissions. When the program reaches an ask operation, it creates a form as specified by the argument of ask, prints it, and terminates. Instead of putting a pointer to a saved state in the form, WASH instead puts the session log into the form.

Submitting a form containing a session log invokes **the same program** on the server. However, since there is now a session log, the input operations do not actually consume input but read the old values from the log. That is, when reaching the above ask operation again, the program is in exactly the same state as in the previous invocation because it replayed the same inputs. In addition, the input for the form generated by this ask is now available, too. Hence, in this round and in all later rounds, ask does **not** produce a web page but rather decodes the input, appends it to the session log, and passes control to one of the callbacks specified for the form. Then execution continues up to the next ask and the next cycle can start.

The working of the io operation is even simpler. If the session log already contains the operation's result from a previous run, then it just returns the result from the log. Otherwise, it performs the IO operation and appends its result to the log. The type of every value that is returned from io is constrained by Read and Show as indicated in Sec.2.1 because such values must be written to the log and potentially read back in.

This implementation of sessions is scalable because it does not require any state on the server. If a server becomes unavailable, then either the session can continue when the server becomes available again or the session can continue on a different server running the same program. Also browser navigation cannot introduce a mismatch between the state of the client and the server state, simply because there is no server state.

One problem with implementing sessions via session logs may be that session logs get too long and the replay time dominates the execution time. However, there are ways of structuring the application (and supporting WASH operators once and forever) so that the session log remains bounded in size [9].

Of course, some applications require server-side state beyond the session log. In many cases, the standard IO interface can handle these efficiently. In addition, there is an abstraction AbstractTable specially tailored for dealing with database accesses [11].

## 5    Conclusion

WASH is a web programming system organized around the ideas of type-safe interfaces, abstract datatypes, and compositionality. This combination enables the modular construction of web applications from pagelets, which are components integrating functionality and appearance. At the same time, the specifications of functionality and appearance may be kept separate, as demonstrated in the paper's example application. A simple graphical notation for designing web applications is put forward. This notation directly reflects the interaction structure as well as the program structure.

While WASH supports the separation of presentation and logic easily, it is debatable if a graphic designer has sufficient expertise to perform the rudimentary programming necessary for the presentation part. A more convincing case could be made if the creation of the presentation part was purely a matter of XHTML editing. Work towards this goal is in progress.

## Acknowledgment

The author is grateful to the second readers for their helpful comments on a draft of this paper, which led to a number of improvements.

## References

1. Apache cocoon project. `http://cocoon.apache.org/`, June 2004.
2. CGI: Common gateway interface. `http://www.w3.org/CGI/`, 1999.
3. R. Fielding, J. Gettys, J. Mogul, H. Frystyk, L. Masinter, P. Leach, and T. Berners-Lee. Hypertext transfer protocol. `http://www.faqs.org/rfcs/rfc2616.html`, June 1999.
4. Paul Graunke, Robert Bruce Findler, Shriram Krishnamurthi, and Matthias Felleisen. Automatically restructuring programs for the Web. In *Proceedings of ASE-2001: The 16th IEEE International Conference on Automated Software Engineering*, pages 211–222, San Diego, USA, November 2001. IEEE CS Press.
5. Paul T. Graunke, Robert Bruce Findler, Shriram Krishnamurthi, and Matthias Felleisen. Modeling Web interactions. In *Proc. 12th European Symposium on Programming*, Lecture Notes in Computer Science, Warsaw, Poland, April 2003. Springer-Verlag.
6. Paul T. Graunke and Shriram Krishnamurthi. Advanced control flows for flexible graphical user interfaces: or, growing GUIs on trees or, bookmarking GUIs. In *Proceedings of the 24th International Conference on Software Engineering (ICSE-02)*, pages 277–290, New York, May 19–25 2002. ACM Press.
7. Haskell 98, a non-strict, purely functional language. `http://www.haskell.org/definition`, December 1998.
8. Philippe Le Hégaret, Ray Whitmer, and Lauren Wood. W3c document object model. `http://www.w3.org/DOM/`, August 2003.
9. Peter Thiemann. An embedded domain-specific language for type-safe server-side Web-scripting. *ACM Transactions on Internet Technology*, 5(1):1–46, 2005.
10. Philip Wadler. Monads for functional programming. In *Advanced Functional Programming*, volume 925 of *Lecture Notes in Computer Science*, pages 24–52. Springer-Verlag, May 1995.
11. Web authoring system in Haskell (WASH). `http://www.informatik.uni-freiburg.de/ thiemann/haskell/WASH`, March 2001.
12. XForms - the next generation of Web forms. `http://www.w3.org/MarkUp/Forms/`, May 2003.

# Refactoring Functional Programs

Simon Thompson

Computing Laboratory, University of Kent,
Canterbury, Kent CT2 7NF, United Kingdom
S.J.Thompson@kent.ac.uk

**Abstract.** Refactoring is the process of improving the design of existing programs without changing their functionality. These notes cover
refactoring in functional languages, using Haskell as the medium, and
introducing the HaRe tool for refactoring in Haskell.

## 1 Introduction

Refactoring [8] is about improving the design of existing computer programs and
systems; as such it is familiar to every programmer, software engineer and designer. Its key characteristic is the focus on structural change, strictly separated
from changes in functionality. A structural change can make a program simpler,
by removing duplicate code, say, or can be the preparatory step for an upgrade
or extension of a system.

Program restructuring has a long history. As early as 1978 Robert Floyd in
his Turing Award lecture [7] encouraged programmers to reflect on and revise
their programs as an integral part of their practice. Griswold's thesis on automated assistance for LISP program restructuring [9] introduced some of the ideas
developed here and Opdyke's thesis [22] examined refactoring in the context of
object-oriented frameworks. Martin Fowler brought the field to prominence with
his book on refactoring object-oriented programs [8]. The refactoring browser, or
'refactory' [3], for Smalltalk is notable among the first generation of OO tools;
a number of Java tools are now widely available. The best known of these is
the refactoring tool for Java in Eclipse [5]. More comprehensive reviews of the
refactoring literature are available at the web page for [8] and at our web site.[1]

Refactorings are one sort of program transformation; they differ from other
kinds of program transformation in a number of ways. Traditional transformations usually have a 'direction': they are applied to make a program more time or
space efficient, say. On the other hand, refactorings are typically bi-directional: a
refactoring to widen the scope of a local definition could equally well be applied
in reverse to localise a global definition.

It is also characteristic of refactorings that they are 'diffuse' and 'bureau-
cratic': that is, their effect is not limited to a particular point in a program, and
they require care and precision in their execution. Consider the example of the
simplest possible refactoring: renaming a component of a program. To effect this

---

[1] http://www.cs.kent.ac.uk/projects/refactor-fp/

V. Varmo and T. Uustalu (Eds.): AFP 2004, LNCS 3622, pp. 331–357, 2005.

change requires not only the component definition to be changed, but also every *use* of the component must be similarly modified. This involves changing every file or module which might use the component, potentially tens or hundreds of modules. Moreover, it is vital not to change any components hidden in other parts of the system which happen to share the same name.

It is, of course, possible to do refactorings 'by hand', but this process is tedious and, more importantly, error-prone. Automated support for refactorings makes them safe and easy to perform, equally easy to undo, and also secure in their implementation. The *Refactoring Functional Programs*[2] [17] project at the University of Kent is building the *HaRe* [12] system to support refactorings for Haskell programs.

HaRe is designed as a serious tool for use by practising programmers: HaRe supports the whole of Haskell 98; it is integrated into standard development environments and it preserves the 'look and feel' of refactored programs. HaRe is built using a number of existing libraries: Programatica [11] on which to build the language-analysis components, and Strafunski [19] which gives general support for tree transformations.

These notes begin presenting overviews of design for functional programs and the HaRe system. The core of the paper is an exposition of the basics of refactoring: a detailed description of generalisation is presented as an example of a structural refactoring in Section 4, and the impact of modules on refactoring is examined in Section 5.

A number of data-oriented refactorings are given Section 6: principal among these is the transformation taking a concrete `data` type into an ADT, which is implemented in HaRe as composition of simpler refactorings. As well as providing a repertoire of built-in refactorings, HaRe provides an API by which other refactorings can be constructed; this is the subject of Section 7. The notes conclude with a discussion of conclusions and directions for the research.

I am very grateful indeed to my colleagues Huiqing Li and Claus Reinke, interns Nguyen Viet Chau and Jon Cowie, and research students Cyris Ryder and Chris Brown for their collaboration in the project. I would also like to thank the referees for their suggestions and corrections.

## 2    The Elements of Design

In designing an object-oriented system, it is taken for granted that design will precede programming. Designs will be written using a system like UML [27] which is supported in tools such as Eclipse [5]. Beginning programmers may well learn a visual design approach using systems like BlueJ [2]. Work on a similar methodology for functional programming is reported in [23], but little other work exists. There may be a number of reasons for this.

- *Existing functional programs are of a scale which does not require design.* Many functional programs are small, but others, such as the Glasgow Haskell Compiler, are substantial.

[2] This work is supported by EPSRC under project grant GR/R75052.

- *Functional programs directly model the application domain, thus rendering design irrelevant.* Whilst functional languages provide a variety of powerful abstractions, it is difficult to argue that these provide all and only the abstractions needed to model the real world.
- *Functional programs are built as an evolving series of prototypes.*

If we accept the final reason, which appears to be the closest to existing practice, we are forced to ask how design emerges. A general principle is the move from the concrete to the abstract, and from the specific to the general. Specifically, for Haskell, we can use the following strategies:

**Generalisation.** A function is written with a specific purpose: it is generalised by making some of the particular behaviour into an argument.

**Higher-Order Functions.** This particular case of generalisation is characteristic of modern functional programming: specific behaviour is abstracted into a function, which becomes a parameter.

**Commonality.** Two parts of a program are identified as being identical or at least similar; they can be replaced by invocations of a single function (with appropriate parameters).

**Data Abstraction.** Concrete, algebraic data types provide an excellent starting point, but are difficult to modify: a move to an abstract type gives the programmer flexibility to modify the implementation without modifying any client code.

**Overloading.** The introduction of a `class` and its `instances` allows set of names to be overloaded: programs thus become usable in a variety of contexts. This can make programs more readable, and also replace a number of similar definitions by a single, overloaded, one.

**Monadification.** This particular case of overloading allows explicit computational effects to become an implicit part of a system; once this transformation has taken place it is possible to modify the monad being used without changing the client code. A number of monads can be combined using monad transformers [14].

The HaRe tool supports many of these 'design abstractions'. Using a refactoring tool allows programmers to take a much more exploratory and speculative approach to design: large-scale refactorings can be accomplished in a single step, and equally importantly can be undone with the same effort. In this way Haskell programming and pedagogy can become very different from current practice.

## 3    The HaRe System

Refactoring for Haskell is supported by the HaRe tool [12] built at the University of Kent as a part of the project *Refactoring Functional Programs*. The system was designed to be a tool useable by the working programmer, rather than a proof-of-concept prototype. This imposes three substantial constraints on the designer.

- It should support a full standard language – Haskell 98 in this case – rather than a convenient subset chosen for demonstration purposes.
- It should work within programmers' existing tools (Emacs and Vim) rather than be stand alone, allowing programmers to augment their existing practice with zero overhead.
- It is our experience that although layout is of syntactic significance in Haskell, different programmers adopt widely different styles of layout, and in most cases programmers would find it completely unacceptable to have had their code reformatted by a 'pretty printer' in the course of a refactoring. The system should therefore preserve the appearance of source code programs. In particular, it is crucial to preserve not only comments but also the particular layout style used by the programmer.

## 3.1   Using HaRe

HaRe supports a growing set of refactorings over Haskell; the details of many of these are presented in the sections that follow. The initial release of HaRe contained a number of 'structural', scope-related, single-module refactorings (October 2003); multiple-module versions of these refactorings were added in HaRe 0.2 (January 2004), and the first datatype-related refactorings added in HaRe 0.3 (November 2004). The third version restructures HaRe to expose an API for

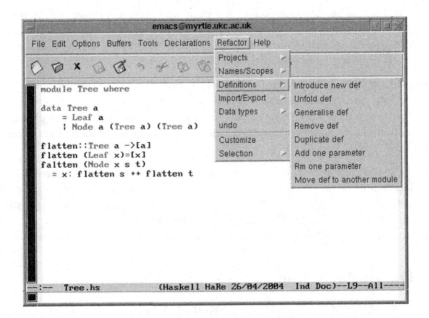

**Fig. 1.** HaRe: the *Refactor* menu

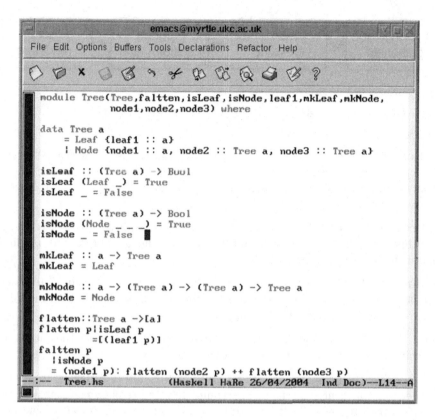

```
emacs@myrtle.ukc.ac.uk

File  Edit  Options  Buffers  Tools  Declarations  Refactor  Help

module Tree(Tree,faltten,isLeaf,isNode,leaf1,mkLeaf,mkNode,
            node1,node2,node3) where

data Tree a
     = Leaf {leaf1 :: a}
     | Node {node1 :: a, node2 :: Tree a, node3 :: Tree a}

isLeaf :: (Tree a) -> Bool
isLeaf (Leaf _) = True
isLeaf _ = False

isNode :: (Tree a) -> Bool
isNode (Node _ _ _) = True
isNode _ = False

mkLeaf :: a -> Tree a
mkLeaf = Leaf

mkNode :: a -> (Tree a) -> (Tree a) -> Tree a
mkNode = Node

flatten::Tree a ->[a]
flatten p|isLeaf p
         =[(leaf1 p)]
faltten p
    |isNode p
    = (node1 p): flatten (node2 p) ++ flatten (node3 p)
--:--     Tree.hs          (Haskell HaRe 26/04/2004   Ind Doc)--L14--A
```

**Fig. 2.** HaRe: the result of 'From concrete to abstract data type'

the system infrastructure used for implementing refactorings and other transformations in HaRe; this is addressed in more detail in Section 7.

HaRe, embedded in Emacs, is shown in Figures 1 and 2. A new *Refactor* menu has been added to the user interface: menu items group refactorings, and submenus identify the particular refactoring to be applied. Input is supplied by the cursor position, which can be used to indicate an identifier to be renamed, say, and from the keyboard, to give the replacement identifier, for instance. Figure 1 shows a program defining and using a concrete data type; Figure 2 shows the result of refactoring this to an abstract data type.

## 3.2   Implementation

HaRe is implemented in Haskell. It can be used as a stand-alone program, and is integrated with Emacs and Vim using their scripting languages. As is apparent from the example shown in Figures 1 and 2, HaRe is more than a *text* editor. Implementing refactorings requires information about a number of aspects of the program:

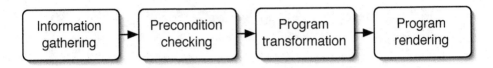

**Fig. 3.** The four stages of a refactoring

**Syntax.** The subject of the refactoring (or program transformation) is the abstract syntax tree (AST) for the parsed program. To preserve comments and layout, information about comments and source code locations for all tokens is also necessary.

**Static Semantics.** In the case of renaming a function f it is necessary to check that this binding of f does not capture any existing uses of f. The binding analysis provides this information.

**Module Analysis.** In a multi-module project, analysis must include all modules. For example, renaming the function f must percolate through all modules of a project which import this binding of f.

**Type System.** If a function g is generalised (as in Section 4) then its type declaration will need to be adjusted accordingly.

It is therefore clear that we require the full functionality of a Haskell front-end in order to implement the refactorings completely and safely. In this project we have used the Programatica front end [11], which supports all aspects of analysis of Haskell 98. The correct implementation of a refactoring consists of four parts, shown in Figure 3.

**Information Gathering and Condition Checking.** The refactoring will only be performed if it preserves the semantics of the program; examples of some of the conditions are given above. Verifying these conditions requires information, such as the set of identifiers in scope at a particular point in the program, to be gathered from the AST by traversing it.

**Transformation.** Once the conditions are verified, it is possible to perform the refactoring, which is a transformation of the AST.

**Program Rendering.** Once transformed, source code for the new program needs to be generated, conforming to the original program layout as much as possible.

Information gathering and transformation consist for the most part of 'boilerplate' code: generic operations are performed at the majority of AST nodes, with the real work being performed by *ad hoc* operations at particular kinds of node. These hybrid generic / specific traversals are supported by a number of systems: in HaRe we use Strafunski [19]; other systems include [15,16].

More details of the HaRe system, including the implementation of a particular refactoring and the details of program rendering, are given in Section 7 and the papers [17,18].

## 4  Structual Refactorings

The first release of HaRe contained a number of refactorings which could be called *structural*. They principally concern the structure of a program, and in particular the objects defined, how they are named and what are their scopes. In summary, HaRe supports the following structural refactorings.

**Delete** a definition that is not used.

**Duplicate** a definition, under another name.

**Rename** a function, variable, type or any other program item.

**Promote** a definition from a local scope to a wider scope, or to the top level of the module.

**Demote** a definition which is only used within one definition to be local to that definition.

**Introduce** a definition to name an identified expression.

**Add** an argument to a function.

**Remove** an argument from a function, if it is not used.

**Unfold** a definition: in other words replace an occurrence of the left-hand side of a definition by the corresponding right-hand side.

**Generalise** a definition by making a selected sub-expression of its right-hand side into a value passed into the function via a new formal parameter.

A number of these refactorings are inverses of each other: promote / demote a definition; add / remove an argument. Others are not quite inverse; the principal example of this is the pair: unfold a definition / introduce a definition. Yet others have inverses yet to be implemented, including generalisation.

We look in more detail here at just one refactoring: generalisation, whose full catalogue entry is given in Figures 4 and 5. Note that, in common with many of these refactorings, generalisation has an effect throughout a module and indeed beyond, since both the definition of the function and all *calls* to the function must be modified.

Each refactoring is only valid under certain conditions. These conditions are covered in more detail in the paper [17] and in the catalogue which accompanies the HaRe system [12].

The most complex conditions are centered on the *binding structure* of the program: that is, the association between uses of identifiers (function and variable names, types, constructor names and so forth) and their definitions. Two examples serve to illustrate the point:

# Generalisation

**Description:** Generalise a definition by selecting a sub-expression of the right-hand side (here "\n") of the definition and making this the value of a new formal parameter added to the definition of the function. The sub-expression becomes the actual parameter at all the call sites.

```
format :: [String] -> [String]        format :: [a] -> [[a]] -> [[a]]
format []    = []                      format sep []    = []
format [x]   = [x]                     format sep [x]   = [x]
format (x:xs)                          format sep (x:xs)
  = (x ++  "\n" ) : format xs            = (x ++ sep) : format sep xs

table = concat . format                table = concat . format "\n"
```

**General comment:** The choice of the position where the argument is added is not accidental: putting the argument at the beginning of the argument list means that it can be added correctly to any partial applications of the function. Note that in the Add Argument refactoring we name the new parameter at the same level as the definition, whereas here we substitute the expression at all call sites.

**Left to right comment:** In the example shown, a single expression is selected. It is possible to abstract over a number of occurrences of the (syntactically) identical expression by preceding this refactoring by

- a transformation to a single equation defined by a case expression;
- the introduction of a local definition of a name for the common expression.

and by following the refactoring by the appropriate inverse refactorings.

In a multi-module system, some of the free variables in the selected sub-expression might not be accessible to the call sites in some client modules. Instead of explicitly exporting and/or importing these variables, the refactorer creates an auxiliary function (fGen, say) in the module containing the definition to represent the sub-expression, and makes it accessible to the client modules.

**Right to left comment:** The inverse can be seen as a sequence of simpler refactorings.

- A definition of a special case is introduced: fmt = format "\n" and any uses of format "\n" (outside its definition) are folded to fmt.
- Using *generative* folding, the definition of format is specialised to a definition of fmt. (Folds in the style of Burstall and Darlington are called generative as they will generate a new definition.)
- If all uses of format take the parameter "\n" then no uses of format remain. Its definition can be removed, and fmt can be renamed to format.

(cont.)

**Fig. 4.** Catalogue entry for generalisation (part 1)

**Left to right conditions:** There are two conditions on the refactoring.

- Adding the new formal parameter should not capture any existing uses of variables.
- The abstracted sub-expression, e say, becomes the first argument of the new function at every use of it. For every new occurrence of e it is a requirement that the bindings of all free identifiers within e are resolved in the same way that they are in the original occurence.

**Right to left conditions:** The successful specialisation depends upon the definition of the function to have a particular form: the particular argument to be removed has to be a constant parameter: that is, it should appear unchanged in every recursive call. The definition of the original function can only be removed if it is only used in the specialised form.

**Analysis required:** Static analysis of bindings; call graph; module analysis. If the type declaration is to be modified, then type inference will be needed.

**Fig. 5.** Catalogue entry for generalisation (part 2)

- If a definition is moved from a local scope to the top level, it may be that some names move out of their scope: this could leave them undefined, or bound to a different definition.
- In the case of generalisation, a new formal parameter is added to the definition in question: this may also disturb the binding structure, capturing references to an object of the same name defined at the top level.

Capture can occur in two ways: the new identifier may be captured, as when f is renamed to g:

```
h x = ... h ... f ... g ...          h x = ... h ... g ... g ...
      where                                where
        g y = ...                            g y = ...

f x = ...                            g x = ...
```

or it may capture other uses, as when a local definition f is renamed to g:

```
h x = ... h ... f ... g ...          h x = ... h ... g ... g ...
      where                                where
        f y = ... f ... g ...                g y = ... g ... g ...

g x = ...                            g x = ...
```

In the next section we explore the impact of modules on the refactoring process for Haskell.

## 5   Modules and Module-Aware Refactorings

The second release of HaRe extends the first in two ways. The structural refactorings are themselves made *module aware*, that is they are extended to have an effect throughout a multi-module project rather than in a single module alone. Various refactorings for the module system are then introduced.

## 5.1   Module-Aware Refactorings

A Haskell module may import definitions from other modules, and re-export them and its own definitions for use in other modules. This has the effect of widening the scope of a definition from a single module to a set of modules. It may be imported just under its name, or in 'qualified' form as `Module.name`. An exhaustive, formal, description of the Haskell module system, developed as a part of the Programatica project, is given in [4].

Returning to our example of generalisation, it is necessary to consider the expression which becomes the new actual parameter at every call site of the function, in every module where the function is used. This expression will use identifiers defined in its home module, and these will need to be accessible. Two options present themselves. First, it would be possible to export all these definitions to all modules using the function, but this has the disadvantage of cluttering up the namespace with extraneous definitions, as well as introducing the possibility of name clashes. Instead, we introduce a new name for the actual parameter in the home module, and export that value together with the generalised function.

The scope of multi-module refactorings is not, of course, universal. In the HaRe project, we build on the Programatica infrastructure, and so we use the Programatica notion of *project* as delimiting the scope of a refactoring. In many cases it is possible to mitigate the effect of refactorings on modules outside the project. For example, if a generalised function is going to be used outside the project, then it is possible to build a 'wrapper' module which exports the original function rather than the generalised version.

## 5.2   Module Refactorings

HaRe supports a number of refactorings related to the module system.

**Clean** the import list, so that the only functions imported are ones that are used in the module.

**Make** an explicit list of those bindings used from each imported module.

**Add** and **remove** items from the export list.

**Move** a definition from one module to another.

Consider the process of moving a top level definition of f from module A to B. First, various conditions need to be satisfied if the move is to happen.

- f should not already be defined at the top level of B.
- The free variables in f should be accessible within the module B.
- The move should not create a circularity in the module dependencies.[3]

---

[3] Whilst Haskell 98 allows recursive modules, the reason for this restriction is the imperfect support for recursive modules provided by current Haskell implementations.

If the conditions are satisfied then the refactoring can be achieved by moving the definition from A to B with some follow-up actions.

- Modify the import/export lists in the modules A and B *and* the client modules of A and B as necessary.
- Change uses of A.f to B.f or f in all affected modules.
- Resolve any ambiguity that might arise.

Other refactorings within the module system include: moving a group of definitions, moving type, class and instance definitions, and merging and splitting modules.

# 6    Data-Oriented Refactorings

This section looks in more detail at a number of larger-scale, data-oriented, refactorings. It is characteristic of all of these that they are bi-directional, with the context determining the appropriate direction. Some of these refactorings are described in the case study of [26]. The section concludes with an overview of other, type-based, refactorings.

## 6.1    Concrete to Abstract Types

One of the principal attractions of almost all modern functional programming languages is the presence of pattern matching.[4] Pattern matching combines selection between alternatives and extraction of fields, allowing definitions of data-processing functions to follow the template provided by the data definition closely. Take the example of a binary tree:

```
data Tree a
  = Leaf a |
    Node a (Tree a) (Tree a)
```

The definition has two cases: a Leaf and a (recursive) Node. Correspondingly, a function to flatten a tree into a list has two clauses: the first deals with a leaf, and the second processes a node, recursively:

```
flatten :: Tree a -> [a]

flatten (Leaf x) = [x]
flatten (Node x s t)
  = x : flatten s ++ flatten t
```

The disadvantage of this approach is the concrete nature of the definition of Tree: in other words, the *interface* to the Tree type is given by a pair of constructors:

---

[4] Scheme is the main exception, and indeed even within the Scheme community it is taken for granted that pattern matching macros are used by scheme programmers in all but the most introductory of contexts.

```
module Tree (Tree, leaf, node, isLeaf, isNode, val, left, right) where

data Tree a
 = Leaf a |
   Node a (Tree a) (Tree a)

isLeaf (Leaf _) = True          val (Leaf x) = x
isLeaf _        = False         val (Node x _ _) = x

isNode (Node _ _ _) = True      left  (Node _ l _) = l
isNode _            = False     right (Node _ _ r) = r

leaf = Leaf
node = Node
```

**Fig. 6.** Tree as an abstract data type

```
Leaf :: a -> Tree a
Node :: a -> Tree a -> Tree a -> Tree a
```

Leaf and Node are not only functions, but also can be used in patterns for the
Tree type. Every Tree is built by applying these constructors, and any function
over Tree can use pattern matching over its arguements.

The alternative is to make Tree an abstract type. The interface to an abstract
type is a collection of functions. Discrimination between the various cases and
selection of components needs now to be provided explicitly by functions. The
code for this case is shown in Figure 6. The selector functions can also be defined
using field names.

```
data Tree a
   = Leaf { val :: a } |
     Node { val :: a, left, right :: Tree a }
```

Each function defined using pattern matching needs to be redefined. Case discrimination is replaced by guards, and selction by explicit selectors (given in this
case by labelled field):

```
flatten :: Tree a -> [a]
flatten t
   | isleaf t = [val t]
   | isNode t
     = val t : flatten (left t) ++ flatten (right t)
```

A refactoring of this sort is often preliminary to a change of representation of the
Tree type; after the refactoring this can be achieved by changing the definition
of the interface functions; no client functions need to be modified.

HaRe supports this refactoring by means of a number of elementary refactorings:

**Add Field Names.** Names are added to the fields of the data type. Names are chosen by the system, but these can be changed using the renaming refactoring.

**Add Discrimiators.** By default, discriminators are named 'isCon' for the constructor Con. If functions of this name already exist, other names are chosen.

**Add Constructors.** Functions con corresponding to the constructor Con are introduced.

**Remove Nested Patterns.** A particular problem is pressented by patterns containing constructors from other datatypes. Using the Tree example again, consider the fragment

```
f (Leaf [x]) = x+17
```

in which a list constructor occurs within a pattern from the Tree datatype. We will have to replace this pattern with a variable, and thus we lose the list pattern match too. So, we need to deal with this *nested* pattern first, thus:[5]

```
f (Leaf xs) = case xs of
                  [x] -> x+17
```

We leave it to readers to convince themsleves that other forms of nesting do not require this treatment.

**Remove Patterns.** Patterns in the Tree type can now be eliminated in terms of the discriminators and selectors. Picking up the previous example, we will have

```
f t
  | isLeaf t = case (val t) of
                   [x] -> x+17
```

**Create ADT Interface.** Move the type definition into a separate file with an interface containing the selectors, discriminators and constructor functions.

Views [28,1] give a mechanism for pattern matching to cohabit with type abstraction. It would be possible to augment the refactoring to include the appropriate view, and to retain pattern matching definitions whilst introducing type abstraction, if the revised proposal [1] were to be incorporated into Haskell.

## 6.2   Inside or Out?

The abstraction of Tree in Section 6.1 gives a minimal interface to the type: values can be constructed and manipulated, but no other functions are included in the 'capsule' or module which delimits the type representation.

Arguably, more functions, such as flatten in our running example. might be included in the capsule. What are the arguments for and against this?

---

[5] It may also be necessary to amalgamate a number of clauses before performing this step, since it is not possible to 'fall through' a case statement.

```
data Tree a
  = Leaf { val::a, flatten:: [a] } |
    Node { val::a, left,right::(Tree a), flatten::[a] }

leaf x     = Leaf x [x]

node x l r = Node x l r (x : (flatten l ++ flatten r))
```

**Fig. 7.** Memoising `flatten` in the data representation

**Inside.** A function included in the capsule has access to the representation, and so can be defined using pattern matching. This may be unavoidable or more efficient if the interface does not export sufficient functionality.

**Outside.** A function defined outside the capsule need not be re-defined when the implementation changes, whereas a function inside must be redefined.

This refactoring extends 'move definition between modules' since the definition itself may also be transformed on moving in or out of the capsule.

### 6.3    Change of Representation: Memoisation

One reason for a change of representation is to support a more efficient representation of a data type. Suppose that `Trees` are repeatedly flattened. There is then a case for including a field in the representation to contain this *memoised* value.

Once data of this sort is included in a type, it is imperative for the consistency of the data representation that the type is abstract, so that values are only constucted and manipulated by functions which preserve the *invariant* property that the particular field indeed represents the memoised value.

This transformation can be supported in a refactoring. The transformed version of the running example is shown in Figure 7. The example shows that the value is memoised in the fields named `flatten`. The `leaf` constructor establises the invariant, and `node` will preserve it.

Incidentally, the memoisation is lazy: the memoised function is as strict or lazy as the original function, so that it is possible, for example. to extract any finite portion of the `flatten` field of `bigTree = node 1 bigTree bigTree`.

### 6.4    Constructor or Constructor Function?

Figure 8 shows two variants of a type of regular expressions. The left-hand definition makes `plus` syntactic sugar: it will be expanded out before any function over `Expr` can be applied, and definitions for regular expressions need not treat the `plus` case separately, so

```
literals (Plus e)
   = literals (Then e (Star e))
   = literals e 'union' literals e
   = ...
```

```
data Expr                      data Expr
  = Epsilon | .... |             = Epsilon | .... |
    Then Expr Expr |               Then Expr Expr |
    Star Expr                      Star Expr |
                                   Plus Expr
plus e = Then e (Star e)
```

**Fig. 8.** Two **data** types of regular expressions

On the other hand, with the right-hand definition it is possible to treat `Plus` explicitly, as in

```
literals (Plus e) = literals e
```

However, it is not just possible but necessary to define a `Plus` case for every function working over the right-hand variant of `Expr`, thus requiring more effort and offering more opportunity for error.[6]

In any particular situation, the context will be needed to determine which approach to use. Note, however, that the transition from left to right can seen as a refactoring: the definitions thus produced may then be transformed to yield a more efficient version as is possible for the `literals` function.

## 6.5   Algebraic or Existential Type?

The traditional functional programming approach would represent a type of shapes as an algebraic type, as shown in the left-hand side of Figure 9. Each function defined over `Shape` will perform a pattern match over shape. Extending the type to include a new kind of shape – `Triangle`, say – will require that all functions have a case added to deal with a triangular shape.

The traditional OO approach will use subclassing or 'polymorphism' (in the OO sense) to implement conditional code.[7] This style is also possible in a functional context, using a combination of type classes and existential types. Figure 9 shows how to achieve this for a type of shapes. It is argued that an advantage of the right-hand representation is that it makes extension of the `Shape` type simpler. To add a triangle shape it is necessary to add a new instance declaration; this single point in the program will contain all the necessary declarations: in this case calculations of the area and perimeter of a triangle.

This approach is not without its drawbacks, however. In the setting of Haskell 98 a full treatment of 'binary methods' becomes problematic. For example it is impossible to define `==` on the existential version of `Shape` using the standard definition by case analysis over the two arguments. Instead, it is necessary to

---

[6] A more persuasive example for this transformation is a range of characters within a regular expression: one can expand `[a-z]` into `a|b|c|...|y|z` but it is much more efficient to treat it as a new constructor of regular expressions.

[7] This is one of Fowler's [8] refactorings: *Replace Conditional with Polymorphism*.

```
data Shape                      data Shape
  = Circle Float |                = forall a. Sh a => Shape a
    Rect Float Float
                                class Sh a where
area :: Shape -> Float            area :: a -> Float
area (Circle f) = pi*r^2          perim :: a -> Float
area (Rect h w) = h*w
                                data Circle = Circle Float
perim :: Shape -> Float
perim (Circle f) = 2*pi*r       instance Sh Circle
perim (Rect h w) = 2*(h+w)        area (Circle f)  = pi*r^2

                                  perim (Circle f) = 2*pi*r

                                data Rect = Rect Float Float

                                instance Sh Rect
                                  area (Rect h w) = h*w
                                  perim (Rect h w) = 2*(h+w)
```

**Fig. 9.** Algebraic or existential type?

convert shapes to a single type (e.g. via show) to turn a case analysis over *types* into a corresponding case over values.

Each representation will be preferable in certain circumstances, just as row-major and column-major array representations are appropriate for different algorithms.[8] The transformation from left to right can be seen as the result of a sequence of simpler refactorings:

- introducing the algebraic 'subtypes' corresponding to the constructors of the original type: in this case Circle and Rect;
- introducing a class definition for the functions: here the class Sh;
- introducing the instance declarations for each 'subtype',
- and finally introducing the existential type: in this example, Shape.

### 6.6 Layered Data Types

Figure 10 illustrates two alternative representations of a data type of arithmetic expressions. The left-hand approach is the more straightforward: the different sorts of arithmetic expression are all collected into a single data type. Its disadvantage is that the type does not reflect the common properties of the Add, Mul and Sub nodes, each of which has two Expr fields, and each of which is treated in a similar way. Refactoring for 'common code extraction' can make this similarity explicit.

On the other hand, in the right-hand definition, the Bin node is a general binary node, with a field from BinOp indicating its sort. Operations which are

---

[8] The reference to array representations is no accident: we can see the two type definitions as presenting clauses of function definitions in row- and column-major form.

```
data Expr = Lit Float |          data Expr  = Lit Float |
            Add Expr Expr |                  Bin BinOp Expr Expr
            Mul Expr Expr |
            Sub Expr Expr        data BinOp = Add | Mul | Sub

eval (Lit r) = r                 eval (Lit r) = r

eval (Add e1 e2)                 eval (Binop op e1 e2)
  = eval e1 + eval e2              = evalOp op (eval e1) (eval e2)
eval (Mul e1 e2)
  = eval e1 * eval e2            evalOp Add = (+)
eval (Sub o1 e2)                 evalOp Mul = (*)
  = eval e1 - eval e2            evalOp Sub = (-)
```

**Fig. 10.** Layered data types

common to `Bin` nodes can be written in a general form, and the pattern matching over the original `Expr` type can be reconstructed thus:

```
eval' (Bin Add e1 e2) = eval' e1 + eval' e2
```

This approach has the advantage that it is, in one way at least, more straightforward to modify. To add division to the expression type, it is a matter of adding to the enumerated type an extra possibility, `Div`, and adding a corresponding clause to the definition of `evalOp`.

Note that moving between representations requires the transformation of all definitions that either use or return an `Expr`.

## 6.7  Monadification

It is commonplace for Haskell programs to incorporate computational effects of various sorts, such as input/output, exceptions and state. Haskell is a pure language, and it is not possible simply to add side effects to the system; instead, expressions with related actions are embedded in a *monad*.

A monad in Haskell is given by a constructor class, which abstracts away from certain computational details of evaluating expressions with associated effects. In its interface lie two functions: `return` which creates an expression with null side effects, and `>>=` which is used to sequence and pass values between two side effecting computations.

A natural step for the programmer is to begin by defining a pure program: one which does no IO, for instance, and later to add IO actions to the program. This necessitates bringing monads to the program. There are two distinct flavours of monadification:

- a non-monadic program is 'sequentialized' to make it monadic; this is the work of Erwig and his collaborators [6];

- a program with explicit actions – such as a state 'threaded' through the evaluation – is made into a program which explicitly uses the monadic operations `return` and `>>=`, or indeed their 'sugared' version, the `do` notation.

An example of what is required can be see in Figures 11 and 12. Figure 11 shows a type of side-effecting expressions, and a `store` type. An example of the side effects are seen in

```
y := (x := x+1) + (x := x+1)
```

Evaluating this expression in a store where x has the value 3 results in y being assigned 9: the first sub expression has the value 4, the second 5.

Figure 12 gives two versions of an evaluator for these expressions. On the left-hand side is an evaluator which passes the `Store` around explicitly. The key case is the evaluation of `Add e1 e2` where we can see that e2 is evaluated in the store `st1`, which may have been modified by the evaluation of e1.

On the right-hand side is the monadic version of the code. How easy is it to transform the left-hand side to the right? It is a combination of unfolding and folding function definitions, combined with the transformation between a `where` clause and a `let`. Unfolding and folding of functions defined in `instance` declarations necessitates a type analysis in order to associate uses of identifiers with their definitions. Existing work on describing monad intoduction includes Erwig and Ren's *monadification* [6] and Lämmel's *monad introduction* [13].

## 6.8    Other Type and Data Refactorings

A number of structural refactorings apply equally well to types: it is possible to rename, delete or duplicate a `type` definition, for instance. Others apply specifically to types:

```
data Expr
  = Lit Integer |        -- Literal integer value
    Vbl Var |            -- Assignable variables
    Add Expr Expr |      -- Expression addition: e1+e2
    Assign Var Expr      -- Assignment: x:=e

type Var = String


type Store = [ (Var, Integer) ]

lookup :: Store -> Var -> Integer
lookup st x = head [ i | (y,i) <- st, y==x ]

update :: Store -> Var -> Integer -> Store
update st x n = (x,n):st
```

**Fig. 11.** Expressions and stores

```
eval :: Expr -> Store -> (Integer, Store)      evalST :: Expr -> State Store Integer

eval (Lit n) st                                evalST (Lit n)
  = (n,st)                                       = do
                                                     return n

eval (Vbl x) st                                evalST (Vbl x)
  = (lookup st x,st)                             = do
                                                     st <- get
                                                     return (lookup st x)

eval (Add e1 e2) st                            evalST (Add e1 e2)
  = (v1+v2, st2)                                 = do
     where                                           v1 <- evalST e1
     (v1,st1) = eval e1 st                           v2 <- evalST e2
     (v2,st2) = eval e2 st1                          return (v1+v2)

eval (Assign x e) st                           evalST (Assign x e)
  = (v, update st' x v)                          = do
     where                                           v <- evalST e
     (v,st') = eval e st                             st <- get
                                                     put (update st x v)
                                                     return v
```

**Fig. 12.** Evaluating expressions with side-effects

**Introduce a type Definition.** Type synonyms make a program easier to read, but have no semantic implication.

**Introduce a newtype.** Oh the other hand, a newtype is a new type, rather than a new name for an existing type. The restrictions that Haskell 98 places on which types may be declared as instances of classes make it necessary to introduce newtypes for composite types as instances.

Other data-related refactorings include:

**Enumerated Type.** Replace a finite set of constants with an enumerated type; that is a data type with a finite number of 0-ary constructors.

**Maybe Types.** Convert a Maybe type to a list or an Either; these can be seen as transformations of particular monads, as can the conversion from (the constant functor) Bool to a Maybe type.

**Currying and Uncurrying.** It is possible to group, ungroup and reorder argument lists to functions and types.

**Algebraic Types.** Convert between tuples and one-constructor algebraic types; between homogeneous tuples and lists.

**Type Generalisation.** A type definition may refer to a particular type, as the right-hand definition of Expr in Figure 10 refers to BinOp; this reference can become an additional parameter to the definition, with compensating changes to be made to the remainder of the program.

Some of these refactorings are already implemented in HaRe; others are being developed. The next section offers users the possibility of implementing refactorings for themselves.

# 7   Designing Your Own Refactorings: The HaRe API

The HaRe system has a layered architecture, illustrated in Figure 13. It is a Haskell program, so ultimately depends on a Haskell compiler for implementation. The Programatica toolset [11] provides the front end functionality, and the traversals and analyses are written using Strafunski [19].

## 7.1   The HaRe API

Using these libraries we have built other libraries of utilities for syntax manipulation: functions to collect all free identifiers in an expression, substitution functions and so forth.

Two library layers are necessary because of our need to preserve program layout and comments. In common with the vast majority of compilers, Programatica's abstract syntax tree (AST) omits comments, and contains only a limited amount of source code location information.

To keep track of complete comment and layout data we work with the token stream output by the lexical analyser, as well as the AST. When a program is modified we update both the AST and the token stream, and we output the

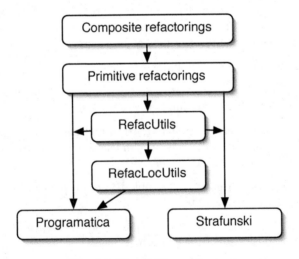

**Fig. 13.** The HaRe architecture

```
inMatch ((HsMatch loc fun pats rhs ds)::HsMatchP)
      | pNTtoPN fun == pn
      = case pats of
          (p1:p2:ps) -> do
                            pats' <-swap p1 p2 pats
                            return (HsMatch loc fun pats' rhs ds)
                  _     -> error "Insufficient arguments to swap."
inMatch m = return m

inExp exp@((Exp (HsApp (Exp (HsApp e e1)) e2))::HsExpP)
      | expToPN e == pn
      = swap e1 e2 exp
inExp e = return e
```

**Fig. 14.** Swapping arguments in a pattern match and a function application

source code program by combining the information held by them both. This necessitates that the utilities we design must manipulate both AST and token stream; we provide two libraries to do this.

RefacUtils: this library hides the token stream manipulation, offering a set of high-level tree manipulation functions which will manipulate syntactic fragments; operations provided include insert, substitute, swap and so forth. These are built on top of our other library, which is described next.

RefacLocUtils: this library provides the functionality to manipulate the token stream and AST directly; it is the user's responsibility to maintain consistency between the two, whereas with RefacUtils this is guaranteed by the library.

In the general course of things we would expect the majority of users to work with RefacUtils.

## 7.2   A Design Example

An illustrative example is given by the refactoring which swaps the first two arguments of a function. The essence of this transformation is the function doSwap:

```
doSwap pn = applyTP (full_buTP (idTP 'adhocTP' inMatch
                                     'adhocTP' inExp
                                     'adhocTP' inDecls
                          ))
```

a bottom-up tree transformation which is the identity except at pattern matches, function applications and type declarations. The adhocTP combinator of Strafunski is *ad hoc* in the sense that it applies its left hand argument except when the right hand one can be applied; the TP suffix denotes that this is a 'type preserving' traversal. The details of the expression and definition manipulation functions are in Figure 14. Note that swap will in general swap two syntactic fragments within an AST, and so will be usable in many contexts. The code in Figure 14 also illustrates the Programatica 'two level' syntax in action: the Exp constructors witness the recursive knot-typing.[9]

The code in Figure 14 makes the 'swap' transformation but raises an error at any point where the function is used with less than two arguments. In a full implementation this condition would be checked prior to applying the refactoring, with two possibilities when the condition fails.

- No action is taken unless all applications have at least two arguments.
- Compensating action is taken in cases with fewer arguments. In this case it is possible to replace these instances of a function `f`, say, with calls to `flip f`, where `flip f a b = f b a`. Note that in particular this handles 'explicit' applications of a function of the form `f $ a $ b`.

Full details of the API and function-by-function Haddock [10] documentation are contained in the HaRe distribution. Details of implementing a number of fusion transformations are given in [20].

### 7.3   A Domain-Specific Language for Refactoring

Users who want to define their own refactorings can potentially interact with the system in two quite different ways. First, it is possible to build refactorings using the API already discussed; this required users to understand details of Strafunski, Haskell syntax in Programatica and the API Itself.

A simpler, but more limited, approach is to provide set of combining forms, or *domain-specific language*, for the existing refactorings, in analogy with the tactic (and tactical) languages of LCF-style proof assistants such as Isabelle[21]. In more detail, users could be offered combinators for

**sequencing** a list of refactorings;
**choice** between a number of alternatives; and
**repetition** of a given refactoring, whilst it is applicable.

Examples of how the DSL might be used are already evident: lifting a definition to the top level (of a module) can be effected by repeatedly lifting it one level; the full ADT refactoring is given by sequencing a number of simpler operations. Building this DSL is a current research topic for the project.

## 8   Reflecting on Refactoring

The work we have seen so far raises a number of questions and directions for future work.

---

[9] The two-level syntax is exemplified by a definition of lists. First a type constructor function is defined, `data L a l = Nil | Cons a l` and then the recursive type is defined to be the fixed point of L, thus: `newtype List a = List (L a (List a))`. Since types cannot be recursive in Haskell, the fixed point introduces a wrapping constructor, `List` here. For example, under this approach the list `[2]` will be given by the term `List (Cons 2 (List Nil))`.

## 8.1    The Refactoring Design Space

In implementing refactorings it becomes apparent that a single refactoring can often have a number of variants, and it is not clear which of these should be implemented. We introduce the different sorts of variation through a series of examples.

**All, One or Some?** In introducing a new definition by selecting an expression, should the definition just replace the single identified instance of the expression, all instances of that expression (in the module) or should the user be asked to select precisely those instances to be replaced?

**Compensation or Not?** In lifting a definition to the top level, what should be done if there are bindings used in the definition which are not in scope at the top level? It is possible to compensate for this by adding extra parameters (λ-lifting), or the implementation may simply disallow this refactoring.

**Modify or Preserve?** Generalisation as outlined in Section 4 modifies the generalised function itself (`format`), changing calls to the function throughout the project. An alternative is to define a generalised function, `format'` say, and to re-define `format` as an instance of this.

One advantage of this approach is that it localises the changes to a single module. Moreover the type of the function is unchanged, so that any uses of the function outside the project will not be compromised. A disadvantage is the proliferation of names: the original function and its generalisation are both visible now.

**How much to Preserve?** A refactoring should not change the behaviour of the program, but underneath this requirement lie a number of possibilities. It would be possible to require that the meaning of every definition was unchanged, but that would preclude a generalisation, which changes not only the function but its type as well.

More realistically, it would be possible to require that the meaning of the `main` program should be unchanged. This allows for a whole variety of refactorings which don't preserve meaning locally, but which do work 'under the hood'. To give two examples:

- The semantics of Haskell draws subtle distinctions between function bindings and lambda expressions, for instance, which are only apparent for partially-defined data values. Arguably these should not be allowed to obstruct transformations which can substantially affect program design.
- More problematic is a refactoring which replaces lists by sets, when the lists are essentially used to store a collection of elements.[10]

To verify the conditions of the last transformation in a tool would be a substantial challenge; this is the point at which a tool builder has to realise that the worth

---

[10] This is illustrated in the case study [26].

of the tool comes from implementing a set of clearly-defined, simple and useful refactorings, rather than attempting to be comprehensive.

**Not (Quite) a Refactoring?** Some operations on programs are not precisely refactorings, but can be supported by the same infrastructure, and would be of value to programmers. Examples include:

- Add a new constructor to a `data` type:[11] this should not only add the constructor but also add new clauses to definitions which use pattern matching over this type.
- Add a field to a constructor of a `data` type: this would require modification to every pattern match and use of this constructor.
- Create a new skeleton definition for a function over a `data` type: one clause would have to be introduced for each constructor.

## 8.2   What Does the Work Say for Haskell?

Building a tool like HaRe makes us focus on some of the details of the design of Haskell, and how it might be improved or extended.

**The Correspondence Principle.** At first sight it appears that there are correspondences between definitions and expressions [24], thus:

|  | *Expressions* | *Definitions* |
|---|---|---|
| *Conditional* | `if ... then ... else ...` | `guard` |
| *Local definition* | `let` | `where` |
| *Abstraction* | `\p -> ...` | `f p = ...` |
| *Pattern matching* | `case x of p ...` | `f p = ...` |

In fact, it is not possible to translate freely between one construct and its correspondent. In general, constructs associated with definitions can be 'open ended' whereas expressions may not.

Take a particular case: a clause of a function may just define values for certain arguments because patterns or guards may not exhaust all the possibilities; values for other arguments may be defined by subsequent clauses. This is not the case with `if ... then ... else ...` and `case`: speaking operationally, once entered they will give a value for all possible arguments; it is not possible to fall through to a subsequent construct.

Arguably this reflects a weakness in the design of Haskell, and could be rectified by tightening up the form of definitions (compulsory `otherwise` and so forth), but this would not be acceptable to the majority of Haskell users.

**Scoped Instance Declarations.** In Haskell it is impossible to prevent an instance declaration from being exported by a module. The lack of scoped class

---

[11] It is arguable that this is a refactoring, in fact. Adding a constructor only has an effect when that constructor is used, although this could arise indirectly through use of a derived instance of `Read`.

instances is a substantial drawback in large projects. The specific difficulty we experienced was integrating libraries from Programatica and Strafunski which defined subtly different instances of the same class over the same type.

**The Module System.** There are certain weaknesses in the module system: it is possible to hide certain identifiers on importing a module, but it is not possible to do the same in an export list, for instance.

**Layout.** In designing a tool which deals with source program layout, a major headache has been caused by tabs, and the different way in which they can be interpreted by different editors (and editor settings). We recommend that all users work with spaces in their source code.

**Haskell 98 / GHC Haskell.** Whilst we have built a system which supports full Haskell 98, it is apparent that the majority of larger-scale Haskell systems use the *de facto* standard, GHC Haskell. We hope to migrate HaRe to GHC in due course, particularly if we are able to use the GHC front end API currently under development.

## 8.3    An Exercise for the Reader

Readers who are interested in learning more about refactoring are encouraged to use the HaRe tool to support exploring refactoring in a particular project. Any non-trivial project would be suitable: the game of minesweeper [25] provides a nicely open-ended case study.

## 8.4    Future Work

High on our priority list is to implement refactorings which will extract 'similar' pieces of program into a common abstraction: this is often requested by potential users. We also expect to migrate the system to deal with hierarchical libraries, libraries without source code and ultimately to use the GHC front end to support full GHC Haskell in HaRe.

## 8.5    Refactoring Elsewhere

These notes have used Haskell as an expository vehicle, but the principles apply equally well to other functional languages, or at least to their pure subsets.

Programming is not the only place where refactoring can be useful. When working on a presentation, a proof, a set of tests and so forth similar redesigns take place. Formal support for proof re-construction could be added to proof assistants such as Isabelle.

In a related context, there is often interest in providing evidence for a program's properties or behaviour. This evidence can be in the form of a proof, test results, model checks and so forth. This raises the challenge of evolving this evidence as the program evolves, through both refactorings and changes of functionality.

# References

1. Warren Burton et al. Views: An Extension to Haskell Pattern Matching. Proposed extension to Haskell; http://www.haskell.org/development/views.html.
2. The BlueJ system. http://www.bluej.org/.
3. John Brandt and Don Roberts. Refactory. http://st-www.cs.uiuc.edu/users/brant/Refactory/.
4. Iavor S. Diatchki, Mark P. Jones, and Thomas Hallgren. A Formal Specification for the Haskell 98 Module System. In *ACM Sigplan Haskell Workshop*, 2002.
5. The Eclipse project. http://www.eclipse.org/.
6. Martin Erwig and Deling Ren. Monadification of functional programs. *Science of Computer Programming*, 52(1-3):101–129, 2004.
7. Robert W. Floyd. The paradigms of programming. *Commun. ACM*, 22(8):455–460, 1979.
8. Martin Fowler. *Refactoring: Improving the Design of Existing Code*. Object Technology Series. Addison-Wesley, 2000.
9. W.G. Griswold and D. Notkin. Automated assistance for program restructuring. *ACM Transactions on Software Engineering and Methodology*, 2, 1993.
10. The Haddock documentation system for Haskell. http://www.haskell.org/haddock.
11. Thomas Hallgren. Haskell Tools from the Programatica Project (Demo Abstract). In *ACM Sigplan Haskell Workshop*, 2003.
12. The HaRe system. http://www.cs.kent.ac.uk/projects/refactor-fp/hare.html.
13. R. Lämmel. Reuse by Program Transformation. In Greg Michaelson and Phil Trinder, editors, *Functional Programming Trends 1999*. Intellect, 2000. Selected papers from the 1st Scottish Functional Programming Workshop.
14. Sheng Liang, Paul Hudak, and Mark Jones. Monad transformers and modular interpreters. In *22nd ACM SIGPLAN-SIGACT Symposium on Principles of Programming Languages: San Francisco, California*. ACM Press, 1995.
15. Ralf Lämmel and Simon Peyton Jones. Scrap your boilerplate: a practical design pattern for generic programming. In *Proceedings of the Workshop on Types in Language Design and Implementation*. ACM, 2003.
16. Ralf Lämmel and Simon Peyton Jones. Scrap more boilerplate: reflection, zips, and generalised casts. In *Proceedings of International Conference on Functional Programming 2004*. ACM Press, 2004.
17. Huiqing Li, Claus Reinke, and Simon Thompson. Tool Support for Refactoring Functional Programs. In *ACM Sigplan Haskell Workshop*, 2003.
18. Huiqing Li, Claus Reinke, and Simon Thompson. Progress on HaRe: the Haskell Refactorer. Poster presentation at the *International Conference on Functional Programming*, Snowbird, Utah. ACM, 2004.
19. Ralf Lämmel and Joost Visser. Generic Programming with Strafunski, 2001. http://www.cs.vu.nl/Strafunski/.
20. Chau Nguyen Viet. Transformation in HaRe. Technical report, Computing Laboratory, University of Kent, 2004. http://www.cs.kent.ac.uk/pubs/2004/2021.
21. Tobias Nipkow, Lawrence C. Paulson, and Markus Wenzel. *Isabelle/HOL: A Proof assistant for Higher-Order Logic*. Springer, 2002.
22. William F. Opdyke. *Refactoring Object-Oriented Frameworks*. PhD thesis, University of Illinois at Urbana-Champaign, 1992.

23. Daniel J. Russell. *FAD: Functional Analysis and Design Methodology*. PhD thesis, University of Kent, 2000.
24. Robert D. Tennent. *Principles of Programming Languages*. Prentice Hall, 1979.
25. Simon Thompson. Minesweeper. `http://www.cs.kent.ac.uk/people/staff/sjt/craft2e/Games/`.
26. Simon Thompson and Claus Reinke. A Case Study in Refactoring Functional Programs. In *Brazilian Symposium on Programming Languages*, 2003.
27. The Unified Modeling Language. `http://www.uml.org/`.
28. Philip Wadler. Views: a way for pattern-matching to cohabit with data abstraction. In *Proceedings of 14th ACM Symposium on Principles of Programming Languages*. ACM Press, January 1987. (Revised March 1987).

# Author Index

# Lecture Notes in Computer Science

For information about Vols. 1–3591

please contact your bookseller or Springer

Vol. 3644: D.-S. Huang, X.-P. Zhang, G.-B. Huang (Eds.), Advances in Intelligent Computing, Part I. XXVII, 1101 pages. 2005.

Vol. 3642: D. Ślezak, J. Yao, J.F. Peters, W. Ziarko, X. Hu (Eds.), Rough Sets, Fuzzy Sets, Data Mining, and Granular Computing, Part II. XXIII, 738 pages. 2005. (Subseries LNAI).

Vol. 3641: D. Ślezak, G. Wang, M. Szczuka, I. Düntsch, Y. Yao (Eds.), Rough Sets, Fuzzy Sets, Data Mining, and Granular Computing, Part I. XXIV, 742 pages. 2005. (Subseries LNAI).

Vol. 3639: P. Godefroid (Ed.), Model Checking Software. XI, 289 pages. 2005.

Vol. 3638: A. Butz, B. Fisher, A. Krüger, P. Olivier (Eds.), Smart Graphics. XI, 269 pages. 2005.

Vol. 3637: J. M. Moreno, J. Madrenas, J. Cosp (Eds.), Evolvable Systems: From Biology to Hardware. XI, 227 pages. 2005.

Vol. 3636: M.J. Blesa, C. Blum, A. Roli, M. Sampels (Eds.), Hybrid Metaheuristics. XII, 155 pages. 2005.

Vol. 3634: L. Ong (Ed.), Computer Science Logic. XI, 567 pages. 2005.

Vol. 3633: C. Bauzer Medeiros, M. Egenhofer, E. Bertino (Eds.), Advances in Spatial and Temporal Databases. XIII, 433 pages. 2005.

Vol. 3632: R. Nieuwenhuis (Ed.), Automated Deduction – CADE-20. XIII, 459 pages. 2005. (Subseries LNAI).

Vol. 3631: J. Eder, H.-M. Haav, A. Kalja, J. Penjam (Eds.), Advances in Databases and Information Systems. XIII, 393 pages. 2005.

Vol. 3630: M.S. Capcarrere, A.A. Freitas, P.J. Bentley, C.G. Johnson, J. Timmis (Eds.), Advances in Artificial Life. XIX, 949 pages. 2005. (Subseries LNAI).

Vol. 3629: J.L. Fiadeiro, N. Harman, M. Roggenbach, J. Rutten (Eds.), Algebra and Coalgebra in Computer Science. XI, 457 pages. 2005.

Vol. 3628: T. Gschwind, U. Aßmann, O. Nierstrasz (Eds.), Software Composition. X, 199 pages. 2005.

Vol. 3627: C. Jacob, M.L. Pilat, P.J. Bentley, J. Timmis (Eds.), Artificial Immune Systems. XII, 500 pages. 2005.

Vol. 3626: B. Ganter, G. Stumme, R. Wille (Eds.), Formal Concept Analysis. X, 349 pages. 2005. (Subseries LNAI).

Vol. 3625: S. Kramer, B. Pfahringer (Eds.), Inductive Logic Programming. XIII, 427 pages. 2005. (Subseries LNAI).

Vol. 3624: C. Chekuri, K. Jansen, J.D.P. Rolim, L. Trevisan (Eds.), Approximation, Randomization and Combinatorial Optimization. XI, 495 pages. 2005.

Vol. 3623: M. Liśkiewicz, R. Reischuk (Eds.), Fundamentals of Computation Theory. XV, 576 pages. 2005.

Vol. 3622: V. Vene, T. Uustalu (Eds.), Advanced Functional Programming. IX, 359 pages. 2005.

Vol. 3621: V. Shoup (Ed.), Advances in Cryptology – CRYPTO 2005. XI, 568 pages. 2005.

Vol. 3620: H. Muñoz-Avila, F. Ricci (Eds.), Case-Based Reasoning Research and Development. XV, 654 pages. 2005. (Subseries LNAI).

Vol. 3619: X. Lu, W. Zhao (Eds.), Networking and Mobile Computing. XXIV, 1299 pages. 2005.

Vol. 3618: J. Jedrzejowicz, A. Szepietowski (Eds.), Mathematical Foundations of Computer Science 2005. XVI, 814 pages. 2005.

Vol. 3617: F. Roli, S. Vitulano (Eds.), Image Analysis and Processing – ICIAP 2005. XXIV, 1219 pages. 2005.

Vol. 3615: B. Ludäscher, L. Raschid (Eds.), Data Integration in the Life Sciences. XII, 344 pages. 2005. (Subseries LNBI).

Vol. 3614: L. Wang, Y. Jin (Eds.), Fuzzy Systems and Knowledge Discovery, Part II. XLI, 1314 pages. 2005. (Subseries LNAI).

Vol. 3613: L. Wang, Y. Jin (Eds.), Fuzzy Systems and Knowledge Discovery, Part I. XLI, 1334 pages. 2005. (Subseries LNAI).

Vol. 3612: L. Wang, K. Chen, Y. S. Ong (Eds.), Advances in Natural Computation, Part III. LXI, 1326 pages. 2005.

Vol. 3611: L. Wang, K. Chen, Y. S. Ong (Eds.), Advances in Natural Computation, Part II. LXI, 1292 pages. 2005.

Vol. 3610: L. Wang, K. Chen, Y. S. Ong (Eds.), Advances in Natural Computation, Part I. LXI, 1302 pages. 2005.

Vol. 3608: F. Dehne, A. López-Ortiz, J.-R. Sack (Eds.), Algorithms and Data Structures. XIV, 446 pages. 2005.

Vol. 3607: J.-D. Zucker, L. Saitta (Eds.), Abstraction, Reformulation and Approximation. XII, 376 pages. 2005. (Subseries LNAI).

Vol. 3606: V. Malyshkin (Ed.), Parallel Computing Technologies. XII, 470 pages. 2005.

Vol. 3604: R. Martin, H. Bez, M. Sabin (Eds.), Mathematics of Surfaces XI. IX, 473 pages. 2005.

Vol. 3603: J. Hurd, T. Melham (Eds.), Theorem Proving in Higher Order Logics. IX, 409 pages. 2005.

Vol. 3602: R. Eigenmann, Z. Li, S.P. Midkiff (Eds.), Languages and Compilers for High Performance Computing. IX, 486 pages. 2005.

Vol. 3599: U. Aßmann, M. Aksit, A. Rensink (Eds.), Model Driven Architecture. X, 235 pages. 2005.

Vol. 3598: H. Murakami, H. Nakashima, H. Tokuda, M. Yasumura, Ubiquitous Computing Systems. XIII, 275 pages. 2005.

Vol. 3597: S. Shimojo, S. Ichii, T.W. Ling, K.-H. Song (Eds.), Web and Communication Technologies and Internet-Related Social Issues - HSI 2005. XIX, 368 pages. 2005.

Vol. 3596: F. Dau, M.-L. Mugnier, G. Stumme (Eds.), Conceptual Structures: Common Semantics for Sharing Knowledge. XI, 467 pages. 2005. (Subseries LNAI).

Vol. 3595: L. Wang (Ed.), Computing and Combinatorics. XVI, 995 pages. 2005.

Vol. 3594: J.C. Setubal, S. Verjovski-Almeida (Eds.), Advances in Bioinformatics and Computational Biology. XIV, 258 pages. 2005. (Subseries LNBI).

Vol. 3593: V. Mařík, R. W. Brennan, M. Pěchouček (Eds.), Holonic and Multi-Agent Systems for Manufacturing. XI, 269 pages. 2005. (Subseries LNAI).

Vol. 3592: S. Katsikas, J. Lopez, G. Pernul (Eds.), Trust, Privacy and Security in Digital Business. XII, 332 pages. 2005.